HERESY AND ORTHODOXY
IN SIXTEENTH-CENTURY PARIS

STUDIES
IN MEDIEVAL AND
REFORMATION THOUGHT

EDITED BY

HEIKO A. OBERMAN, Tucson, Arizona

IN COOPERATION WITH

THOMAS A. BRADY, Jr., Berkeley, California
ANDREW C. GOW, Edmonton, Alberta
JÜRGEN MIETHKE, Heidelberg
M. E. H. NICOLETTE MOUT, Leiden
ANDREW PETTEGREE, St. Andrews
MANFRED SCHULZE, Wuppertal
DAVID C. STEINMETZ, Durham, North Carolina

VOLUME LXXVII

LARISSA JULIET TAYLOR

HERESY AND ORTHODOXY
IN SIXTEENTH-CENTURY PARIS

HERESY AND ORTHODOXY IN SIXTEENTH-CENTURY PARIS

FRANÇOIS LE PICART AND THE BEGINNINGS
OF THE CATHOLIC REFORMATION

BY

LARISSA JULIET TAYLOR

BRILL
LEIDEN · BOSTON · KÖLN
1999

This book is printed on acid-free paper.

Library of Congress Cataloging-in-Publication Data

Taylor, Larissa.
   Heresy and orthodoxy in sixteenth-century Paris : François Le Picart
and the beginnings of the Catholic Reformation / by Larissa Juliet Taylor.
      p.   cm. — (Studies in medieval and Reformation thought, ISSN
0585-6914 ; v. 77)
   Includes bibliographical references and indexes.
   ISBN 9004114033 (hardcover : alk. paper)
   1. Le Picart, François, d. 1556.   I. Title.   II. Series.
BX4705.L5385T39   1999
274.4'36106—dc21
                                                                            99–22833
                                                                            CIP

Die Deutsche Bibliothek - CIP-Einheitsaufnahme

Taylor, Larissa Juliet:
Heresy and orthodoxy in sixteenth-century Paris : François le Picart
and the beginnings of the Catholic Reformation / by Larissa Juliet
Taylor. – Leiden ; Boston ; Köln : Brill, 1999
   (Studies in medieval and reformation thought ; Vol. 77)
   ISBN 90–04–11403–3

ISSN   0585-6914
ISBN   90 04 11403 3

CONTENTS

LIST OF ABBREVIATIONS

Advent Les sermons et instructions chrestiennes, pour tous les iours de l'Advent, iusques à Noël: & de tous les Dimenches & Festes, depuis Noël iusques à Caresme.

Caresme Les sermons et instructions chrestiennes, pour tous les iours de caresme, & Feries de Pasques. Part I.

Caresme-II Les sermons et instructions chrestiennes, pour tous les iours de caresme, & Feries de Pasques. Part II.

Épistre Épistre, contenant un traicté auquel est monstré combien est grande la charité de Iesus Christ en l'institution de la saincte communion de son pretieux corps & sang, au S. Sacrement de l'Autel.

Instruction Instruction et forme de prier Dieu en vraye & parfaite oraison, faite en forme de sermons, sur l'Oraison Dominicale, par M. François le Picart, Docteur en Théologie.

Pasques Les sermons et instructions chrestiennes, pour tous les Dimenches, & toutes les festes des saincts, depuis Pasques iusques à la Trinité.

SL Le second livre du recueil des sermons.

Trinité Les sermons et instructions chrestiennes, pour tous les Dimenches, & toutes les festes des saincts, depuis la Trinité iusques à Advent. Part I.

Trinité-II Les sermons et instructions chrestiennes, pour tous les Dimenches, & toutes les festes des saincts, depuis la Trinité iusques à Advent. Part II.

PREFACE

> Everything in this strange, fascinating book . . . dis-
> turbs, throws into disorder, and tramples underfoot
> earlier certainties. Nothing can be understood as it
> was before, or more precisely, all is finally begin-
> ning to be understood.[1]

> Denis Crouzet's book is destined to occupy a lead-
> ing place in not only the religious but also the spir-
> itual and mental historiography of the sixteenth
> century.[2]

In 1990 a book was published that would profoundly alter the historiography of sixteenth-century France—Denis Crouzet's *Les Guerriers de
Dieu: La violence au temps des troubles de religion (vers 1525–vers 1610)*. The
book has been called revolutionary,[3] and provocative and perplex-
ing,[4] but there can be no doubt that Crouzet has, in the words of
one reviewer, ". . . guaranteed that [the history of the Wars of Religion]
can never again be explained 'sans Dieu'."[5] *Les Guerriers de Dieu* has
been called ". . . nothing less than a complete reinterpretation of the
religious history of the French sixteenth century. . . . There was a
'violence mentale d'avant les violences,' which accounts for the sudden
explosion of religious tension on the eve of the civil wars."[6] Another
reviewer comments that "[h]is best and most original contributions,
those which truly deserve a wider audience, probably lie in his sec-
tions on pre-1562 French astrology and eschatological prophecy."[7]

---

[1] Pierre Chaunu, "Preface," in Denis Crouzet, *Les Guerriers de Dieu: La violence au
temps des troubles de religion (vers 1525–vers 1610)* (Seyssel, France: Champ Vallon, 1990), 10.

[2] Denis Richet, "Preface," in Crouzet, *Guerriers de Dieu*, 15.

[3] J.H.M. Salmon, Review of Crouzet, *Guerriers de Dieu*, in *Journal of Modern History*
63(1991), 775.

[4] Barbara Diefendorf, Review of Crouzet, *Guerriers de Dieu*, in *American Historical
Review* 99(1994), 242.

[5] Mack Holt, "Putting Religion Back into the Wars of Religion," *French Historical
Studies* 18(1993), 539.

[6] Mark Greengrass, "The Psychology of Religious Violence," in *French History*
5(1991), 469.

[7] William Monter, "Review of Crouzet, *Guerriers de Dieu*, in *Sixteenth Century Journal*
22(1991), 558.

With a brilliant analysis of violence and its roots, the book argues
that in sixteenth-century France, the "... violence is the history."[8]
Crouzet asserts that the early part of the century was pervaded by
a sense of eschatological anguish, that it was "... a period haunted
by the fear of God's impending judgment."[9]

Crouzet has reprised this theme in later books. In *La Nuit de la
Saint-Barthélemy*, Crouzet pursues this theme, tracing the origins of
the troubles to

> ... an imagined eschatology, a system of representations put in place
> around the years 1500–1520, and hardening around 1540–1545. The
> decades that preceded the explosion of the wars of religion saw an
> anguish about the future mount irresistibly ... All the channels of infor-
> mation were little by little invaded by the prophetic word, which car-
> ried to the ears of all the knowledge that the violence of God was in
> the process of unfolding on a humanity that had reached the most
> critical time of sin. The sermons prophesied the imminence of the end
> of the world.[10]

In his most recent book, *La genèse de la Réforme française*, Crouzet paints
the world at the end of the Middle Ages in Huizingian hues. He
sees in the late Middle Ages an obsession with death and decay,
arguing that

> [t]he imagination, the presentiment of divine menace moves toward
> an anguish even more pregnant. We must not exaggerate this evolu-
> tion, for the eschatological signs were already present earlier, for exam-
> ple, in the messages of preachers. However, now everything occurs as
> if it were the result of sliding inexorably toward an eschatology more
> full of pathos than ever before, as if there had been a passage toward
> a universe dramatized with very great intensity.
>
> Simultaneously with the appearance of Luther in Christendom, the
> image of a God of chastisement became stronger.... Humanity is
> beyond the signs warning of its corruption and calling for its refor-
> mation. For the wondrous time of God's punishment has begun to
> unfold.[11]

The current study of François Le Picart, the most famous Catholic
preacher in Paris from the 1530s until his death in 1556, was under-

---

[8] Crouzet, *Guerriers de Dieu*, I:53.
[9] Diefendorf, Review of *Guerriers de Dieu*, 241.
[10] Denis Crouzet, *La nuit de la Saint-Barthélemy* (Paris: Fayard, 1994), 489–490.
[11] Denis Crouzet, *La genèse de la Réforme française, 1520–1562* (Paris: SEDES, 1996), 13.

taken in order to delve more deeply into the religious and mental climate of France and its capital in the period before the Religious Wars. Crouzet devotes several pages to the man he calls a *prédicateur panique*, François Le Picart. He situates the preacher "... at the heart of the currents of eschatological thought,"[12] calling him "... a preacher of the violence of God and of the end of Time..."[13] Finding an Old Testament inspiration in his rhetoric, Crouzet claims that it grows with the passage of time.[14] Was Le Picart indeed a prophet? Does a close reading of Le Picart's sermons, the only extensive corpus of sermons printed during this period, support Crouzet's bold thesis? Was France in the first half of the sixteenth century obsessed by frenzied imaginings of God's Judgment?

Le Picart was famous in his time, but "... recognizing that time has begun to efface his renown, and to take him little by little from the memory of men, I have decided to publish this history."[15] So began his seventeenth-century biographer, Hilarion de Coste, a Minim who had published a memorial to François de Paul the year before, quite possibly in the hope of initiating canonization proceedings for Le Picart. *Le parfait ecclesiastique*, printed in 1658, is a work of hagiography, but contains an invaluable collection of sources, some of the originals of which have been lost in the ensuing centuries. Hilarion de Coste was following in the footsteps of the Catholic polemicist Artus Désiré (c. 1510–c. 1579),[16] who noted on the anniversary of Le Picart's death in 1557:

> Have you forgotten the good he did for you
> And the great and perfect love he had,
> I certainly do not think so, for his fame and renown
> Is so great before God that his name is immortal.
> To remind you of his goodwill
> I wanted to let you know this day
> Of that day at the end of the year since his decease,
> So that you and I will have memory of that end.[17]

---

[12] Crouzet, *Guerriers de Dieu*, I:206.

[13] Ibid, I:207, 208.

[14] Ibid, I:208.

[15] F. Hilarion de Coste, *Le parfait ecclesiastique, ou l'histoire de la vie et de la mort de François LePicart, seigneur d'Attily & de Villeron, docteur en théologie de Paris & doyen de Saint-Germain l'Auxerrois* (Paris: Sebastien Cramoisy, 1658), 5.

[16] See Frank S. Giese, *Artus Désiré: Priest and Pamphleteer of the Sixteenth Century* (Chapel Hill: North Carolina Studies in the Romance Languages and Literatures, 1973).

[17] Artus Desiré, *Les regretz et complainctes de Passe partout et Bruictquicourt, sur la mémoire*

So strong had been the love of the people of Paris for Le Picart that his funeral procession was likened to that of a king,[18] while his Calvinist enemies rejoiced that the man whom many felt had been responsible for keeping Paris in the Catholic fold[19] was dead. Yet aside from scholars who study sixteenth-century France, Le Picart's name has been forgotten, eclipsed by the violence and polemic of the Religious Wars that began shortly after his death.

It is in this context that a study of François Le Picart and his works can offer further insight into religious *mentalités* in the critical years before the outbreak of religious war, years that are still too often ignored by scholars. In the decades after 1520, French men and women experienced profound changes in almost every aspect of life, the most significant of which affected religious beliefs and behaviors. For centuries, the landscape of everyday life had been filled with the ever-present reminders of the Catholic Church: the frequent ringing of bells that signaled not only services but also celebration, death or danger to the community; churches, relics, statues and cult sites; and, of course, the markers of life stages through which every human being had to pass—the rituals of baptism, confirmation and extreme unction. In his prologue to Mikhail Bakhtin's *Rabelais and his World*, Michael Holquist writes: "[t]he unique species of historical event we call a revolution occurs when everything changes at once, not excluding the very categories used for gauging and shaping change. . . . It is in the nature of revolutions that no one can be an experienced citizen of the new order they bring into being."[20]

Everything did change in the decades before 1560. There could no longer be any certainties in a world thrown into disarray by challenges to its most dominant institution, challenges that would inevitably have an impact not only on religious belief but on literacy and attitudes to toleration, freedom and equality. Some felt in these times of radical change that God had re-entered the world historical stage. As many throughout Europe became enmeshed in the search

---

renouvellée du trespas et bout de l'an, de feu tres noble et venerable personne Maistre Françoys Picart, docteur en théologie et grand doyen de sainct Germain de l'Aucerroys (Paris: Pierre Gaultier, 1557), fol. Aii.

[18] Ibid.

[19] Émile Doumergue, *Jean Calvin: Les hommes et les choses de son temps* (Lausanne: Georges Bridel, 1899), I:241.

[20] Michael Holquist, "Prologue," in Mikhail Bakhtin, *Rabelais and his World* (Bloomington: Indiana University Press, 1984), xiv.

for answers through astrology and prophecy, the challenge of pre-
dicting the time of the Judgment intensified, especially in the wake
of frightening planetary configurations in the heavens.[21] Others felt
God had turned his back on the human race. Many people, heady
with the wine of the new learning, gloried in the powers of the
human mind and spirit, and began to question long-held truths. To
understand fully the Religious Wars and that which followed, we
must begin by exploring the years between 1520 and 1560. Speaking
of only a six-year period in these four decades, Lucien Febvre wrote:
"the world had moved between 1532 and 1538. And it had moved
very rapidly. . . . These few facts serve as a warning that for those
troubled years of the sixteenth century, when men were living on
the double and ideas were causing things to move with unaccus-
tomed rapidity, it makes no sense to mix up different conditions."[22]

The forty-five years between the outbreak of the Lutheran Reformation and the beginning of the French Religious Wars covers the
period in which William Monter sees Crouzet's most significant historical achievement. These years offer rich details about life, beliefs
and practices. François Le Picart was a leading actor in the events
of these troubled yet exciting times. In a century when "[t]he pulpit was probably the strongest molder of public opinion,"[23] it is
remarkable, as Barbara Diefendorf has said, that ". . . there has been
little serious inquiry into the content of . . . sermons and their relation to subsequent events."[24] Speaking of his own subject, Rabelais,
Febvre wrote: "[t]he approach we are going to use seems obvious:
focus the inquiry on one man, chosen . . . because the state of the
documentation that enables us to reconstruct his thought, the statements contained in his work, and the meaning of the work itself
seem to qualify him specially for such a study."[25] Le Picart's contemporaries, as well as a man living a century later, all believed that
the preacher represented Catholicism in Paris in his time. He was

---

[21] See Robin Bruce Barnes, *Prophecy and Gnosis: Apocalypticism in the Wake of the Lutheran Reformation* (Stanford: Stanford University Press, 1988).

[22] Lucien Febvre, *The Problem of Unbelief in the Sixteenth Century: The Religion of Rabelais*, trans. Beatrice Gottlieb (Cambridge: Cambridge University Press, 1982), 107.

[23] Robert M. Kingdon, *Geneva and the Coming of the Wars of Religion in France 1555–1563* (Geneva: Droz, 1956), 93.

[24] Barbara B. Diefendorf, "Simon Vigor: A Radical Preacher in Sixteenth-Century Paris," *Sixteenth Century Journal* 18(1987), 399.

[25] Febvre, *Problem of Unbelief*, 11.

a man who initiated events that roused the anger of the court, who responded to heretical attacks on the symbols and beliefs of his faith, and who supported those—such as the Jesuits—whom he felt could steer the church back onto the right course. Yet unlike older colleagues on the Faculty of Theology such as Noël Beda, Le Picart was not an intransigent man. Although his passion for Catholicism was acknowledged by all and his orthodoxy was never questioned, he was far from immune to new ideas. His ambivalence about the study of philology, classics and ancient languages all demonstrate the influence humanistic ideals held over him. Without the hagiographical intentions of Hilarion de Coste or Artus Desiré, I hope this book will open a window not merely on the man François Le Picart, who embodied so much about his time, but also on the religious and intellectual climate of Paris in these years. This is not a biography, but rather a study of one man's actions and reactions to unprecedented events, and especially his words—words that speak to us from his sermons of a mind dealing with change; words that themselves change as the situation in France does; words that profoundly affected their hearers. As Elizabeth Marvick states, words ". . . that deviate from the usual forms for the occasion are clues; they suggest latent meanings that prompt a search for nonobvious motives."[26] However much Le Picart was a champion of orthodoxy, one of those scorned *theologastres*[27] of the Faculty of Theology, he was nonetheless a man who experienced the same changes as those around him and was in turn changed by them. His words often surprise the reader who comes to them with preconceived notions. Through him we can come to know more fully what life was like in post-Reformation Paris.

I have incurred numerous scholarly debts in the research and writing of this book. Many scholars offered suggestions and criticisms on the manuscript or the portions that were presented as conference papers, including Fred Baumgartner, Robin Barnes, Barbara Diefendorf, Jeanne Harrie, Katharine Lualdi, Lynn Martin, David McNeil, Ray Mentzer, Virginia Reinburg and Barry Sell. Without the research of James K. Farge, as well as his suggestions and friendship, this book would simply not have been possible. As will be obvious in the pages

---

[26] Elizabeth Marvick, "Psychobiography and the Early Modern French Court: Notes on Method with Some Examples," *French Historical Studies* 19(1996), 944.

[27] See Henri Bernard-Maître, "Les 'théologastres' de l'université de Paris au temps d'Érasme et de Rabelais (1496–1536)," *Bibliothèque de l'humanisme et Renaissance. Travaux et documents* 27(1965), 248–264.

that follow, the scholarship of John O'Malley has helped me understand the connections between Le Picart and the first Jesuits. It
goes without saying that any errors are mine alone. Megan Armstrong obtained copies of original and secondary sources that were
not otherwise available to me, and her insights on Franciscans in
Paris in the later part of the century were invaluable. Denis Crouzet,
with whom I disagree on some fundamental issues, has been both
an inspiration and a generous friend over many years. In Reims,
I owe special thanks to Mme. Claudine Belayche, director of the
Bibliothèque Municipale, Abbé Goy, who pointed me to sources for
Saint-Pierre-des-Dames and Renée de Guise, Dr. J.-P. Fontaine and
M. Brice Gosset. As always, the staff of the Bibliothèque Nationale
and Archives Nationales in Paris were extremely helpful. My special thanks go to my colleagues at Colby College, especially Peggy
Menchen at the Reference Desk and Sunny Pomerleau and the inter-
library loan staff, whose indefatigable efforts to secure even the most
obscure French journal article truly made this book possible. I would
also like to thank my student research assistants, Jamie Smith, John
Sauter, and Tom Donahue, who will undoubtedly be writing their
own books in a few years' time.

Portions of my article, "The Good Shepherd," published in another
form in the *Sixteenth Century Journal* are reproduced here in several
chapters by permission.

I would like to thank Professor Heiko A. Oberman for incorporating the book in his series *Studies in Medieval and Reformation Thought.*

Funding was provided by an NEH Travel-to-Collections Grant, a
Louise McDowell Research Grant from Wellesley College, and a
Harvard University travel grant.

This book is dedicated to my companion and my muse, Kitikat.

*   *   *

Note on Language and Translations

First, a note on terminology. Since the book is written from the viewpoint of François Le Picart, I have used the terms heresy and heretic as he would have used them—in reference to the doctrines and
people he found suspect. Heresy in general refers to practices and beliefs in opposition to what the church decreed in a given time and
place. A heretic was one who, when shown his or her error, persisted

in such practices or beliefs. "Lutheran" was the term most frequently used for the reformers in the early years after the Reformation began, and despite the presence of very few actual Lutherans in France, Le Picart uses it as an all-encompassing term even while recognizing differences among the reformers. When not quoting directly from Le Picart, I have used the more general term Protestant. In reference to the earliest humanists and evangelicals, I have used either those words or referred to them simply as "reformers." Where Calvinists are clearly intended, especially in the later sermons, I have employed that designation. I have not used the term Huguenot because it was not in widespread usage until after the Conspiracy of Amboise in 1560.[28] Le Picart never uses the term.

Similarly, I have used "orthodoxy" to refer to the doctrines and traditions established by the Roman Catholic Catholic Church as accepted and further defined in France in the four decades after the beginning of the Reformation. This was constantly in flux at the time as a result of uncertainties about "Lutheran" belief and changes in the edicts promulgated by the king. Nevertheless, the basic beliefs of the church about the sacraments, belief in the powers of the Virgin Mary and the saints, purgatory, etc., changed very little during these decades. Heterodoxy was an even more fluid term, relating to departures from church practices or beliefs that were seen as potentially dangerous but not necessarily heretical.

I have generally used the term Catholic Reformation in the broadest sense, to describe efforts to reform the church in the wake of the Protestant Reformation. I have not used it in the more specific sense of the set of doctrines enunciated by the Council of Trent, since the final meetings of the council did not take place until after Le Picart's death, and since the French church participated only minimally in the meetings and did not accept its decrees. In this sense, the term Catholic Reformation refers to the continuation of fifteenth-century efforts to reform the church from within, given much greater impetus by the threats posed to the church after 1517. As will be shown, many of Le Picart's beliefs anticipated the Tridentine decrees.

The terms pre- and post-Reformation have been used simply for convenience. Here, pre-Reformation refers to the period before 1517,

---

[28] Janet G. Gray, "The Origin of the Word Huguenot," *Sixteenth Century Journal* 14(1983), 358.

including preachers whose primary efforts were concentrated in that period. The "post" in post-Reformation is not used in the same manner as it is in a word such as "postmodern," but simply to refer to the period after 1517, especially in regard to preachers primarily active after that period and their sermons.

I have attempted to keep translations from the sermons fairly literal except for eliminating repetitions of different French words that have only one English equivalent. It has not been possible or desirable to use entirely gender-neutral language, as this would distort Le Picart's words. Even in paraphrases, I have usually stayed with the "he" that Le Picart normally uses to speak of any human being. To do justice to the verses and songs that appear in Chapters II and III, I have left them in the original French to preserve the rhyme schemes and the plays on words that would be lost in translation. I have standardized the many alternate spellings of Le Picart (LePicart, Picard, Picart and Picardus). Quotations from the Bible have been taken from the *Revised Standard Version*, with use of the Vulgate where appropriate.

L.J.T.
Waterville, Maine
August, 1998

CHAPTER ONE

THE SOURCES

Writing from Paris in December of 1563, in the aftermath of the
uneasy peace ushered in by the Edict of Amboise, 42-year-old René
Benoist, the future "Pape des Halles,"[1] penned an extraordinary document that would be included in the preface to a volume of François
Le Picart's sermons.[2] Although sermons have proved an invaluable
source for our knowledge of *mentalités* and prescriptive behavior, the
problem of determining the relationship, if any, between the preached
Word of God and a written text can be daunting. Thanks to Benoist's
curiosity and the thorough account he left of his investigation, we
have an almost unparalleled glimpse into the process by which Le
Picart's sermons began to appear in print in the years following his
death in 1556.

Benoist begins with an avowal of the complete skepticism with
which he originally greeted the sermon books. Although the first of
Le Picart's sermons were printed in the late 1550s by the Reims
printer Nicolas Bacquenois,[3] Benoist is referring to the Paris publications by Nicolas Chesneau.[4] He gives his reasons for skepticism
about the provenance of the sermons.

---

[1] Émile Pasquier, *René Benoist: Le pape des Halles (1521–1608)* (Paris: Alphonse
Picard, 1913) despite some errors, remains the only biography of Benoist. An excel-
lent discussion of his life and sermons, however, can be found in Barbara Diefendorf,
Beneath the Cross: Catholics and Huguenots in Sixteenth-Century Paris (New York: Oxford
University Press, 1992), 149–152.

[2] René Benoist, "Preface," *Caresme*, fols. iii–vii.

[3] After having worked in Lyon, Bacquenois set up his press in Reims in 1551
and, with the king's privilege and the Cardinal of Lorraine's patronage, was the
official town printer by 1555. Henri Jadart, *Les débuts de l'imprimerie à Reims et les
marques des premiers imprimeurs 1550–1650* (Reims: Imprimerie et Lithographie de
l'Indépendant Rémois, 1893), 6–71. See also Georges Boussinesq and Gustave
Laurent, *Histoire de Reims depuis les origines jusqu'à nos jours. Tome I: Reims ancien des
temps préhistoriques à la mort d'Henri IV* (Reims: Matot-Braine, 1933), 482–484. The
works printed by Bacquenois include the *Instruction* (1557) and *Second Livre* (1560).
The *Premier livre du recueil de sermons* was published by Bacquenois in 1559, but there
are no extant copies.

[4] The four volumes published published by Chesneau in 1566 for the entire litur-
gical year were: *Les sermons et instructions chrestiennes pour tous les iours de caresme, &*

... I considered how by his grace I had familiar access to him and
often saw his library, yet I never heard him say one word to the effect
that he had written, or proposed to write, anything, nor did I see any
sign of writings among his books. What really dissuaded me from
receiving these sermons as his work was that during the year that it
pleased God ... to call him to Him, in the last three months of his
life, that is, June, July and August [1556], he was in Reims in
Champagne, where he had been sent ... by Monseigneur the Most
Illustrious Prince and Most Reverend Cardinal, Charles of Lorraine.
I had been charged to preach in his stead at Saint-Germain l'Auxerrois
on Sundays and feast days. I stayed in his room, and used his books,
among which I saw no sign of composition or even compilation for
the purpose of printing. Similarly, upon his return, in the short time
that preceded his death, I was often with him and neither by words
nor any other sign did he indicate he had something to publish, nor
even that he had any desire to do so. Considering all these things, I
was completely unwilling to believe that these written sermons were
his, and I disdained to read them.[5]

Benoist's suspicions were heightened by the rapidity with which suc-
cessive volumes appeared. "... [S]oon they were seen in the hands
of sincere and faithful Christians, both learned and unlearned, who
held them in great esteem, saying that they had found great consolation and edification in reading them ..." Benoist flipped through
the pages and skimmed a few passages, but felt confirmed in his first
opinion. His cursory examination forced him to admit the sermons
were sound in doctrine, so he decided to spend some time reading
them. "After a short time, I began to develop a taste for them, and
feeling the passion for the faith contained in them, slowly I began
to change my mind."[6] But the excellence and purity of doctrine in
the sermons did not prove they were the work of Le Picart. Benoist
was impressed, however, that they had been published by a long-
time acquaintance of Le Picart, Nicolas Chesneau, the future canon
and dean of Saint-Symphorien in Reims.[7] Chesneau was a man

---

*Feries de Pasques; Les sermons et instructions chrestiennes, pour tous les Dimenches & toutes les
festes des saincts, depuis Pasques iusques à la Trinité; Les sermons et instructions chrestiennes,
pour tous les Dimenches, & toutes les festes des saincts, depuis la Trinité iusques à l'Advent;*
and *Les sermons et instructions chrestiennes, pour tous les iours de l'Advent, iusques à Noël: &
de tous les Dimenches & Festes, depuis Noël iusques à Caresme.*

[5] Benoist, "Preface," *Caresme*, fols. iii–iv.

[6] Ibid, fol. iv.

[7] Also known as Querculus, Chesneau had studied and taught at the Collège de
la Marche in Paris. An author of poems in Latin, Chesneau specialized in printing works of piety and ecclesiastical history in translation. In 1557, the Cardinal of

known for his faith, prudence and probity. Moreover, the care with which the sermons had been collected, edited and printed fit what Benoist knew of the character of the man. Still in some doubt, Benoist decided to speak directly with Chesneau about the matter.

> . . . In view of my belief that Le Picart had written nothing, I wanted to know how he had come into the possession of these sermons. Chesneau explained everything to me—how he had gathered them from those who regularly attended the sermons of this learned man. They had taken the sermons down as diligently as possible, without changing (or only very little, as sometimes happens) a sentence or a word. Chesneau then showed me diverse examples of the said sermons, gathered from several people who had been frequent auditors, and who had assiduously written down and collected them. It simply could not be denied.[8]

Benoist, however well he came to know Le Picart at the end of his life, had had fewer opportunities than many to hear his sermons, as he had only entered the Collège de Navarre for advanced theological studies in 1556,[9] the year of Le Picart's death. As Benoist began a close reading of the sermons, he was struck by their popular nature, surprising to him in view of Le Picart's erudition and reputation as both a preacher and teacher. Then he remembered the criticisms he had heard voiced by heretics, who mocked Le Picart for his simple style, failing to understand that the mark of an excellent preacher was his ability to accommodate himself to the capacity of his listeners.

> My friends, I saw nothing there that persuaded me that the sermons belonged to anyone but the man to whom they were attributed. To prove this to those who want to be more certain, I ask them to refresh their memory about Le Picart's manner of preaching and then read these sermons, and I promise that then they will say these are his true and own works, and will praise God to have given them this good and grace. No longer able to hear the clear sound of this Evangelical Trumpet, they can now read them at their ease and in comfort in their own homes, participating in the same Word of God preached by this learned and virtuous man . . . It should not be thought that these sermons have less authority for having been written down by someone else and not by him . . ., for just as the words of a president

---

Lorraine appointed him as a preacher for the stations of Lent in Reims, and in 1574 he was given the post at Saint-Symphorien. Pierre Desportes, et al., *Histoire de Reims* (Toulouse: Privat, 1983), 231.

[8] Benoist, "Preface," *Caresme*, fol. v.

[9] Pasquier, *René Benoist*, 42.

of *parlement* are written down by several clerks after being pronounced by the said president, they have no less authority and efficacy than if he had written them personally. And just as the president signs the document to verify the writing of the clerk, so these present sermons have been signed and approved as Christian and Catholic by the doctors of the Faculty of Theology. They have decided not to change even some statements that appear puerile, in order that the sermons should live on in their own form, and be truly represented as they were given and faithfully collected, not by one or two only, but by several learned and diligent men. As the writings and reports were sometimes slightly different (because it would be too difficult to have all of them agree on all points), they have been compared and the one closest to what was preached was chosen.[10]

Benoist even offers a hypothesis about why Le Picart chose not to publish the sermons himself.

The greatest and most knowledgeable men customarily have written nothing or only a few things, unless they have been practically constrained to do so, thinking it enough, in fact even more important, to engrave their knowledge on the spirits of men and not amuse themselves by committing it to insensate paper. Because to teach, retain and persuade men by words is a much greater thing than to write something down without resistance at one's convenience. So it was with the great and divine philosopher Socrates. So too with our heavenly doctor Jesus Christ, who didn't write down or give anything to his Apostles to write down, but preached and announced the gospel . . . But God, the author of this knowledge and virtue, wanted these gifts and grace to multiply and profit others, so he would not permit their memory to be effaced. . . . [A]nd so God did not want the memory of this holy and virtuous person our master François Le Picart who, in the judgment of all who knew him, had led a Christian and irreproachable life and edified the Church of Jesus Christ by the preaching of the Word of God, to be extinguished or even lessened by his death.[11]

It was God's will, says Benoist, that the people of Paris and indeed of all Christianity could still hear Le Picart preach through his works. The final pages of the preface are essentially a eulogy, as Benoist exhorts everyone who is able to "love, revere and read diligently the holy works of he who rendered you constant in the Christian religion and faith in this time of danger." Finally, he affirms that ". . . it is certain by the style, method and phrases in these sermons that they

---

[10] Benoist, "Preface," *Caresme*, fol. v.
[11] Ibid, fols. v–vi.

were given by Le Picart. Those who often heard him preach can judge for themselves."[12]

Further explanatory material can be found in the prefaces and dedications. In the same collection in which Benoist wrote his preface, Chesneau states in the dedication that "... I have taken all pains and diligence possible to reread and collect these sermons from several originals and to have them printed correctly."[13] In a lengthy introduction of April 1562 to his volume of sermons from Easter to Trinity that laments the problems of his day, which delayed the project, Chesneau adds, "by the recovery and printing of the present sermons, collected from Le Picart's mouth, word by word, just as they were preached, those who in the lifetime of the author did not have the opportunity to attend his sermons can have them in hand and read them at their leisure."[14]

Similarly, Nicolas Bacquenois states in his dedication to the *Second Livre* that "I have published immediately what I was able to get from the hands of Messieurs the doctors of Reims, to whom you had communicated it, so that after they approved it, all faithful Christians would be able to become participants in such good and holy doctrine."[15] This statement provides another clue to the impetus behind the printing. Bacquenois refers to the person who had given the sermons to the theologians of Reims. The reference is to Renée de Guise, Abbess of Saint-Pierre-des-Dames of Reims (1536–1602).[16] Both of Bacquenois's efforts and three of the four Chesneau editions from 1566 were dedicated to Madame Renée.[17] Daughter of the first Duke of Guise, Claude of Lorraine, Renée was the youngest child.[18] At the age of seven, in 1542, Renée was "elected" abbess of the convent, and during her sixty-year tenure was responsible for reforming the house, re-establishing cloister, and having the portal of the

---

[12] Ibid, fol. vi–vii.

[13] Nicolas Chesneau, "Dedication," *Caresme*, fol. iii.

[14] Nicolas Chesneau, "Dedication," in *Pasques*, fol. viii.

[15] Nicolas Bacquenois, "Dedication," in *SL*, ii.

[16] Although there is still a road named for the rich abbey founded in the seventh century, no trace remains of the convent and church. Maps from the period show the imposing presence of Saint-Pierre-des-Dames.

[17] The only one dedicated to someone other than Renée was the volume of Advent sermons, which Chesneau dedicated to Pierre Rousseau, *prévost* of St. Laurent and canon of Angers.

[18] H. Outram Evennett, *The Cardinal of Lorraine and the Council of Trent: A Study in the Counter-Reformation* (Cambridge: Cambridge University Press, 1930), 11n.

church built.[19] Sister of Marie de Guise, queen-regent of Scotland,
who would be buried at St.-Pierre, Renée was for a time entrusted
with the care of her six-year-old niece, Mary Queen of Scots.[20]
Besides Renée's powerful family connections and her very active part
in building projects and promoting reform, she played a personal
part in ensuring that Le Picart's sermons were published. In the dedication to the *Instruction*, Bacquenois refers to ". . . this book, which
you ordered me to print . . ." He continues: "You will be the reason that a million honorable persons will become participants in a
great good, and will have occasion to learn how it is necessary to
honor, adore and truly recognize one's God, and to understand the
manner of true and perfect prayer."[21] At the beginning of the *Second
Livre*, Bacquenois states that ". . . you have given me, of your grace,
the sermons that he composed on the holy sacrament of the Altar."[22]
Although Renée had not even been born when Le Picart was exiled
to Reims in 1533, Le Picart's role as teacher and friend of her
brother, Charles de Guise, Cardinal of Lorraine, and his frequent
trips to Reims, would have given her direct contact with the great
preacher. She may well have heard him preach in the last months
of his life, when he was preaching and teaching at the fledgling university in Reims founded by her brother by an act of endowment
on April 1, 1554.[23] Chesneau recalls how well she personally knew
Le Picart's probity of life, eminent knowledge and Christian zeal.[24]
Elsewhere, Chesneau refers to her knowledge of Le Picart's great
largesse and charity,[25] and the special regard she had always felt for
him.[26] Since the earliest publications of Le Picart's sermons took
place in Reims, it seems clear that a powerful woman was responsible for their printing, a form of female patronage that was far from
unusual.[27]

[19] Guillaume Marlorat, *Histoire de la ville, cité et université de Reims: Métropolitaine de la Gaule Belgique* (Reims: L. Jacquet, 1846), 236.
[20] G. Crouvezier, *La vie d'une cité Reims au cours des siècles* (Paris: Nouvelles Éditions Latines, 1970), 71. The two sisters were buried close to one another in the choir of Saint-Pierre. Marlorat, *Reims*, 236. See also Joanne Baker, "Female Monasticism and Family Strategy: The Guises and St. Pierre de Reims," in *Sixteenth Century Journal* 28(1997), 1091–1108.
[21] Bacquenois, "Dedication," *Instruction*, fols. 5–6.
[22] Bacquenois, "Dedication," *SL*, i.
[23] Boussinesq and Laurent, *Histoire de Reims*, I:480.
[24] Chesneau, "Dedication," *Caresme*, fol. ii.
[25] Chesneau, "Dedication," *Pasques*, fol. vii.
[26] Chesneau, "Dedication," *Trinité*, fol. ii.
[27] Numerous women in the late Middle Ages had been responsible for the pub-

Chesneau dedicated one other of Le Picart's works to Abbess Renée. This was the *Épistre*, a short work reproduced in its entirety in Appendix A, which Chesneau claims (unfortunately without elaboration),[28] ". . . was written in his own hand, as everyone knows quite well, when he was forbidden to preach in Paris."[29] A treatise on the holy sacrament of the altar, it was composed ". . . upon the request of our good cousin and singular friend, Sister Jehanne of Paris, by letters she sent me. She saw me completely useless as a result of the interdiction against preaching which was made against me, which upset me greatly, so I began to write this . . ."[30] Providing as it does a firsthand glimpse into what Le Picart was thinking at the time of his greatest tribulation, his exile by Francis I in 1533, this short treatise is fascinating evidence. Another work published in the name of François Le Picart may or may not be his work. *Les grans souffrages et oraisons*, undated, was published in Rouen by Nicolas Vaultier. Although Le Picart did preach in Rouen,[31] there were other François Le Picarts, including a Norman poet and a "Franciscus Picard" from Nevers who was principal of the Collège de l'Ave Maria.[32] There is further reason to question Le Picart's connection to this volume. The publisher, either Nicolas Vaultier, who published the full volume, or Thomas Mailard, whose name is attached to *Les grans souffrages* as the second part of the volume, had no known connection to Le Picart. Moreover, this is an edited collections of prayers by other authors, a task that would have required Le Picart's collaboration. Finally, while the subjects chosen in no way eliminate our Le Picart as the redactor, they do not bear a strong resemblance to his choice of topics or subjects in the sermon collections.[33]

---

lication of sermons. In Nuremberg, for example, Johannes Nider had his sermons printed at the request of townswomen. John Dahmus, "Preaching to the Laity in Fifteenth Century Germany: Johannes Nider's 'Harps'," *Journal of Ecclesiastical History* 12(1982), 59.

[28] In all likelihood this *épistre*, presumably in the possession of a family member, only came to light when the publishers began to gather together the sermons for publication.

[29] Chesneau, "Preface," *Épistre*, fol. 3.

[30] Le Picart, *Épistre*, fol. 4.

[31] Feret, P.Y., *La faculté de théologie de Paris et ses docteurs les plus célèbres: Époque moderne* (Paris: Picard, 1900–1910), II:97.

[32] James Farge, *Biographical Register of Paris Doctors of Theology, 1500–1536* (Toronto: Pontifical Institute, 1980), 264.

[33] Prayer was a very important part of Le Picart's program for Catholic piety, and many of those chosen for this collection fit his beliefs, including one on the sacrament of the altar and another on how to live well. Still, the choice of authors

Five complete sermons have been reproduced in Appendix B, including three that are dated—the penultimate sermon given by Le Picart before his death in September, 1556 (B.1), and one for the feast of the Holy Cross in 1555 (B.2). The third is a sermon given at the funeral of his fellow Catholic preacher, the Franciscan Pierre Descornes (B.3), and can be dated to a day or two after 21 May 1549. There are also two undated sermons for the second Sunday after Easter (B.4 and B.5). In addition to these dated sermons, internal references suggest a full range of dates during his preaching career, at least from the 1530s. I have speculated elsewhere that derogatory references to kingship and allowing heretics to preach freely in Paris can only refer to the celebrated events of 1533–34, when Gérard Roussel preached at the Louvre under the sponsorship of Marguerite of Navarre, and which ultimately led to Le Picart's imprisonment and exile.[34] In several places, Le Picart refers to the "recent" taking of Boulogne by the English; elsewhere he mentions how many years France has suffered under the tyranny of heresy. Other dates can be reconstructed from his references, as when he remarks, "The king wanted finally to meet with the Emperor, his brother-in-law at Nice, where by the intervention of Our Holy Father the Pope, they made a truce for ten years."[35] References to Luther as being alive or dead, concrete references to doctrines emanating from Geneva, and other statements in the sermons allow us to posit a range of dates for a number of sermons. Since the printed sermons were taken from listeners' notes, Le Picart's notoriety in 1533–34 may have begun the process. This is further suggested by the hostile *Histoire ecclésiastique*, compiled by Theodore Beza, which notes that "... since [1533] Le Picart has been held to be one of the principal pillars of the Roman Church ..."[36]

---

does not correlate exactly with his use of sources in the sermons. The author of this collection includes works of Aquinas, Gregory, Pope Innocent, William of Paris and Jean Gerson. Included are prayers for St. Brigid, an instruction on better government, a prayer for St. Margaret, and one on the effusions of the blood of Jesus Christ. The latter suggests an earlier authorship than would be consistent with Le Picart's ministry. François Le Picart, *Les grans souffrages et oraisons* (Rouen: Nicolas Vaultier, n.d.).

[34] Larissa Taylor, "Comme un chien mort: Preaching About Kingship in France, 1460–1572," *Proceedings of the Western Society for French History* 22(1995), 157–170.

[35] Le Picart, *Trinité*, fol. 137.

[36] Théodore de Bèze, *Histoire ecclésiastique des églises réformées au royaume de France*, eds. G. Baum and E. Cunitz (Paris: Fischbacher, 1883), I:26–27.

Specific stylistic and linguistic differences strongly support the collation of sermons from different sets of notes. Particularly among the *Trinité* sermons, one can discern fairly easily "early" versus "late" sermons, as well as the idiosyncrasies of different notetakers, evident in spite of Chesneau's editorial expertise. In some cases, especially in the earlier sermons, the publisher would likely have had fewer exemplars from which to produce the printed text. The printed texts of the sermons are in most cases complete or nearly complete sermons, which if delivered would require approximately one hour, the standard length for a sermon. This correlates with internal evidence. Although Le Picart often preached more than once a day, in the morning and in the afternoon, he seems to have adhered to the suggested one-hour limit for sermons. In one sermon he says, "I am running a little late, but I wish the hour were longer, so that I could speak of the honor and dignity of priests; but that's enough for this hour."[37] He points out that if someone complains about the length of a sermon, it is often a sign he is short on devotion.[38] "When someone enjoys a sermon, he will say, 'I don't think the sermon lasted an hour.' Another will say, 'he really bored me! The sermon was too long!'"[39]

Bacquenois's editions are numbered in pages, while Chesneau's are in folio. When converted, the total in 269 sermons and one epistle adds up to almost 3,200 pages. The sermons themselves are a testament to dramatic changes in Catholic homiletic practice during the early sixteenth century in response to both humanism and Protestantism.[40] Different in every way from sermons of preachers only a few years older than Le Picart, the tedious thematic structure of the "modern method" is gone, replaced by a much simplified form.[41] Gone too are the numerous references to non-scriptural sources, bawdy or humorous anecdotes, and zoological exempla—in fact, all of the characteristics of the late medieval sermon. Instead, Le Picart offers simple and easily understood analogies of the following sort:

---

[37] Le Picart, *Advent*, fol. 44.

[38] Ibid, fol. 176.

[39] Ibid, fol. 100.

[40] Larissa Juliet Taylor, "The Influence of Humanism on Post-Reformation Catholic Preachers in France," *Renaissance Quarterly* 50(1997), 115–131.

[41] Le Picart seems to have anticipated the changes coming out of Rome by the second half of the sixteenth century. See Frederick J. McGinness, *Right Thinking and Sacred Oratory in Counter-Reformation Rome* (Princeton: Princeton University Press, 1995).

If a woman, loving her husband greatly, knows that he has come home from a great distance, would it not be very painful for her if she could not see him? If love makes pain, when the heart cannot rejoice in that which it desires, what kind of pain is it to a soul in purgatory, seeing that it is separated from the grace of God, when the vision of God is kept from the soul?[42]

All of the sermons were printed in French—a sharp departure from fifteenth and early sixteenth-century practice, when Latin was the language of printing. In the years of Le Picart's ministry, the French language began to make headway. In 1501, only eight of 88 books printed in Paris had been in French, but by 1530–1549 approximately 25% were in the vernacular. By 1573, a majority of works were printed in French.[43] Francis Higman's research has pointed to the proliferation of Catholic writings published in French in the second half of the sixteenth century, a trend strongest in the 1560s.[44] Typically, such works used justificatory language claiming that it would "be more decent to respond in Latin," lamenting that their opponents made the use of the vernacular necessary.[45] Just a few years after Le Picart's death, in 1560, another Catholic polemicist, Antoine de Mouchy, wrote of a Huguenot work: "[This book] is small in size, but very great in wickedness. Which [tract] is in French, and does not use Latin, so that it may be understood by all, in order to be more harmful and seduce more people, especially the simple and ignorant common folk. Whereby it is necessary to reply in the same language, to prevent such a book from confusing or seducing anyone."[46] Vernacular Catholic writings thus served as an antidote to the new and virulent Protestant poison.[47] Prior to the Reformation, sermons had almost always been printed in Latin for use by other clergymen throughout Europe, *not* the educated laity. Chesneau makes explicit that the printing of these sermons was a new weapon in the

---

[42] Le Picart, *Pasques*, fol. 23.

[43] Lucien Febvre and Henri-Jean Martin, *The Coming of the Book: The Impact of Printing, 1450–1800* (NLB, 1979), 321. Francis I's edict at Villers-Cotterêts of 1539, while limited to governmental publications, certainly had a more generalized impact on the culture of print.

[44] F.M. Higman, "Theology in French: Religious Pamphlets from the Counter-Reformation," *Renaissance and Modern Studies* 23(1979), 130.

[45] Ibid, 131.

[46] Quoted in G. Wylie Sypher, "'Faisant ce qu'il leur vient à plaisir': The Image of Protestantism in French Catholic Polemic on the Eve of the Religious Wars," *Sixteenth Century Journal* 11(1980), 59.

[47] Ibid, 64.

arsenal against heresy. He claims "that all those who amuse themselves and delight in reading these new [heretical] books, would be
far better off to use their time reading, with a pure heart and free
from all bad intentions, the books and excellent works that have
been written against these heresies by the good and holy doctors of
the past."[48] It was a major step when Catholic writers and theologians overcame the bias against publishing in the vernacular, for this
opened up the possibility of the democratization of religious belief,
with all its attendant dangers:

> The wholesale production of religious texts in a long-lived form "made
> it possible to scrutinize discourse in a different kind of way by giving oral
> communication a semi-permanent form", and "thus scrutiny favoured
> the increase in scope of critical activity, and hence of rationality, scep-
> ticism, and logic".... Above all, perhaps, religious discourse laid out
> before the readers' eyes increased the possibility for individual abstract
> thought as opposed to the contemplation of the concrete images visi-
> ble in churches. Utterance in writing could be inspected in detail and
> taken in or out of context, as opposed to preaching, which was tied
> to a particular occasion, person or institution.[49]

Le Picart's sermons are all the more important for understanding
Paris before the Religious Wars because they are unique. In the
period after 1530 and before 1560, there was a precipitous decline
in the printing of Catholic sermons in France. This may well have
been due to a glut on the market—so many sermon books had been
printed during the incunabular period that most preachers would
have had easy access to both model sermon collections and numerous works by near-contemporary preachers. Censorship may also
have had a chilling effect on publication. But there are other issues
involved. It was in the 1530s that the French king decreed that
French would be the language of governmental business. This was
a period of linguistic transition, which would hold true for the printing of sermons as well. Yet the answer is more likely to be found
in the attitudes of reformers toward publishing their sermons.

> ... [T]he reformers showed a certain indifference toward the sermons
> pronounced by their pastors. Thus during an entire century ... they
> hardly thought at all about publishing them. From Farel and Viret we

---

[48] Chesneau, "Dedication," *Pasques*, fol. v.
[49] David J. Nicholls, "The Nature of Popular Heresy in France, 1520–1542,"
The Historical Journal 26(1983), 265.

have no sermon printed during their lifetime. Beza only published his sermons at the end of his career. In German Switzerland it was the same. There were only two exceptions to this rule: Bullinger and Calvin.[50]

Why was this the case? Most likely, it can be attributed to two factors: 1) the newness of the reformed faith, which did not rely on previous exemplars and tradition; and 2) the emphasis on inspiration by the Holy Spirit. It is very likely that this also influenced Catholic sermon printing. Undoubtedly, most Catholic preachers realized that they were in a situation *defined* by its novelty—although this was a critical time for the faith, seeming to necessitate the printing of model sermons, uncertainties about what the next day would bring and differences within the reformed ranks made it an unappealing option. Fixing the Word of God as preached in these early years of the Reformation in print would have been the least effective means of answering the constantly changing Protestant threat, for sermons needed to be fluid in their response. Le Picart and others no doubt felt that their most pressing task was to combat heresy in the most effective way possible—from the pulpit.[51] Thus, during the period from 1530 to 1560, we have almost no Catholic printed sermons.[52] The situation changed in the years after 1560, as war began, and as Calvinism began to be seen as the central threat. That is why Chesneau and Bacquenois chose to publish Le Picart's sermons at that point. They represent the only substantial source for Catholic preaching during the three decades before the wars.

Each of Le Picart's sermons begins with the Biblical reading of the day, given in Latin, which he then translated into French for the listeners. Le Picart would regularly come back to this passage, repeating the Latin. Other Latin sentences appear in the body of the sermon, almost always Biblical texts which are then translated. These should be distinguished from marginal glosses and references, which were aids supplied by the printer for the edification of the

---

[50] Edmond Grin, "Deux sermons de Pierre Viret, leurs thèmes théologiques et leur actualité," *Theologische Zeitschrift* 18(1962), 116.

[51] See Larissa Juliet Taylor, "Out of Print: The Decline of Catholic Printed Sermons in France, 1530–1560," in Robin B. Barnes, Robert A. Kolb, and Paula Presley, eds., *Books Have Their Own Destiny: Essays in Honor of Robert V. Schnucker* (Kirksville, MO: Sixteenth Century Essays and Studies, 1998), 105–113.

[52] There are occasional funeral sermons for these years, as well as a small collection of sermons by Étienne Paris, *Homelies suyvant les matières traictees ès principals festes & solennitez de l'annee* (Paris: Robineau, 1553).

reader/user. The sources mentioned in the body of the sermon were probably in the preached sermon, and were usually identified by origin to the listeners; for example, the preacher might say, "St. Paul tells us," or "as Chrysostom says."

Le Picart's sermons are peppered with trademark phrases. His most famous was "*O* [or *ah*] *Mater Dei!*," which he typically exclaimed when upset or exasperated: "One discovers the hearts of people . . . when one asks for something for the poor: 'My wife isn't here!' *Ah Mater Dei!* This excuse isn't worth anything!"[53] He was so well-known for this expression that it drew ridicule from his Calvinist opponents. Theodore Beza exclaimed, "Oh! Master Le Picart, if you were here, you would certainly say, '*O Mater Dei!*' And the children would all make fun of you! [And you would say:] 'So much does my zeal for our Holy Mother Church excite me, that my bowels are so moved that were it not out of respect for Your *Présente Abbatialité*, they would be loosed in my pants.'"[54] Le Picart would often finish a sermon with "that will be enough for now."[55]

Although Le Picart served as dean of St.-Germain l'Auxerrois from 1548 until his death eight years later, he preached throughout the city of Paris as well as in Reims, Rouen, Meaux and elsewhere in northern France. Sources indicate that even after his appointment he continued to preach at two of the most important Parisian churches, St.-Jacques-de-la-Boucherie and St.-Eustache. Le Picart was above all a popular preacher, rather than one who delivered his sermons to the court or to groups of churchmen or monks. Because Le Picart was far more interested in instructing ordinary people than in training other preachers, as reflected in his lack of interest in printing his sermons, he spends less time than most pre-Reformation French preachers discussing his philosophy of preaching. Yet occasionally he offers a few glimpses into his beliefs on this subject, especially when students or priests made up a substantial part of his audience. In one sermon, he begins, "My friends, seeing that there are several preachers of the Church of God in attendance, I will teach you the art of preaching well."[56] As had almost all of his predecessors, Le

---

[53] Le Picart, *Advent*, fol. 31.
[54] Théodore de Bèze, *Le passavant de Théodore de Bèze, Épître de Maître Benoît passavant à Messire Pierre Lizet* (Paris: Isidore Liseux, 1875), 58.
[55] Le Picart, *SL*, 74, 152.
[56] Le Picart, *Trinité*, fol. 36.

Picart insists that the preacher must lead a good life, and practice
what he preaches: "Do you want to learn to be good preachers? . . .
[P]reachers must lead a more holy life than ordinary people."[57] He
warns that the preacher ". . . must not trust in his own knowledge
no matter how great a clergyman he is, but in the Word and promise
of God."[58] He should not speak in a grand style, but bear in mind
his mission: "The preacher should not use elegant and fancy-sounding
words, as St. Paul tells us: *When I came to you, brothers and sisters, I did
not come proclaiming the mystery of God to you in lofty words or wisdom*
[I Corinthians 2:1]. The preacher must abandon "high theology"
and "difficult doctrines" in his sermons so that everyone can understand him.[59] He continues:

> Do you want to learn how to preach? It's when you realize the peo-
> ple are beginning to understand the justice of God. It's important to
> keep a place for the compassion of God as well, so that people don't
> despair. However, one must present justice to the presumptuous ones
> . . . in order to bring them around, as St. Paul showed . . . giving the
> fear of God to those who trust too much in his mercy, and pulling
> the timid ones away from the depth of this sea of justice toward God's
> compassion.[60]

The main goal of a would-be preacher should be to reproach and
correct faults,[61] speaking ". . . like a dog who barks."[62] Le Picart tells
the students that "when you see these great lords and ladies who
live so delicately and in such voluptuosity, who are so lazy and dis-
inclined to do good, in order to give them courage and reinvigorate
them, you must feed them vinegar, something bitter . . ."[63] The
preacher must be persistent, but Le Picart warns the novice not to
". . . marvel that no one at all converts."[64] A good preacher must be
patient, and never give up.[65] "In what our Lord Jesus Christ said to
the women, just as he said to the Magdalene, it is demonstrated and
taught that one should not hesitate to say a good proposition, a good

---

[57] Ibid, fol. 37.
[58] Ibid, fol. 38.
[59] Ibid, fols. 37, 179.
[60] Ibid, fol. 37.
[61] Ibid, fol. 36.
[62] Le Picart, *Trinité-II*, fol. 70.
[63] Le Picart, *Trinité*, fol. 150.
[64] Le Picart, *Trinité-II*, fol. 38.
[65] Ibid.

word, or a good sermon twice."[66] Against the heretical onslaught, sound preaching was more necessary than ever. "It is essential to teach healthy doctrine, so that one does not engender scandal in anyone. It is not enough to say the truth, but one must say it well . . . so that one gives no occasion for anyone to stray. It is also important for the preacher to say and uncover the cunning and deception of the heretics so that people can be on guard. I would be well content never to speak about this, because it is not edifying, but it is necessary . . ." He adds that the preacher who does not ". . . contradict them . . . renders himself suspect."[67]

To move the audience had been one of the classical Augustinian prescriptions for good preaching, but Le Picart takes it further, relying on the advice of his favorite Church Father: "Today one calls a man a hypocrite if he makes the people cry at a sermon. What do you want to do, make them laugh? If they don't cry at the sermon, they will cry elsewhere, with great pain, as St. John Chrysostom tells us: 'Never let your people leave a sermon without tears in their eyes.'"[68]

An analysis of Le Picart's citation of sources in his sermons shows the degree to which he has adapted his homiletic style to changed circumstances. Two-thirds of all the sources quoted in the 270 sermons are taken from the New Testament (see Table I), an astonishingly high figure compared to all pre-Reformation French preaching and even that of some near contemporaries.[69]

Table I

New Testament Sources

(Total Number = 6513)

Matthew	1211
Mark	160
Luke	795
John	964
Acts	329
Romans	735

---

[66] Le Picart, *Caresme-II*, fol. 185.
[67] Le Picart, *Pasques*, fol. 262.
[68] Le Picart, *Trinité-II*, fol. 188.
[69] Larissa Taylor, *Soldiers of Christ: Preaching in Late Medieval and Reformation France* (New York: Oxford University Press, 1992), 74–79.

(Table I cont.)

Corinthians	805
Galatians	122
Ephesians	168
Philippians	138
Colossians	49
Thessalonians	69
Timothy	230
Titus	38
Philemon	9
Hebrews	305
James	106
Peter	119
John	21
Jude	0
Revelation	140

By contrast, only twenty-three percent of Le Picart's references come from the Old Testament, with 22% of those from the Pentateuch, 9% from the Historical Books, 50% from the Wisdom Books, and 19% from the Prophetic Books (see Table II).

Table II

Old Testament Sources

(Total Number = 2192)

PENTATEUCH

Genesis	276
Exodus	102
Leviticus	13
Numbers	21
Deuteronomy	41
Joshua	21
Judges	6
Ruth	0

HISTORICAL BOOKS

Kings/Samuel	139
Chronicles	10
Ezra	2
Nehemiah	0
Tobit	15
Judith	19

(Table II cont.)

Esther	6
Maccabees	15

WISDOM BOOKS

Job	52
Psalms	748
Proverbs	97
Ecclesiastes	82
Song of Songs	13
Wisdom	51
Sirach	53

PROPHETIC BOOKS

Isaiah	187
Jeremiah	69
Lamentations	5
Baruch	3
Ezekiel	31
Daniel	36
Hosea	12
Joel	12
Amos	9
Obadiah	0
Jonah	7
Micah	5
Nahum	0
Habbakuk	2
Zephaniah	0
Haggai	0
Zechariah	10
Malachi	22

Finally, only ten percent of Le Picart's sources are non-scriptural (Table III).

Table III

Non-Biblical Sources

(Total Number = 1007)

Chrysostom	333
Augustine	156
Jerome	117
Ambrose	58

(Table III cont.)

Bernard	49
Cyprian	42
Rupert	36
Gregory the Great	31
Origen	28
Aristotle	23
Thomas Aquinas	21
Theophylactus	14
Ovid	12
Eusebius	12
Basil	8
Jean Gerson	9
John Damascene	8
Irenaeus	6
Cicero	5
Bede	4
Athanasius	4
Other	31

The thirty-one other references include citations from Clement, Innocent III, Hugo of St. Victor, Cyril, Bonaventure, Virgil, Terence, Horace, Pliny, Boethius, Lactantius, Gregory Nazianzene, Denis Areopagite, Reatus, Arius and Berengarius.

What do these figures tell us? The preponderance of New Testament citations suggests both a continuation of imitation of Christ themes so popular at the end of the Middle Ages as well as an anticipation of the Catholic Reformation's emphasis on the gospels. For Le Picart and many other preachers of the mid-sixteenth century, the New Testament seemed more relevant than the Old.[70] Making Jesus, Paul and the early Church an even more central part of his mission seemed to Le Picart the best way to renew an embattled faith and fight heretics, just as the primitive Church and its Fathers had done. By contrast, Protestants of the late sixteenth century tended to put both Testaments on an equal footing.[71]

The synoptic gospels are heavily represented in Le Picart's sermons, comprising 48% of all New Testament references, with Matthew and

---

[70] On this point, people of such different beliefs as Le Picart, the early Jesuits and Rabelais were in agreement.

[71] Pierre Chaunu, *Église, culture et société: Essais sur réforme et contre-réforme 1517–1620* (Paris: SEDES., 1984), 338.

John quoted most frequently. However, a note of caution is in order. As Chesneau or Bacquenois added the citations to the margins, they would frequently cite all the places in the gospels which said more or less the same thing, thus doubling or tripling certain citations from the spoken version. Similarly, the frequent usage of a gospel passage as the theme, repeated regularly throughout the sermon, multiplied the appearances. The actual references to the synoptic gospels in a delivered sermon was therefore smaller. What is more interesting is Le Picart's extensive use of Paul's epistles, especially the Letters to the Romans and Corinthians, which alone total 24% of the New Testament citations. Although the Pauline epistles were by no means the exclusive preserve of the reformers,[72] Le Picart's engagement with Paul brought him into close contact with the issues raised especially by Luther, and allowed him to use Paul in defense of orthodoxy. That he did so consciously is obvious in the sermons, as he quotes Paul directly to refute heretical doctrines and preaching. Interestingly, only about 2% of the New Testament citations come from the Book of Revelation, arguing strongly against the view that an approaching apocalypse informed Le Picart's vision and preaching.

An analysis of the Old Testament books mentioned in Le Picart's sermons is very revealing. Six books (Psalms, Genesis, Isaiah, Kings/ Samuel [Kings I–IV in the Vulgate], Proverbs, and Exodus) make up 71% of all Old Testament references. One-third of the Old Testament citations come from Psalms. Once again, this suggests that Le Picart is trying to meet the heretics on their own ground in order to refute them. The heavy use of the Wisdom Books indicates a desire to find comfort and draw strength from God in a time of tribulation. Except for the long book of Isaiah, Le Picart shows little interest in the Prophetic Books, again arguing against an identification with the Hebrew prophets. Only one percent of references are taken from the Old Testament's most apocalyptic book, Daniel.

Le Picart's use of non-scriptural sources is equally intriguing. He takes only 10% of all his citations from sources other than the Bible, a very substantial reduction from that of two generations of preachers preceding him, who typically took one-quarter of their references

---

[72] "To quote Saint Paul, to rely on Saint Paul, to be inspired by Saint Paul— this did not mean to be Reformed. . . . Many Catholics who remained Catholics formed their religious thought on his writings." Febvre, *Problem of Unbelief*, 276.

from such sources.[73] The Greek Father Chrysostom (357–407), known as the "Golden-Tongued" was his overwhelming favorite, comprising 33% of all non-Biblical citations. Chrysostom had been used by earlier preachers, but rarely comprised more than 5% of all references.[74] Augustine, the favorite of most pre-Reformation French preachers, is a distant second, accounting for only 15% of references. Le Picart's training in Greek had given him the skills to read Chrysostom and other Greek Fathers in the original language. Moreover, Le Picart would have identified with Chrysostom's struggle to reform his clergy and fight against the Arian heresy. Finally, Chrysostom's unjust exile at the whim of the emperor would have struck a responsive chord.[75] As we shall see in Chapter Five, some of the explanation for the overwhelming reliance on the gospels, and the choice of non-Biblical sources came from Le Picart's friendship and involvement with the early Jesuits.

It takes considerably more imagination to reconstruct Le Picart's actual preaching, although we are fortunate to have many excellent sources. There are testimonials in poems and eulogies from those who admired him as well as denunciations by Calvin and Beza which round out the picture of Le Picart's performance as a preacher. His seventeenth-century biographer Hilarion de Coste wrote, "If he spoke to his auditors of simple things, he did so with a simple form, so that he could say with David, jumping before the arch, I want to appear vile before both God and men; and with Esther he held in horror and abomination the pompous ornaments, artifices and beauties of eloquence."[76] Once again, René Benoist offers helpful information. According to Benoist, Le Picart was a good companion, always humble, true, wise, modest and compassionate. He attests that the method, style, and word choices of the printed sermons reflected the preacher's actual usage in the pulpit.[77] Raban Maur, in his ecclesiastical commentary of 1544, compares him to classical Roman orators: ". . . [Y]ou carry our time with fitting praises,/Certainly

---

[73] Taylor, *Soldiers of Christ*, 75–78.

[74] Ibid, 75–76.

[75] See Timothy E. Gregory, *Vox Populi: Popular Opinion and Violence in the Religious Controversies of the Fifth Century A.D.* (Columbus, 1979), 46; Frederic M. Prethes, *Life of John Chrysostom, Based on the Investigations of Neander, Böhringer, and Others* (Boston: John P. Jewett, 1854), 43–61, 192–197.

[76] Hilarion de Coste, *Parfait ecclesiastique*, 55.

[77] Benoist, "Preface," *Caresme*, fol. vi–vii.

you will give golden names to these times:/Just as tradition reports of Cicero's time . . ."[78] The preacher and polemicist Artus Desiré, who admired and almost certainly knew Le Picart,[79] states in the preface to his memorial volume: "You see now how much he served you/ . . . In the pulpit hardy, like a powerful lion."[80] He continues in the words of Bruictquicourt, one of the two speakers in the poem, "He was the drumbeat of war,/And the great trumpet of France,/Who sounded with such great power/That the sound coming from him/Was heard by all./He was the most expert doctor/And the voice crying in the desert,/Prepare the way and the place/For the great leader Son of God . . . /He was the hammer of the shameless/Who heckled the heretics/And forged the peace/Between the good and the bad./He was the pearl of Paris . . ."[81] About his preaching, Bruictquicourt adds, "He was a faithful servant/Who preached with such great zeal,/That by his preaching/Was caused the conversion/Of innumerable poor souls,/And principally women/Whom he drew away/By his prayer from the brothel."[82] Another would-be poet, Barbier Aubusson de la Maisonneuve, provides similar images of Le Picart's preaching in his eulogy: "Oh cruel death, alas! which caused to die/This great Doctor, the pearl of our age,/Who so made the holy church flourish./Alas! It is Le Picart who helped/To duty by a salutary sermon/ . . . Doctor who was so necessary/To preach Christian charity to you . . . /Whose sermon full of maturity/Converted so many wicked and perverse ones/ . . . Cry for this pillar of the Holy Church./Cry for him who preached without dissimulation . . ."[83] Le Picart's close friend Gabriel Dupuiherbault likewise commemorated his preaching: "Who was . . . more skilful in teaching by faith?/Or more happy in cherishing faith?/Or more lively in watching over the faith?/He would keep teaching the people./Who was more popular or more passionate?/He especially excited the passions of the age/Stimulating many to the love of Christ,/Fixed in his heart, how many heard/The

---

[78] Rabanus Maur, *In ecclesiasticum commentarii, recens in lucem editi* (Paris: Simon Colinoeum, 1544), fol. iiii.

[79] Giese, *Artus Désiré*, 133.

[80] Desiré, *Les regretz et complainctes*, fol. Aii.

[81] Ibid, fol. Aiiii.

[82] Ibid, fol. B.

[83] Barbier Aubusson de la Maisonneuve, *Deploration sur le trespas de noble & vénérable personne monsieur maistre François Picard, Docteur en Theologie, Doyen de sainct Germain de lauxerrois, qui mourut à Paris le dixseptiesme iour de Septembre, l'an mil cinq cens cinquante & six. Par un poete François.* (Paris: Estienne Denise, 1556), fols. Aii–Aiiii.

emotional excitement of his soul/Always speaking with passion?/
...Who ever worked more strongly for a cause?"[84] In his eulogy,
Robert Ceneau, Bishop of Avranches, exclaimed that Le Picart was
like "...a parrot, with a sweet and eloquent song, a talkative bird's
beak, with deaf ears, molested from many parts. But this stainless
and good one was without bile himself."[85] The earliest Jesuits, close
to Le Picart as his friends and students, expressed the views of so
many: "Our most famous master Le Picart['s] name is a cause of
honor, [he] who with a spirit of fervor and piety preaches greatly
with much fruit in Paris. Besides him there is hardly anyone."[86] The
Jesuit Possevino reminisced that "[t]his man was the most celebrated
of his generation, who suffered greatly for his preaching of the
gospels."[87]

Le Picart's Calvinist adversaries offer testimony no less revealing.
Beza describes Le Picart at an execution in Paris in 1548 of a heretic
named Seraphin and four others from Langres:[88]

> François Le Picart, in place of crying out and blustering in his accus-
> tomed manner, exhorted to patience one of the five, who with a smil-
> ing face when these words were said to him, said: "Monsieur our
> Master, praise be to God that you've changed your language: but if
> you were in my place, would you dare to brag about having as good
> a patience as God has given me?"[89]

John Calvin (1509–1564), an almost exact contemporary, refers to
Le Picart in his sermons and treatises. In his 1547 *Acts of the Council
of Trent with the Antidote*, he writes, "it is clear that the master is completely devoid of brains, belongs to the class of fanatics, and is little better than a madman."[90] In 1550 he complained, "Master François

---

[84] Gabriel Dupuiherbault, *De penitence, et des parties d'icelle, selon la verité de l'Eglise
orthodoxe & catholique, & la necessité de salut... auquel sont adiouxtez les Epitaphes de feu
Monsieur Picart.* (Paris: Jean de Roigny, 1556), n.p.

[85] Robert Ceneau, quoted in Hilarion de Coste, *Le parfait ecclésiastique*, 432.

[86] *Fontes Narrativi de S. Ignatio de Loyola et de Societatis Iesu Initiis, II: Narrationes Scriptae
Annis 1557–1574* (Rome: MHSI, 1951).

[87] Antonio Possevino, *Apparatus Sacer* (Venice: Venetian Society, 1603), 505.

[88] Séraphin d'Argences was also known as Robert Le Lièvre and Antoine
Deschamps; in the exemplary punishment designed by the *Chambre Ardente*, Seraphin
was given a taller stake than his disciples. After the actual burning in Paris, he was
burned in effigy in Langres as well as at Sens, Blois, Bourges, Angers and the other
places where he had preached. David Nicholls, "The Theatre of Martyrdom in the
French Reformation," *Past and Present* 121(1988), 54–55.

[89] Bèze, *Histoire ecclésiastique*, I:72–73.

[90] John Calvin, *Tracts and Treatises in Defense of the Reformed Faith*, trans. Henry
Beveridge (Grand Rapids: W.B. Eerdmans, 1958), III:33.

Le Picart, doctor of Paris, crying in his accustomed fashion like a
man who has lost his senses, has dared to say that at Geneva we
deny all religion. He is truly a crazy man out of his mind."[91] But
Calvin's friend and follower Beza is the most vituperative. In the
Histoire ecclésiastique, Beza calls Le Picart a "tempestuous spirit" and
a "choleric rabid dog," but admits he is one of the principal pillars
of the Roman Catholic Church.[92] Elsewhere, playing with rhymes,
he refers to Le Picart as "... *pie bavarde*, because he doesn't know
what he says and he gives you a headache with his chattering ..."[93]
He goes on, "Master Le Picart customarily shakes his purse shouting
Mater Dei against the Lutherans,"[94] and cries that we "... want to
abolish all the ecclesiastical customs. But cry, if that pleases you,
until you crack: the thing is no less false."[95]

Denis Crouzet suggests that Le Picart also tried to incite his crowds
to violence against the reformers. Crouzet points to a passage in the
Histoire ecclésiastique in support of his view:

> [In 1559], almost the same thing happened at St. Eustache. Because
> one of our masters, called the friend of the late Le Picart, preached
> nothing but blood and murder, and incited the Parisians to kill, mak-
> ing pretty promises to those who would so employ themselves. The
> people didn't disappoint him. For it having happened that a poor
> scholar (having come there out of devotion to hear the sermon), laughed
> with one of his companions for some reason when all of a sudden an
> old woman bigot screamed that he was a Lutheran who was making
> fun of the preacher. Hearing her, the people threw themselves upon
> him, without having in any other way heard of this, and taking him
> outside, massacred him miserably till they had torn his eyes out of his
> head with their hands. Another was found who had his horse tram-
> ple over the man's belly three times. The situation merited the atten-
> tion of the magistrat or an inquest, but this notwithstanding, it remained
> unpunished even though testimony wasn't hard to come by (since the
> murderers were proud of what they had done) ...[96]

A gruesome situation, to be sure, from which Crouzet suggests that
Le Picart was not only a man for whom the reform of the church

---

[91] Jean Calvin, *Des scandales qui empeschent auiourdhuy beaucoup de gens de venir à la pure doctrine de l'Evangile, & en desbauchent d'autres* (Geneva: Jean Crespin, 1550), 110.

[92] Bèze, *Histoire ecclésiastique*, I:26–27; Bèze, *Passavant*, 188.

[93] Bèze, *Passavant*, 62.

[94] Ibid, 80.

[95] Ibid, 156.

[96] Bèze, *Histoire ecclésiastique*, I:194; for Crouzet's interpretations, see Crouzet, *Guerriers de Dieu*, I:209; *Genèse*, 432.

was essential, but one "for whom a violent solution was fundamental." Crouzet suggests that because this man was named "Le Picart's friend," he must have been imitating the actions of his predecessor.[97] There are several problems with such an interpretation. As we have seen, Beza and his reformed brethren were no friends of Le Picart, and any testimony from them must be treated as hostile. Furthermore, just because someone is named as a friend of someone else in no way proves identical beliefs or behaviors. Finally, the date of 1559 is all important. Had Le Picart been alive in 1559, he might have shared the sentiments of this unnamed preacher. But he was not. As we shall see later, circumstances between Le Picart's death and the beginning of the Religious Wars had changed dramatically in almost every respect.

Le Picart was aware of the attacks on him, but chose to turn the other cheek. "... It's a regular thing, that when someone is corrected by another, and takes it ill, he says, 'This is a preacher who only knows how to cry and bluster [*se tempester*]; he doesn't preach the gospel.'"[98] In response to the calumnies hurled at him, Le Picart answers, "Here is a man who wants to make me miserable, he injures me, and says the worst that he can about me. I know no better way to vanquish him than not to respond and say nothing, laughing about what he says to me. And when he sees that I don't respond to him, he will be completely confused and leave me alone."[99]

The combined witness of friend and enemy reveals a gifted preacher, a man who let insults and mockery roll off his back, zealous to spread the Word, and passionate in his denunciations of those who were in his view blaspheming against God. Calvin's testimony is perhaps the most compelling; however much he despised Le Picart and his efforts to halt the spread of reformed belief in France, he was forced to admit that "... he has such a reputation among his own, that everything he says is taken as if an angel had spoken."[100] Calvin's biographer, Émile Doumergue, admitted that Le Picart was "the soul of the people of Paris."[101] In the pages that follow, we will examine what he said in those sermons, and the religious climate of Paris in the critical decades before the onset of religious war.

---

[97] Personal communication, 3 January 1998.
[98] Le Picart, *Trinité-II*, fol. 28.
[99] Le Picart, *Instruction*, 233.
[100] Calvin, *Des scandales*, 110.
[101] Doumergue, *Calvin*, I:241.

CHAPTER TWO

THE EARLY YEARS, 1504–1533

Engravings in Aubin-Louis Millet's *Antiquités nationales*, based on no longer extant tomb sculptuary from the church of Notre-Dame-des-Blancs-Manteaux, show the parents of François Le Picart in simple garb. Jean Le Picart wears a togalike garment that probably was his official gown as king's secretary and notary. Jacquette de Champagne wears a modest, fitted gown, belted at the waist. The linings at the end of her sleeves are similar to those worn by Hospitalières in the eighteenth century, known as *sabots à la dévote*. Her hair is completely hidden under a plain headdress like that of a "simple beguine."[1] The inscription on their tombs listed simply their titles and the dates of their deaths, followed by the words, "Pray God for them."[2] Everything we know of their lives supports this picture of a devout and unpretentious couple, all the more surprising in view of their exalted position in Parisian society. The son of Martin Le Picart and Jeanne de Marle, Jean Le Picart[3] was seigneur of Villeron and Atilly, the latter title inherited from his father-in-law.[4] He also served as controller general of Burgundy. Jacquette was the daughter of Clerembaud de Champagne, Lieutenant General of the Artillery[5] and Jeanne de Folmariée.[6] The Le Picart family had been engaged in governmental service since at least 1351, when parlementary records refer to a duel between one Jean Picart and his son-in-law Jean d'Archon, who had accused him of incest.[7] Our Jean Le Picart served as notary and secretary to King Francis I until 1537, when he resigned the

---

[1] Aubin-Louis Millin, *Antiquités nationales, ou recueil de monuments, pour servir à l'histoire générale et particulière de l'Empire François* (Paris: M. Drouhin, 1792), IV:18, 19, 57.

[2] Hilarion de Coste, *Parfait ecclesiastique*, 276.

[3] BN Dossiers bleus, 521, 13638, fol. 37.

[4] BN Ms. Fr. 4752, "Champagne," fol. 52. For the de Marle family, see BN Dossiers bleus, 429, "de Marle," fols. 20–20vo.

[5] Jean Le Picart's costume in the tomb effigy is almost identical to that of Clerembaud, possibly out of respect for his father-in-law. Millin, *Antiquités*, 19.

[6] Hilarion de Coste, *Parfait ecclesiastique*, 7.

[7] Édouard Maugis, *Histoire de parlement de Paris de l'avènement des rois Valois à la mort d'Henri IV* (New York: Burt Franklin, 1914), I:519.

post to his son Jean.[8] The Le Picart family lived on the rue des Blancs-Manteaux on the right bank in the *quartier du Temple*, a part of the city noted for its concentration of members of the new financial aristocracy.[9] Jacquette died on 19 September 1522, having given birth to fifteen children. It was said at the time of her death that all Paris lamented her passing, for her charity had been great, but her husband continued her work.[10] Jean did not remarry, although he lived until 12 July 1549.

Jacquette's fecundity was not unique among Le Picart women and wives. Guillaume Budé's mother Catherine was Martin Le Picart's sister. The famous Greek scholar was among the youngest of eighteen children also born into a family that had prospered as royal servants. Because of the great number of children born to the different branches of the Le Picart family and their roles as royal officials and *parlementaires*, they were connected to every prominent Parisian family by marriage.[11] One relative, "Jean Picart, sieur d'Estelan" and *maître d'hôtel du roi* from 1515–1522 died fighting for Francis I at the Battle of Bicocca in April, 1522.[12]

---

[8] Hélène Michaud, *La grande chancellerie et les écritures royales au seizième siècle (1515–1589)* (Paris: Presses universitaires de France, 1967), 65n.

[9] Jean Favier, *Nouvelle histoire de Paris: Paris au XVe siècle, 1380–1500* (Paris: Hachette, 1974), 118.

[10] Hilarion de Coste, *Parfait ecclésiastique*, 26.

[11] Hilarion de Coste lists the following families that were allied to the Le Picarts: Aubri, Baudichon, Beaucaire, Bernage, Berthemont, Bodin, Boucher, Breban, de la Briere, Briçonnet, Bruslart, Budé, Carnus, Cauchon, Charlet, Charlot de Princé, Charpentier, Clausses de Marchaumont, de Caen, le Coq, les Corbies de Jaigny, Cossart, Courtin, de Greil, Dolu, du Drac, Ferret, Flecelle, Fontenais, Foucault, Fournier, Gelée, Hacqueville, Hallez, Herbelin, Habert, Hubert, Larcher, le Lievre, Longueval, Longueioye, Liorez, le Maistre, de Marle, Marcel, Mareuil, Millet, Moret, de Monceau, de la Motte du Muzeau, Paillart, Picon, Poncher, du Prez, Regnault, de la Rubie, Ruzez de Beaulieu, Sanguins de Livry & Meudon, Salart, Spifame, Sublets de Noyers, Talon, Thumeris, Turquan, du Val, Villemereau, Villemort, Vitri. Hilarion de Coste, *Parfait ecclésiastique*, 249–250. Further names can be gleaned from Châtelet records: Aymery, Barbeau, Barbette, Colletier, Deszasses, La Couppelle, Le Masuyer. Émile Campardon and Alexandre Tuetey, *Inventaire des registres des insinuations du Châtelet de Paris, Règnes de François Ier et de Henri II* (Paris: Imprimerie nationale, 1906), nos. 44, 51, 87–89, 99, 1395, 1480, 1514, 1552, 1889–1892, 2037, 2180–2183, 2211, 2225, 2274, 2352, 2380, 3552, 3600, 4118, 4791–4792, 5152. Michaud's research adds the following: Chevalier, Dupré, Guybert. LePileur, and Saint-Germain. Michaud, *Grande chancellerie*, 176; Farge lists the Harlays, Allegrins and de Thous. Farge, *Biographical Register*, 262. Finally, there were connections to the Basaniers, Disomes, Girards and Guichys. Michel Popoff, *Prosopographie des gens du parlement de Paris (1266–1753)* (Paris: Références, 1996), 792.

[12] V.-L. Bourrilly, ed., *Le journal d'un Bourgeois de Paris sous le règne de François Ier (1515–1536)* (Paris: Alphonse Picard et Fils, 1910), 115.

The third child of the marriage of Jean and Jacquette, François became the eldest son after the death of the first son, Raoul. His elder sister Jeanne married Jean de Salart, Sieur de Beuvron, de Montigny and des Marlotes, a king's counselor and master in the *Chambre des comptes* at Paris. Of his younger brothers, Christophe is the most well-known; born in 1505, he became seigneur of Sevigny in Thiérache.[13] Charles became a *parlementaire*; Jean followed in his father's footsteps; Clerembaud became Seigneur de Neufmoustier, des Chappelles and d'Aigrefin, and served as a captain of the king's army; and Eustache took the titles of Seigneur of Villeron and Atilly as well as that of Vaudargent and de Ver.[14] This is not the same Eustache who was Seigneur of Signy and Montguichet, a war commissar and keeper of the minutes of the Privy Council.[15] The youngest son, Guillaume, became a knight of the order of St. John of Jerusalem, and died in the taking of Algiers in 1541. Of François' younger sisters, Marie married Jean Cauchon, Sieur de Sillery and de Puisieux near Reims; her grandson was the famous Nicolas Bruslard de Sillery. Catherine entered the order of St. Francis and St. Clare at the royal monastery of Longchamps lés Paris, of which she became abbess in 1534. Jacqueline also entered orders, and became a Fontévriste at the convent of Filles-Dieu in Paris.[16]

François was born on April 16, 1504 in Paris, and was initially

---

[13] BN Dossiers bleus, 521, 13638, fol. 38.

[14] Hilarion de Coste, *Parfait ecclesiastique*, 17–20.

[15] François' brother Eustache contracted two marriages, to Marie le Feron and Anne Ruzé; the more well-known Eustache who fills a number of pages in Michaud's study was married to Marie Dupré. However, the latter was obviously a close relative. Even in someone who evidently sought honors and offices, his inventory after decease [AN Minutier central, Et. VI, 1.71, May, 1551] evinced fairly simple tastes. "His capital was probably valued at about 11,000li., divided thus: 2200li. in clothing, silver utensils, jewels and tapestries, 200li. in loans of money and 6800li. in landed property . . . [In] his house on the rue de la Potence . . . [t]here was a tableau painted on wood of the 'History of Lucretia' hanging in the room, valued at 30s. The rug and tapestries throughout the house were worth 668li. The only objects of value were a tapestry of the 'Judgment of Solomon' valued at 350li. and a vase of silver and gems (456li. and 577li.), none of which merited detailed description. If the wardrobe (507li. for husband and wife) included articles of sufficient quantity, fourteen robes for the husband and eleven gowns for the wife, none of these attained a considerable price, the most expensive being a cloak worth 81li. Eustache . . . accorded great importance to his lands. He had inherited . . . a part of the domain of Signy . . . [T]he manor house . . . was very humbly furnished (a Turkish rug in a lower room was 'all torn and ripped') . . ." Michaud, *Grande chancellerie*, 121, 176, 187.

[16] Hilarion de Coste, *Parfait ecclesiastique*, 19–22.

destined, like so many members of the Le Picart family, for a career in jurisprudence.[17] He was baptized by François de Rohan, Archbishop of Lyon, who served as his godfather, in the church of St. Jean en Grève. He was confirmed by his cousin, Étienne Poncher, Bishop of Paris and future Archbishop of Sens, in 1510.[18] Although Hilarion de Coste says that Le Picart began his studies at the Collège de Navarre in 1511, James Farge is surely right to question this assertion, since the boy would have been only seven years old. Farge suggests Le Picart began his arts course at the University of Paris in 1518,[19] a date consistent with the few other details we have of these years, specifically his correspondence with his second cousin, Guillaume Budé (1468–1540).

The study of Greek in Paris had been almost nonexistent before the final quarter of the fifteenth century. At that time, Andronic Callistos and Georgius Hermonymus began to tutor students in the capital, but their own skill levels left much to be desired. In a letter of 1517 to Cuthbert Tunstall in England, Budé reminisced that Hermonymus, who was in Paris in 1494, was ". . . an old Greek . . . who knew just enough of the vernacular to appear literate; he tortured me by unlearning whatever he taught me."[20] Fortunately, Budé's apprenticeship in the language of Homer received a boost when Janus Lascaris took on a number of French students. At the behest of Francis I, Lascaris helped organize the royal library at Blois, for which he acquired numerous Greek manuscripts. Lascaris was so influential that Paris became the earliest center for Greek studies outside of Italy.[21] But it was his student, Budé, who would become the leading Hellenistic scholar in France during the first decades of the sixteenth century.

According to his own statements, Budé wasted much of his youth on horses and hunting.[22] But that changed at the age of twenty-three, when he developed a passion for literature. He devoured the

---

[17] Henri Bernard-Maître, "François Le Picart, docteur de la faculté de théologie de Paris et les débuts de la Compagnie de Jésus (1534–1556)," *Bulletin de littérature ecclésiastique* (1954), 111.

[18] Hilarion de Coste, *Parfait ecclesiastique*, 13.

[19] Farge, *Biographical Register*, 262.

[20] David O. McNeil, *Guillaume Budé and Humanism in the Reign of Francis I* (Geneva: Droz, 1975), 10.

[21] Ibid, 10–11.

[22] BN, *Guillaume Budé*, 5.

books in his father's excellent library and spent most of his money on books in Greek and Latin. Acting in an official capacity for Louis XII, Budé traveled to Venice and Rome in 1501 and 1505 respectively.[23] His 1503 translation from Plutarch's *Moralia* was the first Greek work to be translated by a Frenchman.[24] The accession of Francis I proved singularly important for Budé, as the new king asked him to intercede with Erasmus to help create a college for the study of Greek. Soon Budé, a royal secretary, was named master of the royal library,[25] a position Francis created for him.[26] Budé's enthusiasm for Greek was so intense that he shared his passion for classical studies with his own relatives.

Several extant letters of Budé to his cousin Jean Le Picart show the affection and intimacy which bound the two men. Despite having actively sought favor at court to ease his difficult financial circumstances,[27] Budé complains in these letters that he has become so weighed down by his obligations at court and health problems that he no longer has the time he wishes for reading or letter-writing.[28] In another letter, Budé recalls the friendship that had bound their fathers, and hopes that these letters will testify to future generations of their own esteem and love for one another.[29] Apparently Budé gave Greek manuscripts and books to his cousin Jean, for a manuscript in Leyden containing marginal glosses by Budé is marked on the inside of the cover page, *Ex libris Ioannis Picarti*.[30]

Especially interesting for our purposes are Budé's letters to the oldest Le Picart boys. In a letter to Christophe, who was to study under the famed professor Ravisius Textor,[31] Budé laments that as he grows older he can no longer bring the same zeal to the quest for knowledge that Christophe displays. He begins, "I fear I will no satisfy you with my one letter, you who have written so often beseeching me

---

[23] Ibid; McNeil, *Budé*, 13–14.

[24] Louis Delaruelle, *Guillaume Budé: Les origines, les débuts, les idées maîtresses* (Paris: Honoré Champion, 1907), 1.

[25] BN, *Guillaume Budé*, 19.

[26] McNeil, *Budé*, 98.

[27] Ibid, 93.

[28] Guillaume Budé, *Epistolae Gullielmi Budaei, Secretarii Regii, Posteriores* (Paris: Josse Bade, 1522), fol. 36.

[29] Guillaume Budé, *Epistolae Guilelmi Budaei* (Paris: Josse Bade, 1520), fol. 81.

[30] Louis Delaruelle, *Répertoire analytique et chronologique de la correspondance de Guillaume Budé* (Toulouse: Édouard Privat, 1907), 83n.

[31] Delaruelle, *Répertoire*, 175n.

to write."[32] In Christophe and his brother François he discerned "an exceptional nature" made for learning. Budé ends the letter by saying that since Christophe constantly begs him to write something in Greek, to "consider this Greek end to a Latin letter."[33]

In his letter to François, dated 30 September 1519, Budé greets the fifteen-year-old by saying that the boy's ". . . supplicating and almost obsequious letters constrained me by such obligation . . . through the bonds of the relationship that exists between your father and me."[34] Budé rejoices that François' father has recently begun the study of philology, but fears that he is far too timid and unsure of himself. "Recently [your father] wrote to me from Atilly, letters half in Latin . . . then he made a transition to his native tongue . . . Look at what he says against himself because of his modesty . . . So in the future I will write more simply to him. . . . [H]e is anxious that I not take offense if he becomes more and more familiar with my philology. I would like him to become more confident . . ." Perhaps thinking of his own youth, Budé encourages the boy:

> My François, when I see you and your brother Christophe beginning along this road at your age, which I myself did not follow as an adolescent . . . I will urge you along in this course of study . . . It will be your duty to see that you do not later regret your indulgent parents and this time full of opportunities. Make sure that you do not reproach yourself later for not having shown enough diligence and will.[35]

He sends his greetings to Jean and Christophe, and ends in Greek, "Και διατελει σπουδα ζων περι τα ελληνικα γραμματα, συυ αδελφω σου εμοι αγαπωμευω [And exert yourself strenuously and with love to work along with your brother at Greek literature . . .]"[36]

What works of Greek did they study? Beside pagan works, Greek Church Fathers were of great interest to the earliest French humanists. Germain de Brie, a close acquaintance of Budé, studied Gregory Nazianzene and prepared translations of St. John Chrysostom which appeared in the 1530s.[37] Although the study of Greek would begin to be associated with the reformers in the minds of some by 1523,

---

[32] Budé, *Epistolae (1520)*, fol. 75.
[33] Ibid, fol. 76.
[34] Ibid, fol. 73.
[35] Ibid, fol. 74.
[36] Ibid, fol. 75.
[37] Delaruelle, "Étude du Grec," 144–145.

Budé's orthodoxy was never in doubt. He firmly believed that theology and philosophy went hand in hand, and one scholar has suggested that he was "... not much more enlightened than ... Noël
Beda."[38]

At the time of his correspondence with his second cousin, Le Picart
was enrolled in the arts curriculum of the University of Paris. There
he studied grammar, rhetoric, logic, arithmetic and music, science,
moral philosophy and metaphysics, with Aristotle's works forming
the core of the undergraduate program.[39] Students would also become
familiar with the works of Latin authors, especially Cicero, Horace,
Juvenal, Lucan, Ovid, Seneca, Livy and Virgil.[40] Then there would
have been works that may not have been part of the curriculum,
but were intensely debated by students—especially books and ideas
by Erasmus and Lefèvre d'Étaples.

After finishing his arts course, François Le Picart began to study
theology at Navarre in January, 1522, under the tutelage of Richard
Mareschal.[41] Although many of the colleges of the University of Paris
were in a sad state by the beginning of the sixteenth century, Navarre
had an excellent library. In 1506, the college had revamped the
gallery in which books were kept, and in 1511, King Louis XII had
given 200li. for the construction of a stairway in the new architec-
tural style.[42] Here Le Picart continued his Greek studies under Pierre
Danès (1497–1577), a leader among second-generation Hellenists in
Paris who had studied with Budé, and a man who would later
become one of the king's lectors in Greek.[43] Under his guidance, Le
Picart may have encountered the great dramatists as well as Aristo-
phanes, Isocrates and Herodotus.[44] But for students studying for the
Master's and Doctorate in Theology, the Bible and Peter Lombard's
Sentences formed the basis of instruction. Le Picart, like most students,

---

[38] Linton C. Stevens, "A Re-Evaluation of Hellenism in the French Renaissance,"
in Werner L. Gundersheimer, ed., *French Humanism 1470–1600* (New York: Harper
Torchbooks, 1969), 184–194.

[39] Taylor, *Soldiers of Christ*, 40–41. See also Gordon Leff, *Paris and Oxford Universities
in the Thirteenth and Fourteenth Centuries: An Institutional and Intellectual History* (New York:
John Wiley, 1968); Augustin Renaudet, *Préréforme et humanisme à Paris pendant les premières guerres d'Italie* (Paris: Honoré Champion, 1916).

[40] Guignard, "Imprimeurs," 53.

[41] Farge, *Biographical Register*, 262.

[42] Jacques Guignard, "Imprimeurs et libraires parisiens 1525–1536," *Bulletin de
l'Association Guillaume Budé* 3d sér. (1953), 45.

[43] McNeil, *Budé*, 86.

[44] Stevens, "Re-Evaluation," 182–183.

began to preach during his course of study. Hilarion de Coste notes that "after receiving his bachelor's degree, he dedicated himself wholly to preaching."[45] His first sermon was delivered in 1524, and he was ordained a priest on September 29, 1526 by his cousin, François Poncher, Bishop of Paris.[46] By the following year, he was serving as master for an M.A. graduate of the Nation of France.

Le Picart petitioned the Faculty of Theology in 1529 to allow him to pass his *tentativa* so that he could start to read the *Sentences* in preparation for his license and doctorate in theology.[47] This solemn disputation, based on a set of questions selected by the candidate, would be held before a presiding doctor, regent doctors and bachelors.[48] On February 1, 1529, the Faculty gathered for its regular meeting at Saint Mathurin and took up this matter as well as many others. This was to be the first of a number of occasions in which Le Picart's name was linked with that of the famous syndic, Noël Beda, the *enfant terrible* of the Faculty of Theology. Unlike the other occasions, however, Le Picart and Beda were now on opposite sides. Following a strictly legalist interpretation, Beda argued against allowing an exception to the rules: "The lord syndic Beda argued that the *tentativa* not be given to him, because he [Le Picart] had not had the requisite time according to the ancient statutes and recent faculty conclusions . . ." But on this occasion, the powerful Beda was not able to carry the day. "After deliberation it was stated, having respect to the probity of [Le Picart's] parents who are citizens of Paris, and to his zeal for preaching as well as other things, about which many of our masters gave testimony, that . . . the faculty received him to respond to the *tentativa*, from which conclusion, however, the lord syndic appealed as an abuse."[49] Beda lost the appeal with respect to Le Picart, but was able to insure that no such exceptions would be granted in the future. Thus Le Picart was able to accelerate his theological studies, but had to pay double fees until he received his doctorate in 1535.

The years during which Le Picart worked on his advanced theo-

---

[45] Hilarion de Coste, *Parfait ecclesiastique*, 33.

[46] Ibid, 25.

[47] Farge, *Biographical Register*, 262.

[48] James K. Farge, *Orthodoxy and Reform in Early Reformation France: The Faculty of Theology of Paris, 1500–1543* (Leiden: E.J. Brill, 1985), 19–20.

[49] James K. Farge, ed., *Registre des procès-verbaux de la Faculté de Théologie de l'Université de Paris de janvier 1524 à novembre 1533* (Paris: Aux amateurs du livre, 1990), 208.

logical degrees were momentous ones for France and indeed for all of Europe, as the challenges posed by an Augustinian hermit in Wittenberg began to reverberate throughout Christendom. By 1518, Luther's ideas were known at least among intellectuals in the French capital. In 1519 the theologians of the Faculty of Theology were asked to provide a determination based on Luther's writings, and in April, 1521, they passed judgment against him.

In the wake of Luther's actions, the Faculty of Theology and *parlement* of Paris entered the fray by issuing edicts and determinations regarding censorship of preaching and books. An *arrêt* promulgated in March, 1521 began the decades-long practice of subjecting written works to the scrutiny and approval of one or both institutions. Ironically, this *arrêt* had been prompted by the issuance of an orthodox book that falsely stated it had been printed with permission of the Faculty.[50] As of March 22, 1522, the Faculty required a preliminary authorization before printing.[51] Despite the existence of this statute, prosecutions were rare, with only eleven books and twelve manuscripts condemned between 1520 and 1540.[52] Moreover, it was not difficult to evade censorship by publishing in Lyon[53] or beyond the borders of France. Between 1523 and 1525, Simone de Colines published the gospels, epistles, Acts of the Apostles and Psalms in French. Although the printing of Lefèvre's French version of the Bible was banned in 1523, his New Testament was published in 1528 and the *Sainte Bible* in 1530 at Antwerp.[54]

Not surprisingly Beda, whom Febvre called the "sworn enemy of the humanist race,"[55] was in the forefront of activities against humanist and other "suspect" works in the mid-1520s. Even before 1520, Beda had associated the work of the preachers and scholars Lefèvre d'Étaples and Josse Clichtove with Luther. In 1526 he published his

---

[50] James K. Farge, *Le parti conservateur au XVIe siècle: Université et parlement de Paris à l'époque de la Renaissance et de la Réforme* (Paris: Documents et inédits du Collège de France, 1992), 33.

[51] Febvre and Martin, *Coming of the Book*, 297.

[52] Francis M. Higman, *Censorship and the Sorbonne: A Bibliographical Study of Books in French Censured by the Faculty of Theology of the University of Paris, 1520–1551* (Geneva: Droz, 1979), 49.

[53] The 1524 sermon of Aimé Meigret is a good example. See Taylor, *Soldiers of Christ*, 200–208; Nathanaël Weiss, "Le réformateur d'Aimé Meigret, *Bulletin d'humanisme et renaissance* 39(1890), 245–269; Crouzet, *Genèse*, 163–168.

[54] Febvre and Martin, *Coming of the Book*, 295–305.

[55] Febvre, *Problem of Unbelief*, 35.

Annotations directed against Lefèvre and Erasmus.[56] In this work, Beda firmly tied the "pestilent doctrine" of the Lutherans with that of the "theologizing humanists."[57] Stung by the humanists' attack on scholastic method and its practitioners, Beda summarized the views of these "clandestine Lutherans:" their writings were "contrary to the Christian faith; . . . trouble Christian piety; . . . and trouble the morals of the faithful." He even suggested that Luther may have learned from them rather than the reverse. Despite one scholar's denunciation of Beda's ". . . lack of political sense, let alone political acumen,"[58] his attack was not without some positive points that could be used more effectively by later defenders of Catholicism. The syndic insisted that the second cause of the Reformation was the ambiguity and obscurity of scripture, a point that would be taken up by Le Picart in his sermons. Beda protested that the ". . . arts of the humanists are not intrinsically vicious, but hastened to add that God disapproves of his people becoming attached to pagan elegance . . .,"[59] a point with which Calvin could later agree. Le Picart's cousin, Étienne Poncher, was reported by Pierre Cousturier to have said that "he would trust Erasmus in any point of grammar but in no point of theology."[60] Although Le Picart mocked Erasmus for "his pretty and delicate Latin,"[61] his views were more nuanced than those expressed by Beda. In his sermons, he occasionally displayed knowledge of languages. For example, he explains, "*Missa* is a Hebrew word; it is *liturgia* in Greek and *sacrum misterium* in Latin."[62] Yet he hastens to add that one should not be seduced by classical learning: "What does it profit a Caesar to have so many victories, or a Virgil or a Cicero to have composed so much, and yet be damned?"[63] Classical learning should not be allowed to eclipse the greater gifts God offers: "When we

---

[56] Noël Beda, *Annotationum Natalis Bede, . . . in Jacobum Fabrum Stapulensem libri duo, et in Desiderium Erasmum Roterodamum liber unus qui ordine tertius est. Primus, in commentarios ipsius Fabri super Epistolas beati Pauli. Secundus, in ejusdem commentarios super IV Evangelia. Tertius, in Paraphrases Erasmi super eadem quatuor Evangelia et omnes apostolicas Epistolas* (Paris: Josse Bade, 1526).

[57] Walter F. Bense, "Noël Beda's View of the Reformation," *American Society for Reformation Research* 1(1977), 96–97.

[58] Higman, *Censorship*, 28.

[59] Bense, "Noël Beda," 98.

[60] Henri Bernard-Maître, "Un théoricien de la contemplation à la Chartreuse parisienne de Vauvert: Pierre Cousturier dit Sutor (c. 1480–18 juin 1537)," *Revue d'ascétique et mystique* 32(1956), 183.

[61] Le Picart, *Advent*, fol. 346.

[62] Ibid, fol. 42.

[63] Le Picart, *Trinité*, fol. 82.

think of the great capacity of the soul, the world seems so poor, and philosophy cannot content the heart of man, as Origen tells us."[64] Elsewhere he observes:

> I study profane literature, and as long as it serves to help us know God better, I am content with it. All the study of man must be to learn about his salvation ... So, you have languages, but if you do not use them for your salvation and the edification of the church, your work is not founded in Jesus Christ. You may be reputed wise and prudent, but in truth, you know nothing.[65]

He continues, "if you have the gift of languages, use them well, and you will gain merit before God in working for your salvation. But it would be better never to have seen the alphabet than to use it for ill, as we do so often today."[66] In much the same manner as he would use Saint Paul to confute the heretics, Le Picart mined the "gold" of the humanists: "To confute this false opinion, we see that Plato in his *Timaeus* proved the immortality of the soul . . ."[67] Yet against critics of the Vulgate, Le Picart has a ready response. "If you say that it is more correct in Greek than Latin, I ask you . . . The Latins have never lost their way or been traitors. The Latin Church has not lost its way, as has the Greek, which is not in conformity with us . . . nor do they follow the ways of our Lord. Moreover, the Greek churchmen marry. I know there are good men among them. But for all these reasons it is necessary to stop with the Latin text rather than using the Greek."[68]

Erasmus, who had studied and lectured at the University of Paris in the 1490s, but now referred to it as "a den of brigands,"[69] was the focus of many of the anti-humanist diatribes of Beda and others during the 1520s. Beda and Erasmus had earlier been friends,[70] but in 1525, with the king conveniently in captivity, the Faculty took the offensive. Farge writes that "[s]tymied in its attacks on Lefèvre and Berquin, helpless in the face of Lefèvre d'Étaples' intention to publish French translations of the New Testament, and convinced

---

[64] Ibid, fol. 51.
[65] Le Picart, *Trinité-II*, fol. 139.
[66] Le Picart, *Advent*, fol. 315.
[67] Le Picart, *Trinité-II*, fol. 181.
[68] Le Picart, *Trinité*, fol. 71.
[69] Farge, *Orthodoxy*, 260.
[70] Victor Carrière, "La Sorbonne et l'évangelisme au XVIᵉ siècle," in *Aspects de l'Université de Paris* (Paris: Albin Michel, 1949), 163.

that Erasmus' Greek edition and Latin translation of the New Testament was wreaking havoc in theological studies and in the Church in general, the Faculty decided to attack all new versions of the Bible."[71] Although Beda had been one of four theologians who put together a translation of the Pater Noster, Ave Maria, Creed and Ten Commandments in a work published between 1500 and 1509,[72] the changed circumstances of the 1520s demanded greater caution. Condemning a translation of the office of the Virgin, the doctors stated, "given the conditions of our times, neither this translation of the Hours nor even any translation of the Bible or of parts of it, as we see appearing everywhere, should be allowed; and when they are published they must be suppressed rather than tolerated."[73]

Erasmus did not meekly accept attacks on his work or humanist scholarship more generally, and complained that Beda's charges ". . . better characterized the spirit of a satrap than of a theological discussion." Beda responded patronizingly that what he had done was for Erasmus' own good.[74] The attacks grew more virulent after 1525. On March 12, 1526, the Faculty condemned four books by Erasmus that had been translated into French by Louis de Berquin. Beda had a formidable ally in this work, Pierre Cousturier, who declared Erasmus a "little rhetorician" who should leave off meddling in the affairs of theologians. Cousturier went on the attack with his *De tralatione bibliae et novarum reprobatione interpretationum*, a denunciation of all scriptural translations.[75] Erasmus's successful appeal to the king, to all intents and purposes accusing Beda and Cousturier of sedition, would resonate again in 1533. However, at this time, the king retaliated by ordering all unsold copies of Beda's *Annotations* seized, banning further sales. Beda, undeterred, simply published another work aimed at "closet Lutherans."[76] It was in the context of attacks on scriptural translation that Greek and Hebrew studies

---

[71] Farge, *Orthodoxy*, 177.

[72] Virginia Reinburg, "Popular Prayers in Late Medieval and Reformation France," unpublished Ph.D. dissertation, Princeton University, 1985, 41; Farge, *Biographical Register*, 34.

[73] Farge, *Orthodoxy*, 178–179.

[74] Myron P. Gilmore, "Valla, Érasme et Bédier à propos du Nouveau Testament," in *L'humanisme français au début de la Renaissance* (Paris: J. Vrin, 1973), 178–179.

[75] Farge, *Biographical Register*, 192.

[76] James K. Farge, "Marguerite de Navarre, Her Circle, and the Censors of Paris," in Régine Reynolds-Cornell, ed., *International Colloquium Celebrating the 500th Anniversary of the Birth of Marguerite de Navarre* (Birmingham, AL: Summa Publications), 19.

came under increasing scrutiny. Actions taken by the Faculty in April of 1530 made their intentions clear. They censured two propositions as temerarious, scandalous and impious: that "'Holy Scripture cannot be correctly understood without Greek, Hebrew, or other like languages'; and 'a preacher cannot truly explain the Epistles and Gospels without these languages.'"[77] The early Jesuit Bobadilla quoted the humanistically-trained founder of the Society of Jesus, Ignatius of Loyola, as having said *qui graecisabant, lutheranisabant.*[78] Yet although many began to see the study of classical languages as handmaidens to heresy, others as surely did not, showing that even on such important issues there was no unanimity of opinion. A colleague of Le Picart, Nicolas Maillard, who would pronounce his funeral oration in 1556, wrote to Erasmus in 1531 saying that at his instigation he had been studying Greek for six years. Two years later, Maillard considered working with the German Protestant Johann Sturm on a paraphrase of Saint Paul's letter to the Romans.[79] The Dominican inquisitor Mathieu Ory, not known for leniency towards heretics, held the study of Greek and Hebrew in high regard.[80]

It was preaching that came under the most intense scrutiny in the years immediately following the condemnation of Luther. In conjunction with the fast-moving events in the Empire, the nascent French evangelical movement now came under suspicion. In 1521, desperate to remedy the problems he had found in his diocese of Meaux, which was "... 'starved of divine food' and poisoned by the superstitious claptrap of the local Franciscans,"[81] Bishop Guillaume Briçonnet had assembled around him a group of men imbued with humanist and evangelical ideals. They included Lefèvre d'Étaples, Guillaume Farel,[82] Michel d'Arande and Gérard Roussel. What had begun as an effort to reform the religious houses in the diocese soon acquired its own

---

[77] Farge, *Orthodoxy*, 197.

[78] Henri Bernard-Maître, "La préréforme humaniste de l'Université de Paris aux origines de la Compagnie de Jésus (1525–1536) in *L'homme devant Dieu: Mélanges offerts au Père Henri de Lubac* (Paris: Aubier, 1964), 229.

[79] Farge, *Biographical Register*, 297–298.

[80] Henri Bernard-Maître, "L'inquisiteur Dominican Mathieu Ory et son *Alexipharmacon* contre les hérétiques," *Revue des sciences religieuses* 30(1956), 258.

[81] R.J. Knecht, *Renaissance Warrior and Patron: The Reign of Francis I* (Cambridge: Cambridge University Press, 1994), 156.

[82] For a thorough discussion of Farel, see Comité Farel, *Guillaume Farel 1489–1565: Biographie nouvelle écrite d'après les documents originaux par un group d'historiens, professeurs et pasteurs de Suisse, de France et d'Italie*. Neuchâtel and Paris: Éditions Delachaux & Niestlé S.A., 1930.

momentum, and led to a widespread effort to reform the church along the lines of the primitive church. Evangelical preaching was instituted; regular visitations took place; synods were held to educate parish priests; and the Bible became the focus of study based on new philological and humanistic methods. It was in Meaux that Lefèvre had begun the work on his French translation of the Bible. And while the beliefs of the group of Meaux ran the full gamut from orthodoxy to heresy, the *Bourgeois de Paris* expressed what was undoubtedly the view of many when he reported that ". . . the great majority of the group of Meaux were infected with the false doctrine of Luther . . ."[83]

Troubles arising as a result of the new biblicism and evangelism practiced at Meaux made confrontation inevitable. Briçonnet admitted that "the least important people of the city" were singing a song that made fun of the Paris theologians:

> Pource quilz picquent les gros et les bigotz vivans en ypocrisie,
> Disans quilz ont estudie le temps passe en leur grande theologie,
> Lire, lire, lironpha,
> Disans quilz ont estudie le temps passe en leur grande theologie
> Dont ilz ont bien pratique sans charite.[84]

Evangelical preaching in the diocese soon attracted unwelcome notice. In 1522, Francis I's confessor, Guillaume Petit, protested at the sermons being preached by Marguerite of Navarre's almoner, Michel d'Arande. In addition, Pierre Caroli had preached that "holy scripture is now understood better than ever before, and was not well interpreted in the past." More potentially disruptive was his belief that preaching was not the exclusive right of priests and monks, for "God can illuminate the heart of a woman with the true sense of scripture if she has simple goodness in her."[85] In 1524, he was denounced for telling his parishioners to bring translations of St. Paul to his sermons. Jacques Pavannes, another of Briçonnet's protegés, preached against purgatory and sacramental confession, and claimed that offering candles and prayers to the saints was idolatrous. He justified iconoclasm and preached that the mass ". . . does nothing

---

[83] Bourrilly, *Bourgeois de Paris*, 233.
[84] Farge, *Orthodoxy*, 240.
[85] Charles Duplessis d'Argentré, *Collectio judiciorum de novis erroribus qui ab initio duodecimi saeculi . . . usque ad annum 1632 in ecclesia proscripti sunt et notati . . .* (Paris: A. Cailleau, 1727–1736), 26.

to add in the remission of sins."[86] Bertrand Coquelet was forced to recant assertions made in his sermons, and was imprisoned.[87] Martial Mazurier, using the philological and exegetical methods and ideas of Lefèvre, stated his belief in the plurality of Magdalenes in 1521, a doctrine condemned earlier by the Faculty of Theology. The day before the censure of 104 of Luther's propositions, Mazurier's position was condemned. It is interesting to note that a few years later, Mazurier was one of the first to be led in the *Spiritual Exercises* by Ignatius of Loyola, who arrived in Paris in 1528.[88] The man who for Le Picart would prove to the most important alumnus of the Meaux group, Gérard Roussel (1480–1550), challenged the Vulgate Bible on the basis of poor translations from the Hebrew original, and criticized belief in the assumption of the Virgin and the veneration of the saints.[89]

The Faculty recommended the prosecution of Lefèvre as a heretic, but the king's protection made further efforts against the brilliant scholar impossible. Others associated with the Circle of Meaux were not so fortunate, especially when the king's absence or captivity allowed the Faculty and *parlement* a freer hand. From June, 1525 to November, 1526, Briçonnet had to answer charges stemming from the actions of the preachers in his diocese and the spread of "Lutheranism" there. On October 3, 1525, the *parlement* issued warrants for all of the leading members of the Circle. Most fled or sought the protection of the king's reform-minded sister, Marguerite of Navarre (1492–1549). Roussel went to Strasbourg, from whence he wrote to Briçonnet excitedly about his reactions to reformed preaching in the imperial city.[90] If a number of those associated with the Circle of Meaux remained committed to a reformed Catholicism, it is nonetheless significant that the city of Meaux was considered a "Protestant stronghold" through the early 1560s.[91]

The Faculty of Theology and *parlement* were determined, beginning as early as 1523, to stem the rising tide of heresy with measures that went beyond censorship of books and preaching. On May

---

[86] Ibid, 30–34.
[87] McNeil, *Budé*, 121.
[88] Bernard-Maître, "Préréforme humaniste," 230.
[89] Farge, *Orthodoxy*, 173.
[90] A.-J. Herminjard, *Correspondance des réformateurs dans les pays de langue français* (Geneva and Paris, 1886–1897), I:406–407.
[91] Nicholls, "Popular Heresy," 268.

13, 1523, the house of Louis de Berquin was searched and his books
confiscated. Found among his books and papers was Luther's *De
abroganda missa privata*, Berquin's own translations of Luther and Ulrich
von Hutten, and a satire aimed at the Faculty. As the Faculty was
preparing to condemn Berquin, the young aristocrat appeared with
letters from the king forbidding continued prosecution. Despite the
royal intervention, the Faculty sent their conclusion on to the *parlement*, claiming that their deliberations had been completed. Berquin
was jailed in August, 1523, forcing Francis to demand his release.[92]
In January, 1526, Berquin was incarcerated once again in the Concier-
gerie ". . . because he was a Lutheran, and had been questioned at
an earlier date by the court since he held to the doctrine of the
Lutherans."[93] Claiming their accusations were spurious, he appealed
directly to the king, who was still in Spain. On July 11, Francis
wrote, remanding Berquin into royal custody at the Louvre, until he
could personally judge the case. The *parlement* refused, and it was
only when the provost of Paris intervened, accompanied by the king's
archers, that Berquin was removed to the Louvre. Berquin was
arrested once again in the summer of 1528, and tried by a commission that included Budé. Even Erasmus had become largely unsup-
portive by this time, telling Beda that "Berquin means nothing to
me."[94] In April, 1529, sentence was pronounced, by which

> . . . he was condemned to make an *amende honorable*, his head uncov-
> ered, a blazing wax taper in his hand . . . crying for the mercy of God,
> the king, and justice, for the offense he committed by becoming part
> of the Lutheran sect and the evil books he had written against the
> majesty of God and His glorious mother. . . . [T]hen after to be led
> on foot, his head uncovered, to the place de Grève where in his pres-
> ence his books would be burned . . . Afterwards, he was to be con-
> ducted to the great Church of Notre-Dame, where he would also make
> an *amende honorable* to God and the glorious Virgin Mary, his mother,
> and from thence he would be led to the prisons of Monsieur of Paris,
> to be enclosed behind its wall for all of his life.[95]

After the ceremony was completed, Berquin was to be fined and
imprisoned for life. Rashly trusting in the ability of the king to release
him once more, he appealed to the *parlement*. Frustrated, it changed

---

[92] Farge, *Orthodoxy and Reform*, 173–174.
[93] Bourrilly, *Bourgeois de Paris*, 234.
[94] McNeil, *Budé*, 121–122.
[95] Bourrilly, *Bourgeois de Paris*, 320.

his sentence to death. "He was condemned to die and be burned alive in the place de Grève at Paris, and before his death, in his presence, his books were to be burned; this was done and expedited the same day so that he could not have recourse to the king or Madame the Regent, who was at Blois . . ."[96]

Although the Faculty of Theology, working for the most part in concert with the *parlement* of Paris, acted vigorously to repress heresy in the 1520s, royal policy made their work difficult. Francis I's patronage of humanists and reformers encouraged many to test the limits of official tolerance, while others claimed the king ". . . was of one heart with the evangelists and only dissimulated for political reasons."[97] However, his preoccupation with international and military initiatives, especially his Italian ventures, aided the conservatives in Paris. Yet Francis was not so singleminded in his patronage of scholars and humanists that he did not react to genuine challenges to orthodoxy. Executions for heresy, while infrequent in these years, did occur. In August of 1523, the "first French martyr," Jean Vallière, a hermit, was condemned to make an *amende*, have his tongue cut out, and be burned alive for having contended that Jesus was born of Joseph and Mary after having been conceived in the ordinary way.[98] In December, 1526, the king expressed his shock and outrage at the public mockery of the theologians when a group of ". . . seven men dressed as demons [led] a horse mounted by a woman and surrounded by 'men dressed in the garb of doctors of theology who had signs both front and back which read 'Lutherans.'"[99] More shocking still was an act of iconoclasm committed against a statue of the Virgin on the corner of the rue de la Culture-Sainte-Catherine and the rue des Rosiers. In the small hours of the morning on June 1, 1528, the statue was smashed by iconoclasts. The *Bourgeois de Paris* describes the scene:

> It was here that several heretics came on the holiday between Monday and Tuesday to attack an image of Our Lady in stone, holding her child, which was against the wall of the house of Master Louis de

---

[96] Ibid, 321.

[97] Jean Lamat, "Picrochole est-il Noël Beda?" *Travaux d'humanisme et renaissance* 8(1969), 19.

[98] Bourrilly, *Bourgeois de Paris*, 397–398.

[99] Farge, *Orthodoxy*, 262; J.M. DeBujanda, Francis M. Higman, and James K. Farge, eds., *Index de l'Université de Paris 1544, 1545, 1547, 1549, 1551, 1556* (Sherbrooke: Librairie Droz, 1985), 48.

Harlay. . . . [T]hey stabbed the image several times with their knives, cutting off her head and that of her small child, Our Lord; but the perpetrators were never discovered. When the king was advised of this, he was so enraged and angry that it was said that he wept copiously.[100]

Francis ordered an inquest and arranged for several expiatory processions, efforts later praised by Le Picart: ". . . The king, moved by a good spirit, wrote to the prelates in his realm ordering them to make processions and general prayers throughout the cities, with sermons, to move the people to devotion."[101] On the ninth, the rector of the university led a procession of the faculty, accompanied by students, each carrying a taper in his hand, from the church of Saint Gervais to the place where the image had been destroyed; from there, joined by the mendicants, they walked solemnly to the church of Saint Martin-des-Champs.[102] Two days later, the king personally led a procession ". . . carrying a wax torch, his head uncovered, with great reverence, having with him men playing trumpets and clarinets. And with him were the Cardinal of Lorraine and several prelates and great lords, each of the gentlemen carrying a white candle in his hands, and all the archers . . ."[103] The following day the king led yet another procession, this time dressed in full regalia, carrying a splendid new silver statue of the virgin that he had commissioned and which he placed in the spot where the statue had been desecrated.[104] This statue would be stolen in 1545.[105]

Lucien Febvre's characterization of the period before 1534 as one of "magnificent religious anarchy"[106] is close to the mark. Much of the chaos derived from the problem of defining heresy in the years after Luther. Separated by well over a millenium, both St. Jerome and Erasmus (in 1517) had praised France as one of the few countries untouched by heresy. But in the 1520s, no one except the most strident theologians could be quite sure who was or was not a heretic, least of all Francis I. Nicola Sutherland claims that the king simply

---

[100] Bourrilly, *Bourgeois de Paris*, 291.

[101] Le Picart, *Trinité*, fol. 137.

[102] Bourrilly, *Bourgeois de Paris*, 291.

[103] Ibid, 292.

[104] Ibid, 292–293.

[105] Émile Doumergue, "Paris protestant au XVIᵉ siècle," *Bulletin de la Société de l'histoire de protestantisme français* 45(1896), 118.

[106] Lucien Febvre, *Au coeur religieux du XVIᵉ siècle* (Paris, 1957), 66.

"... evaded the long-term implications of heresy ..."[107] The biographer of Francis I, R.J. Knecht, articulates the king's position:

> While he professed to be opposed to heresy and issued decrees banning the publication and sale of Lutheran books, he impeded the efforts of the Faculty of Theology and *Parlement* to silence various scholars and preachers whose views seemed to them dangerously at variance with traditional dogma. He protected Lefèvre, Berquin and some other scholars and preachers from presecution. Rightly or wrongly, he did not regard them as heretics.[108]

Francis I's vacillation exacerbated what Chaunu describes as the polarization of each position after Luther.[109] For men such as Beda, the king's attitude was disastrous, and needed to be circumvented whenever and however possible, even if this meant civil disobedience. Although many of the actions taken in the 1520s against heresy are repugnant to the modern mind, the theologians and *parlementaires* recognized more than most others in the early years of the Reformation the potential dangers posed by both humanism and heresy. As Farge has written, "[t]o take account of the opinions of the enemies of the Faculty of Theology without doing the necessary work to try and understand their point of view is to truncate the knowledge of the great intellectual and religious questions of the Renaissance and Reformation."[110] In the view of Beda and his colleagues, the floodgates were opened in the 1520s.

The great majority of Parisians, no matter their class or position, held beliefs somewhere between those propounded by Beda and the partisans of reform. It was not unusual for members of the same family to hold different religious beliefs. As Barbara Diefendorf has shown,

> A complex web of kinship bound up Protestants and Catholics in the city of Paris. . . . There were probably few French Protestants who did not have a sibling, a parent, or even perhaps a spouse who remained Catholic. . . . . A more important question, then, might be how many

---

[107] Nicola Sutherland, *The Huguenot Struggle for Recognition* (New Haven: Yale University Press, 1980), 3.
[108] Knecht, *Renaissance Warrior*, 164.
[109] Chaunu, *Église*, 345.
[110] Farge, *Parti conservateur*, 30.

Catholics had families touched by schism. . . . [F]ully one-third of the
ninety city councillors in my study had one or more close relatives
who stood on the other side in the religious disputes.[111]

Although she points out that ". . . religious differences placed a heavy
psychological burden on the family,"[112] they may also have fostered
a degree of understanding that would have seemed utterly foreign
to the *Bedaistes*. The sons of Guillaume Budé, the humanist who sat
in judgment on Berquin, emigrated to Geneva. Étienne Poncher, Le
Picart's cousin, was considered by some to be "soft on heresy." In
spite of the reputation he would earn as the most ardent Parisian
defender of Catholicism in the years after Beda's death, François Le
Picart would also bear the imprints not only of his humanist training but also the more intangible effects of a personal knowledge of
heresy in his extended family.

---

[111] Barbara Diefendorf, "Houses Divided: Religious Schism in Sixteenth-Century
Parisian Families," in Susan Zimmerman and Ronald F.E. Weissman, eds., *Urban
Life in the Renaissance* (Newark: University of Delaware Press, 1989), 82.
[112] Ibid, 92.

CHAPTER THREE

THE DEFINING MOMENT, 1533–1534

> A woman sits in her bedroom sewing, occupying herself with domestic activities appropriate to her sex. Suddenly, she is confronted by Megaera,[1] a Greek Fury, who urges her to begin reading the Bible. Worked into a frenzy, she strikes out, tormenting and oppressing all around her as she preaches her newfound knowledge.[2]

The audience for this stage play of October, 1533, students and professors at the Collège de Navarre, erupted into applause at the none-too-subtle depictions of the king's sister, Marguerite of Navarre and her preacher, Gérard Roussel.[3] Apprised of the satire, Marguerite

---

[1] Megaera was a play on the name Magister Gérard—Gérard Roussel.

[2] This was not merely a parody of Marguerite, but also a reference to preachers who "encouraged" women to preach. In February, 1532, the Faculty condemned the doctrines of Étienne Lecourt, who preached that soon women would take over the offices of bishops and bishops those of women. Women, he said, would preach the gospels. Duplessis d'Argentré, *Collectio judiciorum*, 97.

[3] Alexander Ganoczy, *The Young Calvin*, trans. David Foxgrover and Wade Provo (Philadelphia: Westminster Press, 1987), 77–78. Farcical plays were not the exclusive preserve of Catholics. *La farce des theologastres*, probably written by Berquin or one of his circle between 1526 and 1528 and first published in 1531–32, mocked "theologastres"—a term of derision coined by Luther in 1518—and friars for wounding faith and scripture. The character Raison speaks:

> Le seiner de Berquin
> Il leur exposoit le latin
> De Erasme qu'ilz n'entendent point
> Mais ilz le mirent par ung point
> En prison et par voye oblicque
> Le cuiderent dire heretique
> Sans monstrer erreur ne raison
> Pourquoy, qui est grant desraison (76–77).

The farce, which mentions Beda and Lizet by name, exalts the truth coming from Germany, a truth the bigots of the Sorbonne cannot understand and only want to extinguish:

FOY: Nennin, non, c'est en Allemaigne,
                  Où elle fait sa reisdence.

had the college raided. The *prévost* showed up at the college with a hundred of his men and arrested the principal and his assistants after being first greeted by the students with a shower of stones.[4] Navarre's grand master, Doctor Étienne Loret, and the grammar principal, Jean Morin, were taken into custody.[5] In the aftermath, a 24–year-old student who had come to Paris to study Greek, Hebrew and classics, wrote of the incident with some amusement to his lawyer friend, François Daniel of Orléans, expressing at the same time his admiration for Master Gérard.[6] The student's name was John Calvin.

The years 1533 and 1534 were momentous ones for France, and no less so for François Le Picart. The satirical play was only one of many shocking events that would radically transform the religious atmosphere in Paris. The year 1533 had begun with the king away in Picardy, leaving the king and queen of Navarre to hold court in Paris. At Marguerite's request, her almoner, Gérard Roussel, was preaching at the Louvre to enormous crowds eager to hear the new doctrines. Roussel, who had traveled to Strasbourg to learn at the feet of some of the leading reformers after the Circle of Meaux had been forcibly dispersed in the mid-1520s, had been close to the queen of Navarre at least since that time.[7] During Lent of 1531, Roussel

---

FRATREZ:	Elle fait dieu qui la mehaigne,
	Où cheux Luther.
THEOLOGASTRES:	Ho! Pestillence!
	Taisez ce mot.
FOY:	Querez par tout
	Et celuy qui ma santé toult
	Soit bruslé comme ung heretique
	A ce faire chascun s'applique
	Maistre Nostre Theologastre
	Et vostre compaign Frere Fratrez . . . (59–60).

Claude Longéon, ed., *La farce des theologastres* (Geneva: Droz, 1989). A short analysis of the farce with an English translation of a portion of it can be found in Charles Garside, Jr., "La farce des théologastres: Humanism, Heresy, and the Sorbonne, 1523–1525," *Rice University Studies* 60(1974), 45–82.

[4] John Calvin, *Opera quae supersunt omnia*, ed. G. Baum, et al, 55 vols. (Braunschweig and Berlin: Schwetschke, 1863–1890), X:2, 27–28; Herminjard, *Correspondance*, III:94.

[5] Farge, *Orthodoxy*, 203–204; V.-L. Bourrilly and Nathanaël Weiss, "Jean du Bellay," *Bulletin de la société de l'histoire du protestantisme français* 52(1903), 210.

[6] Herminjard, *Correspondance*, III:108.

[7] Marguerite may have known Roussel as early as 1521 through her connections to Briçonnet, although she states in a letter to Anne de Montmorency in May of 1533 that she had only known him for five years. Herminjard, *Correspondance*, III:53. For the date of 1521, see A. Hyrvoix, "Noël Bédier d'après les documents inédits, 1533–1534," *Revue des questions historiques* 72(1903), 582.

had been charged by the Faculty of Theology with preaching heresy in the presence of Marguerite. At that time, Francis I managed to placate the theologians by asking Roussel to give him advance notice of what he was going to preach.[8] By 1533, however, Pierre Siderander was able to write to Jacques Bédrot in Strasbourg that

> ...so many people wanted to attend the sermons on the Word of God preached by Gérard, that no sermons could be given, because four to five thousand people were present. Three times the location had to be changed, and it was very difficult indeed to find a place large enough to accommodate the crowd. However, he preached daily throughout Lent, with the king and queen [of Navarre] being present.[9]

Roussel may have been the most famous of the evangelical preachers, but he was not alone in offering a new kind of sermon to the people of Paris—another well-known preacher, Coreau, was also expounding evangelical ideas.[10]

On March 29, 1533, the Faculty of Theology conferred at the Sorbonne to determine what course of action they should take to refute "the errors that have been publicly preached in churches throughout Paris during Lent."[11] The theologians decided to fight fire with fire, delegating six bachelors to preach against the "perverse doctrines of the Lutherans."[12] Among the preachers were François Le Picart, the Mathurin Louis Lescudier and a Franciscan, Geoffroy Thomas.[13] According to Oswald Myconius, who wrote to Heinrich Bullinger on 8 April,[14] Le Picart exclaimed with exasperation from the pulpit, "Only little old ladies come to my sermons! The men all go to the Louvre!"[15] He is also alleged to have called the king of Navarre a heretic.[16] If he did so, he was acting against

---

[8] Knecht, *Renaissance Warrior*, 308.

[9] Herminjard, *Correspondance*, III:55.

[10] Marcel Royannez, "L'eucharistie chez les évangeliques et les premiers réformés français (1522–1546), *Bulletin de la société de l'histoire du protestantisme français* 125(1979), 564.

[11] Léopold Delisle, "Notice sur un régistre des procès-verbaux de la faculté de théologie de Paris pendant les années 1505–1533," *Notice et extraits des manuscrits de la Bibliothèque Nationale et autres bibliothèques* 36(1899), 398.

[12] Walter F. Bense, "Noël Beda and the Humanist Reformation at Paris, 1504–1534," unpublished Ph.D. dissertation, Harvard University, 1967, 804.

[13] Bourrilly and Weiss, "Jean du Bellay," 197.

[14] The date on the letter is 1534, but surely refers to the events of 1533, as Farge suggests. Farge, *Biographical Register*, 263.

[15] Herminjard, *Correspondance*, III:161.

[16] Ibid, III:56.

the letter of the Faculty of Theology's mandate, which "expressly forbade them from specifically naming persons or places."[17] Evidence from the sermons suggests that Le Picart did not regret his actions. Perhaps responding directly to this charge, he maintains in one sermon, "If I talk here in general my words are less useful and efficacious than to speak in particular . . . Particular warnings and exhortations are more necessary . . ."[18] From this point on, the situation in Paris grew daily more tense. Masters were instructed to bring to the Faculty's attention any errors they found in sermons so the theologians could find an appropriate remedy.[19]

A few days after Easter, Le Picart, Beda and others were confined to their lodgings by the king of Navarre. When reports came to him that Beda had been seen riding his mule through the streets of Paris in defiance of the order,[20] Navarre rode out to see Francis I, then at Meaux, to warn him of the seditious preaching in the capital, reminding the king of the Faculty and *parlement's* action against Berquin in 1529.[21] The king sent his confessor, Guillaume Petit, and Cardinal Antoine DuPrat to Paris to examine the preachers, collect a list of the heretical doctrines preached by Roussel, and ". . . bring anyone to justice who could be proven to preach or to hold to the doctrine of the Lutherans."[22] According to a later letter of the king, the bachelors maintained that they had preached against Roussel ". . . because the people murmured against the said Master Gérard and [Jean de la Rétif] . . ."[23] Siderander claimed that "Le Picart and others, who are held in high esteem here . . . in their preaching attacked and insulted the king . . . confident of the authority of the Sorbonne. Next they tried to create an uproar, and arouse the people so that they would not suffer heresy . . ."[24] Following an interrogation by Guillaume Poyet, Le Picart was imprisoned in the monastery prison of Saint-Magloire, where he was forbidden to preach or teach.[25] Despite the

---

[17] Delisle, "Notice," 398.

[18] Le Picart, *Trinité-II*, fol. 29.

[19] Delisle, "Notice," 398.

[20] Charles Schmidt, *Gérard Roussel: Prédicateur de la reine Marguerite de Navarre, mémoire servant à l'histoire des premières tentatives faites pour introduire la Réformation en France* (Geneva: Slatkine Reprints, 1970), 88.

[21] Hyrvoix, "Noël Bédier," 582.

[22] Bense, "Noël Beda," 804.

[23] Herminjard, *Correspondance*, VI:446.

[24] Ibid, III:56.

[25] Ibid, 73.

injunction, which upset Le Picart greatly,[26] students continued to flock to him to hear lectures and seek his guidance.[27]

On April 16, the Faculty met once again to consider letters from Francis I seeking redress from "those preachers who were so indiscreet as to preach as if they wanted to arouse the people against Master Gérard Roussel, who had preached Lent before the illustrious Queen of Navarre in the Louvre." The theologians were also ordered to forward all questionable articles preached by Roussel.[28] Two bachelors, Nicolas Boissel and Jean de Sallignac, were asked to testify about Roussel's suspect propositions. The former refused to cooperate unless the proceedings were convened before judges,[29] but de Sallignac responded

> ... audaciously that he had never heard Roussel preach or say anything about merit or veneration of the saints, about faith, the Church and its authority or other matters which is not said or taught in the schools of the Faculty or which is not read in the ancient doctors of the holy Church. Having heard this, our doctors were amazed, and it was suggested that they decide later what should be done about these things.[30]

Five days later, Nicolas Leclerc, Valentin Liévin and Jean de Gaigny were deputed to go to the king, although Gaigny was unable to join the others.[31] They returned with assurances that the king was determined to extirpate the Lutheran heresy.

On May 13, the king wrote from Moulins to his councillors in Paris about those "preachers of Paris, of whom some say they were preaching propositions against the faith, and the ones who were accusing them tried to move the people to sedition, each one scandalizing the other without worthwhile foundation . . ."[32] Roussel was forbidden to preach until he was cleared of having preached heresy, but was to be ". . . confined to the custody of our very dear and

---

[26] He states that he was "fort marry." Le Picart, *Épistre*, fol. 4.
[27] Hilarion de Coste, *Parfait ecclesiastique*, 74.
[28] Delisle, "Notice," 399.
[29] Ibid., 348.
[30] Sallignac's exculpation of Roussel must be viewed in the light of later actions against him. Seven months after this response, Sallignac was investigated by the Faculty, and a year later a search of his rooms turned up suspect books. Farge, *Biographical Register*, 401.
[31] Ibid.
[32] Herminjard, *Correspondance*, VI:445.

beloved sister, the queen of Navarre, to hold him until our return."[33]
The light measures taken against Roussel infuriated the theologians
and astonished the public.[34] Le Picart, Thomas and Lescudier were
to be exiled to thirty leagues from Paris and from each other;
Siderander reported that some thought they would be banished in
perpetuity.[35] Beda was also ordered into exile, not in this case for
having preached seditious sermons, as claimed by Siderander,[36] but
for having ". . . tried to lead the Faculty astray," primarily through
his opposition to the divorce of Henry VIII.[37] This set off a veritable war of placards in the capital among the partisans and opponents of the exiled preachers that would continue well after the men
had departed.[38] Siderander wrote that "daily these proclamations are
affixed pro and con."[39] A number of them were directed against
Pierre Descornes, one of the strongest defenders of the preachers,
for whom Le Picart would give the funeral oration sixteen years
later. Another, in response, was affixed near the theological colleges
and directed at the "Lutheran dogs." It read:

> Au feu, au feu cest hérésie
> Qui jour et nuyt trop nous grève!
> Doibz-tu souffrir qu'elle moleste
> Saincte Escripture et ses édictz?
> Veulx-tu bannir science parfaicte
> Pour soubstenir Lutériens mauldictz?
> Crains-tu point Dieu qu'il permette
> Toy et les tiens, qui sont floris, faire péril?

> Paris, Paris, fleur de noblesse,
> Soubstiens la foy de Dieu que on blesse,
> Ou aultrement fouldre et tempeste
> Cherra sur toy, je t'advertis.
> Prions tous le roy de gloire
> Qu'il confonde ces chiens mauldictz,
> A fin qu'il n'e[n] soit plus mémoire
> Non plus que de vielz oz pourris.

---

[33] Ibid, VI:446–447.
[34] Bourrilly and Weiss, "Jean du Bellay," 204.
[35] Herminjard, *Correspondance*, III:56.
[36] Larmat, "Picrochole," 18.
[37] Bense, "Noël Beda," 813.
[38] Herminjard, *Correspondance*, III:58.
[39] Ibid, III:57.

Au feu, au feu! c'est leur repère!
Faiz-en justice! Dieu l'a permys.[40]

This was followed the next day by a similar placard, specifically aimed at Roussel, who had been freed upon the king's departure for the Midi and was preaching again in Paris.[41] Among the responses was one by Clément Marot, reprinted in his *Oeuvres* of 1535:

En leau, en leau, ces folz seditieux
Lesquelz en lieu de diuines parolles
Preschent au peuple vn tas de monopolles,
Pour esmouuoir debatz contentieux,
Le Roy leur est vn peu trop gracieux
Que na il mys a bas ce testes folles?
   En leau.
Ilz ayment tant les vins delicieux,
Quon peult nommer cabaretz leurs escolles,
Mais refroydir fauldroit leur chauldes colles
Par le rebours de ce quilz ayment mieulx
   En leau.

   Dizain a ce propos.
Au feu, en leau, en lair, ou en la terre
Soient prys et mys ces folz predicateurs,
Qui vont preschant Sedition et Guerre
Entre le peuple et les bons precepteurs,
Ilz ont este trop long temps seducteurs,
Et mys le monde en trouble et desarroy,
Mais dieu de grace, a voulu que le Roy
Aye entendu leur sophisticq parler,
Qui les fera punir selon la loy
Au feu, en leau, en la terre, ou en lair.[42]

Near the end of May, the time came for Beda and the three preachers to depart for exile. In anticipation, supporters of the syndic had crowded around the Collège de Montaigu waiting for him to leave Paris. He finally left on March 27 for Montargis, southeast of Paris.[43] Le Picart's departure aroused similar feelings. Conducted to the city gates by large, weeping crowds, Le Picart left for Reims, where he

---

[40] Ibid, III:58–59.
[41] Schmidt, *Roussel*, 92.
[42] Herminjard, *Correspondance*, III:59–60.
[43] Bense, "Noël Beda," 814–815.

had maternal relatives. Some, however, rejoiced at their fall and hoped this was a sign that Francis I favored the reform.[44]

Although not yet the Catholic stronghold it would become in later years under Guise domination, the Champagne to which Le Picart now travelled was not untouched by Protestantism. Reims had been fairly quiet in these years,[45] but there had been some recent problems. In 1525, reformers ". . . broke with stones the lantern placed before the statue of the Virgin at the portal of the Cathedral. They overturned the crosses on the parvis at the church of the Magdalene and in the cemetery of Saint-Jacques. The cross of Fust, between Saint-Martin and Saint-Timothée, was thrown down three or four times."[46] But most of the Reims Protestants ". . . kept to themselves and [held services] in their own homes."[47]

While in Reims, Le Picart found solace writing his *Épistre* and quite possibly preaching to the sisters of Saint-Pierre-des-Dames. Although Le Picart later expressed anger at being considered a *mutin* and a *séditieux*, this treatise displays no bitterness over his exile. Indeed, it might be argued that this marked a turning point for him, a defining moment in which he came to terms with the pride and arrogance that had contributed to his fall. He may have read more of the Church Father who was to become his favorite, Chrysostom, whose life story would have consoled Le Picart. As in his own case, the condemnation of Chrysostom and his exile had led to popular demonstrations of support.[48] Chrysostom's words resonate throughout both the *Épistre* and the sermons of Le Picart's later years. The bishop of Constantinople had expressed the view that "the more my troubles increase, the greater is my consolation."[49] In later sermons, Le Picart tells his listeners "Saint Chrysostom says that the evils and punishments of this world are truly the grace and compassion of God."[50] He adds that according to Chrysostom, ". . . the nature of tribulation is . . . that the man who is tried remains in liberty not to give into temptation."[51]

---

[44] Herminjard, *Correspondance*, III:57.
[45] A.N. Galpern, *The Religions of the People in Sixteenth-Century Champagne* (Cambridge: Harvard University Press, 1976), 136.
[46] Boussinesq and Laurent, *Histoire de Reims*, I:473.
[47] Desportes, *Histoire de Reims*, 175.
[48] Gregory, *Vox Populi*, 55.
[49] Prethes, *Life of John Chrysostom*, 193.
[50] Le Picart, *Trinité*, fol. 33.
[51] Le Picart, *Trinité-II*, fol. 38.

Responding to the challenge, Le Picart rejoices in this test of his faith. At one point in the *Épistre* he declares,

> My sisters, we have a great and long road to travel. Therefore let us come together in our Lord, and then nothing will be impossible for us. The thorns and the thistles, the trees and the mountains, and all the other obstacles in our path cannot harm us. And once having traversed this dangerous passage with the help of our Lord . . . we will know that it is not possible to avoid the dangers of the world without our companion Jesus Christ, who is faithful and loyal. He is not merely our companion, but our servant in times of need.[52]

Le Picart puts his own problems in the context of Jesus' passion: "I owe my whole life to our Lord Jesus Christ, because he gave his life for me, and sustained such bitter sorrows in order to save me from damnation. What then can I find hard to endure, when I have the memory of our Lord Jesus Christ? . . ."[53]

The text of the *Épistre* suggests that during this exile Le Picart seems to have struggled with the question of why he was being tested, eventually finding comfort and an answer. He says that "when I have done with and endured all chastisements, pains, prisons, exiles and death, yet will I not be worthy."[54] He asks, "what can be hard for me, when I have memory and record of Jesus Christ?"[55] Through reflections of this type, Le Picart was able to make of his banishment an opportunity to imitate Christ.[56]

Le Picart was in Reims through the end of 1533. In June, Melanchthon heard from Latomus in Paris that the banishment of the preachers had so debilitated the conservative cause that their only hope lay in the death of the queen of Navarre, who was pregnant.[57] By August 23, Sturm was writing with great optimism of the possibilities that France would be gained for the reform. He wrote to Bucer that "except for some greybeards of the age of Priam, there is no one who supports these Phrygian priests . . . Gérard Roussel is so modest that the greatest number of those with judgment go to hear him."[58]

---

[52] Le Picart, *Épistre*, 21–22.
[53] Ibid, 12.
[54] Le Picart, *Épistre*, fol. 14.
[55] Ibid, fol. 11.
[56] Ibid, fols. 11, 21.
[57] Bourrilly, 43–47.
[58] Herminjard, *Correspondance*, III:72–75.

It was, however, a good time to be away from Paris. The city had been afflicted by plague since 1531, which became particularly virulent in the late summer and early fall of 1533. The *parlement* issued a decree that was to be cried out in all the quarters and cross-roads of the capital:

> All houses which have been afflicted by the plague during the past two months must make this known for twelve months by means of two wooden crosses. All who were, or are, sick with the plague, or who have those who are sick living with them, must carry a white staff on the street. Whoever visits, attends, washes, or serves those suffering from the plague must not associate with others for forty days. The Faculty of Medicine is appointing four doctors, two surgeons, and six barbers who, at the expense of the city, are to devote themselves exclusively to the care of the pest-ridden. The public baths will be closed till Christmas. No one may purchase or carry off clothes from those who are sick. The streets are to be repaired and kept clean. Morning and night householders must pour water in front of their houses so that the filth is washed away. Chamber pots must not be emptied out of the windows but poured into gutters and the filth flushed away with at least three pails of water. Those who fail to do this will be subject to corporal punishment. Refuse must be carried out into the fields or at least placed in baskets at assigned places for hauling away. Pigs, rabbits, chickens, and doves must not be kept within the city or suburbs, but must be sent out into the country. Dirty linen must not be hung out of the windows to dry. Individuals should be appointed in every parish to carry off and bury those who have died of the pestilence, and to air out their houses and mark them with crosses. Tanners, under the threat of exile, must not exercise their trade in the city or in the suburbs. For this they must go to the bank of the Seine beyond the Tuileries and Saint-Germain-des-Prés and there stretch out their hides, and the dyers should there also spread out their wool to dry. A similar prohibition is leveled against butchers and salt-fish handlers, and these are further forbidden to throw their refuse into the river or quays.[59]

A self-proclaimed "pilgrim" in Paris at the time, Ignatius of Loyola, came into close contact with the plague, as he relates in his *Autobiography:*

> . . . a friar came to ask Doctor Frago that he try to find him a house, because in the one where he had lodging many people had died of the plague, he thought (for the plague was then beginning in Paris). Doctor Frago and the pilgrim wished to go see the house. They took

---

[59] Quoted in Georg Schurhammer, *Francis Xavier: His Life, His Times. I: Europe, 1506–1541* (Rome: Jesuit Historical Institute, 1973), 191.

a woman well versed in these matters, and on entering she confirmed that it was the plague. The pilgrim also chose to enter. Coming upon a sick person, he comforted him and touched his sore with his hand.

After he had comforted and encouraged him a while, he went off alone. His hand began to hurt so that it seemed he had caught the plague. This fancy was so strong that he could not overcome it until he thrust his hand forcefully into his mouth and moved it about inside, saying, "If you have the plague in the hand, you will also have it in the mouth." When he had done this, he was rid of the fancy and of the pain in his hand.

But when he returned to the college of Sainte-Barbe, where he then had lodging and was attending the course, those in the college who knew that he had entered the plague-ridden house fled from him and would not let him enter. So he was forced to remain out for some days.[60]

But neither the plague nor the exile of some of their leaders deterred the conservative theologians of the Faculty from further attacks on the queen of Navarre and her protegés, for heretical ideas still resounded from the pulpits of Paris. Beza claimed that thanks to Marguerite, Gérard Roussel, Jean Courtauld and François Bertault were "announcing the truth a little more boldly than they had been accustomed to."[61] In addition, other reports indicated that "[a] certain Augustinian preaches the gospel at the door of the Louvre [probably Saint-Germain l'Auxerrois] before a huge crowd of people; at the Louvre itself, it was the Carmelite from Italy, whom the pope had given to his niece, who preaches Christ very freely . . . The queen, sister of the king, governs the niece of the pope . . ."[62] Feelings had been running strongly against Marguerite for several months, and one monk, Toussaint Lemand, suggested she should be tied up in a sack and thrown into the Seine.[63] The performance at the Collège de Navarre was only one of the indignities to which Marguerite was

---

[60] Ignatius of Loyola, *The Spiritual Exercises and Selected Works*, ed. and trans. George E. Ganss (New York: Paulist Press, 1991), 103–104.

[61] Bèze, *Histoire ecclésiastique*, I:26.

[62] Hyrvoix, "Noël Bédier," 589. Catherine de Medici's marriage to the dauphin Henri was celebrated in October, 1533.

[63] F. Genin, ed., *Lettres de Marguerite, d'Angoulême, soeur de François I, reine de Navarre* (Paris: J. Renouard, 1851), 56. This was a familiar threat, hurled against the Franciscan Olivier Maillard by an angry Louis XII. It would be repeated during the Religious Wars by the Sixteen against the preacher Panigarole. Alexander Samouillan, *Olivier Maillard: Sa prédication et son temps* (Toulouse: Privat, 1891), 26; Charles Labitte, *De la démocratie chez les prédicateurs de la Ligue* (Paris: Joubert, 1841), 87.

subjected in the autumn of 1533. The theologians now attacked the new edition of her *Miroir de l'âme pécheresse*,[64] published by Antoine Augereau, one of several actions that would lead to the printer's eventual execution.[65] Although the book was not officially condemned it was listed as suspicious.[66] Containing no mention of justification by works, purgatory or prayer to the saints, Marguerite had also referred the *Salve Regina* to Christ, not the Virgin Mary.[67] After hearing of the theologians' attack on her book, the queen of Navarre complained to her brother in Marseilles, who demanded an explanation. Nicolas Leclerc explained that the book had been set aside as suspicious for the technical but legally correct reason that it had been printed without the Faculty's authorization.[68] The tide seemed to turn once again against the conservatives when Francis I retaliated by depriving the Faculty of its right to nominate preachers for individual parishes, turning this over instead to the reform-minded bishop, Jean DuBellay.[69] At this point, reformed hopes were at their apogee. With Marguerite and her husband in control of Paris along with the bishop, booksellers were openly selling heretical works.[70] The reformer Martin Bucer wrote excitedly of events in Paris: "We have begun to preach Christ openly . . ."[71]

The tide would soon turn again. On November 1, the Feast of All Saints, the newly-elected rector, Nicolas Cop, stunned the University of Paris with his inaugural sermon. Cop, a friend of Calvin, had the previous month delivered a harangue against those who had censored the *Miroir*. In his speech to the assembled faculties, Cop referred obliquely to Le Picart and Beda, clamoring against those who "cursed good men or slandered princes."[72] At the forefront of those who denounced Cop was the Franciscan Descornes, who claimed six of his statements were heretical. Besides attacking salvation by works, Cop had exclaimed, "[t]he world and the wicked are wont to label as heretics, imposters, seducers and evil-speakers those who strive

---

[64] The first edition had been published in Alençon in 1531.
[65] Guignard, "Imprimeurs," 72.
[66] Delisle, "Notice," 350.
[67] Bèze, *Histoire ecclésiastique*, I:23–24.
[68] Schurhammer, *Francis Xavier*, 194.
[69] Calvin, *Opera*, X:2, 29–30.
[70] Herminjard, *Correspondance*, III:75.
[71] Hyrvoix, "Noël Bédier," 583–584.
[72] Schurhammer, *Francis Xavier*, 196.

purely and sincerely to penetrate the minds of believers with the Gospel . . ."[73] Although a copy of Cop's speech exists in Calvin's handwriting, no contemporary source attributed the speech to the future reformer, and many modern scholars do not believe it was his work.[74] After receiving a warning that he would be arrested, Cop fled Paris with a bounty of 300 *écus* on his head. Whether or not he had taken part in the composition of the sermon, Calvin felt by the end of November that the situation had become too dangerous for him in Paris, and fled.

> On December 19, Francis I wrote from Lyon, despairing that the accursed, heretical sect of Luther had taken root and grown in his good city of Paris, the capital of his kingdom and the seat of the chief university of Christendom. He ordered an example to be made of these heretics: they should be relentlessly sought out, and two members of the council should be designated to give their exclusive attention to this. Measures, moreover, should be taken against the preachers who had favored these errors . . .[75]

Within a week, more than fifty suspects had been rounded up, and an edict was passed ordering those convicted of heresy to be burned at the stake.[76] Exaggerating the degree of persecution, the reformers wrote "that there are nearly three thousand prisoners in Paris,"[77] blaming this not on their own missteps but on the wedding that had taken place in October between Catherine de Medici and the dauphin Henri.[78]

It was in this changed climate that Le Picart was the first to be recalled from exile, thanks largely to his family connections. Although it was "not the most prudent thing to do," Jean Le Picart had written to Guillaume Preudhomme, Francis I's *receveur-général* of the treasury, asking for his help in having his son recalled from exile. Preudhomme wrote back on December 26, acknowledging Le Picart's letters of 19 December, and reporting with pleasure that after consultation with another of Le Picart's friends, the Cardinal de Veneur, the king had been persuaded to allow François ". . . to return to

---

[73] Quoted in Knecht, *Renaissance Warrior*, 311.
[74] Ganoczy, *Calvin*, 80; Alister McGrath, *A Life of John Calvin: A Study in the Shaping of Western Culture* (Oxford: Basil Blackwell, 1990), 66.
[75] Schurhammer, *Francis Xavier*, 199; Herminjard, *Correspondance*, III:114.
[76] Schurhammer, *Francis Xavier*, 199; Herminjard, *Correspondance*, III:129–130.
[77] Herminjard, *Correspondance*, III:129.
[78] Hyrvoix, "Noël Bédier," 584.

Paris to preach, as he is accustomed to doing."[79] Just as Chrysostom's
return had been met with joyous celebration,[80] François Le Picart's
return was greeted with jubilation. Calvin's biographer, Doumergue,
states that "in glory he left for exile: in greater glory he returned
from it. The return was a triumph. All the city trembled with joy
and public celebration, and he resumed his passionate lessons and
preaching."[81] Academics, *parlementaires*, city leaders and his large family came out to meet him. "In this city of Paris, the eagerness and
joy was universal: because a good man had been taken back from
his enemies . . ."[82] Although his early release and relatively lenient
treatment were undoubtedly due to his family connections, Le Picart
apparently learned an important lesson: "There are in this world
many who call themselves your friends, showing themselves to be
your servants and promising much, but in need they will abandon
you."[83] Le Picart may also have learned how to temper his message,
or at least aim it more carefully. In one sermon he exclaims, "You
have a good Catholic king and the Faculty of Theology, but the
men at court are cowards."[84]

Le Picart was quickly caught up in the academic life and pastoral
obligations that his exile had interrupted. On January 2, Nicolas
Frizon was designated to preside over Le Picart's *magna ordinaria*.[85]
During Lent of 1534, Le Picart was again preaching in Paris. But
the troubles were not over. A work falsely attributed to Beda, enti-
tled the *Oraison faite au roi de France par les trois docteurs de Paris bannis
et relégués requérans d'estre rappelés de leur exil*, had been given to the
king. This treatise, with a dedicatory preface to Francis I which compared the author to St. Paul, contained numerous propositions that
were defamatory and seditious, and it was to ascertain whether Beda
was really the author that he was allowed to return to Paris. On
April 22, Étienne Dolet wrote, "I am amazed and indignant to learn
that the monstrous and vicious beast Beda, that execrable pest, has

---

[79] Quoted in Jean de Launoy, *Regii Navarrae Gymnasii Parisiensis Historia* (Cologne: Fabri and Barillot, 1731), IV:412.

[80] Gregory, *Vox Populi*, 58.

[81] Doumergue, *Calvin*, I:240.

[82] Launoy, *Regii Navarii*, 412.

[83] Le Picart, *Pasques*, fol. 43.

[84] Le Picart, *Trinité*, fol. 165.

[85] Farge, *Biographical Register*, 263.

been recalled from exile. There has been a rumour here that he has again attempted some wickedness . . ."[86] The king was not initially convinced that Beda had not penned this "scandalous libel,"[87] since it fit everything Francis had come to expect from the syndic. However, Beda immediately disavowed the work, whose real author has never been conclusively determined.[88] Every copy the authorities could locate was burned, and Beda and other preachers were ordered to denounce the book in their sermons. But Beda simply could not leave well enough alone, and chose to accuse the king's lecturers in Greek and Hebrew of crimes against the Vulgate Bible, and meddling in theological matters.[89] Although Francis I claimed there were "a hundred reasons" for the second arrest and final exile,[90] it was probably Beda's intransigence regarding Henry VIII's proposed divorce that led to his final incarceration. Walter Bense speculates that Beda had written that ". . . neither the king of England nor the king of France lived like good Christian princes should, and that this statement was found among the materials taken from his room during his [first] exile."[91] In March of 1534, Beda, now joined by Nicolas Leclerc, was back in prison, and both men remained for much of 1534 on the charge of *lèse majesté*. At some time after that, likely the result of further incendiary preaching, Le Picart was ordered to join them in prison.[92] As a result, Le Picart did not receive his license with his class in June of 1534. Despite the efforts of the papal nuncio,[93] the three men would remain in captivity until late November. Roussel was still free, although he had been forbidden to preach.[94] Despite the prohibition, Master Gérard tried to preach at Notre-Dame on April 1, but the seeds planted by the theologians began to bear fruit, and an angry crowd refused to allow him to speak,

---

[86] Quoted in Farge, *Orthodoxy*, 205–206.

[87] Gabrielle Berthoud, *Aspects de la propagande religieuse* (Geneva: Droz, 1957), 152.

[88] Antoine Marcourt, Pierre de Vingle and Pierre Caroli are all possibilities. Gabrielle Berthoud, "La 'confession' de Maître Noël Beda et le problème de son autheur," *Bibliothèque d'humanisme et renaissance* 29(1967), 373–397; Bense, "Noël Beda," 831.

[89] Farge, *Orthodoxy*, 205.

[90] Ibid, 268.

[91] Bense, "Noël Beda," 836–837.

[92] Ibid, 836–841.

[93] J. Lestocquoy, ed., *Correspondance des nonces en France: Carpi et Ferrerio 1535–1540 et légations de Carpi et de Farnèse* (Paris: E. de Boccard, 1961), 19–20.

[94] Schmidt, *Roussel*, 107.

shouting "Down with him!" Pelted by stones, Roussel had to be res-
cued by the police. It was his last attempt to preach in Paris.[95]

The summer of 1534 remained a trying one for the preachers and
theologians of the Sorbonne and Navarre. Beda, Le Picart and Leclerc
were still in prison. In July, Francis, whom Beza characterized as
"having begun to taste a little bit of the truth,"[96] spurred on by the
DuBellay brothers, approached Melanchthon and Bucer about a possible reconciliation between the faiths. This was closely tied to events
on the international stage, as Francis was willing to do anything that
would annoy Charles V. Ambassadors at Henry VIII's court speculated around this time that the French king was favorable to the
reformed faith.

But these efforts came to nothing, for on the night of October
17–18, placards denouncing the mass and expounding a Zwinglian
interpretation were affixed all over Paris and even on the king's bed-
chamber door in the château at Amboise. Placards were also posted
in Tours, Blois and Orléans. These *Articles véritables sur les horribles,
grandz & importables abuz de la Messe papalle,* written by Antoine Marcourt
and printed in Neuchâtel by Pierre de Vingle, attacked the mass on
four points: 1) Christ was sacrificed once and for all on the cross,
and this action could not be repeated; 2) the mass declares that
Christ is really present in the eucharist, which is impossible, for the
Bible says that He is with God the Father; 3) transubstantiation is
a human invention; and 4) the mass is a memorial service and not
a miracle.[97] The mass was described as a sham created by the Catholic
priesthood to seduce the people and destroy the world. The work
ended, "be not surprised then that they defend it with force. They
kill, burn, destroy, and murder as brigands all those who contradict
it; for, without force, they are defenceless. Truth menaces, compels,
follows and chases them and it will find them out. By it shall they
be destroyed. Fiat. Fiat. Amen."[98] The placards had been ". . . smuggled into France by Guillaume Feret, a servant of the king's apothe-
cary, and displayed in Paris by a group of radical dissenters who
may have wanted to show their implacable hostility towards any

---

[95] Schurhammer, *Francis Xavier,* 202.
[96] Bèze, *Histoire ecclésiastique,* I:28.
[97] Knecht, *Renaissance Warrior,* 315.
[98] Quoted in Mark Greengrass, *The French Reformation* (Oxford: Basil Blackwell,
1987), 25.

Protestant compromise with Rome at a time when Francis was seeking to heal the religious schism in Germany."[99] With this one ges-
ture, the early reformed movement in Paris was effectively killed.
Beza wrote afterwards that "all this [progress] was interrupted by
the indiscreet zeal of certain men . . ."[100]

Not unlike the response to events in the years between 1557 and
1562, rumors spread like wildfire throughout the city. Some said that
the heretics were going to burn down the churches and massacre
the faithful during mass; others that the Louvre would be sacked.
Foreigners, especially those who spoke German, were targeted by
frightened Parisians, and a Flemish merchant was lynched by a mob.
Fires were lit on the Place Maubert, the Place de Grève and elsewhere throughout the city and the kingdom. On November 13 and
14, a shoemaker's son, known as the "Paralytic," and a well-to-do
draper were sent to the stake. Before the month was over, a printer,
weaver, bookseller and mason would follow them.[101]

Mark Greengrass summarizes the effects of the Affair of the Placards:

> The affair thus both helped define orthodoxy and gave it new allies
> among the clergy and royal corporations whose task it was to preserve
> order. It also made it more difficult for those of heterodox opinion
> within France either to voice their opinions or enjoy protection in high
> places. Even Marguerite d'Angoulême faltered, having withdrawn from
> her brother's court to become queen regent of Navarre . . . Finally, it
> swelled the numbers of exiles abroad. . . . But the extent to which the
> Placards mark a watershed should not be exaggerated, for the overall
> pattern of the 1530s was a cyclical one of repression followed by remis-
> sion. . . . Finally, the attitudes of Francis I cannot be said to have been
> irredeemably and substantially altered by the affair. One protestant in
> exile—John Calvin—thought the king might still be persuaded after
> 1535 to accept a measure of evangelical truth—at least this was the
> purpose of dedicating to him the famous treatise, the *Institution of the
> Christian Religion* . . . in 1536.[102]

Crouzet challenges the view held by many historians that the Placards
constituted a major turning point in the history of the French
Reformation. He says instead, "[they were] only a parenthesis, with
minor implications."[103] Be that as it may, for Le Picart, the incident

---

[99] Knecht, *Renaissance Warrior*, 315.
[100] Bèze, *Histoire ecclésiastique*, I:28.
[101] Knecht, *Renaissance Warrior*, 316.
[102] Greengrass, *French Reformation*, 26–27.
[103] Crouzet, *Genèse*, 229.

had important results. On November 21, 1534, the university, vindicated by these events, petitioned for the release of Beda, Leclerc, and Le Picart.[104] Le Picart and Leclerc were freed a few days later, but the king's anger against Beda had not dissipated. After performing an *amende honorable* at Notre-Dame, the man who had symbolized Catholic reaction was exiled to Mont St.-Michel, where he would die on 8 January 1537.

Crouzet situates the real turning point at an event on January 13, 1535, which he refers to as "the second affair." In mid-November, Antoine Marcourt had published his *Petit traicté tres utile et salutaire de la saincte eucharistie de nostre seigneur Jesuchrist*, which amplified statements made in the Placards. Crouzet hypothesizes that it was this book, distributed clandestinely at the Louvre and throughout Paris on the morning of the thirteenth that prompted severe repressive measures.[105] This view warrants serious attention, as it fits the timing of the response much more closely than does the Affair of the Placards. In all likelihood, it was this second act of bravado, coming on the heels of the Placards, that convinced Francis I of the need to take radical steps to stop the spread of heresy. In any case, both events proved auspicious for the Catholic faithful. In their wake, the king even remarked that the Faculty of Theology ". . . has always been a shining light, held in high esteem for its sacred studies . . ."[106] On January 21, 1535, the king, the religious orders, and the corporations of the city staged a great procession in honor of the Blessed Sacrament, with all of the relics of the city and kingdom brought out and honored. The tension could be cut with a knife:

> To prevent disorders, the principals of the colleges were told to keep their students at home during the festivities. The side streets emptying into the one taken by the procession were shut off with barriers; and the police, dressed in military tunics adorned with silver and the coat of arms of the city (a white ship on a red ground), kept order with white staves. In the early morning the parishes of the city and suburbs headed with the crosses, banners, and relics towards Saint-Germain l'Auxerrois near the Louvre. From there the procession was to go to the Rue Saint-Honoré past the cemetery of Les Saints-Innocents, Saint-Jacques-de-la-Boucherie, and the bridge of Notre-Dame to the cathedral.[107]

---

[104] Farge, *Biographical Register*, 263.
[105] Crouzet, *Genèse*, 232–233.
[106] Farge, *Orthodoxy*, 207.
[107] Schurhammer, *Francis Xavier*, I:229.

Later that evening, as the celebratory mood continued, six Protestants were burned at the stake, three at Les Halles and three at the Cross of Trahoir.[108] Three large sacks of heretical books found in their possession were also burned.[109] Le Picart alludes to this event in one of his sermons: "In the beginning, we were so fervent to punish them, that at one time, after mass, we burned six of them. After that they were muzzled by fear, so that some said they no longer existed."[110] A week earlier, Francis I had issued an edict stating that "... no one from this day forward, may print or cause to be printed in our kingdom any book, and this under pain of hanging."[111] Although the king would modify the decree six weeks later, anyone who was discovered to have printed books in defiance of the order was threatened with death. On 24 January 1535, a royal proclamation called for seventy-three Lutherans, including Pierre Caroli, to give themselves up, and less than a week later it was made a capital crime to protect heretics. The events of 1534–1535 marked a triumph for those who had watched with dismay the unchecked gains of the reformers. Although the king would continue negotiations with the German reformers well into 1535, his motives by this time were largely political. Even more importantly, as Farge has noted, "Marguerite's influence was on the wane,"[112] perhaps one of the most gratifying of the victories achieved by the theologians.

Le Picart was able to receive his license in theology on February 3, 1535, and passed his doctoral disputation three weeks later. He was then assigned to preach the Lenten series at St.-Eustache in both 1535 and 1536.[113] The last verbal encounter between Le Picart and Roussel was still to come, in February, 1536, after Marguerite de Navarre obtained the appointment of Gérard Roussel as Bishop of Oloron. Le Picart, preaching at the church of Saint-Benoît near the university, shouted from the pulpit, "Choose one from your midst!" which many in his audience inferred to be a reference to Roussel.[114] In one sermon, he exclaims: "We read in the fourth book of the register of Saint Gregory a letter that he wrote to Childebert,

[108] Marcel Fosseyeux, "Processions et pèlerinages parisiens sous l'ancien régime," *Bulletin de la société de l'histoire de l'Ile-de-France* 71–72(1944–45), 26.
[109] Febvre and Martin, *Book*, 310.
[110] Le Picart, *SL*, 148.
[111] Farge, "Marguerite de Navarre," 21.
[112] Ibid.
[113] Farge, *Biographical Register*, 262–263.
[114] Schurhammer, *Francis Xavier*, 264.

King of France, in which he took the king to task for appointing
bishops without examining them well."[115]

Le Picart's sermons bear the strong imprint of these years. Even
if statements taken from undated sermons cannot be proven to have
come from 1533–1534, there can be little doubt that it was those
events that inspired them. Several themes emerge. Le Picart is quite
critical of royalty, and while he does not mention Francis I, Marguerite
de Navarre or her husband by name, the implications are clear.
There are equally obvious references to Roussel, as well as to the
bishops and others who licensed him to preach. Finally, Le Picart
reflects on the purpose of tribulation, with what are certainly personal reminiscences of his experience of prison, exile and disgrace.

Le Picart does not mince words when referring to kings. "When
the governor of a republic is a fool, it is difficult for his people to
live well. We see this in the book of Kings."[116] Le Picart warns such
kings that if they do wrong, they ". . . will have a judgment more
harsh and bitter than that of others."[117] He leaves little doubt what
he thinks of such a king:

> O, Sire, you are the sovereign king of heaven and earth, but I, how-
> ever much I am King of France, I am only a small servant compared
> to you. And that I am King before you, oh no! I am only your serv-
> ant and officer. The king must consider and say "I am the leader of
> the people of God—he has given me this office. But compared to my
> master I am nothing but a dead dog."[118]

Kings may have great estates and castles and be hailed by all, yet
"they are small with regard to God, for they are only men."[119] With
a sinister reference to John the Baptist, Le Picart says, "Saint John
arrived in the court to meet the king. What did he say to him? 'You
are an adulterer, a bawd, one who commits incest . . .'"[120] His words
ring with implied threats: "It is a grievous sin to introduce another
God than God the Creator; it would be like having another king
than the King of France."[121] He reminds the king that the dignity
of the priesthood is greater than that of kings or emperors: "If I am

---

[115] Le Picart, *Trinité-II*, fol. 14.
[116] Ibid, fol. 13.
[117] Le Picart, *Pasques*, fol. 37.
[118] Le Picart, *Advent*, fol. 235.
[119] Le Picart, *Pasques*, fol. 161.
[120] Le Picart, *Trinité-II*, fol. 7.
[121] Le Picart, *Trinité*, fol. 77.

a good man and of good faith, I must believe myself to be more as priest than if I were a king, an emperor or some other great prince."[122] However powerful the king might be, the church was greater: "Excommunication is the knife of the church. This power is much greater than that of the king, because it concerns the soul, and the power of the king only extends over the body."[123] If one had to make a choice, "one should obey God and not the king."[124]

Le Picart examines how royal wrongheadedness or inaction allowed heresy to gain a foothold. After some initial repression,

> they hid themselves, and afterwards the chickens came in and multiplied in such great number that there have never been more in the world than at present. If someone dies of the plague, we mark the house, in order to avoid evil and danger. It is necessary for us to do the same thing to heretics, who are far worse than they were in the beginning, for there are now sacramentarians and worse . . .[125]

In a later reference, he is less willing to condone policy in the early years: "If the heretics had been punished for their lesser errors in the beginning, they would not have gotten to the point of committing great ones."[126] Le Picart holds the king directly responsible for the preaching of diverse doctrines.[127] Probably thinking of the light punishment Roussel had received compared to his own, Le Picart complains that ". . . yet we endure it, and don't punish them at all . . . For this reason, many are damned."[128] For those who may have shied away from confrontation in light of the heavy punishment meted out to Catholic preachers, Le Picart offers encouragement, saying: "We are heirs, not of the king of France, but of God . . ."[129]

Some of Le Picart's attacks on kingship target the virtual idolatry in which the king is held by the people, who make him a God on earth. "When we go before the king, we tremble before His Majesty, and yet we do not tremble before God."[130] Even in Paris, the most

---

[122] Le Picart, *Pasques*, fol. 34.
[123] Le Picart, *Advent*, fol. 109.
[124] Le Picart, *Instruction*, 160.
[125] Le Picart, *SL*, 148.
[126] Le Picart, *Caresme-II*, fol. 40.
[127] Le Picart, *Caresme*, fol. 22.
[128] Ibid, fol. 136.
[129] Le Picart, *Trinité*, fol. 69.
[130] Le Picart, *SL*, 88.

Catholic city in the kingdom, "if the king passes, each person goes outside of their house to see him, yet when one carries Our Lord, we do not budge from the house."[131] When the king commands something, "each one fears and obeys him, as we must do. But I tell you it is more important to obey God than the king."[132] He muses, "I will hold myself well for two hours on both knees before the king, or before some prince, and will not say that it hurts my knees. And yet I can't hold myself on my knees a half hour before God."[133] If people discovered a conspiracy to burn down the city or poison the king, Le Picart is sure that they would warn the king, yet nothing is done to those guilty of the worst of all crimes, heresy.[134] "If someone commits a crime against the king, he will be hanged forthwith. This is justice. But to take the name of God in vain, and that which concerns the honor of God, is ignored."[135] If a man's honor is challenged, "I will raise my arm to strike the man who insults me, but when we insult Our Lord Jesus Christ no one says a word."[136] Le Picart compares the French situation unfavorably with that of Spain:

> In some countries, as in Spain, when one carries our Lord to the sick in the city, the great ones and the emperor himself accompany it to the house of the sick person, and afterwards they once again conduct our Lord to the church, and there are many or more lighted torches than we have in this city of Paris on the day of God's feast. When the king passes, everyone goes out of his house to see him.[137]

Le Picart blames the French king for not upholding similar standards. Later, in 1554, when he had mellowed considerably and made his peace with the events of 1533–34, Le Picart could say that "[t]he king for a time played the part of a Lutheran, as one of them, in order that based on that they would take the occasion to assemble everywhere, and that one could strike a blow at them and purge them from the realm."[138]

---

[131] Le Picart, *Pasques*, fol. 303.
[132] Le Picart, *Instruction*, 160
[133] Le Picart, *SL*, 190; cf. *Trinité-II*, fol. 65.
[134] Le Picart, *Trinité*, fol. 57.
[135] Le Picart, *Advent*, fol. 83.
[136] Le Picart, *SL*, 148–149.
[137] Ibid, 236.
[138] Labitte, *Les prédicateurs de la Ligue*, 3.

In his comparisons of good and bad preaching, Le Picart could only have been thinking of his personal rivalry with Roussel. He says, "Someone will say to the king, 'Sire, don't you have any good prophets in your realm?' 'Yes, he will answer, but I don't like him at all, because he never has any good prophecies for me. He never says anything that my heart wants to hear.'"[139] He is incensed that ". . . vices reign because one does not dare to say the truth to princes."[140] Stung by his imprisonments and exile, Le Picart exclaims that "today, if during a sermon one reprimands those who are full of vice, they will say, 'this preacher is a *mutin*, a *seditieux*!"[141] For speaking the truth a man was hated and persecuted,[142] for lying was taken as truth, and truth a lie.[143] Flatterers and outright liars were everywhere.[144] Le Picart says that "if the world says, 'here is a good preacher,' that is a sign that he is not."[145] Playing the part of royalty, he cries, "'O! Saint John [the Baptist] is indiscreet! One must not speak thus to kings and princes.' This is what the world says: but God believes that Saint John is discreet."[146] Even if it is the king or some other great person who commits a sin, he must be reprimanded publicly, "as we see by the example of Saint Paul, who reproached Saint Peter in public . . ."[147]

The problem was most serious when it was not merely flattery, but heresy that prompted a preacher. "You have a heretical preacher, who cannot prove his assertions, and yet one believes him rather than one who can prove what he says?"[148] Openly scornful, he asks, "Do you think that until now there have never been men in Paris who perfectly understood and preached the gospel?"[149] In a passage that undoubtedly refers to his own situation, he exclaims, "[these preachers] are in great danger, being in the good graces of a prince: it is necessary to pray that they are chased away and dismissed, put

---

[139] Le Picart, *Advent*, fol. 241.
[140] Le Picart, *Trinité-II*, fol. 74.
[141] Le Picart, *Pasques*, fol. 91.
[142] Le Picart, *Caresme-II*, fol. 62.
[143] Le Picart, *Advent*, fol. 241.
[144] Le Picart, *Trinité-II*, fol. 74.
[145] Ibid, fol. 84.
[146] Ibid, fol. 69.
[147] Ibid.
[148] Le Picart, *Trinité*, fol. 16.
[149] Ibid, fol. 60.

in prison, in order that they will have the chance to recognize God
the Creator."[150]

Le Picart challenges those who have received preferments and
patronage at the hands of the king and Marguerite: "It is necessary
to be reputed a fool according the world, in doing acts of true wisdom, according to God, in rejecting for oneself all goods and worldly
honors."[151] Even those who should know better, bishops in the church,
had helped men like Roussel preach. Briçonnet and DuBellay may
have been in Le Picart's mind: "You say that you have the permission of the bishop, and that he allows this. I assure you, over
some things the bishop has no power. He cannot, for example, give
a man a dispensation to marry during Lent."[152] Today "there are a
great number of bishops, archbishops and prelates who are diligent
in making their way in the world and accumulating pomp . . . But
for bringing wandering sheep back to the sheepfold, they don't want
anything to do with it. And what is more, I, a bishop or prelate,
permit a heretic or one suspected of heresy to preach in my diocese!"[153]
A simple man could be excused for his ignorance, "but one constituted in an office or a dignity, like a doctor or curé, if he preaches
an error through ignorance one must impute this to his malice."[154]

Le Picart affirms his role in the confrontation with Roussel. "When
the sin is public, one must reprimand it publicly, especially when it
is a great scandal to the church!"[155] One must not wait to do so,
but rather challenge such a preacher in the pulpit, so that "he can
confess his error, that he has preached badly . . ."[156] Roussel may
not have realized it, but Le Picart was doing him a favor. "If you
know that I damn myself by preaching as I do, shouldn't you come
tell me, and reproach me publicly?"[157]

Many comments in the sermons speak directly to Le Picart's personal experience of prison, and he takes Paul as his model. He warns
that "men can be bound, but not the Word. The greatest part of
the epistles of Saint Paul were written in prison."[158] He goes on,

---

[150] Le Picart, *Advent*, fol. 190.
[151] Le Picart, *Trinité-II*, fol. 80.
[152] Le Picart, *Instruction*, 161.
[153] Le Picart, *Caresme*, fol. 21.
[154] Le Picart, *Pasques*, fol. 184.
[155] Le Picart, *Trinité-II*, fol. 69.
[156] Le Picart, *Pasques*, fol. 73.
[157] Ibid, fol. 295.
[158] Le Picart, *Trinité*, fol. 74.

"Keep in mind that our Lord Jesus Christ was resurrected, for which I labor even to the point of being bound and made prisoner, like a malefactor: because saint Paul when he wrote to Timothy was a prisoner, and by his example we must not be scandalized if a good man, for having done and said the truth, is imprisoned."[159] A true preacher of the Word of God "must be prepared to lose everything—all his goods—rather than turn from the truth."[160] To be punished publicly, to be burned at the stake, to be hanged[161] was the price a man of integrity had to be willing to pay. "St. Paul never experienced such freedom as when he was imprisoned and beaten."[162]

Le Picart had learned the moral lesson God had been trying to teach him, understanding that a preacher of the truth would have to endure great tribulations.[163] This was a sign of God's love. "If someone strikes me, I must not strike him back...but leave the vengeance to God."[164] In fact, Le Picart owed a debt of gratitude to Francis and Marguerite, who taught him the lesson that "we must esteem our enemies as our great friends, because it is thanks to them that we will gain paradise."[165] One must not murmur against God or one's persecutors but love them and pray for them,[166] embracing the tribulations, because "when someone persecutes another, and by this persecution he comes to know God better, the persecution turns out to be for his salvation. He becomes more humble and is confirmed in the fear and love of God." What more could a person ask than the companionship of Christ? "He nourishes me. I was in prison, and he visited me, he testified through his death."[167] Even more, "...tribulation serves to prepare us for our inheritance: because if there are no enemies and no war, there can be no victory, and no crown."[168] Faith and the assistance of the Holy Spirit were all that was needed to find joy in adversity.[169]

Le Picart had many feelings to sort through as a result of the events of 1533–1534. He felt tremendous anger that heretical views

---

[159] Le Picart, *Trinité-II*, fol. 79.
[160] Le Picart, *Trinité*, fol. 40.
[161] Ibid, fols. 128, 234.
[162] Le Picart, *Trinité*, fol. 119.
[163] Ibid, fol. 39.
[164] Ibid, fol. 24.
[165] Le Picart, *Advent*, fol. 168.
[166] Le Picart, *Instruction*, 213; *Advent*, fol. 36.
[167] Le Picart, *Trinité*, fol. 252.
[168] Le Picart, *Instruction*, 242.
[169] Le Picart, *Trinité*, fol. 10; *Instruction*, 285.

were being preached openly with the sanction of royalty, and that
defenders of the true faith were punished. Yet he also had to reflect
on the sin of pride and what such tribulations meant for a Christian
man. Ultimately these troubles strengthened him as a man and as
a preacher. It has been said of great spiritual figures that they experience a defining moment—the climax of a period in their life when
they have been broken, and have put themselves back together again,
renewed in their faith in God and stronger than before. François Le
Picart seems to have had such a defining moment in the period from
March, 1533 to December, 1534. He entered this phase a brash
young man, about to take his doctorate in theology at one of the
premier universities in Christendom. He associated himself with the
leaders of the conservative reaction in Paris—Beda, Leclerc and others,
and lashed out not only at the evangelicals and the heretics whom
he believed were trying to destroy the faith, but also at royalty—a
king and his sister who not only had allowed this to happen but
even helped heresy to gain a foothold in the most Catholic city of
France. Things were out of control in these middle years of the
1530s, and Le Picart responded with a defense of what had always
mattered most to him—his Catholic faith. We cannot know for certain if these troubles humbled him, but the testimony of his own
words in the sermons and his actions in the years that followed suggest it. After his exile and imprisonment, he was able to focus his
attention on what truly mattered to him: a defense of the Catholic
faith and the extirpation of heresy. Never again in trouble with the
authorities, Le Picart was able to pour his heart and soul into his
preaching. The years 1533–1534 therefore marked a turning point
for France, and also for François Le Picart. In his own words, he
summed up the experience: "The tribulation that God sent me was
so that I would come to know myself..."[170]

---

[170] Le Picart, *Instruction*, 226, 228.

CHAPTER FOUR

THE FAITH EMBATTLED

On the feast of the Nativity of the Virgin, September 8, 1546, a
group of blasphemers was discovered, thanks to an informer, wor-
shipping in the house of Estienne Mangin of Meaux. Pierre Leclerc
stood before them, expounding a passage from St. Paul's Epistle to
the Corinthians. When interrupted, they offered no resistance, but
began singing Psalms, especially the 79th: "Oh God, the heathen
are come!" The congregation of men and women was led away to
Paris, where several were condemned to death. The prisoners, except
for Mangin and Leclerc, were placed in tumbrils by Gilles Berthelot,
Provost Marshal, who was to accompany them, along with his archers
and lieutenants, to the town of Meaux, where sentence would be
carried out. The two leaders were dragged on hurdles.[1] Accompanying
them, mounted on mules, rode two doctors from the Paris Faculty
of Theology, François Le Picart and Nicolas Maillard, who continually harangued the prisoners in the hope of effecting their conversion. Pierre Leclerc, angered by their attempts, turned to Le Picart,
and shouted, "Get away from us, Satan, and do not hinder us from
remembering and thinking about the benefits our God has given
us." The men and women received unexpected support during their
journey. As they wended their way through the forest of Livry, a
master weaver appeared, following the vehicles conveying the prisoners, and exhorted them to be strong in the face of such harassment.
Fearing he would not be heard, the man shouted, "My brothers,
remember He that is in Heaven above!" Hearing this, the retainers of
Berthelot took and bound the man, and put him in with the others.
As the procession reached Livry, the people of the town came forth,
and recognizing one of their own, shouted that he was an unrepentant Lutheran who deserved punishment more than those among
whom he had been placed.

---

[1] David Nicholls, "Inertia and Reform in the Pre-Tridentine French Church: The
Response to Protestantism in the Diocese of Rouen, 1520–1562," *Journal of Ecclesiastical
History* 32(1981), 62.

Upon their arrival in Meaux nearly a month after their arrest, the prisoners were interrogated on the rack. One hardy soul yelled out not to spare the body that so resisted the Creator's will. The house of Estienne Mangin, where the conventicles had been held, was razed to the ground. In the Grand Marché fourteen gibbets were erected, surrounded by straw, faggots, brimstone, gunpowder and timber. Close at hand were platforms for those who would not suffer burning at the stake.

On October 6, Le Picart and Maillard conversed with the prisoners, hoping some would admit to the Real Presence in the Sacrament of the Altar. Leclerc demanded of them, "When you take the host and drink of the cup, do you taste flesh or blood?" The prisoners were offered a deal; if they confessed, they would obtain some favor. Seven accepted.

The following day, at 2:00 o'clock in the afternoon, the fourteen condemned heretics were brought to the Grand Marché, followed on foot by those who were to be spared. The fourteen were bound with ropes and iron chains to a gibbet. As they were raised into the air, facing each other, those whose tongues had not been cut out sung Psalms. To drown out the voices of the heretics, the priests and the crowd sung the *Salve Regina* and *O Salutaris Hostia*, until the bodies had been burnt and fallen into the fire.

On the 8th of October, a general procession was held in Meaux. The entourage, composed of scholars, children from Meaux, the monks of Notre-Dame, other local religious, chaplains, vicars, and canons all walked in solemn entourage carrying torches. Behind them, the body of Christ was carried aloft for the reverence of the people. Finally came the prisoners, walking two by two, followed by the officials of Meaux and three thousand citizens of the town. François Le Picart climbed to his pulpit in the midst of the Grand Marché, which had been covered with a golden canopy, from whence he delivered a sermon on the Holy Sacrament of the Altar. The heretics stood on the platform not far from the preacher, the men in their shirts holding torches, the women barefoot, holding tapers. Attending the sermon were an "almost infinite number of people, from Paris and other places, who had arrived the day before."[2] Beza claims that after becoming thoroughly worked up, Le Picart angrily insisted

---

[2] Simon Fontaine, *Histoire catholique de nostre temps, touchant l'estat de la religion chrestienne, par F. Simon Fontaine de l'ordre de S. François & Docteur en Theologie à Paris. Enrichie de plusieurs choses notables depuis l'an 1546 iusques à l'an 1550* (Paris: Claude Frémy, 1562), 234.

that those who died the day before had been ". . . condemned to the pits of hell, and that even if an angel descended from the sky to say the contrary, it must be rejected, for God would not be God if he didn't damn them eternally."[3] When the sermon was over, the body of Christ was escorted once again to the church of St. Étienne, where the heretics were forced to kneel in expiation of their crimes.[4]

*　*　*

In the aftermath of the Affair of the Placards, the Faculty of Theology and the *parlement* were far less stymied in their attempts to eradicate heresy by royal interference. Moreover, many of the protagonists of the early battles—including Lefèvre, Erasmus, Beda and Budé—would die between 1535 and 1540, leaving the struggle to younger men. The leading figures in our story after 1536 were François Le Picart, John Calvin and Ignatius of Loyola.

Some historians have maintained that the French church at least before 1542 was ineffectual in its response to heresy. David Nicholls contends that "[i]nertia, coupled with a few signs of reform, governed the Church's specific responses to Protestantism . . ."[5] In Normandy at least, he found that the threat of Protestantism was not taken very seriously and special sermons against heresy were rare.[6] Part of the problem, as we have seen in Chapter Three, was royal policy. But in the capital, the French church had made a concerted effort to deal with the problem of heresy. As early as 1528, the Council of Sens had been convened to deal with the problem. Although the Faculty was not directly involved, the humanist-turned-orthodox-theologian Josse Clichtove (1472–1543) drew up articles that were published the following October in an attempt to define Catholic orthodoxy and specify erroneous doctrines. Condemned by name were Luther, Melanchthon, Karlstadt, Oecolampadius, the Frenchman François Lambert, and others involved in this "execrable conspiracy."[7]

---

[3] Bèze, *Histoire ecclésiastique*, I:69–70.
[4] The original documents on which this account is based come from Jean Crespin's *Histoire des Martyres*, and Claude Rochard's *Antiquitez de la Ville de Meaux*. Partial English translations of these sources can be found in the appendices of H.M. Bower, *The Fourteen of Meaux* (London: Longmans, Green and Co., 1894), 36–47.
[5] Nicholls, "Theatre of Martyrdom," 189.
[6] Ibid, 191, 196.
[7] Farge, *Orthodoxy*, 241.

Cardinal DuPrat, who had presided over the meetings, was one of the first French churchmen to call attention to the disunity within the reformed movement, especially the disagreements between Luther and Zwingli over the mass.[8]

In January of 1536 the *parlement* of Paris order a "reformation" of the Faculty of Theology as part of a constructive response to the "Lutheran" threat. The sixth provision required four lectures on the Bible to be delivered daily from November 12 to August 31, two ". . . in the morning at the Collège de Navarre, and the two others were to be in the afternoon at the Collège de Sorbonne. The first lecture, at 7 a.m., was to cover the Epistles and the Apocalypse; the second at 8 a.m., was to be on the prophets. The afternoon lectures were to begin at 1 p.m. with a lecture on the Gospels and continue at 2 p.m. on the Pentateuch and the 'géographes.' . . . No lectures on the *Sentences* could take place at the same hour as any of these new Scripture lectures."[9] Faculty who did not lecture were to preach in Paris or nearby towns, and students for the license had to prove they had attended the lectures on Scripture for three years. Le Picart was one of the first four lecturers named for the year 1536;[10] then in 1541, when the Sorbonne did not have enough qualified regent doctors to fill the afternoon lectures, he was named to speak there.[11] These efforts, intended to restore the University of Paris to its reputation as queen of theology, reflected some of the early positive influences of both humanism and Protestantism on the Faculty.

The 1540s marked a hardening of royal policy against heresy. On June 1, 1540, the edict of Fontainebleau gave the *parlements* complete jurisdiction over heresy cases. The spread of heresy was compared to a public fire, the dousing of which was part of every citizen's responsibility.[12] Even more important was the Faculty's promulgation of "Articles of Faith" in 1542 that were intended primarily as guidelines for preachers. The lack of a clear definition of heresy in the 1520s had helped the reformed faith gain a foothold, and even

---

[8] Sutherland, *Huguenot Struggle*, 20.

[9] Farge, *Orthodoxy*, 52.

[10] The others were Michel Doc, Guillaume Ribou and Jerónimo Frago y Garces, although Frago y Garces had to be replaced by Jean d'Abres. James K. Farge, *Registre des conclusions de l'université de Paris (1533–1550)* (Paris: Klincksieck, 1994), II:93–94, 94n. Each lecturer was paid 30li.6s.6d. for the year. Farge, *Orthodoxy*, 53n.

[11] Pasquier, *Benoist*, 51n.

[12] Knecht, *Renaissance Warrior*, 328.

orthodox preachers could make mistakes, as their sermons were now subjected to far closer scrutiny than they had been in earlier years. Antoine Heyraud, provincial of the Dominicans in Provence and assistant to Bishop Jacopo Sadoleto of Carpentras, had made ambiguous statements about justification and predestination that the bishop had felt compelled to refute.[13] By 1542, the situation had grown more serious, as pulpits during Lent and Advent had rung out with the heretical sermons of François Landry, Jean Barenton, François Perucel and Claude d'Espence.[14] Letters patent of Francis I introduce the twenty-five articles with this justification:

> In order to provide a much needed and required remedy for the many scandals and schisms which have heretofore come about, even in the recent Advent season, by means of and on the occasion of contentions, altercations and contradictions of certain preachers preaching and publishing diverse and contrary doctrines, and in order that such novelties and pernicious enterprises bring no inconveniences and irreparable damages to our religion, . . . our esteemed friends the dean and doctors of the Faculty of Theology of our daughter the University of Paris, convened and assembled following our will and persuasion, in order to give advice on this business, have by mature and sincere deliberation, agreed, made and decided upon the articles which follow word-for-word, in which they have faithfully deduced what is to be believed and preached regarding the points which have fallen into dispute . . ."[15]

François Le Picart was one of the Faculty members directly involved in the formulation of these articles, and he refers to them occasionally in his sermons: "It is one of the articles of the Faculty of Theology that . . . one can speak to the saints before going to God, and that this is holy and meritorious."[16] The articles reaffirm the traditional interpretation of the seven sacraments (1,3,5–10), uphold belief in the powers of the saints and the Virgin (11–16), free will (2), good works (4), purgatory (17) and the infallibility and tradition of the church (18–25).[17] The language of the articles shows the degree to which the theologians were responding point-by-point to heretical preachers. For example, article 20 states that "[m]any things

---

[13] Marc Venard, "L'église d'Avignon," *thèse d'état* presented to the Université de Paris IV, 1977, I:457.

[14] Higman, *Censorship*, 56.

[15] Farge, *Orthodoxy*, 209.

[16] Le Picart, *Pasques*, fol. 68.

[17] See Farge, *Orthodoxy*, 210–211.

which the Church has received by tradition are not expressly and explicitly stated in scripture."[18] The promulgation of these articles, renewed in 1545, gave both *parlement* and the Faculty a specific weapon with which to deal with the problem of heretical preaching. If the primitive features of the French Reformation had consisted of fideism, biblicism and illuminism,[19] attacks on specific doctrines in the 1530s now resulted in men and women being charged with attacks on the Catholic faith and the Christian religion,[20] accusations facilitated by the Articles.

In addition to such positive steps, the *parlement* and Faculty continued and extended their efforts in the realm of censorship. Even before the Placards, in 1531 and 1532, the *parlement* had sent representatives to booksellers to check on what they were publishing and selling, and had found a large number of books worthy of the flames. Although the draconian measures taken by Francis I in 1535 had not lasted long, new edicts and decrees appeared in the final twelve years of the king's reign. In 1538, the king led the way, ordering his own printer of Greek works, Conrad Néobar, not to publish anything without the authorization of the Faculty.[21] But it was an edict of July 1, 1542, that went the farthest. One of its specific aims was to rid the kingdom of all copies of Calvin's *Institutes*, which were to be turned in within twenty-four hours on pain of death. The edict further decreed that all clandestine printing must cease, and in all published works the printer's name and city had to be clearly displayed. Before being offered for sale, all books were to be examined by members of the Faculty. Printers were forbidden from commenting on any aspect of Christian doctrine in books covering grammar, rhetoric, logic or literature,[22] so that such works could not be used surreptitiously to evade the censorship laws. The *parlement* also ordered Parisians to denounce preachers or curés who expounded heretical doctrines.[23] A committee of six doctors of the Faculty, including Le Picart, was to be informed of the activities of any "secret heretics."[24]

---

[18] Ibid, 211.

[19] Pierre Imbart de la Tour, *Les origines de la réforme* (Geneva: Slatkine Reprints, 1978), III:416–454.

[20] Nicholls, "Popular Heresy," 271.

[21] Farge, "Marguerite," 22.

[22] Higman, *Censorship*, 50.

[23] DeBujanda, *Index*, 66.

[24] The others were Henri Gervais, Nicolas Leclerc, Pierre Richard, Robert Bouquin, Jean Benoist. Bèze, *Histoire ecclésiastique*, I:46.

Unlike many of the earlier decrees, this edict showed a new aware-ness of problems associated with books being smuggled into France from abroad as well as other clandestine publishing activities.[25] Six Parisian booksellers or publishers were put on trial between 1541 and 1544, two of whom were burnt at the stake. *Colporteurs* selling books throughout France found themselves in an especially precari-ous situation,[26] as traveling from place to place made them suspect of conveying forbidden works smuggled into France. In 1544 a spec-tacular demonstration of the authorities' intentions to prosecute under the new law was given, when *parlement* ordered books by both Calvin and Étienne Dolet to be burned in front of Notre-Dame while the cathedral bells were rung. During the same year, the first of several indexes of forbidden books was issued, which would involve the cen-sure of 528 books.[27]

Tensions in the capital mounted during the final months of Francis I's reign in 1546–1547. Even before the discovery of the heretics of Meaux had caused an uproar, several heretics were burned in the Place Maubert between July and September, 1546, including Dolet.[28] More executions followed in January of 1547, as well as a proces-sion following the mutilation of a statue in the Cemetery of the Innocents. And then, on 31 March 1547, the man known as "le grand roy Françoys" died, ending an age.

Flooding of the Seine was severe in the spring and summer of 1547, overflowing the place de Grève and the rues de Bièvre and de la Harpe, so that "one could not pass to the rue de la Hachette."[29] People suffering from the strains and tensions of the recent years attributed the floods to the spread of heresy. But King Henri II's strong measures against heresy reassured the people of the capital, who gave him the credit for the receding of the waters.[30] In November, Mathieu Ory was confirmed in his role as Inquisitor of the Faith. The following month, the king issued an edict that went further than many of its predecessors:

---

[25] Higman, *Censorship*, 52.
[26] Knecht, *Renaissance Warrior*, 509.
[27] Farge, "Marguerite," 23.
[28] Nathanaël Weiss, *La chambre ardente: Étude sur la liberté de conscience en France sous François Ier et Henri II (1540–1550)* (Paris: Fischbacher, 1889), xxxvii.
[29] Ibid, lxvi.
[30] Ibid, lxvii.

One of the things we have most in our heart is, by all the best means possible to us, to extirpate errors and false doctrines, which have multiplied and still multiply at present in our realm ... And because it seems to us ... that one of the first and principal means is to take away from our subjects the books that are the foundation and occasion of the said errors. ... We ordain, inhibit and prohibit ... under pain of confiscation of body and goods, to print or have printed, to sell or publish, any books concerning holy scripture, and especially those brought from Geneva, Germany and other foreign places, when they have not first been seen, looked at and examined by the Faculty of Theology of Paris ...[31]

Henri was so concerned with heresy that he gave the *Chambre Ardente* far-reaching powers to deal with malefactors in 1547–1548. But the high point of cooperation between the king, the *parlement* and the Faculty of Theology came in 1551 with the issuance of the Edict of Châteaubriant, which provided a comprehensive program for the eradication of heresy. Châteaubriant marked a decisive shift in policy from prohibition to persecution, with positive prescriptions for appropriate religious behavior.[32] The first article spells out how closely linked in the public mind sedition and heresy had become, ordering *parlementaires* to seek out Lutherans and "punish them as fomentors of sedition, schismatics, disturbers of public harmony and tranquility, rebels, and disobedient evaders of our ordinances and commandments."[33] Article 10 prohibited the sale or translation of the Bible or Church Fathers without prior approval.[34] A new incentive was offered for turning in heretics—informers were to receive one-third of the property confiscated from convicted heretics.[35]

In the events of these years, François Le Picart was a major actor in his role as preacher, lecturer and theologian. Besides his part in the drawing up of the Articles of Faith, he presided over the execution of heretics at Meaux and in Paris.[36] Beza mocked his role in these proceedings, asking, "Oh Master Picard! Oh Master Maillard! Master Leclerc ... won't we burn these heretics?" Furthermore, as

---

[31] DeBujanda, *Index*, 72.

[32] Sutherland, *Huguenot Struggle*, 47.

[33] Mack Holt, *The French Wars of Religion, 1562–1629* (Cambridge: Cambridge University Press, 1995), 30.

[34] DeBujanda, Higman and Farge, *Index*, 73.

[35] Sutherland, *Huguenot Struggle*, 46.

[36] Bèze, *Passavant*, 84; see also Jean Crespin, *Histoire des martyrs persecutez et mis à mort pour la veritee de l'evangile, depuis le temps des apostres iusques à present (1619)* (Toulouse: Société des livres religieux, 1885), I:518.

evidence of how much had changed since 1533–1534, he was selected by the university to congratulate Henri II on his accession.[37] He listened to denunciations of those suspected of heresy, and his name can be found in books as the authority who approved publication. A 250-page "livret" of 1548 by Nicole Grenier explaining different points of Catholic doctrine contains a note on the last page that it was "seen and read by Master François Le Picart."[38] Henri Busson has suggested that Le Picart also spearheaded the persecution of Rabelais, claiming that he was the motivating force behind, and perhaps even the author of, Gabriel Dupuiherbault's attack on Rabelais.[39]

---

[37] Marie-Louise Concasty, ed., *Commentaires de la faculté de médecine de l'université de Paris (1516–1560): Documents inédits sur l'histoire de France* (Paris: Imprimerie nationale, 1964), 416.

[38] Nicole Grenier, *Le bouclier de la foy, en forme de dialogue, extraict de la saincte escripture, et des sainctz peres, et plus anciens docteurs de l'eglise, dedié au roy tres chrestien Henry, deuxiesme de ce nom, nouvellement imprimé à Paris en 1548 nouvellement reveu et augmenté par l'autheur* (Paris: Vivant Gaulteroit, 1548), n.p.

[39] Henri Busson, "Les églises contre Rabelais," *Études rabelaisiennes* 7(1967), 1–81. Busson makes his case based on what he believes are inconsistencies between the personality of "the gentle and inoffensive poet theologian [Gabriel Dupuiherbault]" and the strident tone of part of his *Theotimus*, which attacked Rabelais. Busson contends that Le Picart was the actual author, suggesting that Le Picart had been infuriated by Rabelais' attacks on his friend Pierre Descornes. In Book III of *Gargantua and Pantagruel*, Rabelais writes, "Ho, ho, ho: our horny Pierre Cornu—except that fat Franciscan just has the name and you'll have the real thing—God keep and protect you! Give us a little Franciscan preaching, will you, and I'll go around begging for alms!" François Rabelais, *Gargantua and Pantagruel*, trans. Burton Raffael (New York: W.W. Norton, 1990), 280. But Busson's argument is undermined by his mistaking of Descornes' death for 1542, instead of 1549, and his assumption that Le Picart was outraged at a posthumous assault on his friend and fellow preacher. In fact, a comparison of the beliefs of Le Picart and Rabelais shows that they were not nearly as far apart as Busson would have us believe. Pantagruel says, "If God be for us who can be against us?" Quoted in Febvre, *Problem of Unbelief*, 251. These words echo Le Picart's own in his *Épistre* and sermons, for example, when he asks, "If God is for us, we should fear no creature." Le Picart, *Instruction*, 73; cf. ibid, 74. Rabelais' emphasis on prayer, the goodness of God, and his formulation of the relation of faith to salvation are not very different from Le Picart's understanding, and his emphasis on *fides charitate formata* would have been equally acceptable to Le Picart, Lefèvre and perhaps even Roussel. Febvre, *Problem of Unbelief*, 284–294. If as Febvre remarks, ". . . the Virgin and the saints. . . are given a very lowly place" in Rabelais (Ibid, 305), the difference from Le Picart is one of emphasis, for the latter is very concerned to make sure his listeners understand that it is Jesus Christ who saves. This is not to suggest that Le Picart would have been happy with Rabelais' novel. The original censure of the work in 1533, according to Nicolas Leclerc, had not been for heresy, but for obscenity. (Ibid, 104). The scatological imagery of *Gargantua and Pantagruel* and the ridicule of the church would have put Le Picart and Rabelais at odds under any circumstances, but Busson's hypothesis is largely without foundation.

Robert Estienne claimed that along with Jean de Gaigny and Jean Guyencourt, Le Picart was responsible for bringing charges against him that led to his flight to Geneva.[40]

As the great Catholic defender of the faith in Paris in the years following the Affair of the Placards, François Le Picart found himself subject to both physical and verbal assaults. In the forties and fifties, as Calvinist partisans grew in number even in the city of Paris, Le Picart in his person came to symbolize the Catholic faith. One day in March, 1546 when Le Picart was preaching in Paris, Jean de la Vacquerie reports that

> one of them, who seemed dazed and impatient in his rage, tried to strangle the venerable doctor and excellent preacher, Master François Le Picart, while he was preaching in the church of St.-Jacques-de-la-Boucherie in Paris. After trying to put his enterprise into effect, he was stopped by the people gathered around the pulpit, who threw him out of the church and killed him in their excitement.[41]

This potential for martyrdom may have worked in Le Picart's favor. In one of his sermons, he alludes to the incident: "I am not ashamed nor do I fear to expose holy scripture according to the sense of the church. But the heretics do not dare to speak publicly. And even if they kill me for expounding the Bible according to the doctrine of the church, it's all the same to me, for their doctrine is wicked, and that of Our Lord is true."[42]

Le Picart's sermons are full of references to heresy. Although some churchmen feared that speaking of heretical doctrines from the pulpit would aid in their diffusion, Le Picart believed it was essential to warn people about heresy. He even preached that people should interrupt him during his sermons if they detected any errors in his words: "If I preach an error, don't wait until the end of the sermon to correct me, because those who hear me preach will get the wrong idea, or they will be scandalized if they do not wait around to hear you correct me after the sermon. So reprimand me publicly, in the pulpit, and tell me my mistake."[43] However tongue-in-cheek this pro-

---

[40] Farge, *Biographical Register*, 180.

[41] Jean de la Vacquerie, *Remonstrance adressé au roy, au princes catholiques, et à tous Magistrats & Gouverneurs de Republiques, touchant l'abolition des troubles & emotions qui se sont auiourd'huy en France, causez par les heresies qui y regnent & par la Chrestienté* (Paris: Jean Poupy, 1574), fols. 36–37.

[42] Le Picart, *SL*, 203.

[43] Le Picart, *Caresme*, fol. 127.

nouncement was, Le Picart was adamant about silencing heretical preachers. In his public role since 1535 as examiner of suspect works, he had become thoroughly conversant with the opinions of French evangelicals, most of whom had been forced to choose sides, as well as those of Luther, Zwingli, Calvin and the other reformers. His preaching followed closely the simple doctrines enunciated in the Articles of Faith.

Le Picart frequently comments on the times in which he is living. He lays the *malheur des temps* squarely at the feet of the heretics. "All manner of evil abounds today. Do we have any reason to rejoice, seeing how many heresies and evils reign? Yet we laugh and revel in life. We see schism and dissension in Christianity, and yet we do not grieve."[44] Using medical metaphors, he compares heresy to a cancer that grows silently but continuously in the body.[45] There is no longer "any health in the body, there is no corner on which there is not a leper; it has infected almost the entire body of the church."[46] The symptoms of sickness include the divisions that are found everywhere. ". . . [I]n a kingdom that is divided and in confusion, the devil rules, and it will be ruined and desolated. As you see when there is dissension between husband and wife, the house will come to destruction."[47] Children fight against their fathers, and girls against their mothers.[48] Heresy is responsible for both war and the recent onslaught of the Turks:

> [First,] Christianity is menaced by the infidel, whom Christians are unable to resist, if they are not of one accord, which cannot happen without peace. Second, this is because of the errors and heresies which spread from day to day throughout the realm, which we cannot abolish or extirpate without peace. Because in time of war what one constructs the other destroys and demolishes. Third, it is the cause of great oppression and excessive charges which fall on the poor people in times of war and which cannot be discharged without living in peace.[49]

God, he asserts, is punishing Christians for having deserted Him.[50]
Le Picart traces the cause of these ills to a falling away from God.

---

[44] Le Picart, *Trinité-II*, fol. 171.
[45] Le Picart, *SL*, 56.
[46] Le Picart, *Trinité*, fol. 122.
[47] Le Picart, *SL*, 37.
[48] Le Picart, *Trinité*, fol. 161.
[49] Ibid, fol. 136.
[50] Ibid, fol. 177.

"Today, oh how awful! There are people so bad who say there is
no God, nor providence of God. These people are called *athei*, that
is, without God."[51] Although he likely had Protestants in mind, his
description certainly encompasses true atheism, possibly the outcome
of heresy: "Today there are people who don't know God at all; they
think and believe that there is no God, which is a great error."[52] In
this unbelieving generation, he compares the heretics and nonbe-
lievers to the Jews of old:

> Therefore, Christians, don't be like them! Don't ask for signs, like the
> Jews did, and like the heretics of today do, who demand signs and
> want literally to see Our Lord Jesus Christ in the holy sacrament of
> the altar. If they don't, they don't believe He is there. Oh incredu-
> lous and adulterous generation! Don't you know that faith is about
> things unseen?[53]

The condition of the times was especially disturbing, for things had
once been otherwise. "In past times we lived well, in great peace
and tranquillity in the church. But now there are all these new doctors, and even without seeing them, we believe what they say!"[54]
This was especially lamentable in France, which had once been
notable for its purity: "You see that all of France, practically all of
Christianity is infected. Saint Jerome praised this country of France,
because in his time there were no [heretics] at all, and now they
are everywhere. There is not a city in France that does not have
some, and when one finds three people together, one is bound to
be infected."[55] He is particularly troubled that such monsters are
even found in Paris, the most Catholic of cities.[56] "The faith once
flourished so much in Paris, and yet now it has been deserted so
that I have heard from those who know that there are more than
thirty thousand Lutherans in Paris."[57] Elsewhere, he states that in the
past there were only one or two heretics, but now there are "... almost
as many as there are monsters in the sea."[58] Probably speaking in
the early 1540s, Le Picart exclaims, "[Y]ou have been able to see for

---

[51] Ibid, fol. 2.
[52] Ibid.
[53] Le Picart, *Caresme*, fol. 52.
[54] Le Picart, *Advent*, fol. 134.
[55] Le Picart, *Instruction*, 294.
[56] Ibid, 295; Le Picart, *Pasques*, fol. 41.
[57] Le Picart, *Trinité*, fol. 113.
[58] Ibid, fol. 17.

twelve or twenty years all of the false prophets in this city of Paris."[59]
He warns that the acceptance of false prophets—with men such as
Gérard Roussel in mind—will provoke the ire of God.[60]

Le Picart insists that divisions within the Catholic Church, which
allow the new doctrines to flourish, must end. "Christians, we see
how the evil ones and heretics get together against us. And yet we
are divided, full of dissension and quarrels! This is a sign that we
do not have charity."[61] He wavers between optimism and pessimism
over the chances of ending these divisions. "We write many good
books, but the heretics won't be overcome by them, because they
bring up our abuses; but if we live well, we will confound them,
and the foundation of their errors will be eradicated, and will dis-
appear like smoke. Yet when I look around at so many abuses, I
am in despair about whether these heresies will cease . . ."[62] Yet his
basic optimism and faith triumph:

> As you see, the heretics try to abolish and destroy the truth. Nevertheless,
> by their fight against and contradictions of the truth, God will make
> the truth more widely known. In imagining that they are going to
> abolish the truth, they will make it shine forth and appear. . . . So you
> will see that the more the heretics try to destroy the truth, the more
> God will incite the good to study and be more vigilant in confound-
> ing them and their errors.[63]

Although Le Picart sometimes follows the convention of his times in
referring to all heretics as Lutherans, he shows a clear awareness of
the distinctions between the different groups. Recognizing that one of
the foundations of their heresy was their interpretation of the mass,
he offers a historical framework. He tells his audience that the first
to speak ill of the holy sacrament of the altar was Berengarius, who
was followed by John Wyclif and Jan Hus.[64] The church, he points out,
had been in existence for a thousand years before someone dared
to speak ill of the sacrament of the altar. But at least when his error
was condemned by a council, Berengarius recanted.[65] The same could
not be said of those who came after him. Le Picart explains that

---

[59] Ibid, fol. 60.
[60] Le Picart, *Advent*, fol. 136.
[61] Le Picart, *Caresme*, fol. 136.
[62] Le Picart, *Pasques*, fol. 90.
[63] Le Picart, *Caresme*, fol. 127.
[64] Ibid, fol. 52.
[65] Le Picart, *SL*, 32–33.

theirs was different from the error of Berengarius. Because he said that
the holy sacrament of the altar was nothing but bread and wine, and
that the precious body of Our Lord Jesus Christ was not there. But
these two [Wyclif and Hus] fully admitted that the precious body
of Our Lord Jesus Christ was present in the holy sacrament of the
altar. Their error was in saying that in the holy sacrament, the bread
and wine remained in their nature and substance, and were not converted or transubstantiated into the precious body of Our Lord. They
were anathematized and condemned at the Council of Constance...
and since their time no one had spoken ill of the holy sacrament of
the altar until about thirty years ago when that contemptible and
unhappy man Luther, worse than the devil, who has more disciples
than Mohammed, renewed the heresy of those two wretched English-
men [sic].[66]

The different dates of the sermons can be seen in Le Picart's references to Luther. In one sermon, he talks about the suffering await-
ing Luther if he "dies in his sin,"[67] and questions what reparation
he can possibly make for all the evils he has caused.[68] In other places,
he speaks of how even "Luther will admit to the importance of confession from the heart."[69] But elsewhere he refers to Luther in the
past tense, as having died suddenly[70] and living twenty-eight years
with a nun before his death.[71]

Le Picart distinguishes between Luther and other reformers. He
refers on occasion to Zwingli, whom he knew was killed in battle,[72]
and there are brief references to Bucer[73] and Melanchthon (usually in
connection to Luther). In one diatribe, Le Picart attacks Melanchthon's
arrogance and love of glory in taking such a name.[74] Aside from
Luther, Le Picart devotes the most time to Oecolampadius. "Isn't it
remarkable, he asks, how they can't agree among themselves? Luther
has one faith, one doctrine, Oecolampadius has another, so who
speaks the truth?"[75] This was an important point, which he stresses.
"There are those disciples of Martin Luther who say and do worse

---

[66] Ibid, 35–36; *Pasques*, fol. 257.
[67] Le Picart, *Trinité-II*, fol. 164; *SL*, 260.
[68] Le Picart, *Trinité*, fol. 98.
[69] Ibid, fol. 87.
[70] Le Picart, *Trinité-II*, fol. 179.
[71] Ibid, fol. 187.
[72] Ibid, fol. 179; cf. ibid, fol. 187.
[73] Le Picart, *Trinité*, fol. 97.
[74] Ibid, fol. 96; *Trinité-II*, fol. 179.
[75] Le Picart, *Trinité*, fol. 97; cf. ibid, fol. 96; *Trinité-II*, fol. 187.

than him: because he admits that Our Lord Jesus Christ is truly present in the holy sacrament of the altar, but he is mistaken and errs in saying that the bread and wine in the sacrament remain in their substance and nature."[76] He explains:

> Here we have the heretic Luther, and his disciple Melanchthon, and Oecolampadius, and all of them have contrary opinions. Is this not a marvel and evident sign that they are deaf and mute, and that their edifice will not grow higher, but will fall into ruin? Luther says rightly that the body of Jesus Christ is in the holy sacrament of the altar, but he says that the bread is there too, which is false. Oecolampadius says that there is only bread, which is a complete error. God is not with those who are so divided . . .[77]

Continuing on this subject, Le Picart tells his listeners

> there are five or six different opinions. One says it is only bread, the other that Jesus Christ is there but that the substance of the bread remains and is not transubstantiated. Another says, that it is only the body and blood of Our Lord, and not a sacrifice and oblation. Yet another says that the sacrifice only profits the one who receives it, and not all the living and dead. Another says that it is necessary to give the sacrament in both kinds to the laity. The division and variety of opinions that they hold is an argument and obvious sign that they do not have the Holy Spirit in them, but they speak in the spirit of Satan and the devil.[78]

Although the Catholic Church was not without problems, it did not suffer from the same kind of doctrinal bickering. "When one sees the union and harmony in our congregation, which comes from the grace of God, we must conclude that our congregation is the house of God, since there is unity, concord and common consent in the faith. . . . My doctrine is not particular, singular or private—it does not engender schism or division at all."[79]

Le Picart challenges the admiration in which these "brilliant" new men are held. "One says today that Calvin is very erudite: that he is as knowledgeable a man as Luther. What is this you say, a knowledgeable man, ha! Knowledge does not consist of language or speculation, but of practice and works."[80] Le Picart spends considerable

---

[76] Le Picart, *SL*, 37–38; *Pasques*, fol. 258.
[77] Le Picart, *Trinité*, fol. 96.
[78] Le Picart, *Pasques*, fol. 87; cf. *Advent*, fol. 111; *SL*, 37.
[79] Le Picart, *Trinité-II*, fol. 41.
[80] Ibid, fol. 139.

time on the doctrines emanating from Geneva. He tells his listeners
searching for the truth that they can go to Geneva, but they won't
find it there—instead they will find only corruption and infection,[81]
for there they ignore the mass and the other sacraments of the
church.[82] The books smuggled in from Geneva show how far the
Calvinists are from the truth.[83] Their lives are spent in debauchery,[84]
evident even in their preaching: "Do you think that it would be nice
to see me here in my pulpit dressed like those of Geneva, all in fak-
ery, and wearing my plume behind my ear? I would be damned if
I lived or dressed otherwise than my estate requires!"[85]

Le Picart takes on the Calvinist doctrine of predestination. For
those curious to know if they are among the elect,[86] he warns:

> It is not for me to investigate the will of God and what He has delib-
> erated for me. Rather I must believe that I am predestined to a cer-
> tain end and that God has decided in advance what will happen. I
> must not inquire or look into what God has predestined for me. But
> I should believe God has elected me to predestination in order to be
> saved. But how will I know, whether I am predestined to salvation?
> By guarding the commandments, you will know that you are predes-
> tined. The observance of God's commandments is the only certitude
> you need of your salvation.[87]

Le Picart expresses contempt for Genevans who claim they are among
the elect. "I would very much like to ask them how they know that,
and how it was revealed to them!"[88] The problem was not simply
their pride and arrogance, but their tendency to antinomianism. "By
this they abandon themselves to all manner of vices, thinking nothing of their salvation. You will not be able to conceive of any vice
greater than this. It is a very dangerous thought: because the judgments of God are of a wisdom too profound for us. . . . If you really
want to know if you are predestined to be saved or damned, look
to your works, and your life . . ."[89] He continues, "there is danger that
hope will be converted into temerity and audacity under the cover

---

[81] Le Picart, *Advent*, fol. 346; cf. ibid, fol. 333.
[82] Le Picart, *Pasques*, fol. 41.
[83] Le Picart, *Trinité-II*, fol. 22.
[84] Ibid, fol. 20.
[85] Ibid, fol. 5.
[86] Le Picart, *Trinité*, fol. 201.
[87] Le Picart, *Instruction*, 121–122.
[88] Le Picart, *SL*, 166.
[89] Le Picart, *Caresme*, fol. 170.

of the mercy of God. Just as with those who eliminate purgatory and satisfaction for sins, you see that that hope is converted into freedom to sin . . ."[90] But the good Catholic who does his best and follows God's commandments as well as he can "is as confident as a lion, who fears nothing."[91] Interestingly, contemporary Calvinists such as Pierre Viret were coming to some of the same conclusions regarding the problem of antinomianism. A prolific writer and contemporary of Le Picart, the pastor of Lausanne attacks false Evangelists who use the gospel as a cloak for their debauchery.[92]

Based on his knowledge of the writings and actions of the great heresiarchs of his age as well as his encounters with French reformers, Le Picart constructs a profile of the typical heretic that he regularly describes in his sermons. Frequently recalling the accusation that had been hurled at Luther at the Diet of Worms, Le Picart argues that these men and women privilege their own interpretation over that of the Church Fathers and other learned men. The church's doctrine had stood for fifteen hundred years, yet these arrogant fellows believe they have all the answers. "The heretics are peculiar people, apostates, prideful men, to whom the Holy Spirit has not revealed itself."[93] They strive to be different, saying otherwise than the church of God, which he attributes to their desire to gain fame and be highly esteemed.[94] What else could one think, when "they say they have the Holy Spirit, and the true understanding of scripture, and that we err and do not really understand holy scripture. For the love of God, you see the error, the presumption, and the temerity of these

---

[90] Le Picart, *Advent*, fol. 50.

[91] Le Picart, *Caresme-II*, fol. 58.

[92] "They are good Evangelists, meaning that it offers them nothing more than the ability to eat meat every day and do similar things, turning the freedom of the gospel into carnal license . . . It is certain that there are many such Evangelists who are foolish, temerarious, presumptuous, and mock both God and men . . . They do not know Jesus Christ . . . Often such Evangelists are more debauched, engaging in more dissolutions than anyone else, and for them the gospel is only a farce and source of merriment . . ." Pierre Viret, *De la communication des fideles qui cognoissent la verité de l'Evangile, aux ceremonies des Papistes, & principalement à leurs baptesmes, mariages, messes, funerailles, & obseques pour les trespassez* (Geneva: No publisher given, 1547), 140–142; cf. Pierre Viret, *La necromance papale, faites par dialogues en maniere de devis* (Geneva: No publisher given, 1553), 71; Pierre Viret, *Dialogue du desordre qui est à present au monde, et des causes d'iceluy, & du moyen pour y remedier: desquelz l'ordre & le tiltre sensuit* (Geneva: No publisher given, 1545), 810–811.

[93] Le Picart, *SL*, 14.

[94] Le Picart, *Trinité*, fol. 8; cf. *Pasques*, fol. 105.

people! Where is the Holy Spirit in them?"[95] Unlike those who have
never been taught the truth, the heretic, knowing the beliefs of the
church, chooses not to believe.[96] His arrogance is such that he does
not realize that the power of God cannot be comprehended because
of the weakness of human understanding.[97]

Le Picart confronts the apparent holiness of life of so many heretics,
especially when compared to what he sees as a major problem for
the Catholic church—the abuses of many clergymen. "You will see
a heretic and on the surface it seems that he lives well—he does
works that it would be very difficult for a good Christian to do. But
this is to deceive people."[98] Sometimes the heretics give more to the
poor and show greater brotherly love toward their neighbors:[99] "The
heretics give alms freely, as we see today by experience, and it often
seems that they exhibit more charity among themselves than we
Catholics do... They are more well off than we are, and it seems
that their way of living is superior to ours... You will see them
giving much to the poor... They have the appearance of religion
about them."[100] Amazingly, in view of their insolence, they often
appear gentle and simple, humble and gracious.[101] But this appearance of virtue is only a facade, intended to attract converts and
deceive simple people:[102] "It is marvelous that under the pretext of
love of charity, they take [the name of] Jesus Christ in order to
abolish charity and Jesus Christ."[103] Their appearance of justice is
nothing but hypocrisy;[104] it always turns out in the end that heretics
have acted out of cupidity and ambition.[105]

Although Le Picart insists that under their sheep's clothing, the
heretics are plundering wolves, he complains that they delight in
presenting a pious image of themselves.[106] They walk around with
the Bible on their tongues even more than good Catholics,[107] and
often study harder than Catholics, not to make the truth known, but

---

[95] Le Picart, *Pasques*, fol. 87.
[96] Le Picart, *Advent*, fol. 261.
[97] Le Picart, *Trinité*, fol. 126.
[98] Le Picart, *Caresme-II*, fol. 62.
[99] Le Picart, *Advent*, fols. 112–113.
[100] Ibid, fols. 112–113.
[101] Le Picart, *Trinité*, fol. 60.
[102] Ibid, fols. 8, 64.
[103] Ibid, fol. 216.
[104] Ibid, fol. 182.
[105] Ibid, fol. 60.
[106] Le Picart, *Advent*, fol. 152; *Trinité-II*, fol. 47.
[107] Le Picart, *SL*, 58.

to destroy it.[108] They "mix their doctrine, which is nothing but water, with the doctrine and Word of Our Lord and of His church, which is the good wine,"[109] in the manner of poison being added to food or drink.[110] He compares them to "tavernkeepers who mix water with wine. Just so, the heretics mix their doctrine, which is only water, with the doctrine and Word of Our Lord, which is good wine. They mix water in the wine and sell it among the good wines. They mix their doctrine with the gospel, in order that it will appear to have a good taste and be accepted, for otherwise it would not pass muster."[111] This allows them to catch people off guard who, thinking they are hearing solid preaching, are seduced by their simulated piety and flatteries.[112] Too often they succeed:

> They take a poor simple man, a worker, and say to him, "Come here, and I will teach you about your salvation." "That sounds good, sir, teach me." "What do you call that which hangs above the altar?" And the poor man responds simply, according to what he believes, and according to the truth, and says that that is the *cymboire*, in which is contained the precious body of our Lord. And they say to him, "Come, come, you're wrong, it's nothing." And afterwards they take him to a sermon, and give him a little book, in which you won't even find the name of the printer, and this book is entitled *The Summary of Scripture*.[113]

He imputes an organized plan to the heretics:

> There are three types of people in their sects. They have told me so themselves. There are visitors, receivers and distributors. Here you have these gentlemen who make their visitations in order to preach to poor simple people, and attract them to their sect. Then we have the distributors, who do not allow any of their sect to die of hunger. This is a great temptation to many. Then there are those who give out the books of their sect without charging for them, and these books plant a thousand falsehoods and diabolical ideas in the minds of the people they deceive and mislead.[114]

Although by reputation and by the words in his sermons, Le Picart was usually temperate in his responses, he occasionally retorts with the same type of characterizations Calvin and Beza used against him:

---

[108] Le Picart, *Advent*, fol. 240.
[109] Le Picart, *Pasques*, fol. 29.
[110] Le Picart, *Advent*, fol. 363; *Caresme-II*, fol. 24.
[111] Le Picart, *Pasques*, fol. 29.
[112] Ibid, fol. 103; *Advent*, fol. 231; *Trinité-II*, fol. 6.
[113] Le Picart, *SL*, 249.
[114] Ibid, 150–151.

Christians, you see the wrong and injury that these unhappy heretics
do to God when they deny and contradict that which we have shown
here. They are so out of their senses, reason and understanding, that
by their foul and stinking mouths and tongues, they make Jesus Christ
a liar and false prophet, no matter how much they make use of His
name and always have it on their lips.[115]

Of course those "foul and stinking" tongues would often be cut out
in preparation for burning at the stake, as was fitting for these devils on earth.[116] If, at their punishment, heretics displayed unusual for-
titude, this was not the steadfastness of a true martyr, but only a
continuation of their deceptions.[117] He explains that

when God permits a heretic, in his obstinacy, to go to his death joy-
ously and in such a manner that it seems to show constancy, this is
a temptation that God puts before you, to see if you love Him with
all of your heart, and are loyal and firm in your faith. Yes, you say,
but look at the constancy of that one! He has no fear of death! Oh,
good Christian, this is not constancy, but hardness and stubbornness!
These men are the martyrs of the devil![118]

One must not be swayed by them: "They die in the fire, without
moving at all, or changing their color. You should not marvel at all
of this: this is not the virtue of constancy, but rather obstinacy and
presumption."[119]

Like so many of his contemporaries at mid-century, Le Picart
characterizes the heretics as immoral. He describes them as "earthy
people, who preach free love, which is true servitude. They make
their priests marry, and their women are held in common. Oh what
carnal and sensual people!"[120] Scripture is only a cover for their
wickedness, just as their inability to be chaste leads them to argue
for clerical marriage.[121] Similarly, their gluttony motivates them to
challenge the church's teaching on eating meat during Lent or on
Fridays.[122]

Oblivious to the inconsistency in his argument, Le Picart tells his
listeners that a further characteristic of the heretic is secrecy. As

---

[115] Ibid, 10–11.
[116] Le Picart, *Trinité-II*, fol. 126.
[117] Ibid, fol. 194.
[118] Le Picart, *Advent*, fol. 361.
[119] Ibid, 113.
[120] Le Picart, *Trinité*, fol. 58; cf. *Advent*, fol. 32.
[121] Le Picart, *Pasques*, fol. 29.
[122] Le Picart, *Caresme*, fol. 5, 156; *Advent*, fol. 337; *Trinité*, fol. 52; *Trinité-II*, fol. 119.

Calvinist communities began to grow in the 1550s, clandestine behavior had been increasingly necessary to protect congregations. Meetings and *prêches* were held at night, under cover of darkness, usually in the home of one of the converts. Besides hearing sermons, the gathered worshippers would often take mass in both kinds and sing Psalms. The Catholic memoirist Claude Haton describes such a meeting in Provins:

> ... in the home of one of the members ... [they] hold the service of the Lord and sing his praises. One of them reads a chapter from the Old or the New Testament from a French Bible, which delights the assembly. Then they read another chapter, from the book of Exodus or Deuteronomy, which tells of the laws God gave to Moses on stone tablets. These Lutherans claim to be the true observers of the Law. To move the hearts of each other and especially the new adherents, they sing some of the Psalms of David, translated into French by Clément Marot, two or three times. These praises are sung at the beginning, middle and end of the ceremony, which they call a *prêche*. Then they all embrace one another and the preacher speaks of the love they must have for each other.[123]

Perhaps with Roussel and Marguerite in mind, Le Picart asks, "Those who preach in secret [*soubs la cheminée*] before noblewomen, when will they mend their ways?"[124] He explains that this secrecy derives from cowardice and fear: "These people here, these heretics, say nothing publicly, but always secretly, and they never speak to two people together ... but only to one, whom they swear to secrecy."[125] They teach their novices to lie, and engage in one-on-one conversations so that no one can bear witness against them.[126] Most of their teaching takes place in conventicles, corners or other secret places.[127] On the occasions when they come out of hiding, they dissimulate in their preaching,[128] using special code words known only

---

[123] Felix Bourquélot, ed., *Mémoires de Claude Haton* (Paris: Imprimerie impériale, 1857), I:49–50.

[124] Le Picart, *Trinité*, fol. 98.

[125] Le Picart, *Pasques*, fol. 295; *SL*, 201.

[126] Le Picart, *Advent*, fol. 136; *Pasques*, fol. 84.

[127] Le Picart, *SL*, 56–57; *Advent*, fol. 362.

[128] Henry Heller examines the case of one of the reformers of Meaux, Pierre Caroli, and remarks that "[a]ware of the presence of spies in the church Caroli tried to shock and confuse them ... Obviously his technique was meant to prevent listeners from pinning down exactly what he had said." Henry Heller, "Marguerite of Navarre and the Reformers of Meaux," *Bibliothèque d'humanisme et renaissance* 33 (1971), 273.

to initiates.[129] Comparing their sneaking around and whispering to a snake waiting to strike, Le Picart says their secrecy is "a sign that their merchandise is worth nothing, if they are not willing to show it in public."[130] By contrast, the preaching of Christ is not done in shadows or in hiding, but in public. "True preaching must not be done in the shadows, but in the sunlight . . ."[131]

After drawing a portrait of the heretic so that his audience can recognize such people in their midst, Le Picart delves into their doctrines. Like most of his colleagues on the Faculty of Theology during the troubled years of the 1520s and 1530s, he believes that the Protestant insistence on *sola scriptura* is among the most dangerous of their beliefs, for from it proceed the others. "The foundation of their errors is that they say that we must not believe anything that is not explicitly stated in scripture . . ."[132] He asks them how they know that ". . . scripture and the Gospel was written by Saint Matthew or the other evangelists, if the apostles hadn't said so and passed it on, and it came to us from hand to hand."[133] But they go beyond that, insisting that every man and woman has the right to read and interpret scripture. This is nonsense, as scripture itself proves. "As Saint Paul wrote to the Ephesians, it was only the bishop who was to read the epistle and declaration to the people."[134] The church appoints prelates because they are able to understand and interpret the Bible according to the consensus of the church.[135] In a masterful stroke, Le Picart is able to turn the heretics' opinions and arguments against them. "Come here, Luther, you say that holy scripture is so easy that it is necessary to have the New Testament in French. If it is so easy, there should be no diversity of opinions . . . Oecolampadius says the same, yet it follows that holy scripture is not as easy as you say, and so it is a bad thing to translate it into French."[136]

But the heretics "understand and interpret [scripture] badly, because they follow their own particular sense . . .,"[137] claiming arrogantly

---

[129] Le Picart, *Pasques*, fol. 283.
[130] Le Picart, *Trinité-II*, fol. 105.
[131] Le Picart, *Trinité*, fol. 38.
[132] Le Picart, *SL*, 12; *Trinité*, fol. 216; *Advent*, fol. 360.
[133] Le Picart, *Trinité*, fol. 94.
[134] Ibid, fol. 168.
[135] Ibid, fol. 67.
[136] Ibid, fol. 96.
[137] Le Picart, *Pasques*, fol. 29; *Trinité-II*, fol. 194.

that Christians have been blind up until this time.[138] To act as one's own priest is to ignore one's station in life:

> Our Lord demonstrates to us here that it is not given to all indifferently to treat holy scripture. In vain we raises our eyes to all the goods, riches and offices that we cannot have. A woman desires in vain to be a bishop and take on the office of a public magistrate. So if we are not capable of understanding holy scripture, why do we desire to meddle in it? Our estate and condition is not given to this. It is enough for simple folk who do not have any duties in the church to be taught by their superiors who have them in their care. Since Our Lord made these distinctions among His own, how can we do differently?[139]

Le Picart insists that lay people who want to read scripture should consider how this exceeds the limits of the gifts God has given them.[140] Even "Saint Peter, speaking of the epistles of Saint Paul, said that there many things in them that are difficult to understand."[141] Le Picart uses the analogy of food to explain how one must feed people the Word of God, each according to his or her capacity:[142] "Bread that is not broken will choke little children. Just so it is necessary to break up scripture . . ."[143] On the other hand, those who are full-grown can be given beef, mutton, and solid meat to sustain them, not milk or bouillon, as is given to children. But "the Lutheran does not do anything in a measured way; he gives the whole loaf of bread, and in so doing he makes the children gag."[144] Possibly mindful of Marguerite de Navarre, as well as the censured beliefs of the Circle of Meaux, Le Picart asks, "My ladies, how will you understand scripture, if we don't show you? Yet they say that God can instruct a little lady just as well as a doctor of Paris."[145] Taking his statements almost directly from articles condemned by the Faculty in the 1520s, he says, ". . . some say women can understand better than the great doctors of the church,"[146] and warns that "it does not belong to a woman to remit sins, but to priests."[147] Just

---

[138] Le Picart, *Trinité*, fol. 58.
[139] Le Picart, *Caresme*, fol. 84, *Advent*, fol. 253.
[140] Le Picart, *Advent*, fol. 247.
[141] Ibid, fol. 202.
[142] Le Picart, *Pasques*, fol. 55.
[143] Le Picart, *Trinité*, fol. 57.
[144] Le Picart, *Pasques*, fol. 157.
[145] Le Picart, *Trinité*, fol. 167.
[146] Ibid, fol. 67.
[147] Le Picart, *Advent*, fol. 41.

as Marguerite had read scripture and begun to preach in the student play of 1533, so other women might try to do the same. But
there was no scriptural or traditional precedent for this:

> [The Samaritan Woman] went into the city to tell everyone what Jesus
> Christ had said to her, saying, "Is He not the Christ? Is He not the
> Son of God, the true Messiah promised in the law? He told and
> declared to me everything I have done in my life." From this passage
> the Lutherans want you to believe that women are authorized to preach
> and that the Samaritan Woman preached. The Samaritan Woman did
> not speak in the manner of preaching, but only out of the admiration
> she felt for Our Lord . . .[148]

Again brandishing Saint Paul, Le Picart insists that women cannot
preach, for "to preach is to have authority, and the natural and proper
condition of women is to be subject [to men]."[149]

The dangers of allowing every person to interpret scripture were
evident to one who had seen ordinary people lose both their lives
and their goods. "Scripture is like good wine. But there is danger
that those who don't have a good head for it will get drunk, because
they just can't handle it."[150] Unwilling to accept the interpretations and
glosses of trained theologians, the heretics "expound scripture according to their own fantasy."[151] Le Picart then turns the heretics' arguments on their head by claiming that they add things to holy scripture
that are not there and falsify them.[152] He tells his audience that they
must not take every word of scripture literally, as the heretics advise.
"Saint John Chrysostom tells us that we must not take the words of
the gospel according to the letter, but rather the sense and interpretation . . ."[153] Since there are so many apparent contradictions in
scripture, it is necessary to compare passages, and reconcile them,
something that must be left to those trained in theology.[154] While the
reformers' fundamentalism precluded discussion of ethical issues,[155]
the sermon of a properly-constituted preacher applied scripture to
the lives of men and women, leading them to amendment.[156]

---

[148] Le Picart, *Caresme*, fol. 172.
[149] Ibid, fol. 173.
[150] Le Picart, *Trinité*, fol. 179.
[151] Le Picart, *Caresme*, fol. 168.
[152] Le Picart, *SL*, 12; *Trinité-II*, fol. 126.
[153] Le Picart, *Trinité*, fol. 76.
[154] Le Picart, *Pasques*, fol. 38; cf. ibid, fol. 14; *Caresme-II*, fol. 25.
[155] Le Picart, *Advent*, fol. 360.
[156] Le Picart, *Caresme-II*, fol. 25.

Closely associated with the problem of *sola scriptura* was the heretics' insistence that the Bible be translated into the vernacular. Le Picart mocks the reformers, saying "to translate into French the Book of Revelation and the epistles of Paul is strange indeed, yet they say that the scriptures are easy."[157] He argues that a preacher who uses Greek or Latin with women or children simply wastes everyone's time.[158] "The heretics say that it is necessary to have it in French; yet when we say it in French, and you don't understand, it doesn't profit you any more than if it is in Hebrew, or in Spanish, or in some other language that you don't understand."[159] To the women of Paris who want the scriptures in French,[160] he suggests they follow the example of their ancestors: "Do you believe that the merit of your prayer comes from intelligence? No, all the fruit and merit of prayer comes from the heart, the affections and goodwill. Yet, do you think they are worth more than those of past times because you have books of Hours in French?"[161] "Do you think that your heart is more raised to God and with Him when you say your Hours in French rather than in Latin?"[162]

There were several problems with translations, not the least of which were incorrect renderings of words and meaning:

> Christian, I will say a word in passing for the love of God, to demonstrate the novelty of those who translate holy scripture into French . . . And to show their malice, at the beginning of the New Testament, translated from Greek to French . . . they translate it incorrectly from the Greek. Where we find the words "do not be idolators," they refer to the adoration of images, and say: "Do not be servants to images." In Greek the word is *ycon*. They would have it understood as idol or image. If they want to meddle so much with translations, why don't they translate faithfully? There is a considerable difference between an image and an idol.[163]

Even when the translations are acceptable, putting them in the hands of simple folk is dangerous,[164] for "there are a number of passages in scripture that when translated into the vulgar tongue give more

---

[157] Le Picart, *Trinité*, fol. 57.
[158] Le Picart, *Advent*, fol. 254; *Trinité-II*, fol. 32.
[159] Le Picart, *Pasques*, fol. 227.
[160] Le Picart, *Trinité*, fol. 67.
[161] Ibid, fol. 56.
[162] Le Picart, *Caresme-II*, fol. 94.
[163] Le Picart, *Trinité*, fol. 71.
[164] Le Picart, *Caresme-II*, fol. 6.

occasion for error than for good because of the simplicity and weakness of people."[165] He does not blame these people, for ordinary folk commit fewer misdeeds than those with a knowledge of letters,[166] but that is all the more reason to protect them. To make his point more forcefully, Le Picart invokes the case of the Vaudois, which would have been well-known after the massacre of April 1545 in which at least 2,700 men and women were put to death and others sent to the galleys.[167] Le Picart laments that "it often leads more to ruin than profit, as happened to the Vaudois, the Poor of Lyon, who fell into error because they wanted to have holy scripture translated word-for-word into French."[168] He urges people to put aside their curiosity, for this plays into the hands of sly and cunning heretics. "We want to hear new things, to have new books without titles, and so it is not surprising if we are seduced."[169] Le Picart advises that the fundamentals of the faith can be found in a few simple beliefs, and that reading scripture is unnecessary: "Read the whole Bible, and everything you will find is already contained in the Lord's Prayer."[170] He insists that all that learning ". . . will profit us not at all, but if we know Jesus Christ well, we know everything . . . But if you know all the other sciences and know nothing of Jesus Christ crucified, you know nothing at all."[171]

Le Picart also spends a great deal of time on individual points thrown into dispute by the "Lutherans." Closely tied to the problem of scripture alone was the role of the church. He provides a complete defense of the church even if, as we shall see later, this does not extend to his treatment of individual churchmen. "The truth is so manifest, and for all that, your eyes are fascinated, and all that we have had for 1550 years is brought into doubt."[172] The church has been, since the time of the apostles, an impregnable edifice, a sign of invincible truth.[173] Le Picart explains that "the church came before scripture, so one must believe in the tradition,

[165] Le Picart, *Trinité*, fol. 56.
[166] Ibid, fol. 17.
[167] Knecht, *Renaissance Warrior*, 513–516.
[168] Le Picart, *Trinité*, fol. 254; *Pasques*, fol. 185.
[169] Le Picart, *SL*, 145.
[170] Le Picart, *Instruction*, 59.
[171] Le Picart, *Caresme*, fol. 1.
[172] Le Picart, *Pasques*, fol. 183.
[173] Le Picart, *Caresme*, fol. 52.

interpretation, sense and understanding that the church has given to the words. "It's God who built and planted the Church, and who sustains it. So the Church truly is the house of God. Its foundation is stable and firm, so it is impossible to ruin or demolish the church, for as the house of Our Lord it is permanent, stable and eternal."[174] He commands his listeners: ". . . since we are on the field during bad times, let us return to our house, which is the church, and follow the doctrine it has taught 1,555 years and which will endure till the end of the world, despite Satan and his disciples."[175] Sounding very much like Montaigne would several decades later, he asks, "why refuse to follow the common manner, which we have been accustomed to for so long in the church of God? Do you want to be particular?"[176]

Le Picart employs his humanistic training and the new philology to defend tradition: "You know that Saint John wrote his gospel long after the other three evangelists. [Many incidents mentioned in his gospel] . . . are not mentioned by the other evangelists at all. To whom, therefore, should one turn, and how was one to believe before John wrote this? Surely by tradition, and the words of the apostles and the church."[177] He goes on:

> The other gospels, such as those of Saints Bartholomew, Barnabas and Nicodemus were written down, but we rejected them and held them as apocryphal by the authority and teaching of the church, which tells us that we must believe in the truth of the gospels of Saints Matthew, Mark, Luke and John, and the other scriptures. The Word of God and His will is made known through scripture in such a way that if the church (that is, God through His church) does not tell us and reveal that such scripture is holy and true (which you must then receive), and the others are apocryphal, then we would not know that such writings are not to be received.[178]

Both scripture and tradition are inseparable components of Christianity. He describes the church in symbolic terms:

> The ship on which there is a mast, a great piece of wood raised overhead, signifies the church in which one finds the cross. We experience winds and tempests, overpowering waves and storms, just as in the

---

[174] Le Picart, *Trinité-II*, fol. 149.
[175] Ibid, fol. 193.
[176] Ibid, fol. 85.
[177] Le Picart, *SL*, 51–52.
[178] Ibid, 52–53.

sea. These are heresies, sins and temptations. Who steers this ship? It
is the wood that is in the middle of the church that keeps it together.
And when Ulysses was bound to the mast of the ship he and his companions escaped many great dangers. Since Our Lord was bound to
the cross, we have had the power to escape from the heresies and
temptations, floods and storms of this world . . .[179]

The church could be buffeted, but not brought down by these storms,
for unlike individuals who can make mistakes, the church was infal-
lible.[180] "The heretics and Lutherans say that these are only traditions
and commandments of men. I say to you, they come from God. He
has given them to us through the commandments and ministry of
men, the superiors who represent the person of God."[181] It is inap-
propriate for men and women to discuss or examine the commandments handed down to them, for simple obedience is their part.[182]

Le Picart defines membership in the church. "What is the church?
It is the congregation of Christians. Who is outside? The infidel,
Turks, pagans, Jews, heretics and those who have been justly excommunicated."[183] Besides the metaphor of the ship, he also compares
the church to Noah's ark[184] and to a house—anyone outside the
house is outside the way of salvation.[185] This includes "the Greeks,
who . . . are schismatic, because they left the Roman Church and the
pope, who is head of the universal Catholic church."[186] But Le Picart
concentrates on heretics who have willingly separated themselves
from the community. "The person who doesn't love the church and
is not ready to die for it denies God. He who turns away from the
church turns away from God."[187] The church is the mother, and
God the father,[188] so the "heretic and his ilk are no more part of
the mystical body of Jesus Christ."[189]

Le Picart recognizes that abuses in the church have given strength
to the heretics. "Look around here, you will see our new heretical

---

[179] Le Picart, *Trinité-II*, fol. 104.
[180] Le Picart, *Advent*, fol. 255.
[181] Le Picart, *Caresme*, fol. 155.
[182] Ibid, fol. 44.
[183] Le Picart, *Advent*, fol. 107.
[184] Ibid, fol. 107.
[185] Le Picart, *Trinité-II*, fol. 41.
[186] Le Picart, *SL*, 243.
[187] Ibid, 21.
[188] Le Picart, *Instruction*, 294.
[189] Le Picart, *SL*, 230.

doctors who say that those who do not live well have neither authority nor power in the church of God. And yet we see the contrary,
because however much Judas was a traitor he was still an apostle."[190]
Le Picart would put forth an entire program for reforming the clergy,
yet insists that the existence of bad-living priests and bishops does
not mean that the church itself is evil. Abuses were not an excuse
for leaving its obedience: "Jesus Christ showed us the opposite by
his own deeds, when he willingly obeyed and was subject [to God's
will]."[191] Priests, who are ministers and lieutenants of God must be
obeyed.[192]

The issue of ecclesiastical compulsion had been a charged one for
French evangelicals and reformers as early as the 1520s,[193] but Le
Picart argues that the heretics' claim that the rules of the church
constrain the liberty of the Christian is specious.[194] He asks with
some asperity, "Alas! Today we have come to a time when the ceremonies of the church are eliminated. Will the traditions of the
Church Fathers and holy councils be abolished? Next thing they will
tear out the beard and hair of Our Lord!"[195] After all, they challenge everything else: "Today our new apostate doctors say it is only
the church. If they want to celebrate a marriage in Lent, they say
it is only the church that prohibits it. And so they take no account
at all of the church, which is the spouse of God."[196] As usual, he
quotes from Saint Paul to show how ceremonies founded in tradition have a legitimate place in the Christian life. "The heretic says
that it is not necessary to follow the ceremonies [of the church]. But
Saint Paul says the opposite in I Corinthians 2, when he tells us
that women must pray with their heads covered, men with their
heads uncovered."[197] When in doubt, one should follow a simple
rule: "If you see that we do certain things that are not contrary to
faith or morality, you should do them as well."[198] For example, if
the church commands belief in purgatory or abstinence from meat

---

[190] Le Picart, *Advent*, fol. 354.
[191] Ibid, fol. 252.
[192] Le Picart, *Caresme-II*, fol. 56.
[193] Taylor, *Soldiers of Christ*, 198–208.
[194] Le Picart, *Trinité*, fol. 118.
[195] Le Picart, *Advent*, fol. 229.
[196] Le Picart, *SL*, 21.
[197] Le Picart, *Instruction*, 58.
[198] Ibid, 59.

during Lent, one should simply obey without question, profiting from
the example of the Fall: "When the church commands fasting, it
does not condemn meat . . . The vice is not in the meat, but in the
will and desire that one has to do offense. . . . [The heretics say] the
church cannot compel one to fast, and that it is permissible to eat
meat with their blessing . . . Didn't God command Adam not to eat
the forbidden fruit?"[199] Selectivity of belief is unacceptable—if the
church commands something, one cannot say, "I believe in one
article of faith, but not the others."[200] Le Picart sees in the rebellion
against the church an effort to flatter kings and princes, for many
heretics argue that the secular power must be obeyed, but not the
ecclesiastical.[201] But he warns that if they have their way, all obedience to higher powers will be in jeopardy.[202] Perhaps thinking of the
German Peasants' War of 1525, he remarks that ". . . if they could,
the Lutherans . . . would make everyone equal, and would reduce
order to confusion."[203]

From the subject of church tradition, Le Picart turns to faith and
good works. He rejects justification by faith alone and the heretics'
dismissal of free will,[204] in the process showing a reasonably nuanced
understanding of the reformers' beliefs. He tells his listeners that the
heretics maintain works are ineffectual because Jesus Christ already
atoned for humanity's sins; they believe the church's position suggests this was insufficient.[205] Le Picart explains: "It is true that your
work, coming purely from yourself, is not at all satisfactory . . . But
the merit of Jesus Christ on which your work is founded makes your
work satisfactory for the remission of your sins and is as pleasant
and agreeable to God as if Jesus Christ Himself had done it."[206] Le
Picart accepts that human beings can do nothing good of themselves,
that they are totally dependent on the grace of God.[207] "Yet in saying this petition, we use the verb *Da*, by which we recognize our
indigence. Because if we had no need, we would not ask. Remember
therefore, that all our work, all our industry is in vain without the

---

[199] Ibid, 52.
[200] Le Picart, *Advent*, fol. 113.
[201] Le Picart, *Pasques*, fol. 36.
[202] Le Picart, *Trinité*, fol. 97.
[203] Le Picart, *Pasques*, fol. 36.
[204] Ibid, fol. 53; *Trinité*, fol. 68; *Advent*, fol. 313; *SL*, 227; *Caresme*, fol. 166.
[205] Le Picart, *SL*, 178.
[206] Le Picart, *Caresme*, fol. 65.
[207] Le Picart, *Instruction*, 176.

grace of God."[208] Yet he insists that each person must cooperate with that grace while attributing the glory to God and the salvific work on the cross.[209] God "is the principal worker in us, but through His grace we can cooperate with Him."[210] He continually emphasizes God's action: "And yet when a man labors and works while leaning on God, the land that he works and cultivates will bear fruit. But if God does not give his blessing, it will produce nothing. By this it is necessary to know and understand that without the grace of God our labor is in vain and is nothing at all . . ."[211] Good works done in the grace of God and hope based on a living faith offer assurance of salvation.[212] Against the heretics' "Mohammedan paradise," in which one could be saved without works, Le Picart makes it an essential act of devotion to add one's own penitence to that of Jesus Christ on the cross.[213] He presents examples such as the sinner in the house of Simon the Pharisee: "'Woman, your sins are pardoned.' Christians, here it is demonstrated to us how the heretics are wrong and deceived in attributing the justification of man to faith alone. We see here the opposite, because Our Lord Jesus Christ attributed it to her charity and love of God, which is never found without a good work."[214] Similarly, didn't God consider the works, the fasting and the penitence of the people of Nineveh, when he deferred his judgment? The exterior work bears witness to the good will and heart of a man.[215] Finally, he points to the practical results of the heretics' doctrine: "These contemptible heretics are like mad dogs, because they say that man cannot do a work agreeable to God, but rather that works displease Him. This is insanity and madness and shows how they have lost all reason. They say that the more a man repents of his sin, the more he is a hypocrite. Isn't this a belief that will truly discourage man from doing good?"[216]

One of the most fundamental aspects of a Christian's good behavior derived from his or her participation in the sacraments. Le Picart

---

[208] Ibid, 154, 177.
[209] Le Picart, *Advent*, fol. 268; *Pasques*, fol. 59; *Trinité*, fol. 26.
[210] Le Picart, *Caresme*, fol. 66; cf. ibid, fols. 68, 99.
[211] Le Picart, *Instruction*, 176.
[212] Le Picart, *Trinité*, fol. 7.
[213] Le Picart, *Advent*, fol. 266; *Caresme*, fol. 64; *Pasques*, fol. 93.
[214] Le Picart, *Caresme-II*, fol. 86.
[215] Le Picart, *Caresme*, fol. 53.
[216] Le Picart, *Advent*, fol. 105.

refutes the Anabaptist position saying, "to be rebaptized would be
a testimony that Jesus Christ died more than once. And this is what
the Anabaptists of today would have us believe!"[217] Similarly, although
he spends considerable time in his sermons on the positive aspects
and proper forms of sacramental confession, he dismisses the heretical view of confession quickly. "The heretics claim that confession to
a priest is a human invention, and say that one must instead make
a general confession."[218] He questions their sincerity: "A Lutheran
will constantly say, 'I repent, I am a great sinner,' and yet he will
declare nothing in particular."[219]

Most of Le Picart's attention to the heretical treatment of the
sacraments focused on the interpretation of the mass, for it was one
of the only sacraments recognized by various Protestant communities. It also most clearly demonstrated the disagreements and divisions among them. Although research has shown that early French
heretics placed little emphasis on interpretations of the mass,[220] Swiss
and German theology on the subject as well as actions by the relatively few sacramentarians in France could not help but galvanize
orthodox Catholics because of the degree of blasphemy involved. Le
Picart insists that the mass "is not a human invention, as those block-
head apostasizing heretics want us to believe. They say that men
invented the sacrament of the altar for the purpose of making
money."[221] Rather "it is the tradition and invention of Our Lord
Jesus Christ, who was the first to celebrate and say mass, and who
made His apostles priests in order to say it."[222] Against all their speculation, Le Picart says that the mass is a great mystery. "When you
ask how [the accidents of the mass] exist, I respond that I don't
know. One should not ask, because where God has put Himself, we
should not inquire about it, but simply believe."[223] When the bread
was transubstantiated, "it isn't bread any longer, however much the
appearance of bread remains."[224] Jesus Christ was totally present in
each and every part of the host, "even when it is divided into a

---

[217] Ibid, fol. 27.
[218] Le Picart, *Pasques*, fol. 17.
[219] Le Picart, *Advent*, fol. 331.
[220] Royannez, "L'eucharistie," 575.
[221] Le Picart, *SL*, 131.
[222] Ibid, 22.
[223] Ibid, 39.
[224] Ibid, 92.

thousand parts and pieces."[225] Le Picart offers a rationale for the church's doctrine of transubstantiation: "God wanted His precious body to be invisible to us in the holy sacrament of the altar because it is an abhorrent thing to eat the flesh of a man visibly."[226] Yet responding to Swiss accusations regarding the materiality of Catholic doctrine, Le Picart explains:

> However much Our Lord Jesus Christ is really and essentially present in the holy sacrament of the altar, one must not imagine that He descends out of the sky (because He stays there always), or that He is formed once again, when the bread is transubstantiated into His precious body. But this bread that the priest holds in his hand is changed into the self-same body of Jesus Christ, which was formed in the virginal body of the blessed Virgin Mary by the operation of the Holy Spirit. His body is not formed two times, nor over again in the holy sacrament of the altar.[227]

He goes farther, explaining that "when we say that [Jesus Christ] is in heaven, that is not to say that He is enclosed in a certain place like I am enclosed in this pulpit: because holy scripture makes it clear that He fills heaven and earth. We know that God is everywhere."[228] Le Picart demands of his listeners more than belief in the Real Presence, to which even Luther subscribed. "It is not enough to believe that the holy body of Jesus Christ is in the holy sacrament of the altar, because however much Luther is a heretic, he believes that. But it is necessary that our faith in it be whole and complete."[229]

Le Picart explains the heretics' belief that the Catholic doctrine of transubstantiation is a form of idolatry, claiming the mass is nothing but a representation.[230]

> They insist on calling the holy sacrament of the altar the Lord's Supper. And however much that is good in itself, nevertheless, he who uses those words alone, saying only the Lord's Supper, is suspect of heresy, since no one uses those words alone, except for the heretics, who do not want to use the words that the church uses . . . We never use the terms or words that the heretics use, however much the word itself is good.[231]

---

[225] Ibid, 94.
[226] Ibid, 90.
[227] Ibid, 83.
[228] Le Picart, *Instruction*, 71–72.
[229] Le Picart, *Pasques*, fol. 278.
[230] Le Picart, *Trinité-II*, fol. 193.
[231] Le Picart, *SL*, 143.

The church's interpretation is the only true one, for it remains faithful to the words of institution, when "Our Lord Jesus Christ said: 'Here is my body, here is my blood . . .' "[232]

Le Picart was especially angered by the lack of reverence shown to the body of Christ by Protestants. "Yesterday when we carried the precious body of Our Lord Jesus Christ in great honor and reverence around the city, they mocked it and called us hypocrites."[233] Some even trample on the body and blood of Christ.[234] "If a man strikes a councillor or a president, he will be punished, and well; that's as it should be. But I wish that we had the same courage to respond to the injury against Our Lord. Yet one does nothing even to a sacramentarian! *O Mater Dei!* When we are before God, we will see what He has to say about this!"[235] If nothing is done, the consequences will be dire, for "they think to take from us this precious ring, this great treasure, our entire spiritual life . . ."[236] Where the heretics attempt to do away with the mass, Le Picart suggests that good Catholics become ever more observant—"we will do it three times as much!"[237] When the host is carried aloft in procession, "the more the heretics impugn it, the more we will honor it!"[238] This could involve direct action. If a person comes upon some form of blasphemy, he must defend the Lord without fear.[239] Otherwise the dangers will increase: "I am not saying that we will always have it in this country or in this city. For because of our sins and demerits, God may take it from us, as has been done to the people of Geneva, Germany, England and many other places. But in some place, wherever it may be, the mass will always be said and celebrated until the end of the world."[240]

Le Picart insists on the honor due to the Virgin, the saints and the angels,[241] although he devotes less attention to this subject than one might expect from a post-Reformation Catholic preacher in France. A good example can be seen in the penultimate sermon

---

[232] Ibid, 11.
[233] Ibid, 58.
[234] Le Picart, *Trinité*, fol. 165.
[235] Le Picart, *Trinité-II*, fol. 170.
[236] Le Picart, *SL*, 69.
[237] Ibid, 140; cf. ibid, 92.
[238] Le Picart, *Trinité*, fol. 241.
[239] Le Picart, *SL*, 57.
[240] Le Picart, *Pasques*, fol. 268; *SL*, 81.
[241] Le Picart, *Trinité-II*, fol. 127.

delivered by Le Picart for the Nativity of the Virgin (Appendix B.1). Despite its dedication, the sermon spends very little time on the Virgin. "These unhappy heretics," he explains, "say that the saints can't help us."[242] "You, heretic, you mock the fact that we pray to the saints, and you say they don't know what we say to them, nor what we do down here, because they are too far away."[243] Le Picart refutes the Lutheran claim that images are idols by citing Paul's Letter to the Corinthians [I:8], insisting they are not idols because they simply represent something else.[244] Through God's action, the bones and the relics of the saints can and do perform miracles. He provides the example of John Chrysostom, who prayed for good health so he could make a trip to Rome to touch the ashes of Saint Paul.[245] In a sermon devoted to Saint Martin, Le Picart reminds his listeners that miracles do happen:

> A good man with a sick daughter, who had received a letter from Saint Martin, putting his confidence in God that He would do something through Saint Martin, took this letter and put it on his daughter, who was immediately cured. I know well that the Lutheran will laugh at this. Let him laugh! . . . And the handkerchiefs of Saint Paul placed on the sick cured them. The fringe of the robe of Our Lord cured the woman who was sick with a bloody flux.[246]

Yet Le Picart is equally concerned with promoting correct practice and belief. He exclaims:

> We pray God that His name should be known everywhere, and in all places and that all idolatry should be abolished and gone from the world, and that all idolators should return to the knowledge of the one true God, whom we adore. We also pray God that the Jews will recognize our Lord Jesus Christ to be the true God and true man. Similarly, don't we pray God and ask that there be no superstition? We find that when a man or an animal is sick and someone says words over him to effect a cure. Sometimes a person will use a prayer and put [a paper with the words on it] on the sick person, and if he is cured, that is superstition. This cure proceeds from the devil to your great detriment and damnation.[247]

---

[242] Le Picart, *SL*, 162; *Trinité-II*, 164.
[243] Le Picart, *SL*, 59–60; *Pasques*, fol. 38.
[244] Le Picart, *Advent*, fol. 347.
[245] Le Picart, *Caresme-II*, fol. 148; cf. *Pasques*, fol. 293.
[246] Le Picart, *Trinité-II*, fol. 211; *Caresme*, fol. 59.
[247] Le Picart, *Instruction*, 157–158.

Because of the desecration of images of the saints and Virgin that had taken place all over France, it was important that the king set the kind of example he had in 1528:

> When our prince made an *amende honorable* to God for the sin of that evil person who dishonored the image of the Virgin Mary near the rue Saint-Antoine, and for the irreverence shown to the holy sacrament of the altar in this city of Paris, it provided great consolation and instruction for the people, because when a great one is the first to do what God commands, it makes an impression on others.[248]

Le Picart uses the same language to condemn heretical attacks on the Virgin. As with so many of their beliefs, the heretics' unwillingness to accept church tradition on an equal footing with scripture leads to these errors. "Our new Christians, the heretics, have no shame in calling the Council of Basel, in which it was decreed that the Virgin Mary was conceived without sin, the congregation of Satan."[249] They even cast doubts on her virginity, which demonstrated the need for tradition:

> There are a number of articles of faith that we are held to believe that are not written down in scripture. Look, for example, at the virginity of the Virgin Mary. It is an article of faith that she remained a virgin after giving birth. There are writings and arguments sufficient to prove that she gave birth to Our Lord Jesus Christ. But scripture doesn't say that she remained a virgin, or that it is necessary to believe this . . .[250]

Le Picart also defends practices that have evolved over the centuries, such as the use of music in church services:

> It is necessary for us to sing from our hearts, with our mouths, against the evil heretics who say that it is vain to sing songs to God . . . We sing in church in order that our thoughts will incite us to spiritual devotion. And if through this one is moved to dissolution or vainglory, it is against the intention of the church . . . This is important, because through singing many simple and rude folk are made more devout. David played the harp so that an evil spirit would be expelled from Saul.[251]

---

[248] Le Picart, *Pasques*, fol. 132.
[249] Le Picart, *Advent*, fol. 62.
[250] Le Picart, *Trinité*, fol. 216; *Instruction*, 231; *Caresme-II*, fol. 148.
[251] Le Picart, *Trinité*, fol. 195.

Here again, Le Picart explains that the Catholic church's interpretation takes into account the practical effects of its actions on ordinary believers.

Knowing the doctrines of the heretics was only the first step in extirpating their errors. In his pastoral role, Le Picart suggests a plan for dealing with the heretics. The church and the king must address the problem directly, because "these are sins that harm others; just as when I hear someone is going to burn down your house—it is similar to preaching heresy and seducing the people."[252] Le Picart gives his listeners numerous practical suggestions. First, the heretics are to be separated from others, so they cannot infect the community with their poison.[253] One must continue, however, to pray for their conversion.[254] He supports the use of the Inquisition and the punishment of nobles and other leaders of society, for through their influence many others are corrupted.[255]

Ordinary men and women are advised to attend the sermons of orthodox Catholic preachers, listening to their words and making them part of their lives.[256] By gaining a thorough knowledge of the truth, they can then correct the preachers who spread heresy, for however much a preacher seems to speak well, he must be stopped at all costs if he preaches heretical doctrines.[257] "We hear a nasty comment against the faith. I say nothing. My silence confirms the others in their errors!"[258] Standing up for the faith sometimes requires disobedience to one's family. "Even if it happens that a father orders his son to go hear a preacher or other suspect person, or do something against the honor of God, the child must not obey him, but separate himself from his company."[259]

Le Picart offers clues to help determine a preacher's orthodoxy. "See if he preaches in another form and manner than the church has always taught"[260] or uses gestures and words that are different.[261] More specifically, "see if he doesn't bother to rail against vices and

---

[252] Ibid, fol. 155.
[253] Ibid, fol. 98.
[254] Ibid, fol. 97.
[255] Ibid, fol. 190.
[256] Le Picart, *Advent*, fol. 253.
[257] Le Picart, *Caresme*, fol. 163.
[258] Le Picart, *Trinité-II*, fol. 192.
[259] Le Picart, *Pasques*, fol. 28.
[260] Le Picart, *Caresme*, fol. 137.
[261] Le Picart, *Advent*, fol. 278; *Trinité-II*, fol. 192.

sins in his preaching, and if he says that you don't have to confess
to a priest and make satisfaction. If he tells you it is not necessary
to pray to the saints in paradise, or if he says there is no purgatory, and that it is not necessary to pray for the dead, then he is a
false preacher."[262] Le Picart reminds his listeners of what happened
to Eve when she heeded the serpent,[263] and tells them to ignore or
fight back against a heretic who claims that Jesus Christ is not truly
present in the mass.[264] But in general, one should flee from heretics,
for they are more dangerous than all the devils in hell.[265]

Le Picart's advice applied equally to heretics who were not preachers, and this could sometimes mean ignoring the precepts of Christian
brotherhood. "Saint John tells us that we must no more be friends
with a heretic than with a devil. . . . He forbids us from extending
hospitality to a heretic, even if he is dying of hunger."[266] Le Picart
tells men and women to "flee the heretics and Lutherans, more than
a man with a thousand plagues. Don't converse with them or listen
to them, because their doctrine brings corporal and spiritual death—
they kill the body and soul, and will lead you into hell."[267] This
applies even to friends,[268] for otherwise, one participated in their
crimes:[269] "*O Mater Dei!* I don't flee from and avoid a heretic or one
suspect of heresy, but frequent their company. And if I am a good
woman, yet I spend my time with a woman of bad reputation, I
will render myself suspect, and will lose the good opinion that others have of me."[270] While heretical preachers had to be stopped, Le
Picart warns men and women not to get too involved in disputing
with heretics, for the best way to deal with them is by simplicity,
good conversation, and humility.[271]

Heretical books were to be shunned, but if found they should be
burned.[272] People should exercise caution even with apparently orthodox works. Le Picart had experienced the consequences personally

---

[262] Le Picart, *Trinité*, fol. 59.
[263] Le Picart, *SL*, 201; *Trinité-II*, fol. 192.
[264] Le Picart, *Caresme-II*, fol. 176.
[265] Le Picart, *Advent*, fol. 261.
[266] Ibid, fol. 178; *Caresme-II*, fol. 181.
[267] Le Picart, *Pasques*, fol. 82.
[268] Le Picart, *Advent*, fol. 323.
[269] Ibid, fol. 281.
[270] Le Picart, *Caresme*, fol. 130; cf. *Trinité*, fol. 121.
[271] Le Picart, *Pasques*, fol. 89.
[272] Le Picart, *Trinité-II*, fol. 48; cf. *Trinité*, fol. 98.

in 1534 after the appearance of the *Confession et raison de la foy de maistre Noël Beda*. He also recalls: "You know of a good man, named Descornes, who I believe to be among the numbers of the blessed. The evil heretics have made books using his name so that they would not be published. They dare not print anything in their own name."[273] The best response in these uneasy times is "to go to your spiritual father, curé or vicar, or to some other good man, so that you can find out what you ought to do."[274]

Le Picart confesses that his own sins and those of other churchmen have contributed to the growth of heresy.[275] Although "I have not yet become a heretic by the grace of God," he worries that "there is still time for me to fall."[276] He suggests that a heretic willing to admit his errors could be pardoned.[277] The range of punishments for heresy ran the gamut from simple warnings and *amendes honorables* to whipping and having one's tongue cut out. But for particularly obdurate and dangerous heretics, burning at the stake was the most fitting penalty, for such executions were "... exemplary sentences at the heart of public ceremonies designed to purify a community and present openly the dangers of heresy."[278] For impious men and women who were disloyal to God, Le Picart and most of his contemporaries felt that the ultimate penalty, as had been meted out to the blasphemers of Meaux, was necessary.[279] Because of the heretics' obstinacy, Le Picart sanctioned the use of torture.[280] He recounts his experiences interviewing heretics, saying "I have spoken to some in prison worthy of the flames. I asked them who had taught them. They answered, 'the Holy Spirit.'"[281] Such people had to be burned alive,[282] for by their actions they were spitting at the cross.[283] Le Picart claims this is not vengeance, but the accomplishment of

[273] Le Picart, *Pasques*, fol. 104; this is a reference to the *Epitaphia honorandi magistri nostri Petri a Cornibus . . . edito a compluribus orthodoxis & catholicis . . . quibus eius tumulum adornarunt in ecclesia Fratrum Minorum Parisiensium* (Paris: Adam Saulnier, 1542). Farge, *Biographical Register*, 111.

[274] Le Picart, *SL*, 147.

[275] Le Picart, *Advent*, fol. 283.

[276] Le Picart, *Trinité*, fol. 33.

[277] Ibid, fol. 121.

[278] Greengrass, *French Reformation*, 36.

[279] Le Picart, *Trinité-II*, fol. 169; *Advent*, fol. 283.

[280] Le Picart, *Trinité-II*, fol. 14.

[281] Le Picart, *Trinité*, fol. 67.

[282] Ibid, fol. 147.

[283] Le Picart, *Trinité-II*, fol. 194.

God's commandments.[284] Still, most accused heretics in France were *not* burnt at the stake, especially before the 1550s.[285] Henri II's *Chambre Ardente* prosecuted 323 people for heresy between May, 1548 and March, 1550, condemning only thirty-nine to death. Of those, only six were burned as unrepentant heretics; the remainder, after confessing their guilt and admitting their errors, were hanged.[286]

In her brilliant study of Catholicism in Paris between 1557 and 1572, Barbara Diefendorf remarks that "[w]e cannot understand the French Catholic reaction to religious schism unless we can comprehend that, for the sixteenth-century Parisian, religious unity—personally felt and publicly displayed—was not just an ideal, but a vital condition for individual and collective salvation. Society was perceived as an organic whole, 'one bread, and one body.'"[287] Heresy was an attack on both the political and the sacral body, and as such had to be eradicated. Yet during the two reigns in which the reformed faith had made inroads even in Paris, the monarchy had not followed a consistent policy of repression. Before 1535, Francis I's policy had been characterized by ambivalence, but in the last years of the reign persecution intensified. Henri II's reign, from 1547 to 1559, has usually been portrayed as marking a shift toward harsh repression. This was largely true in terms of the king's domestic policy, but Henri II's wars, his diplomatic needs and his conflict with Pope Julius III all interfered with his ability to rid the realm of heresy. As Frederic Baumgartner has shown, "Henry's attitude against the Protestants was, therefore, rather more ambivalent than it usually has been portrayed. On one hand determined to eradicate heresy, on the other prepared to make allowances for high rank and the needs of diplomacy, Henry was not able to pursue the goal of religious conformity with single-minded intent."[288] In these circumstances, it was frequently left to the *parlement*, the Faculty of Theology and individual preachers to eliminate or minimize the threats posed by Protestantism. François Le Picart was in the forefront of these efforts in Paris from 1533 until his death in 1556. His work in drawing up

---

[284] Le Picart, *Pasques*, fol. 80.
[285] Nicholls, "Theatre of Martyrdom," 51.
[286] Holt, *French Wars of Religion*, 28.
[287] Diefendorf, *Beneath the Cross*, 38.
[288] Frederic J. Baumgartner, *Henry II: King of France 1547–1559* (Durham: Duke University Press, 1988), 131–132.

the Articles of Faith, censoring books, hearing denunciations, and
working for the conversion of heretics was critical in keeping Paris
within the Catholic fold. Yet it was his role as a preacher—the most
popular in Paris—that not only made him beloved by the people,
but also allowed him to disseminate knowledge about the actions
and beliefs of the heretics which he believed was crucial if men and
women were to remain faithful to the church.

    To the modern mind, burning at the stake is one of the most
inhumane and revolting tortures ever devised. That François Le
Picart presided over the burning of heretics and supported the punishment for recalcitrant heretics cannot be denied. Yet if we are to
understand the *mentalités* of Parisians in the middle of the sixteenth-
century, we must try to understand his beliefs. He did not derive
pleasure from the excruciating death of heretics, and like most secular and ecclesiastical authorities, he would have been very sparing
in the use of this final punishment, since it was likely to create martyrs for the Protestant cause. Yet sometimes it was necessary for the
greater good of society. As David Nicholls writes:

> The purpose of executing heretics was total obliteration: heresy had
> to be driven out of society like disease from the body and the social
> body completely cleansed of all impurities. . . . Guilty of the ultimate
> religious and political crime of *lèse-majesté divine*, even their memory was
> meant to be destroyed along with all physical evidence of their exis-
> tence on earth and in this polity. . . . Unlike other criminals, whose
> bodies could be exposed and left to rot, the heretic had to be utterly
> destroyed.[289]

Denis Crouzet's brilliant exposition of the culture of violence that
was an intrinsic part of religious conflict best captures its meanings
for sixteenth-century people. Protestants were animated by a need
to destroy the symbols—the host, statues, altars—of a faith they felt
had lost sight of God and the Word. In annihilating the bodies of
heretics, Catholics felt they were acting at God's behest:

> The stoning and burning of the bodies of the enemies of God restored
> the order of God, the order created by God, and this recreation could
> only be from God . . . Sacrificial offering of obedience or the will to
> put in concrete form a collective experience of belonging, the last
> sequence of the unfolding ritual is isolated like a revelation from

---

[289] Nicholls, "Theatre of Martyrdom," 50.

God. . . . The end of a heretic was a spectacle, because it was a vic-
torious sign from God. . . . The body of the enemy was not only the
body of the enemy: it was magnified into a reality of Evil . . .[290]

Like the cancer to which Le Picart compared it, heresy had to be
surgically excised because it was a crime against God. The very salvation of Christianity was at stake. And even after the destruction
of the body and memory of the heretic, further purification had to
be carried out through expiatory processions. Yet this ferocious oppo-
nent of heresy had another side to him. Le Picart filled his sermons
with examples of the goodness of God and his love for his people.
The hope and optimism of his sermons owe much to events that
transpired in the early 1530s that have not yet been discussed.

---

[290] Crouzet, *Guerriers de Dieu*, I:78, 80.

CHAPTER FIVE

FRIEND OF THE SOCIETY

On 15 August 1534, the Feast of the Assumption
of the Virgin, seven friends crossed the Seine from
the Latin Quarter, walking by the Cathedral of
Notre-Dame and the bustling markets of Les Halles.
Passing through the city gates, they climbed the hill
to Montmartre, to the tiny Martyrs' Chapel dedicated to the patrons of Paris, Sts. Denis, Rusticus
and Eleutherius.[1] The recently-ordained Pierre Favre
said mass in the quiet darkness of the crypt, holding
forth the Host as each of the men took vows of
poverty and chastity, and agreed to make a pilgrimage to Jerusalem.[2] To this last promise they added
the proviso that if that became impossible they
would submit themselves to the will of the Pope.[3]
After the service, they retired to a fountain on the
side of the hill, where they spent the remainder of
the day enjoying a picnic and rejoicing in their
commitment. Forty-three years later, Simão Rodrigues wrote, ". . . whenever I think back on that occasion, as I have often done, I am filled with intense
fervor, renewed with a growth of piety, overtaken
by wonder unspeakable."[4] Afterwards all of the men
recounted that this had been a crucial turning point
in their lives, but insisted that at the time they had
no intentions of founding a new order.[5]

As we have seen, the years 1533–1534 were challenging and life-
altering ones for François Le Picart. For the better part of nineteen

---

[1] William V. Bangert, *To the Other Towns: A Life of Blessed Peter Favre, First Companion of St. Ignatius* (Westminster, MD: Newman Press, 1959), 36.

[2] William V. Bangert, *A History of the Society of Jesus* (St. Louis: Institute of Jesuit Sources, 1972), 16.

[3] Henri Bernard-Maître, "Les fondateurs de la compagnie de Jésus et l'human-isme Parisien de la renaissance (1525–1536)," *Nouvelle revue théologique* 72(1950), 828.

[4] Quoted in William V. Bangert, *Claude Jay and Alfonso Salmerón: Two Early Jesuits* (Chicago: Loyola University Press, 1985), 9.

[5] John W. O'Malley, *The First Jesuits* (Cambridge: Harvard University Press, 1993), 32.

months, Le Picart lived in prison or in exile, although the terms of his confinement were never harsh. But in addition to the personal growth that likely accompanied his tribulation and testing, there were other positive developments in these years that helped to shape his apostolate and career as a preacher. In the course of his teaching at the university since the mid-1520s, Le Picart had encountered many students who would prove to be important in his life. Among those who had come to study at the University of Paris in the late 1520s and early 1530s were the men who would become known as the first Jesuits, men who would be profoundly influenced by François Le Picart and would in turn leave their mark on him.

The story of the Jesuits in Paris does not begin with Ignatius of Loyola, but with Pierre Favre, a Savoyard born in the same year as Le Picart. Favre matriculated at the University of Paris in 1525, at the age of nineteen. He soon made the acquaintance of Francis Xavier, with whom he would room beginning in 1526. Writing later to new recruits studying in Paris, Favre wrote, "We did not know how to discern in the light of truth what was good in our intellectual pursuits, and as a consequence we often took to be an end what was really a means and vice versa. . . . We did not think that the Cross deserved to have a place in our studies . . ."[6] Like so many coming of age in these troubled times, both Favre and Xavier were confused and deeply distressed, unsure of the direction their lives should take. Then in 1529 they made the acquaintance of the future founder of the Jesuit order, Iñigo de Loyola. Ironically, Iñigo's spiritual pilgrimage had begun on a battlefield fighting French troops at Pamplona, when a serious wound ended his military career.[7] During his recuperation in the castle at Loyola, Iñigo began reading the *Golden Legend* of Jacobus da Voragine, a book that inspired him to reshape his own life in imitation of the saints. Leaving Loyola on what he had begun to conceive of as a pilgrimage to Jerusalem, he discarded his sword and donned the garb of a beggar. At the monastery of Montserrat, under the guidance of the novice master, Iñigo began his new life. He then stopped at the town of Manresa to reflect on his experiences, and it was in a cave there that he began making notes that would form the essence of the *Spiritual*

    ⁶ Bangert, *To the Other Towns*, 24–25.
    ⁷ The most brilliant interpretation of this turning point can be found in W.W. Meissner's psychoanalytic study, *Ignatius of Loyola: The Psychology of a Saint* (New Haven: Yale University Press, 1992), Parts V–VI.

Exercises.[8] He followed this up with close study of the medieval best-seller, Thomas à Kempis's *Imitation of Christ*, and started to practice flagellation, fasting and prayer. During his stay at Manresa, which tempered so much of his future outlook, he wavered between feelings of consolation and desolation.[9] Realizing that he needed greater knowledge to attain more fully his spiritual goals, Iñigo began studying Latin grammar, and two years later enrolled in the University of Alcalá. The choice of Alcalá was significant, for the recently-founded university was known as a center of Erasmian and humanistic studies.[10] Cardinal Francisco Ximénes de Cisneros had gathered some of the leading proponents of the new learning there, and the university became known for its study of scripture in the original languages, which had resulted in the Complutensian Polyglot Bible. Also translated into Castilian at Alcalá was Ludolph of Saxony's *Life of Christ*, another book that would have a profound impact on Iñigo.[11] While at Alcalá, Iñigo acted as a spiritual director to both men and women.

A little later, after he fell under suspicion of heterodoxy in Salamanca, Iñigo decided to continue his studies at the University of Paris. In a letter of March 3, 1528, at the age of thirty-seven, he wrote: ". . . In a favorable amount of time and in perfect health, by the grace and bounty of God Our Lord, I arrived, the second of February, in this city of Paris, where I will study until the day the Lord ordains that I do something else."[12] He began his studies at Noël Beda's Collège de Montaigu, from which John Calvin had only recently departed for law studies at Orléans.[13] During the year and a half he spent at Montaigu, which was so dark and damp that it was known as the "cleft in the buttocks of Mother Theology," Iñigo endured days filled with study, prayer and memorization that began at four in the morning and ended at nine in the evening.[14] For much of his first year

---

[8] O'Malley, *First Jesuits*, 24–25.

[9] Joseph de Guibert, *The Jesuits: Their Spiritual Doctrine and Practice: A Historical Study* (Chicago: Loyola University Press, 1964), 29.

[10] O'Malley, *First Jesuits*, 27; friends of Iñigo, the Eguías, were Erasmus's publishers at Alcalá. Guibert, *Jesuits*, 164.

[11] John C. Olin, *Catholic Reform from Cardinal Ximénes to the Council of Trent, 1495–1563* (New York: Fordham University Press, 1990), 5–6.

[12] I. Rodriguez-Grahit, "Ignace de Loyola et le collège Montaigu: L'influence de Standonk sur Ignace," *Bibliothèque d'humanisme et renaissance* 20(1958), 388.

[13] Ganoczy, *Young Calvin*, 63.

[14] David Mitchell, *The Jesuits: A History* (London: MacDonald Futura Publishers, 1980), 32.

in Paris, Iñigo was reduced to penury, forced to beg on the streets. But he was satisfied with his decision. He wrote in 1532 to his brother Beltrán, urging him to send his son to study in Paris, saying "I do not think you will find anywhere in Europe greater advantages. . . . He will be able to accomplish here in four years what it would take him six to do elsewhere or even more."[15] Still, his lack of orthodoxy was noted, and he was denounced to Mathieu Ory. The inquisitorial process dragged on, but he was acquitted in September of 1529.[16] By October 1, he had moved on to the Collège de Sainte-Barbe, where he shared a room with Favre and Xavier, and helped them earn their board by tutoring.[17] Here he began calling himself Ignacio or Ignatius. He may have done this under the mistaken assumption that this was a variant of Iñigo[18] or simply because of an error made by the registrar at the university.[19] Sainte-Barbe, funded by the king of Portugal, would not exist much longer, but in the years of their residence it was a battleground between conservatives and progressives.[20] The man who would later be one of the greatest friends of the Society in Paris, the headmaster Diego Gouveia, was initially hostile to Ignatius:

> In Paris a slander campaign began against the pilgrim, especially among the Spaniards. Our Master de Gouveia said that he [the pilgrim] had turned Amador, who was a member of his college, into a madman, and was determined, so he said, that the first time he [the pilgrim] set foot in Sainte-Barbe, he would give him a public whipping in the hall for being a seducer of students.[21]

But Ignatius was able to turn Gouveia's anger into love and humility: "When the time came for the punishment to be exacted, to the surprise and edification of all, the principal fell to his knees at Iñigo's feet and begged his pardon."[22] This was to prove the beginning of a long and warm friendship. In December of 1532, Ignatius received his bachelor of arts, and four months later he passed the licentiate.[23]

---

[15] Quoted in Thomas H. Clancy, *An Introduction to Jesuit Life: The Constitutions and History through 435 Years* (St. Louis: Institute of Jesuit Sources, 1976), 35.

[16] Bernard-Maître, "Fondateurs," 821.

[17] J.C.H. Aveling, *The Jesuits* (London: Blond & Briggs, 1981), 77.

[18] O'Malley, *First Jesuits*, 29.

[19] Aveling, *Jesuits*, 58.

[20] Bernard-Maître, "Fondateurs," 823.

[21] Joseph N. Tylenda, ed., *A Pilgrim's Journey: The Autobiography of Ignatius of Loyola* (Wilmington, DE: Michael Glazier, 1985), 89.

[22] Meissner, *Ignatius*, 149.

[23] Bernard-Maître, "Fondateurs," 825.

By 1533, Francis Xavier, who had harbored ambitions of becoming a famed professor or counselor to princes like his father,[24] had been converted to the pastoral and missionary ideals of his friends, and in the only extant letter from this period showed appreciation to Ignatius for turning him away from "bad company." This was probably a reference to his acquaintance, Nicolas Bourbon, who would get into trouble with the authorities over the publication of his *Nugae*.[25] Incredibly, during one of the most momentous periods in Parisian history, there are virtually no mentions in any of the early Jesuits' correspondence from 1533–1535 of the conflicts between the reformers and the theologians, perhaps because of the insulation of their quarter of the city or language difficulties.[26]

During the course of their studies, Ignatius, Favre and Xavier drew others to their spiritual cause. Ignatius attracted two new Spanish arrivals to Paris in 1533, Diego Laínez and Alfonso Salmerón.[27] By early 1534 the five were joined by two others, Simão Rodrigues, who had arrived in Paris in 1527,[28] and Nicolás Alfonso de Bobadilla.[29] All but Francis Xavier had made the *Spiritual Exercises* by August of 1534. To "make" the *Exercises* meant to follow a four-week program, guided by a spiritual director; it was what one historian has called a "... shock-tactic spiritual gymnastic to be undertaken and performed at some particular moment—perhaps of inward crisis—when new decisions and resolutions in life are called for or held to be desirable."[30] Not concerned with propagating any particular theological viewpoint,[31] their avowed purpose was "preparing and disposing our soul to rid itself of all its disordered affections and then, after their removal, of seeking and finding God's will in the ordering of our life for the salvation of our soul."[32] They prepared the individual to "... experience and to discern the affects that accompany the practice of living the 'memory' of Christ's life, death, and resurrection ..."

---

[24] Meissner, *Ignatius*, 152.
[25] Bernard-Maître, "Préréforme humaniste," 229.
[26] Bernard-Maître, "Fondateurs," 826; O'Malley, *First Jesuits*, 29.
[27] O'Malley, *First Jesuits*, 30.
[28] Schurhammer, *Francis Xavier*, 136.
[29] Ibid, 140, 155, 159.
[30] H. Outram Evennett, *The Spirit of the Counter-Reformation* (Cambridge: Cambridge University Press, 1968), 45.
[31] O'Malley, *First Jesuits*, 42.
[32] Quoted in O'Malley, *First Jesuits*, 37.

using "the sensuous imagination" to evaluate the spiritual meanings of consolation and desolation.[33] By the end of summer, 1534, united in their spiritual quest, the seven companions made the symbolically important pilgrimage to Montmartre. A few months later they attracted another recruit—Claude Jay, a boyhood friend of Favre from Savoy.[34]

Toward the end of 1534, Ignatius was once again denounced to the Inquisition. Because of Ory's absence from Paris, a copy of the *Exercises* was taken to Valentin Liévin. This actually worked to his benefit, for Liévin concluded that both the work and all of the companions were fully orthodox.[35] In spring, 1535, after having finalized plans for joining up with the companions in Venice en route to Jerusalem, Ignatius left Paris for his final visit to his homeland.[36] On August 15, 1535, the anniversary of the first vows at Montmartre, Favre and the remaining group of men repeated the experience.[37] During 1536, Favre guided two further recruits through the *Spiritual Exercises*: Paschase Broët, a priest from Picardy, and Jean Codure, a Provençal.[38] In mid-November of 1536, Favre and his companions left Paris in two groups, and were reunited with Ignatius in Rome in April of 1538.[39] When the group had dispersed for street preaching throughout Italy, they had decided that if asked who they were, they would respond that they were of the Company of Jesus, since they had no other superior.[40] The term Jesuit was often used pejoratively in the early sixteenth century to refer to a religious hypocrite,[41] but this did not deter the companions.

John O'Malley writes that "[t]he brevity of the account of the Parisian years in [Ignatius's] *Autobiography* belies their importance for the future Society of Jesus."[42] The formative experience and shared dreams at the University of Paris would influence every aspect of the Society's program in the years to come. The earliest Jesuits "began by taking everywhere they went the methods in which they had

---

[33] Antonio T. DeNicholas, *Powers of Imagining: Ignatius de Loyola* (Albany: State University of New York Press, 1986), x.

[34] Bangert, *Jay and Salmerón*, 9.

[35] Bernard-Maître, "Fondateurs," 829.

[36] O'Malley, *First Jesuits*, 32.

[37] Bangert, *Jay and Salmerón*, 10.

[38] Ibid, 15.

[39] Ibid, 16, 25.

[40] O'Malley, *First Jesuits*, 34.

[41] Ibid, 69.

[42] Ibid, 28.

been initiated at the colleges of the University of Paris . . . [I]t was always to a Parisian prototype that they referred, while introducing modifications suggested by experience."[43] Yet their university years were enlightening in ways that were not always flattering to their *alma mater*. In 1535, critical of the education students were receiving, Francis Xavier wrote,

> Often I want to cry out against the universities . . . and with all my power to vomit out abuse as a fool and out of my senses, and especially against the University of Paris, the Sorbonne. . . . I greatly fear that many of those who study at the University look more toward acquiring dignities, bishoprics, benefices and offices, than doing what is just and necessary as canons regular and bishops. The common saying goes, "I want to study letters in order to have some good benefice in the Church, and then afterwards I will live for God." These certainly are brute beasts who only follow their sensuality and what their appetites ordain; these unchaste ones . . . [instead of] desiring that the will of God be done, do not confide in Him and put themselves entirely in His counsel and solicitude, because they fear that what they desire God won't want, and that if they obey and comply with God's will, they will be constrained to abandon their badly acquired benefices.[44]

A second-generation Jesuit, Jerónimo Nadal (1507–1580) would ask, "Why in so infinitely large a population of Paris are doctors who preach and work zealously for the salvation of souls so rare?"[45] The early Jesuits' response to the scholastic culture of the University of Paris was ambivalent, and however much their ideas were given structure and form by the teaching at Paris, numerous other influences came to bear on the development of Jesuit thought. In varying degrees, all of the earliest ten companions had imbibed the spirit of humanism at Alcalá or the Collège de Sainte-Barbe.[46] Of no one was this more true than Salmerón. Thoroughly conversant with Erasmian views, Salmerón was fluent in classical Greek and Latin, and had studied all of the classics.[47] Laínez believed that humanist pedagogy was an absolutely indispensable element of the Jesuits' educational program.[48] Favre was equally adept in Greek and Latin, but

[43] Bernard-Maître, "François Le Picart," 92.
[44] Quoted in ibid, 93–94.
[45] Quoted in ibid, 97.
[46] O'Malley, *First Jesuits*, 98.
[47] Bangert, *Jay and Salmerón*, 154.
[48] Augustin Renaudet, "L'humanisme et l'enseignement de l'Université de Paris au temps de la Renaissance," in *Aspects de l'Université de Paris* (Paris: Albin Michel, 1949), 155.

he added something else to the formative influences on the group—
a personal gentleness and sweetness that strongly affected the future
Society's emphasis on consolation. In 1577 Simão Rodrigues wrote:

> There was an especially rare and delightful sweetness and charm in
> his relations with other men which I must confess to this very day I
> have not discovered in any other. In some way or other, he so won
> the friendship of other men and gradually stole into their souls that
> by his whole manner and the gentleness of his words he irresistibly
> drew them to a love of God.[49]

Favre's ideal of love and companionship with Christ and his concept of service, so evident in his *Memoriale*,[50] left an indelible mark
on the nascent movement and on those with whom he had formed
friendships in Paris.

Strong bonds had also been forged during the years 1525–1536
with one of the masters at the University of Paris, François Le Picart.
During most of their years in Paris, the early Jesuits attended the
new lectures in theology at the Collège de Navarre and the Sorbonne.[51]
Le Picart is the Parisian doctor most often mentioned in the Jesuit
writings and correspondence, but other names also appear. Favre
wrote from Rome, "it would be worthwhile for you to commend us
to the most observant of our masters, [Jacques] Barthélemy, [Pierre]
Descornes, [François] Le Picart, [Robert] Wauchope, [Thomas]
Laurent and [Jean] Benoist, all highly renowned, who express great
pleasure at being called our preceptors and us their disciples and
sons in Jesus Christ."[52] During the remainder of his life, especially
after the Jesuits' return to Paris, Le Picart was intimately involved
in forwarding the prospects of the beleaguered Society.

After the group had reunited in Italy, it became clear that the
pilgrimage to Jerusalem would have to be abandoned as a result of
the Turkish advance. The first Jesuits therefore followed the alternate
course proposed by Ignatius and volunteered their services to the
pope. On 27 September 1540, Paul III gave official approval to the

---

[49] Quoted in Bangert, *Jay and Salmerón*, 21.

[50] Brian O'Leary, "The Discernment of Spirits in the *Memoriale* of Blessed Peter
Favre," *The Way* 35(1979), 1–140.

[51] O'Malley, *First Jesuits*, 245.

[52] Quoted in Bernard-Maître, "François Le Picart," 99. For these doctors, information can be found in Farge's *Biographical Register*, 39–40, 42–43, 110–112, 242–243,
437–441.

new religious order. They returned to Paris on November 30,[53] paying their first visit to their ancient master at the Collège de Sainte-Barbe, Gouveia. Then "we then went to visit our master Le Picart, and he is so attached to the Company that he says that if it were not for his bad leg, he would join us."[54] Jerónimo Domenech, who had studied in Paris but only made the *Exercises* in 1539, reported that

> Le Picart is on such good terms with us that he seems only to think about speaking with us on this subject. The other day I went to talk to him. He speaks to us with such humility and openness of all his affairs that he seemed to be confessing to me and declaring his desires, "Would that I could be one of your Society!" We have not actually engaged him to make the *Exercises*, because we see the moment is not very favorable to him. We will therefore prepare him now for when the moment comes. It is an incredible thing, his attachment to the Company and the good feeling he has about all our business.

Domenech also credited Le Picart with reclaiming many "who had been infected with heresy . . ."[55]

Through all of the difficult years between 1540 and 1556, the Jesuits had no stronger friend and supporter than François Le Picart. He was also their role model. Reflecting concerns that had been part of the reformation of the Faculty of Theology in 1536, Nadal asked:

> Why is it necessary to have such a large crowd of doctors here? Why not minister the Word in many other parts? . . . Why do those not go out in the nearby cities and villages according to the example of Christ and the apostles to announce the reign of Heaven? Because among such an infinite population of Paris, rare are the doctors who preach and serve zealously for the salvation of souls! We see in our lifetime our most famous master Le Picart, whose name is a cause of honor, who with a spirit of fervor and piety preaches greatly with fruit in Paris. But besides him, there is hardly anyone![56]

In 1549, at a time when the Jesuit community in Paris comprised only thirteen members,[57] Polanco recorded that "Doctor Le Picart

---

[53] A. Lynn Martin, *The Jesuit Mind: The Mentality of an Elite in Early Modern France* (Ithaca: Cornell University Press, 1988), 1.

[54] *Fontes Narrativi de S. Ignatio de Loyola et de Societatis Iesu initiis: Narrationes scriptae ante annum 1557* (Rome: MHSI, 1943), I:253, 255.

[55] Joanne Alphonso de Polanco, *Vita Ignatii Loiolae et rerum Societatis Jesu* (Madrid: MHSI, 1894), I:94.

[56] *FN*, II:56.

[57] O'Malley, *First Jesuits*, 54.

promotes to the limit both with his counsel and his authority all our
works with sincerity and love."[58] Francis Xavier wrote to his brothers from India that he hoped to enlist the aid of Le Picart and
Descornes in spreading the Word in India,[59] but Le Picart's main
preoccupation in the 1540s and 1550s had to be the reform of the
Catholic Church and the return to the fold of those who had turned
to heresy.

The Jesuits were able to reciprocate through their contacts with
Rome. In a letter of October, 1552 to Ignatius of Loyola, Broët
asked:

> Our teacher François Le Picart, so affectionate to our Company, rec-
> ommends himself greatly to the prayers of Your Reverence and to all
> the fathers and brethren of the house, and he has begged me to write
> to Your Reverence asking for the love of Our Lord Jesus Christ to
> extend to him the grace of obtaining a license giving him the power
> to read heretical books, so that he will be able to disprove their errors
> in his sermons, and to please give him the authority to absolve heretics
> in both their consciences and in writing . . .[60]

Both Le Picart and Broët were persistent in their efforts to gain this
privilege. A few weeks later, Broët wrote to Ignatius again, saying
that "François Le Picart, teacher of theology and great friend of the
Company, has asked me to write with the utmost affection to . . . beg
with all his heart that you obtain for him a license to absolve heretics
and to have the right to read heretical books."[61] The right to absolve
heretics, bypassing the Inquisition, was a privilege Julius III had
accorded the Jesuits.[62]

More recruits had begun to study in Paris even before the Company's official sanction, but their presence was to remain small thanks
to formidable opposition from the *parlement*, the University of Paris
and the bishop, who were concerned with the papal protections and
privileges of the Jesuits. The Society had no legal existence in France,
and despite the efforts of the Bishop of Clermont, who established
the first Jesuit college in France, they could not own property.[63]

---

[58] Polanco, *Vita Ignatii Loiolae*, I:419.
[59] Hilarion de Coste, *Parfait ecclesiastique*, 169–170.
[60] *Epistolae PP. Paschasii Broëti, Claudii Jaji, Joannis Codurii et Simonis Rodericii* (Madrid: Gabrielis Lopez del Horno, 1903), 75.
[61] Ibid, 78.
[62] O'Malley, *First Jesuits*, 144.
[63] Martin, *Jesuit Mind*, 1.

Another friend and student of Le Picart, Charles de Guise, Cardinal of Lorraine, acted as the Society's protector in France and set out to secure the necessary *droit de naturalisation*, but this provoked immediate opposition from Bishop DuBellay of Paris.[64] When Broët naïvely produced the papal bulls, the *parlement* reacted in its usual fashion whenever Gallican liberties were threatened. The Faculty of Theology followed suit and condemned the Jesuits on 1 December 1554. Placards appeared everywhere in the city, and preachers denounced the group in their sermons. Throughout the conflict with the bishop, *parlement* and Faculty, Le Picart's support was essential and deeply valued. Broët wrote on 4 March 1553, "... there is great difficulty with the *parlement,* who say you need to consider well and ponder and deliberate with mature counsel. Neither Monsieur Le Picart nor Monsieur Gouveia have any difficulty with this. They favor us greatly for the love of God, but against these two are more than fifty others."[65] Feelings against the Society were indeed running high, and many despaired of gaining a foothold in Paris.[66]

> Too few have godly feelings toward the Society, and we are accused of arrogance ... ... [T]he grace of the gospels, the public administration of the sacraments ... are not conceded to us ... The rest, who are easily numbered, conduct themselves by fighting strenuously in defense of our rules, and they preach supporting our Society ... who we will name by the grace and honor of their actions:
>
> In the first place, there is Doctor Gouveia, of the Portuguese nation, a theologian of the first rank who is eighty-six years old;
>
> Near him comes the celebrated churchman, Doctor François Le Picart, a native of Paris, and also among the first ranks of theologians.
>
> Third, merit is conceded to Doctor Francisco Joverio, a man of rare erudition, who incurred suspicion on account of his defense of our profession when the name of Jesuit was made into a joke. He responded with true humility of soul: "I am not one of their number, nor worthy to join their company."
>
> In fourth place we would call Doctor Sebastian Rodriguez, a Portuguese, a man noted for his piety. These four men look after us. There are others who have sincere affection for the Society out of their love of Christ, but they have nothing to do with us, deterred by the abundance of our adversaries.... Others greatly extol our *Institutes,*

---

[64] Evennett, *Cardinal of Lorraine*, 58–59. Interestingly, Le Picart's old Greek teacher, the humanist Danès, was also a strong supporter of the Society. Ibid, 60.

[65] *Epistolae Broëti*, 87.

[66] Polanco, *Vita Ignatii Loiolae*, II:297.

but do not at all approve of the privileges conceded to us by the holy
pontiff, and several warn the bishops to oppose the Society . . .[67]

While expressing exasperation with the position of the Faculty of
Theology as a whole, Broët states that "only Doctor Le Picart, about
whom other mention has been made, a man renowned for learning and piety, and Doctor Gouveia . . . favored us earnestly."[68] Many
others, unfortunately, ". . . fear to be associated with us, that along
with us they will be thought to be evil."[69]

The following May, Broët learned that the Jesuits had been forbidden from practicing their ministry in Paris under pain of excommunication.[70] After their right to communicate and hear confessions
in the church of Saint-Germain-des-Prés was challenged, Broët sought
Le Picart's advice as to how they should proceed. Le Picart's counseled them to temporarily halt the services, but not to refuse any
who came in search of consolation.[71] It would only be the "Calvinist
arrogance" displayed at the Colloquy of Poissy in 1561 that turned
the tide, leading to a parlementary decree according the Jesuits legal
status in France.[72]

In the last years of his life, Le Picart's name was again linked
with that of Gérard Roussel. In 1553, Roussel had been mentioned
as a candidate for the cardinal's hat. The Jesuits were consulted,
and painted an extremely unflattering portrait of Roussel. Laínez
recalled the day when ". . . Master Le Picart, preaching at Saint-
Benoît, had, in developing his theme, *Eligite unum ex vobis*, criticized
those who chose heretics for bishops, so that many hearers believed
this was said about the new and wicked election of Master Gérard
[to the bishopric of Oloron]."[73] But this proposal may have inspired
the Jesuits. After the election of Pope Paul IV on May 23, 1555,
they proposed Le Picart for the red hat.

We have discussed before the Pope the promotion to the cardinalate
of our Master Le Picart on the recommendation of our Doctor Olave
and others of the Company who know what a learned and good serv-

---

[67] *Litterae quadrimestres ex universis praeter Indiam et Brasiliam locis in quibus aliqui de
Societate Jesu versabantur Romam missae* (Madrid: Augustinus Avrial, 1895), II:294–295.
[68] Polanco, *Vita Ignatii Loiolae*, III:291; *Epistolae PP Broëti*, 89.
[69] Ibid, V:335.
[70] O'Malley, *First Jesuits*, 288–289.
[71] *Epistolae PP Broëti*, 102.
[72] Martin, *Jesuit Mind*, 2.
[73] Quoted in Bernard-Maître, "François Le Picart," 103.

ant of God he is. And when a certain prelate expressed some opposition, thanks to the witness of so many of us who had known him, it was decided that our Master Le Picart would be, with great edification, one of the first cardinals of Rome . . . If his claudication is not an obstacle . . . it will be easy to make him a cardinal.[74]

Le Picart's unwillingness to go to Rome, using his vascular problems as an excuse, and his subsequent death, prevented his elevation. Ironically, he was following one of the Jesuits' own precepts that said when presented with a possible dignity, ". . . every manner and means of resisting and impeding such an intention of the Pontiff are to be expended and exercised, every stone to be turned, lest a dignity be imposed."[75] Many in the Society did not find it at all surprising that Le Picart died only a couple of months after the death of Ignatius on July 31, 1556, for the parallels were numerous between the two men. Both had suffered imprisonment for their beliefs in early adulthood[76] and both men had had to come to terms with problems of pride. Just as the story was told of how François Le Picart gave his cloak and alms to a poor man, the same was said of Ignatius: "On the eve of our Lady's feast in March, in the year 1522, he went at night, as secretly as he could, to a poor man and, removing all his clothing, he gave it to the poor man and dressed himself in the garment he so desired to wear . . ."[77] Both showed particular concern for women, not only offering spiritual guidance to women, but directing a significant portion of their ministries to the conversion of prostitutes. Le Picart rejected the inheritance he could have had; it was said (inaccurately) that Ignatius had renounced a huge inheritance.[78] On a purely physical level, both men limped.[79]

Juan Polanco (1517–1576) noted under 17 September 1556: "A good friend of the Society, famed as a pious and learned preacher,

---

[74] Quoted in ibid, 103–104.

[75] O'Malley, *First Jesuits*, 310.

[76] Tylenda, *Pilgrim's Journey*, 78. Both men were visited in prison by people yearning for instruction, and both used the experience as an opportunity for growth. Ignatius said to a woman who expressed compassion for his situation, "In this you show that you do not desire to be a prisoner for the love of God. Why does prison seem so great an evil for you? I will tell you that there are not bars enough or chains enough in Salamanca but I would desire more for God's love." Meissner, *Ignatius*, 136.

[77] Tylenda, *Pilgrim's Journey*, 26.

[78] Ibid, 27.

[79] O'Malley, *First Jesuits*, 24.

Doctor Le Picart has left Paris for a better life . . ."[80] Nicolas Orlandinus wrote that "we must not let go by Doctor François Le Picart, a man of nobility and virtue, true constancy and benevolence: his true and sincere soul always supported the cause of the Society against our adversaries, and he never stopped struggling with all hope for us."[81] Writing in 1583, Bobadilla recalled, "as to preachers, I have heard all the great ones of my time. In Spain, Dionisio Palomo, Vives, Thomás de Guzmán, and de la Cruz; in France, Le Picart and others one cannot name; in Flanders, Alfonso de Castro and Osunna; in Germany, Domingo de Soto and Pedro de Soto, who preached to the Emperor Charles V . . ."[82] Ponce Cogordan (1500–1582) claimed that two years after Le Picart's death, he had a great number of imitators in more than thirty churches in Paris."[83] Finally, Antonio Possevino (1533–1611), responding to the appearance of Le Picart's sermons in print, wrote a fitting epitaph:

> François Le Picart, Paris theologian . . . published sermons in French for the gospels of the entire year, which are alive with extraordinary piety. This man was the most celebrated of his generation, a man who suffered greatly on account of his preaching of the gospels. Hereafter who reads them will understand that the words of Ezekiel apply: *And where the spirit was, in that place will he walk.*[84]

From the evidence of his sermons, the teacher had become the disciple, a position utterly in keeping with Le Picart's renowned humility. How much he was changed by his friendship and conversations with the earliest Jesuits can be seen in every aspect of his preaching, from sermon structure and style to content. In order to examine the influence in Le Picart's sermons, we must first look more closely at Jesuit spirituality as expressed in their writings.

Bobadilla had been a student of Le Picart. Based on his diaries from this period, Schurhammer relates that

> . . . Bobadilla listened to the sermons of Dr. Le Picart and others. In his room he read the works of the Church Fathers, especially those of "the four Doctors of the Church," . . . and the writings of St. John Chrysostom and other exegetes. After taking vows on Montmartre in

---

[80] Polanco, *Vita Ignatii Loiolae*, VI:486.
[81] Launoy, *Regii Navarrae Gymnasii*, IV:428.
[82] *Bobadilla Monumenta* (Rome: MHSI, 1970), 561–562.
[83] Bernard-Maître, "François Le Picart," 103.
[84] Antonio Possevino, *Apparatus sacer* (Venice: Venetian Society, 1603), 505.

1534, he filled page after page with excerpts from their works with a tireless industry that was only interrupted once by a sickness in the summer of 1535. He finally put these pages together into a thick volume of a thousand pages. They were written in black and red ink with titles and borders and with the names of the authors inscribed on the margins in either red or black. He first made brief summaries on Genesis using Eugubinus as his source, who had based his commentaries on the primitive Hebrew. He then added some brief notes on the Psalms. These were followed by lengthy extracts on the Gospel of St. Matthew. His main sources for these were St. Jerome and St. John Chrysostom, the Commentaries of Johannes Major, St. Thomas, and Theophylactus; but he cited other sources as well, including Albert the Great, the Venerable Bede, Augustine, Gregory, Hilary, Nicholas of Lyra, Origen, John Damascene, Dionysius, Symmachus, Scotus, Seneca, and the *Glossa ordinaria* and *marginalis*. These in turn were followed by passages dealing with the Gospel of St. Luke taken from Ambrose and Dionysius; on the Gospel of St. John from Chrysostom, Augustine, and Thomas; and, finally, on the Epistles of St. Paul from Augustine, Anselm, and Theophylactus.

At the conclusion to his extracts of the Epistle to the Romans, Bobadilla states that "in his preaching, [Le] Picart has said that the whole of Sacred Scripture is like a single book of lamentation, praise, promise, and joy."[85]

Bobadilla's attendance at Le Picart's sermons in these years poses an interesting problem related to his diary entries: to what degree did Le Picart influence the early Jesuits and to what degree was he influenced by them? A study of the citations in Le Picart's sermons shows that the sources Bobadilla mentions were those most favored by Le Picart (see Chapter I). Ignatius particularly recommended the study of Chrysostom for preachers.[86] Paul was a favorite of both Le Picart and the Jesuits. Nadal, who had taken the Renaissance dictum of *ad fontes* very seriously by studying Hebrew with rabbis in Avignon,[87] wrote in his journal: "Study Paul!"[88] As one of the primary teachers of the early Jesuits, it may be argued that Le Picart's was the greater influence, but a mutually beneficial interaction seems most likely. But the exchange went well beyond the sources, to the content. The writings of the first companions can be compared with Le Picart's sermons.

---

[85] Schurhammer, *Francis Xavier*, 257–258.
[86] O'Malley, *First Jesuits*, 260.
[87] James Brodrick, *The Origin of the Jesuits* (Westport, CT: Greenwood Publishers, 1971), 200.
[88] Quoted in O'Malley, *First Jesuits*, 109.

Bobadilla left numerous writings, including a treatise in 1551 on frequent and daily communion, a project for reform of the church (1555), in which he invited the pope to start at the top and attack the problem of nepotism, and an autobiography of his travels and preaching through Europe (1589).[89]

Francis Xavier's letter of 1544 describing his missions contained an appeal to the universities to use their knowledge to gain souls. He consecrated a number of his works, especially those directed to novices, to the central need for prayer in a Christian's life. Yet one of the overriding themes of the saint's letters and writings was the need for humility. "Experience will teach you many things," he writes in his 1549 guide for the apostolate at Ormuz, "if you are humble and prudent."[90] Le Picart's learning experience of 1533–1534 immediately comes to mind. In the same year, Xavier wrote in his "Confidence of the Apostle," that not presumption or hollow enthusiasm, but humility and a solid confidence were needed for inward growth. Finally, in Xavier's "Work of the Missionary" of 1552, he wrote, "First, for as much as you have it in you, work with all your power to make yourself loved."[91] All the Catholic descriptions of Le Picart describe a man who matched in every detail Xavier's ideal.

Pierre Favre dedicated most of his writings to the cultivation of the inward Christian life. In his 1541 "Directions on the Faith and Morals," he offered not only practical religious guidelines, but described the necessary spirit that must inform them. He spoke of the importance of prayer and the sacraments. In his "Studies of the Student" of the same year, he told those already in the company or those contemplating joining that they must turn their studies to the glory of God and the salvation of souls. He suggested they examine their own experiences, without hiding their doubts or their suffering. In his "Fraternal Charity" of 1542, Favre explained that brotherly love was the foundation of the order. One must seek peace for oneself and one's brother, and take responsibility for one's own guilt. His "True Reform" of 1543, based on his experiences in Germany, discussed the reasons for the crisis in Christianity, laying the blame firmly on the decline of the religious life among Catholics, especially

---

[89] Gilmont, *Écrits spirituels*, 160–161.
[90] Ibid, 131–133.
[91] Ibid, 135.

the clergy. He urged preachers to make their sermons an invitation to personal reform. His works exemplify the kindness and goodness that characterized his own ministry and made him so well loved. Favre also penned a manual for confessors in 1544, in which he identified confession as the critical moment in producing radical inward renewal in the penitent. He urged confessors to show their goodwill toward the penitent, and to be comforting and compassionate.[92] Favre's complete corpus of writings and advice bear the imprint of his personality, even his treatise on how to deal with Protestants, written in 1546. Most Jesuits during this period were not exercising a ministry aimed at converting heretics,[93] but Favre's work in Germany had exposed him more directly than most to the problem. He insisted to others of the Company that above all they must love heretics, and make themselves loved by them. "To convert them, discussions on faith must give way to the work of conversion of morals. Strengthen wills that are weak, and lead them to practice good works and nourish crippled souls—that [is] what must be done above all!"[94] Favre's diary, overflowing with the passion of his beliefs, was composed between 1542 and 1546, and served as a light and a guide for the many who read it in the difficult years that followed. Favre's whole being was his contribution to the nascent Jesuit movement. His works ring with hope and optimism, and a

---

[92] Ibid, 118–123.

[93] O'Malley, *First Jesuits*, 70; however, in a letter of August, 1554 to Peter Canisius, Ignatius wrote "On the Society's Duty to Oppose Heresy." His words sound remarkably like those of Le Picart. "Seeing the progress that the heretics have made in so short a time, spreading the poison of their evil teaching throughout so many countries and peoples, and making use of the verse of the Apostle to describe their progress, *and their speech will eat its way like gangrene* [2 Tim. 2:17], it would seem that our Society . . . should not only be solicitious in preparing the proper remedies but should be ready to apply them . . . The heretics have made their false theology popular and presented it in a way that is within the capacity of the common people . . . Their success is largely due to the negligence of those who should have shown some interest; and the bad example and the ignorance of Catholics, especially the clergy, have made such ravages in the vineyard of the Lord. . . . The heretics write a good many pamphlets and booklets, by which they aim to remove all authority from the Catholics . . . It would seem imperative, therefore, that ours also write answer in pamphlet form, short and well written so that they can be produced without delay and purchased by many . . . These works should be modest, but stimulating; they should point out the evil that is abroad and uncover the deceits and evil purposes of the adversaries. Joseph N. Tylenda, ed., *Counsels for Jesuits: Selected Letters and Instructions of Saint Ignatius of Loyola* (Chicago: Loyola University Press, 1985), 97, 99.

[94] Gilmont, *Écrits spirituels*, 123.

spirit of consolation and compassion. At the heart of his spirituality
was an affective embrace of God, most important when despair
threatened:

> That same day, as I was going through the streets, and without any
> joy from what met my gaze, but rather distractions and temptations
> from vain and evil thoughts, I experienced sadness as a result. Then
> I had a reply: "You must not sadden yourself because you do not find
> peace and consolations in empty things, but rejoice with thanksgiving
> because of it."[95]

Favre taught that optimism must be embraced, for it produced apostolic activity and fruit, while its converse, pessimism, had to be
rejected because it was apostolically sterile.[96] His work has been
described "as one of the most tender confessions of an interior lyri-
cism found in mystical literature."[97]

Alfonso Salmerón, like Le Picart a great preacher, wrote in 1546
"The Mission of the Bishop, a Work of Love," a treatise dedicated
to the dual work of the missionary and the bishop. He writes of the
love and self-abnegation needed for a true imitation of Christ. As
part of the meeting of Trent in 1545, he delivered a sermon on one
of Le Picart's favorite themes: "Physician, cure thyself."[98] Although
the loss of all his teeth in 1569 forced him to give up preaching,
Salmerón spent his remaining years collecting and editing his notes
for sermons. In these are found admonitions against preaching abstract
theological doctrines. The first sixteen volumes demonstrate Salmerón's
great love for the New Testament. They are a virtual resumé of Le
Picart's themes:

    I. De prolegomenis in sacrosancta Evangelia (principles of exegesis)
    II. De Verbi ante incarnationem gestis (first chapter of St. John)
    III. De infantia et pueritia D. N. Iesu Christi
    IV. De historia vitae D. N. Iesu Christi usque ad dominicam Coenam
    V. De sermone D. N. Iesu Christi in monte
    VI. De miraculis Domini
    VII. De parabolis Domini
    VIII. De disputationibus Domini

---

[95] O'Leary, "Discernment of Spirits," 91.
[96] Ibid, 112.
[97] Brodrick, *Origin of the Jesuits*, 38.
[98] Gilmont, *Écrits spirituels*, 155.

IX. De sermone in Coena ad Apostolos habito.
 X. De passione et morte D. N. Iesu Christi
 XI. De resurrectione et ascensione Domini
XII. De Ecclesiae nascentis exordiis, in Acta apostolorum
XIII. In Epistolam ad Romanos
XIV. In Epistolas ad Corinthios, Galatas, Ephesios, Philippenses,
     Colossenses et Thessalonicenses
 XV. In Epistolas ad Timotheum, Titum, Philemon et Hebraeos
XVI. In Epistolas canonicas et in Apocalypsim.[99]

Simão Rodrigues compiled fewer works, but his treatise on "Suffering and Perfection" of 1547 would have resonated with Le Picart. Known for his passionate enthusiasm, Rodrigues pushed himself to the limits. "Love of Christ crucified, love of the vocation, submission in tribulations were realities that cannot leave us indifferent," he wrote, adding that "with knees bent, hands and heart reaching to heaven, I ask God the Father the grace to suffer for you and your brothers."[100]

In Diego Laínez's writings, we find the closest approach to Le Picart's philosophy of life and mission, not surprising in view of Laínez's great talent as a preacher. He offered advice on preaching and study as well as sermons and religious instructions. Although many of his works appeared shortly after Le Picart's death, they show how the beliefs of the early Jesuits and Le Picart intersected. At the request of Ignatius of Loyola, Laínez composed a manual for novice preachers. He began with the goal of sacred eloquence: the need to win souls, listing as the subjects of preaching the Last Things, love, providence, redemption, the sacraments, sin (especially pride and lack of shame). He emphasized the importance of grace. His guide for the spiritual and intellectual progress of students of 1560–1561 asserted that all true wisdom came from God, who gave it most abundantly to the pure of heart. Integrity of life was critical.[101] In other works, he counseled continual prayer, prompt and unquestioning obedience, the importance of the ministry of confession, the need for personal sanctification, the willingness to give one's life to serve God, and the necessity of trusting God alone and putting no

---

[99] These form Salmerón's "Commentary on the New Testament," written between 1569 and 1580. Ibid, 157.
[100] Ibid, 138.
[101] Ibid, 146.

faith in worldly power. In his "Apostolate to the Orthodox" (1561), Laínez urged priests to avoid confrontations and opposition, but to remain firm in matters of doctrine.[102] In a treatise on apostolic prudence sent in response to some criticisms from Trent in 1562, Laínez replied that "our preachers are not dumb dogs [*chiens muets*]. They truly bark, but with discretion! Condemnation of vices must conform to charity, for zeal unregulated by prudence gets in the way of the common good and hinders the fruits of divine service."[103] Like Le Picart, Laínez was unconcerned with worldly honors. When his relatives and parents asked him to secure a benefice for one of his nephews, he refused, saying this was "against all justice and honesty." He continued, "for thirty years I have taught that such situations [appointing children to cures] are an abuse! Let it be God's will that I never, however much I am a sinner, allow such a contradiction between my words and my actions!"[104] Finally, he insisted on the necessity of poverty, "which defends us against the numerous adversaries to our perfection." As his editor adds, Laínez preached by example.[105]

Finally, we must turn to the writings of Ignatius of Loyola. Although Le Picart never made the *Exercises*, that does not mean they did not influence him, for in his conversations with the Jesuits it is clear that they "paved the way" for a possible future retreat in their discussions. It is impossible to know for certain what these discussions entailed, or how precisely Le Picart reacted. Nonetheless, certain hypotheses can be suggested. The aim of the *Spiritual Exercises* was ". . . the conquest of self and the regulation of one's life in such a way that no decision is made under the influence of any inordinate attachment."[106] What did this mean to Le Picart? Unlike so many of his contemporaries, he had not sought benefices or worldly honors.[107] If there was one aspect of his character not in line with the

---

[102] Ibid, 144–152.

[103] Ibid, 152–153.

[104] Ibid, 153.

[105] Ibid.

[106] Ignatius of Loyola, *The Spiritual Exercises of St. Ignatius: Based on Studies in the Language of the Autograph*, ed. and trans. Louis J. Puhl (Chicago: Loyola University Press, 1951), 11.

[107] The only indication that Le Picart ever applied for a benefice is a note in Launoy for 1526, which lists one François le Picart among the names of those desiring a benefice. Jean de Launoy, *Opera omnia* (Cologne: Fabri & Barillot et Marci-Michaelis Bousquet, 1732), IV:480.

precepts of Christian charity or the Jesuit ideal, it was his behavior in 1533–1534, when he had publicly judged others, including the royal family. It is therefore especially significant that Le Picart came to know the early Jesuits in these years. The third kind of humility called for in the *Exercises* seems to describe Le Picart in the last twenty years of his life: ". . . I desire and choose poverty with Christ poor, rather than riches; insults with Christ loaded with them, rather than honors; I desire to be accounted as worthless and a fool for Christ, rather than to be esteemed as wise and prudent in this world. So Christ was treated before me."[108] The *Exercises* portray God as the loving consoler who gives all for his creation:

> This is to reflect how God dwells in creatures: in the elements giving them existence, in the plants giving them life, in the animals conferring upon them sensation, in man bestowing understanding. So He dwells in me and gives me being, life, sensation, intelligence; and makes a temple of me, since I am created in the likeness and image of the Divine Majesty.
> . . . This is to consider all blessings and gifts as descending from above. Thus, my limited power comes from the supreme and infinite power above, and so, too, justice, goodness, mercy, etc., descend from above as the rays of light descend from the sun, and as the waters flow from their fountains, etc.
> Then I will reflect on myself, as has been said.[109]

It was through "knowing, loving, and serving [God] on earth" that humans could find their way back to God, the ultimate end of creation.[110] In the *Discernment of Spirits*, Ignatius contrasts consolation with desolation:

> I call it consolation when an interior movement is aroused in the soul, by which it is inflamed with love of its Creator and Lord, and as a consequence, can love no creature on the face of the earth for its own sake, but only in the Creator of them all. It is likewise consolation when one sheds tears that move to the love of God, whether it be because of sorrow for sins, or because of the sufferings of Christ our Lord, or for any other reason that is immediately directed to the praise and service of God. Finally, I call consolation every increase of faith, hope, and love, and all interior joy that invites and attracts to what is heavenly and to the salvation of one's soul by filling it with peace and quiet in its Creator and Lord.

---

[108] Ignatius of Loyola, *Spiritual Exercises*, ed. Puhl, 69.
[109] Ibid, 102–103.
[110] Ignatius of Loyola, *Spiritual Exercises and Selected Works*, ed. Ganss, 11.

I call desolation what is entirely the opposite of what is described
in the third rule, as darkness of soul, turmoil of spirit, inclination to
what is low and earthly, restlessness rising from many disturbances and
temptations which lead to want of faith, want of hope, want of love.
The soul is wholly slothful, tepid, sad, and separated, as it were, from
its Creator and Lord. For just as consolation is the opposite of desolation, so the thoughts that spring from consolation are the opposite
of those that spring from desolation.[111]

The same work also explains why God sends tribulations:

The second reason is because God wishes to try us, to see how much
we are worth, and how much we will advance in His service and
praise when left without the generous reward of consolations and signal favors. The third reason is because God wishes to give us a true
knowledge and understanding of ourselves, so that we may have an
intimate perception of the fact that it is not within our power to acquire
and attain great devotion, intense love, tears, or any other spiritual
consolation; but that all this is the gift and grace of God our Lord.[112]

But it was in his *Diary* that Ignatius revealed his most intimate
relationship with God. He wrote, "During this period of time I kept
on thinking that humility, reverence, and affectionate awe ought to
be not fearful but loving. This thought took root in my mind so
deeply that I begged over and over again: 'Give me loving humility, and with it reverence and affectionate awe.' After these words
I received new visitations. Moreover, I repulsed tears in order to
attend to this loving humility and so forth."[113] Such revelations typically came to Ignatius during moments of prayer or at mass.[114] From
these experiences, he began to feel the depth of God's love: "All
through these hours I found in myself such intense love and such
perception of seeing Jesus that I thought that in the future nothing
could come and separate me from him, or make me doubt about
the graces or confirmation I had received."[115] In other letters, Ignatius
promoted church practices that would be favored by Le Picart.
Writing in November, 1543 to Teresa Rejadell, Ignatius counseled:

Regarding daily Communion, we should recall that in the early Church
everybody received daily, and that since that time there has been no

---

[111] Ignatius of Loyola, *Spiritual Exercises*, ed. Puhl, 142.
[112] Ibid, 144.
[113] Ignatius of Loyola, *Spiritual Exercises and Selected Works*, ed. Ganss, 263–264.
[114] Ibid, 231.
[115] Ibid, 250.

ordinance or document of our Holy Mother the Church or of the holy
doctors, either positive or scholastic, against a person's being able to
receive Communion daily if so moved by devotion . . . That is, given
that all things are lawful for you in our Lord, if—barring obvious mortal sin or anything you can deem to be such—you judge that your
soul derives more help and is more inflamed with love for our Creator
and Lord, and if you receive Communion with this intention, having
found by experience that this spiritual food offers you sustenance, peace,
and tranquility, preserving and advancing you in his greater service,
praise, and glory, so that you have no doubt about this, then it is licit,
and indeed would be better, for you to receive Communion every day.[116]

The early Jesuit writings appear to be a summary of François Le
Picart's life and preaching. The themes enunciated of personal sanctity, a simple preaching based on the New Testament aimed at win-
ning souls, correction of abuses within the church,[117] the importance
of proper and empathic confession for both priest and penitent[118]
and frequent communion[119] all dominated Le Picart's ministry.
Sometimes the words are almost identical. Just as Le Picart counseled that where the eucharist was under attack good Catholics must
frequent it all the more, Laínez wrote, ". . . you condemn confession, and I will confess my sins all the more frequently."[120] For both
the Jesuits and Le Picart, their mission was overwhelmingly one of
consolation, for they ". . . believed in a world in which God's grace
was abundant. God willed all to be saved and had embraced the
world with even greater love because of the life, death and resurrection of Jesus Christ."[121] The Jesuits frequently expounded on the
theme of human dignity.[122] Not content to spout platitudes, they
worked to help the needy, and consecrated a significant part of their
mission to the poor and the outcast.[123] Even on specific points, Le
Picart's sermons are very close to what all of the early Jesuits were
saying. While Jesuits focused on practices attacked by Protestants,[124]
Mary played a lesser role than she had in late medieval Catholicism.[125]

---

[116] Ibid, 340–341.
[117] O'Malley, *First Jesuits*, 277, 305.
[118] Ibid, 142.
[119] Ibid, 96, 153.
[120] Quoted in ibid, 278.
[121] Ibid, 84; cf. ibid, 19, 82, 141.
[122] Ibid, 250.
[123] Ibid, 72, 167.
[124] Ibid, 272.
[125] Ibid, 266–267, 269.

And in striking contrast to many contemporaries, the Jesuits showed little interest in predictions of the "end times" or apocalyptic thinking.[126] Their pedagogical methods reflected how they had learned from Le Picart—they both preached and lectured, but according to the *Constitutions*, ". . . when Jesuits preached or delivered 'sacred lectures,' they were not to do so in 'the scholastic manner.' "[127] Their cardinal rule of preaching was to make it fit the circumstances of the audience.[128] Nadal argued for the study of Hebrew and Greek but ". . . added that those languages should be used to defend the Vulgate against its calumniators."[129] Finally, Lynn Martin has remarked that a ". . . somewhat surprising aspect of the Jesuit confrontation with Protestantism was the moderation of their sermons . . ."[130]

Le Picart's sermons convey an almost wholly positive and reassuring image of God. Absent is the intentional ambivalence of late medieval preaching, in which the promise of heavenly paradise was juxtaposed against terrifying depictions of hell, purgatory, and the Judgment.[131] Le Picart's God is presented in relational terms, most often as a loving father. "We are adopted into the family of God, and are made His children, because through the inspiration that the Holy Spirit gives us, we cry for God, as a child cries for his father."[132] A child who is with his father or his mother is happy, and does not fear bad things will happen to him, just as one who is loved by the king fears no ill from his master.[133] Through the merits of Jesus Christ and faith "we are adopted children of God, and are certain that God is completely good . . ."[134] Le Picart uses physical, affective imagery to describe God's love. "He embraces and kisses us,"[135] he says. "We are enfolded in the arms of God our father."[136] Le Picart cannot

---

[126] Ibid, 269, 372.

[127] Ibid, 98.

[128] Ibid, 112.

[129] Ibid, 257.

[130] A. Lynn Martin, "The Jesuit Émond Auger and the Saint Bartholomew's Massacre at Bordeaux: The Final Word," in Jerome Friedman, ed., *Regnum, Religio et Ratio: Essays Presented to Robert M. Kingdon* (Kirksville, MO: Sixteenth Century Essays and Studies, 1987), 120; cf. O'Malley, *First Jesuits*, 71.

[131] Sermons by Vincent Ferrier and Jean Tisserand typify this kind of preaching. See Taylor, *Soldiers of Christ*, 93–101.

[132] Le Picart, *Instruction*, 15; cf. ibid, 154; *Trinité*, fol. 77; *Trinité*, fol. 37.

[133] Le Picart, *Advent*, fol. 127.

[134] Le Picart, *Instruction*, 12.

[135] Le Picart, *Trinité*, fol. 20.

[136] Le Picart, *Advent*, fol. 285.

understand women and men who do not rejoice in this great good: "Why are you so sad? Consider that you are a daughter of God, who shows you so many signs of love, and who only asks for your salvation! He is your justification, your sanctification, and your salvation."[137] This model provides a prescription for Christian behavior, for "a good child does what he knows will please his father, and flees from that which will displease him; he adapts himself to the will of his father."[138] In a happy family, it is a father's consolation to see his children living well,[139] and this is reciprocal—no one is more dear to the child than his father.[140] Why then does God send trouble and tribulations to his children? Although God does not want to do this, it is a sign of love. "When a father punishes his child, he shows that he loves him well"[141] for otherwise the child will abandon himself to all sorts of evils.[142] He gives an example that would be relevant to many of his listeners: "When a father doesn't want to give his son money to play tennis, as so many students do instead of their lessons, . . . this is certainly not a sign of hatred, but of goodwill."[143] Sometimes it is even necessary for a good father to tempt, vex and try his child.[144] "If the father doesn't correct him, it is a sign that he is a bastard, and that his father doesn't love him. So God, who is our good father, who loves us, and does all for the profit and salvation of his own, sends adversities and tribulations to those he loves and has made his children."[145] Taking the analogy farther, he adds that "when the child is legitimate, he resembles his father."[146]

God wants his children to approach him:

> If I were at the table of the King, I would tremble in seeing His Majesty, and would not dare to say a single word. But if he said to me, "speak boldly, I give you leave, and order you to speak," then I would no longer be shy. Our Lord Jesus Christ is so great a master

---

[137] Le Picart, *SL*, 70.
[138] Le Picart, *Pasques*, fol. 22. Cf. "The small child presents himself to his father with humility, in the faith he has in him, and shows him that he loves him. So assure yourself of God, who is your good father . . ." Ibid, fol. 23.
[139] Le Picart, *Trinité*, fol. 232.
[140] Le Picart, *Instruction*, 65.
[141] Le Picart, *Trinité*, fol. 33.
[142] Le Picart, *Pasques*, fol. 42.
[143] Le Picart, *Trinité*, fol. 234.
[144] Le Picart, *Instruction*, 236.
[145] Le Picart, *Pasques*, fol. 42.
[146] Le Picart, *Trinité*, fol. 222.

and lord and we are so small, so little in regard to Him, that it is like
a grain of sand next to a mountain. And if I consider my indignity
and the majesty of God, I tremble, and dare not go to Him. But God
doesn't want that, and He gives us the privilege that a father gives to
his son to come to him. He tells us to call him Our Father, which is
a name of love and assurance.[147]

Prayer is simply a talk with God. Le Picart exclaims, "Our Lord
Jesus Christ says, "Ask and you will receive, look and you will find,
knock on the door and it will be opened to you."[148] One should not
demand things of God, but ask with humility or state one's problems, as when Martha and Mary approached the Lord on the
approaching death of their brother Lazarus. "They did not demand,
'Come with us!' but said simply, 'Your friend is sick.'"[149] God never
denies what is good for his children, but always knows what is best.

> You often see a child asking for something from his father. If he doesn't
> get what he wants, he shouldn't think his father doesn't love him. The
> father did this because he knew that what the child asked for was not
> for his good and salvation. So when Our Lord does not give us what
> we ask for, this does not mean He doesn't love us, but is rather a
> sign that what we have asked for is not good.[150]

Quoting Chrysostom, Le Picart assures his listeners that when a father
see his child in necessity, he gives him what he needs, but not
"strange or extravagant" things that will only cause him harm.[151] He
tells his listeners that they must trust in God's wisdom and promise:
"Our Lord Jesus Christ gives us the example of the father in a family. If his child asks for bread, he doesn't give him a stone. If he
asks for fish, he doesn't give him a snake. If he asks for an egg, he
doesn't give him a spider. And if you—which is no small thing—
know how to give good things to your children, how much more so
does your celestial Father!" Patience and tenacity are the keys to
effective prayer. He continues: "However much He refuses us, it is
necessary to put a good face on it, when He closes the door just as
when He opens it."[152] Sometimes one must ask several times, but if
God continues to refuse it is a sign that the object of the prayer is

---

[147] Le Picart, *Pasques*, fols. 274–275.
[148] Le Picart, *Instruction*, 146.
[149] Le Picart, *Trinité*, fol. 186.
[150] Le Picart, *Instruction*, 150; cf. ibid, 19.
[151] Le Picart, *Trinité*, fol. 51.
[152] Ibid, fol. 88.

detrimental to one's salvation.[153] The simple act of speaking with God is beneficial. Just as the ability to speak with the king all day and night shows the favor in which one is held, so speaking with God is the most special form of grace.[154]

Although paternal imagery dominates in the sermons, Le Picart also refers to God as a good friend, a teacher, and a loving brother.[155] He uses the favorite medieval analogy of the body, saying "we are the limbs, and He is our head, and our life depends on it, just like our limbs live and depend on the head and the heart."[156] But God also has agents who look out for human beings. Le Picart frequently mentions guardian angels, "who watch over and lead each person, to aid the free will of man and help him find salvation."[157] He asks his listeners,

> Haven't you wanted to go someplace or other, and someone tells you not to go, and then some bad thing happens, so you will say that the good angel kept you from going there? Sometimes you don't want to go to a sermon, and someone tells you, "My friend, let us go to the sermon," and afterwards you will say, "I certainly don't regret going." It's the good angel who told you to go and hear the words of the preacher.[158]

He compares guardian angels to tutors,[159] sent to help and console human beings in times of tribulation.[160]

Le Picart's God is above all a consoling figure. He explains that "the Holy Spirit is called the *paraclite*, that is, consoler, because it consoles our souls, it assures our consciences that Paradise is for us, and brings us full testimony that we are children of God."[161] God's only will and intention is to deliver human beings from evil, and restore to them the great goodness of his love.[162] "Isn't it a marvelous thing," he asks, "that in place of punishing us He gives us an abundance of mercy?"[163] God's promise means that all who turn

---

[153] Le Picart, *Instruction*, 149.
[154] Le Picart, *Trinité*, fol. 235; *Instruction*, 34.
[155] Le Picart, *SL*, 111.
[156] Le Picart, *Trinité*, fol. 65.
[157] Le Picart, *Caresme*, fol. 109; cf. *SL*, 88.
[158] Le Picart, *Trinité-II*, fol. 126.
[159] Le Picart, *Caresme-II*, fol. 165.
[160] Le Picart, *Trinité-II*, fol. 125.
[161] Le Picart, *Trinité*, fol. 10.
[162] Le Picart, *Caresme*, fol. 65.
[163] Le Picart, *Trinité*, fol. 125.

to him, just or sinners, will not be rejected.[164] For unlike humans,
God "never dismisses or leaves those who place their heart and hope
in Him, because He is faithful, and has promised this, and without
any question He will do this through His grace and great goodness."[165] God's fidelity stands in stark contrast to the faithlessness of
earthly men and women: "Everyday He is injured by us, blasphemed,
and condemned, and yet He never stops nourishing us . . ."[166] Le
Picart again draws an analogy with kingship: "Just as when the
Emperor comes to France, the king confers on him benefices and
offices, so God does this for each of His creatures."[167] Like a good
king who ". . . has his palace open, go to Him, He will give you
what you need . . . One must not fear, because Jesus Christ will assure
you . . ."[168] The good Christian should believe firmly that God is
good, and does everything for our benefit, so that we will not fall
into despair.[169]

Le Picart describes how God's love and wrath work, dividing God's
behavior according to the old and the new covenants:

> The law of Moses was a law of fear and servitude. And the law of
> the gospel is a law of grace, liberty and remission. It is a law that
> frees us from fear and puts us in full confidence of Jesus Christ. In
> the new law, our Lord does not want to hold us by fear. That's not
> to say it is not necessary to have some fear, but the point is that he
> wants to gain us by love. . . . A person who is in a state of grace does
> things freely and with good heart; he has no difficulty following the
> law because he does it from love and not fear.[170]

He insists that the Jews followed the law only through force and
fear,[171] not voluntarily. In almost every sermon, Le Picart asserts that
rigor is ineffective, that love is the only way to gain hearts.[172] Furthermore, he affirms that "since the coming of our Lord it is easier to
be saved than in times past."[173] The Law of Moses, which menaced
people,[174] was defective, because it was only a figure, a representa-

---

[164] Ibid, fol. 18.
[165] Le Picart, *Caresme*, fol. 175.
[166] Le Picart, *Advent*, fol. 182.
[167] Ibid, fol. 103.
[168] Le Picart, *Trinité*, fol. 248.
[169] Ibid, fol. 175; *Instruction*, 152, 183.
[170] Le Picart, *Advent*, fol. 40.
[171] Le Picart, *Caresme-II*, fol. 4; Le Picart, *Instruction*, 61.
[172] Ibid, fol. 129.
[173] Le Picart, *Advent*, fol. 10.
[174] Le Picart, *Caresme-II*, fol. 7.

tion of the Gospel, "in which we are delivered from this servitude and made children of God."[175] If the Jews lived in fear, by contrast Christians live by love, in freedom.[176] Since the Christian era began, God has not wanted to exert force, because such a love will be empty.[177] "To obey by fear, out of fear of being punished, renders a man a serf. He does not enjoy true liberty. But to obey by love and charity frees a man from slavery . . ."[178]

Still, in his role as preacher and confessor, Le Picart was regularly faced by men and women whose consciences were troubled.

> If we have good faith and hope in God, we will not have so much anxiety in our spirits . . . You see some who in one day go four or five times to confession, and at the last they are as anxious as at the first. Have good faith in God, and resolve not to commit mortal or venial sins. In having hope and goodwill, do not be disturbed. Yet it is amazing how agitated and fainthearted we are![179]

Le Picart warns his flock that despair is "the consummation of all evil and sin,"[180] a great fault that indicates a person has no experience of God.[181] He soothes them with the knowledge that no spiritual malady or sin is incurable,[182] for God never asks something that a person cannot do: "Whatever poverty or weakness that he sees in himself, he must always have more confidence and hope in the goodness and compassion of God, who is all powerful and completely good, and who wants to help him so that he can do his duty as best he can, and so that he will never despair nor doubt the bounty and compassion of God."[183] Le Picart asks his listeners if they believe God is a tyrant or an executioner:[184] "Have confidence in and lean on our Lord Jesus Christ. Believe in the good counsel he has given you. Believe that God is good. Do you really believe he wants to damn you if you do the best you can in light of human weakness? That the justice of God is more cruel than the justice of men?"[185] He offers the examples of great sinners like Magdalene who through

---

[175] Le Picart, *Advent*, fol. 194.
[176] Le Picart, *Trinité*, fol. 117.
[177] Le Picart, *Caresme*, fol. 99.
[178] Le Picart, *Pasques*, fol. 62.
[179] Le Picart, *Instruction*, 152.
[180] Le Picart, *Pasques*, fol. 330.
[181] Le Picart, *Caresme*, fol. 57; *Trinité*, fol. 51.
[182] Le Picart, *Caresme*, fol. 158.
[183] Ibid, fol. 20.
[184] Ibid, fol. 90; *Advent*, fol. 285.
[185] Ibid, fol. 157.

faith, love, and repentance rose from the depths to be among the highest in God's esteem.[186] Men and women must know that God places no limits on repentance, but always waits with open arms:[187] "He does not put a time limit or a term or a required place for us to repent."[188] By contrast, the devil incites humans to despair: "The devil puts our faults before our eyes to discourage us from going to God. Look therefore more to His bounty and liberality than to your faults and sins. Then you will find yourself reassured in Him. Consider the great boon He gave to the thief on the cross!"[189] Doubt and despair cause agitation and disquiet in the soul:[190] "A heart that is filled with good hope is always joyous, but one with no hope is always sad, and melancholy."[191] Le Picart insists there is no reason for dejection: "You say you would rather die than do evil. Why then do you fear and upset yourself? Be assured of God and you will find contentment and tranquility of spirit."[192] If the magnitude or multitude of one's sins seems insurmountable, Le Picart counsels the penitent to start with small steps, changing the will from evildoing to good.[193] "If I undertake to go to Rome, I should do it little by little . . ."[194]

Le Picart offers consolation by discussing the nature of man. Naturally, he begins with the Fall. Yet in his sermons there is surprisingly little emphasis on the disobedience in the Garden of Eden.[195] Le Picart says that man in the postlapsarian state is "unstable, weak and impotent,"[196] by inclination more prone to evil than good.[197] Oddly, this can be the basis for reassurance: "By these examples,

---

[186] Le Picart, *Trinité*, fol. 69; *Caresme*, fol. 10.
[187] Le Picart, *Trinité-II*, fol. 107.
[188] Le Picart, *Pasques*, fol. 264.
[189] Le Picart, *SL*, 112.
[190] Le Picart, *Instruction*, fols. 16, 148.
[191] Le Picart, *Advent*, fol. 34.
[192] Ibid, fol. 265.
[193] Le Picart, *Caresme*, fol. 64.
[194] Le Picart, *Pasques*, fol. 24.
[195] One of the few examples is fairly matter of fact: "If Adam had persisted in the righteousness in which God created him, however much Eve might have sinned, still their children would not have lost their rectitude and innocence. But since Adam offended, he is constituted the chief of all sin, but Eve helped him. He left his children this mortgage; he wasted the inheritance of his children." Le Picart, *Advent*, fol. 59.
[196] Le Picart, *Pasques*, fol. 77.
[197] Le Picart, *Advent*, fol. 3.

you can see and know the fragility of man, who so often succumbs to temptation."[198] When a person recognizes his own weakness, he can then turn to God. Sounding remarkably like Luther, Le Picart says, ". . . we are all sinners . . . There is not one of us who is just before Him . . ."[199] But when "we see that we are bad and inclined to evil, we should humble ourselves with contrition in our heart and offer our poverty [of soul] to Our Lord."[200]

At the same time, this formulation allows Le Picart to emphasize the inherent dignity of human beings, for God created human beings to be saved and does not wish to damn anyone.[201] In terms that show his humanistic training and a knowledge of Pico della Mirandola's work,[202] Le Picart explains this is natural in view of why and how God created man: "When it came to creating man, he did not say, *Fiat!* But he put his own hand to it and said *Faciamus!* . . . 'We make man in our image and similitude.' It is as if God said, 'This is my masterpiece, it's here I will stop and put my grace more abundantly than in all other creatures.' Man was created last, as the end of all creatures."[203] Created in the image of God, human beings are capable of reaching upward to God, something given to no other creature.[204] This is the great happiness of man, that he has an *a priori* conception of God: "You see that there is no difference between the brute beasts and man, except that man is capable of God, he has reason and knowledge of God . . . He can raise his senses to know God. Oh! In this consists the happiness and the life of man!"[205] Le Picart tells his listeners that "we are the temple of God,"[206] with "the vestige of the Holy Trinity imprinted on the soul."[207] People must

---

[198] Le Picart, *Instruction*, 254, cf. ibid, 257.

[199] Le Picart, *Caresme*, fol. 3; *Instruction*, 199.

[200] Le Picart, *Advent*, fol. 207.

[201] Le Picart, *SL*, 98; cf. Ibid, 101; *Trinité*, fols. 18, 201; *Instruction*, 183; *Caresme*, fol. 40.

[202] Such a familiarity would have been natural for any student at the University of Paris. Pico had studied there in 1485, and contemporaries of Le Picart trying to refute the criticisms of Erasmus and Lefèvre would point out that Pico had not disdained the beliefs of the Middle Ages. Renaudet, "L'humanisme," 135, 153. Interestingly, this also shows connections between Le Picart and Lefèvre d'Étaples, who had been in close contact with Pico. Denis Crouzet states that "Christ is, for Lefèvre, goodness." Crouzet, *Genèse*, 95.

[203] Le Picart, *Pasques*, fol. 49.

[204] Ibid, fol. 72; *Instruction*, 64.

[205] Le Picart, *Trinité*, fol. 1.

[206] Ibid, fol. 65.

[207] Le Picart, *Advent*, fol. 52.

give thanks, for "... you see the birds, who pray to God in their songs ... The birds and other creatures praise God, but man doesn't appreciate that God has given him such great grace."[208] He adds, "even without seeing the worker, the painter, if you only see his painting, you can see that he is a good and very industrious painter."[209]

Since the Fall, humans have been like "strangers and pilgrims, travelers in a strange land,"[210] who should desire nothing more than reunion with God. Quoting Chrysostom, Le Picart claims that the greatest pain of all is this separation from God.[211] He employs familial imagery, asking,

> isn't this a terrible pain for a man to be excommunicated and separated from the society of Christians? And how much more to be separated from the vision of God? Never to see God in the face, God who is all perfection, bounty, joy, beauty and felicity, God who is so great that one does not how to speak of it or even think of it? What sadness for a child to be separated from his father and mother![212]

Still, the feelings a person has for the absent loved one can make difficult things tolerable.[213] It helps to remember that the world is illusory—"it is like a mirror that promises many things that turn out not to be true. The true mirror is holy scripture."[214] On earth, one can only see God as if reflected in a mirror, his image obscured;[215] the commission of venial sins delays the moment when a man or woman will see God without filters or illusions.[216] Le Picart compares the human condition to that of

> the children of Israel ... when they were captives in Babylon ... wondering, "How will we sing the song of the Lord in an alien land? So we who are in this world on earth and in a foreign country on the banks of Babylon, in a transitory world, how will we be able to rejoice?" You too will say, "How will I be able to rejoice in a strange land, full of miseries and calamities, in which we are always in danger of offending God and being damned forever without end?" I say that it is necessary to rejoice in the good hope of our Lord, that it will please

---

[208] Le Picart, *Pasques*, fol. 172.
[209] Le Picart, *Trinité*, fol. 3.
[210] Le Picart, *Pasques*, fol. 31.
[211] Le Picart, *Trinité*, fol. 63.
[212] Le Picart, *Trinité*, fol. 63.
[213] Le Picart, *Trinité-II*, fol. 135.
[214] Le Picart, *Trinité*, fol. 50.
[215] Le Picart, *Advent*, fol. 196; *Trinité*, fol. 1.
[216] Le Picart, *Instruction*, 265, 268.

Him through His grace, goodness and pity to return us to our homeland, which we had to leave.[217]

Like Ignatius, Le Picart regularly uses the imagery of pilgrims trying to find their way back to God. "You are not of Paris," he shouts,
"but pilgrims!"[218] He asks his people, "If you lose a dog, or a legal
pouch, or some similar thing, isn't it true that you will spare nothing to have it cried through the streets and the quarters of the
city? . . ."[219] More than anything, he urges his listeners to ask God
to restore the great good they have lost.[220]

Occasionally, Le Picart's oratory verges on the mystical. He speaks
of "my heart inflamed in God . . .,"[221] telling his listeners to "give
Him your body, your soul."[222] The process of living in God is all-
consuming: "Charity transforms a person in God, it makes him be
more in God than in himself. For a man who loves someone, all
his thoughts, his heart, his affection is spent on his friend, and he
can think of nothing else. He is therefore more part of the one he
loves than of himself."[223] Le Picart calls on his listeners to return to
the greatest good possible for a human being—union with and adher-
ence to the spirit of God.[224] Prayer and meditation bring a person
closer to God, as does participation in the eucharist, for in the mass
". . . the precious body of Jesus Christ is so intimately united to us
that we are made as one, Jesus Christ and us. What goodness! What
surplus of love He shows us by this!"[225]

What then could be known of God? Le Picart describes God as
the source from which all things proceed,[226] but admits that it is
difficult to imagine God: "It is easier to say what God is not, than
what He is, because one cannot explain or define the name of God.
He is ineffable, Christians!"[227] God, he says, is immortal, impassive,
immutable, all powerful, all good, and aids humans in their tribulations

---

[217] Le Picart, *Pasques*, fol. 5.
[218] Le Picart, *Trinité*, fol. 66; cf. *Trinité-II*, fol. 176; *Pasques*, fol. 32; *SL*, 88.
[219] Le Picart, *Caresme-II*, fol. 167.
[220] Le Picart, *Caresme*, fol. 65.
[221] Le Picart, *Instruction*, 153.
[222] Le Picart, *SL*, 213.
[223] Le Picart, *Pasques*, fol. 101.
[224] Le Picart, *Advent*, fol. 29.
[225] Le Picart, *SL*, 185.
[226] Le Picart, *Trinité*, fol. 6.
[227] Ibid, fol. 3.

and necessities.[228] But he warns against conceptualizing God in anthropomorphic terms. God is not enclosed in a space, but is ". . . everywhere . . . God is spirit, a spiritual substance . . ."[229] If we accept God's omnipresence, "it expands our heart to love Him, and turns our affection to Him."[230] "It is often said, that God gets angry, but not like a man or by feelings, but by effects. Because one finds no passion in God."[231]

The sermons are so filled with the examples of God's goodness that it would be impossible to overstate the case. Adjectives such as good, merciful, compassionate, supportive, sustaining, faithful, bountiful, liberal, kind, consoling, gracious and forgiving leap out from almost every page. Le Picart adduces as proof of God's great love for his creation his willingness to send Jesus Christ to die for the sins of humanity and help man return to his original dignity: "Our Lord Jesus Christ was crucified and died in order to gather us together and reunite us, we who had been dispersed, divided and alienated from our God."[232] His coming announced to every single person the remission of their sins and the grace given by God.[233] Le Picart presents Jesus as the companion one needs on this grand pilgrimage:

After having passed through the dangerous passages and escaped them,

> we will know that we could never have done so without having Jesus Christ as our companion, who is faithful and loyal. He was not content to be simply our companion, so He gave himself fully to us, as a servant in our necessity. This is incredible charity, not only to want to be our companion on the road, but also to serve us in our necessity.[234]

People should lean on God who,[235] like a great lord "takes a village and puts it under His protection, so that passing soldiers will do no evil there."[236]

To Le Picart, Jesus is the doctor of the soul. "If there is a doctor in the city who cures all maladies, everyone would go to him!

---

[228] Le Picart, *Instruction*, 78.
[229] Le Picart, *Trinité*, fol. 3.
[230] Le Picart, *Instruction*, 72.
[231] Le Picart, *Trinité*, fol. 199.
[232] Le Picart, *Caresme-II*, fol. 92; cf. *SL*, 100.
[233] Le Picart, *Caresme*, fol. 19; *Instruction*, 158.
[234] Le Picart, *Épistre*, fol. 22.
[235] Le Picart, *Instruction*, 152.
[236] Ibid, 82.

This doctor is Jesus Christ . . ."[237] Speaking of the sick men who followed Jesus, Le Picart asks, "And what was their faith? They had heard that Jesus Christ was a man who was compassionate, clement, friendly, flexible, full of goodness, ready to relieve and aid those who came to Him."[238]

Jesus is also a friend. "He is near us. He is in us. He lives in us. He loves us sincerely. And when He sees that we are in need and necessity He helps us."[239] Whenever and wherever a person comes to Him with a contrite heart, Jesus will pardon his sins.[240] He even looks the other way: "Our Lord Jesus Christ pretends and acts like He does not see our faults, much like when a school teacher doesn't punish someone right away, so that it seems that he has not noticed."[241] This is an incredible boon for humanity. When you believe, "all [your] bad fantasies will vanish; you will fear no more, and will feel complete assurance."[242] Le Picart cannot help adding that God is *so* good that he even wants Martin Luther to be saved![243]

It is this knowledge of and belief in God that prepares one for the trials and tribulations of the world. Having endured his full share of slings and arrows, Le Picart counsels people to rejoice in tribulation as a sign of God's grace.[244] "When He afflicts you, He always makes His grace and mercy exceed the punishment and affliction."[245] One must suffer in patience, like Job, rather than murmuring against God,[246] for the greater the cross, the more agreeable the human action.[247] He uses the analogy of a pregnant woman to prove his point: "A woman would rather suffer the pains of childbirth than to carry her child forever!"[248] But what should one make of bad things happening to good people? They provide assurance of the life to come: "God is just, and the prosperity of evil ones and the tribulations of the good lead us to understand that there will be another

---

[237] Le Picart, *Trinité*, fol. 20; cf. ibid, fol. 101.
[238] Ibid, fol. 111.
[239] Le Picart, *Advent*, fol. 127.
[240] Le Picart, *Caresme-II*, fol. 3.
[241] Le Picart, *Advent*, fol. 51.
[242] Le Picart, *Pasques*, fol. 11.
[243] Le Picart, *Caresme*, fol. 111.
[244] Le Picart, *Trinité*, fol. 196.
[245] Ibid, fol. 125.
[246] Le Picart, *Instruction*, 28.
[247] Le Picart, *Trinité*, fol. 52.
[248] Le Picart, *Pasques*, fol. 43.

time, that of the future resurrection, and without which we could not endure."[249] He doubts that those who prosper in this world have much hope of eternal life:

> Saint Ambrose, traveling through the country, sometimes happened to lodge in the house of a rich man. . . . He asked his host about his estate, and the man told him that he had everything that he desired and that God loved him well, for he had never had any adversity and his goods had multiplied marvelously. His wife never contradicted him in anything, and he had good children. Saint Ambrose, hearing these words, said to his people and his companions, "Let us leave here . . . because where there is no tribulation and adversity, it is a sign that God is not there." . . . [After that,] fire descended from the sky and destroyed the house and those who were within it.[250]

These words offered great comfort to faithful Catholics who felt increasingly threatened. But Le Picart wanted people to do everything in their power to make themselves ready to meet God, both in the eucharist and the afterlife. He tells his listeners it is almost impossible to go through this mortal life without committing venial sins:[251] "if we say that we have not sinned we are deceived and have very little truthfulness in us. Who is the man who can say he is without sin?"[252] Yet he urges his listeners not to jump to the conclusion that they have committed a mortal sin, for ". . . before a sin can be mortal, there must be deliberation. When there is no deliberation, God excuses it, if the person does not regularly do bad things."[253] God judges intentions:[254] "Sin does not harm a person when he wants to amend himself."[255] However insufficient it is for salvation, the Law nonetheless provides a place to begin, followed by the message of the gospels.[256] Emphasizing the moral of the Great Commandment, Le Picart advises that concern for one's neighbor is the mark of a true Christian. "Just like your celestial Father is merciful to you, so be merciful to your neighbor."[257] If he has committed an offense,

---

[249] Le Picart, *Trinité*, fol. 152.
[250] Le Picart, *Instruction*, 241.
[251] Ibid, 202.
[252] Ibid, 200.
[253] Ibid, 270.
[254] Le Picart, *Advent*, fol. 288; *Trinité*, fol. 31.
[255] Le Picart, *Advent*, fol. 298.
[256] Le Picart, *Trinité*, fol. 93.
[257] Ibid, fol. 34.

pardon him, just as you wish God to pardon you.[258] When a person accepts his frailty and weakness, he can begin to comprehend his need for God, and can rely on God's promise.[259] The serenity of spirit that results from turning yourself over completely to God is a sign that God has called for you.[260] "So you must have a good heart and be firm in your belief in God, because when the devil sees that through some temptations we are not at all moved, he will go away, leaving us alone. But if we vacillate and dispute among ourselves and are troubled, then the devil will rejoice . . ."[261]

We cannot know who gained the most from the interaction between the early Jesuits and François Le Picart. It is perhaps more fruitful to ask what they found in each other. Why, when Bobadilla railed against scholastic theology and the lack of pastoral care shown by the theologians of Paris, did he single out Le Picart as one whose preaching and teaching was different? The angry Le Picart of 1533–1534 who has often been referred to as a comrade of the reactionary Noël Beda does not seem like the type of man who would have appealed to these earnest, humanistically-trained men who had embarked on a personal spiritual and mystical quest. Yet appeal to them he did, a testament to the complexity of the man. More than most of the earliest Jesuits, Le Picart was engaged in the fight against heresy, because he had to deal with its consequences every day. At the same time, we must not forget the young man who had been encouraged by his cousin Guillaume Budé to persevere in his study of Greek. Everything in Le Picart's sermons shows how fully he had imbibed the humanist criticism of the church, and was incorporating the new learning into his preaching. As a "humanistic non-humanist," a man who had studied Greek and the classics, and integrated the new learning into his own preaching, Le Picart was able to criticize the excesses and irresponsibility he saw in men such as Erasmus. Yet Le Picart's attention to his pastoral duties, his simplicity of style, and his optimistic outlook made him a man of a new generation.[262] He had been formed in what Jean-Claude Margolin calls they "heyday of French humanism, 1480–1540," a period marked by ". . . an

---

[258] Le Picart, *Instruction*, 207.
[259] Ibid, 39, 148.
[260] Le Picart, *Advent*, fol. 220.
[261] Le Picart, *Instruction*, 27.
[262] Taylor, "Influence of Humanism," 133.

emphasis on the study of authors and texts, [when] certain historical traditions were called into question, myths were scrutinized, and
a critical approach was adopted in all areas of research, including
sacred biblical texts.[263] If he did not accept uncritically all that humanism professed, that does not change Le Picart's fundamental orien-
tation toward new methods. For the early Jesuits who had also learned
and grown in that climate, Le Picart was a model of what a Catholic
preacher and teacher could and should be in the wake of the Protestant
Reformation. If he was still somewhat unique in France, other Catholic
preachers of the time, especially in Italy, were incorporating ideals
of humility, criticism of abuses, and humanism into their preaching.[264]

Thanks to his friendship and work with the Jesuits, Le Picart broad-
ened his conception of God's goodness and imbued his listeners with
a sense of consolation and hope even in the troubled times in which
they were living. In almost every subject treated in his sermons except
perhaps heresy, Le Picart expressed views that exactly paralleled
those of the earliest Jesuits. In their fledgling movement, Le Picart
saw the remedy for so many of the ills of the Catholic Church,
which he believed had allowed heresy to spread roots. In one sermon, he seems to refer directly to the mission that he was not personally able to undertake: "The holy land of Jerusalem is now in
the hands of the infidel. I fear too that we are wavering, and that
Christianity is instead going to the islands, and to new lands . . ."[265]

---

[263] Jean-Claude Margolin, "Humanism in France," in Anthony Goodman and
Angus MacKay, eds., *The Impact of Humanism on Western Europe* (New York: Longman,
1990), 164.
[264] See Corrie E. Norman, *Humanist Taste and Franciscan Values: Cornelio Musso and
Catholic Preaching in Sixteenth-Century Italy* (New York: Peter Lang, 1998). Musso's dates
(1511–1574) make him a slightly younger contemporary of Le Picart.
[265] Le Picart, *Trinité*, fol. 165.

CHAPTER SIX

CATHOLIC REFORM

> Going to preach one day, Le Picart ran into a
> poor man completely naked and wet; he called to
> him, drew him aside and gave him the habits he
> was wearing to clothe him, and not satisfied with
> this he gave him alms as well.[1]

It would be easy to dismiss this incident as evidence of the zealous
partisanship of contemporary Catholics and a seventeenth-century
hagiographer, but even hostile sources admitted that "... to his faults
must be added virtues no less popular. This terrible persecutor was
a gentleman, and a very good man. He never wanted to receive any
compensation from the church. He had a charity so perfect that he
was considered the father of the poor and the downtrodden."[2]

Never had the Roman Catholic Church needed men who led by
example as much as it did in the wake of the Protestant Reformation.
Efforts to reform the church from within had been attempted since
the middle of the fifteenth century with little long-term success.
Observantine monastic leaders and men whom Augustin Renaudet
dubbed "prereformers," including Olivier Maillard, Jean Raulin and
Jan Standonck, had all tried in the fifteenth and early sixteenth century to lift the church and churchmen out of the morass into which
they had sunk as a result of the crisis of the fourteenth century.[3]

---

[1] Hilarion de Coste, *Parfait ecclesiastique*, 57.

[2] Doumergue, *Calvin*, I:241.

[3] See Renaudet, *Préréforme et humanisme*; M. Piton, "L'idéal épiscopal selon les
prédicateurs français de la fin du XVᵉ siècle et du début du XVIᵉ," *Revue d'histoire
de l'église de France* (1966), 77–118, 393–423; Marcel Godet, "Consultation de Tours
pour la réforme de l'église de France (12 novembre 1493)," *Revue d'histoire de l'église
de France* 2(1911), 175–196, 333–348; Marcel Godet, *La congrégation de Montaigu
(1490–1580)* (Paris: Honoré Champion, 1912); Bernard Chevalier, "Olivier Maillard
et la réforme des Cordeliers (1482–1502)," *Revue d'histoire de l'église de France* 65(1979),
25–39; Raymond Darricau, "La réforme des reguliers en France de la fin du XVᵉ
siècle à la fin des guerres de religion," *Revue d'histoire de l'église de France* 65(1979),
5–12; G. Godineau, "Statuts synodaux inédits du diocèse de Bourges promulgués
par Jean Coeur en 1451," *Revue d'histoire de l'église de France* 72(1986), 49–66; Arlette

The results were less than inspiring. While on the one hand the French church had prodigious wealth and lands on the eve of the Reformation, the lower clergy was too often uneducated and poverty-stricken, causing one historian to refer to this large group as a "clerical proletariat."[4] Most bishops did not reside in their dioceses; absenteeism and pluralism were rampant. Nor were these the only sins. Baumgartner gives the following examples, which were all too common:

> The Parlement of Provence once had to compel an archbishop of Arles to give alms to the victims of a great flood of the Rhône. Drunkenness was another problem, exemplified by the prelate called "the Cardinal of Bottles." But as usually has been the case, sexual incontinence was the most common vice. Concubines and illegitimate children were common for the prelates. Brantome, the eager gossipmonger who loved to tell tales on the hierarchy, told of one bishop who, "in order to build up his harem," gave pensions to ten-year-old girls so they would be available to him when they were older. Although the lower clergy did not share in the opulent life-style of the prelates, the same vices were very evident.[5]

Part of the problem was that reform-minded individuals, such as Josse Clichtove, were unwilling to take specific individuals to task for their failings. Although he regularly criticized the lower clergy, ". . . with respect to his superiors, his criticism was occasional, reserved and rendered in private."[6] This kind of reticence did not necessarily indicate timidity or fear of reprisals, but rather concern at making a bad situation worse—after the Reformation criticism of the hierarchy could not only open one to charges of Lutheranism, but also give ammunition to the heretics. Yet the hierarchy, especially, the bishops, were a major part of the problem. As Baumgartner has shown, French bishops not only did *not* set the example they should, but also took few steps to stem the rising tide of Protestantism.[7] The latter problem was especially severe in the capital. Bishops Étienne Poncher, Le Picart's cousin, and Jean DuBellay were very open to

---

Jouanna, *La France du XVIᵉ siècle 1483–1598* (Paris: Presses universitaires de France, 1996), 284–288.

[4] Baumgartner, *France in the Sixteenth Century*, 36.

[5] Ibid, 37.

[6] Michael J. Kraus, "Patronage and Reform in the France of the Prereform: The Case of Clichtove," *Canadian Journal of History* 6(1971), 63.

[7] Frederic J. Baumgartner, *Change and Continuity in the French Episcopate: The Bishops and the Wars of Religion, 1547–1610* (Durham: Duke University Press, 1986), 203.

reform. Jean and Guillaume DuBellay had tried to lure Melanchthon to Paris in hopes of finding a compromise between Lutherans and Catholics, and their brother René, later bishop of Le Mans, had allowed Roussel and other evangelicals to preach in Paris in 1533.[8]

There were few large-scale efforts at reform before 1530, although some individual bishops carried out reform programs in their dioceses.[9] Chastened into a thoroughly orthodox position, Guillaume Briçonnet of Meaux nevertheless continued his efforts at reform in 1525. On 14 December 1525, he called together in his episcopal palace all of the curés or their vicars in his diocese in order to inquire about both observance and orthodoxy. This gathering showed the effects of the earlier evangelization. While large numbers of parishioners were described as good Christians, there were problems in certain parishes over confession, the invocation of the saints, and Purgatory; at the same time, satirical songs directed against the Faculty of Theology and the *parlement* remained popular. Interestingly, however, there was virtually no mention of Luther or Lutheran doctrines.[10]

Attempts to correct abuses on the national level were hindered by almost continual conflict between French kings and popes over the course of the sixteenth century. The French political and military involvement in Italy was the source of many of these ills. A French council assembled at Tours in 1511 had authorized King Louis XII to call a general council to reform the church; when a year later French prelates met at the Council of Pisa, Pope Julius II excommunicated them along with their king.[11] Although this situation was resolved by Julius's death in early 1513, it set the tone for later problems. Although the pope who conceived of the council of Trent, Paul III, was hardly anti-French, his initial convocation in 1544 of the great council that would set the agenda for Catholic reform provoked strong opposition from Francis I, who objected to its location.[12] Francis was more interested in thwarting the Emperor's aims than in dealing with the problems facing the Catholic Church. The

---

[8] Ibid, 24.
[9] François d'Estaing, Bishop of Rodez (1464–1530), was one leader with both vision and the practical skills needed to carry out reform. See Nicole Lemaître, *Le Rouergue flamboyante: Le clergé et les fidèles du diocèse de Rodez 1417–1563* (Paris: Cerf, 1988), 217–392.
[10] Michel Veissière, "Croyances et pratique religieuse à Meaux au temps de Guillaume Briçonnet (1525)," *Revue d'histoire de l'église de France* 67(1981), 59.
[11] Baumgartner, *France in the Sixteenth Century*, 43.
[12] Ibid, 145.

king sent a few cardinals, but the French position during the first
meetings at Trent was at best defensive, and dramatically worsened
when the meetings were reconvened by Julius III.[13] Following in the
footsteps of his earlier namesake, Julius provoked what has come to
be known as the Gallican crisis of 1551. Henri II, strongly supported
by his court, accused the pope of openly favoring the imperial side,
ordering his bishops to return to their dioceses to collect the information that would be needed to call a general council of the French
church.[14] According to the royal letter of February 18, 1551, each
bishop was to live in his diocese for six consecutive months, visiting
each of the parishes. The purpose was threefold: 1) to interro-
gate curés and vicars about the beliefs and behaviors of their parishioners; 2) to inquire about the doctrine of Lenten preachers; and 3) to
identify and punish heretics. In addition, bishops were to arrange
for processions and prayers to ask God for peace and tranquility.[15]
The timing of this attempt at reformation seemed highly suspect to
the pope, who had called for the Council of Trent to meet again
later in the year. Julius, believing this was nothing but attempted
sabotage, denounced "the pretended assembly of a national council
for all of France, against the authority of the Holy Apostolic See,
in contempt of the general council to be held at Trent, to the great
detriment of the accustomed order of the church universal."[16] As
with the earlier problems, the dispute between Henri and Julius cen-
tered almost entirely on political and military issues. Henri announced
his support of Ottavio Farnese, a rebellious subject of the pope who
claimed the Duchy of Parma. Accompanied by French troops, Farnese
invaded the Papal States. At the same time, the king cut off all
diplomatic relations with the papacy and refused to allow ecclesiastical revenues to flow from France into papal coffers.[17] Julius promptly
summoned Henri "before the tribunal of God" and threatened
him with deposition and excommunication.[18] Henri's envoy, Jacques
Amyot, informed the prelates gathered at Trent in September of

---

[13] Evennett, *Cardinal of Lorraine*, 29–35.
[14] Ibid, 35–36.
[15] Marc Venard, "Une réforme Gallicane? Le projet de concile national de 1551,"
Revue d'histoire de l'église de France 67(1981), 201.
[16] Quoted in ibid, 203.
[17] Thomas I. Crimando, "Two French Views of the Council of Trent," *Sixteenth
Century Journal* 19(1988) 172–173.
[18] Evennett, *Cardinal of Lorraine*, 37.

1551 that Henri did not recognize their meeting as a true council, and therefore France would not accept its decrees. The military nature of the conflict was confirmed by its end—an armistice between the pope and the king signed in April, 1552.[19] If Henri's project for a national council had been intended primarily to intimidate the pope, it nevertheless had some positive results. The visitations provided considerable information that gave members of the hierarchy greater awareness of problems in their dioceses. Besides searching for traces of Protestantism, the visitors assessed the level of the parish clergy, and showed particular concern over their lack of education and inability to teach others. The bishop of Autun devised a system for rating his curés as capable, incapable or tolerable; the vicar of Beauvais judged that ignorance among his clergy was the norm.[20] Monasteries were classified as good or bad.[21] If many of the findings and recommendations offered hopeful signs that the French church was capable of reform, there were unfortunately equally strong divisions that would require more than a century for effective implantation.[22]

If France rejected the Council of Trent and its decrees, some of the ideas and programs agreed upon there did exert some influence upon the hierarchy in France. Most important was the discussion of the proper role and content of preaching, which proved a lively topic of discussion in Rome as well. Session Twenty-Four of the Council decreed that each bishop's primary responsibility was to preach the gospel[23] and both Tridentine and Italian Counter-Reformation writers recommended that the Catholic preacher ". . . become an exemplum of his message, the eloquence of a life lived in virtue."[24] The preacher's life was to become his message.[25] Le Picart's student and patron, the Cardinal of Lorraine served as such an example:

> His diocesan reforms were of but local import: his fame as a preacher was European. . . . In a period when few bishops and still fewer cardinals preached, when pulpit eloquence was everywhere left mainly to the hired services of friars and monks, the Cardinal of Lorraine preached

---

[19] Crimando, "French Views," 173.
[20] Venard, "Une réforme Gallicane," 216.
[21] Ibid, 221.
[22] Ibid, 225.
[23] Francesco C. Cesareo, "Penitential Sermons in Renaissance Italy: Girolamo Seripando and the Pater Noster," *Catholic Historical Review* 83(1997), 3.
[24] McGinness, *Right Thinking* 23.
[25] Ibid, 41.

continually—to select fashionable assemblies, to his canons, to the good people of Reims, to the most remote rustic congregation of his arch-diocese.[26]

Moreover, the scholastic style that had been favored by most late medieval preachers was to be abandoned; preachers were forbidden to engage in scholastic subtleties, to show off their learning, or to threaten the social and political order; instead they were to rely primarily on scripture.[27] As we have seen, these changes had already appeared in Le Picart's sermons. The early Jesuits played an important role in these discussions and the propagation of the new homiletic theory. Like Le Picart, the Jesuits defined the Reformation as first and foremost a pastoral problem, making a point of defending practices under attack by the Protestants, and prescribing good examples as the best way to counter the threat.[28]

Until his death in 1556, Le Picart preached to ordinary men and women in cities and villages throughout Normandy, Champagne, and Brie, but his primary field of action was Paris. If in 1533 he had complained that only old ladies came to his sermons, this was not true in the years that followed, as his preaching attracted large crowds. He delivered sermons regularly in Paris at the major churches, including St.-Jacques-de-la-Boucherie, St.-Eustache and St.-Benoît, and in August of 1548, he was appointed dean of the royal parish church, Saint-Germain l'Auxerrois. Saint-Germain l'Auxerrois was one of the oldest cult sites on the right bank of the Seine. The fourth church to be erected on the location, Saint-Germain had been begun in the mid-thirteenth century. During the years when Le Picart was dean, the commission of a magnifice *jubé* was given to Pierre Lescot, Henri II's Louvre architect. A group of tapestries was added in the same period for the decoration of the choir during Easter and other great feasts of the church year along with stained glass windows in the transept. The deanery, where Le Picart had his lodgings, was situated at an angle to the parvis and the sacristy along the rue des Prêtres Saint-Germain l'Auxerrois. The parish chapel was dedicated to the Virgin, and a contemporary statue of St. Mary of Egypt was particularly appropriate in view of Le Picart's interest in the con-

---

[26] Evennett, *Cardinal of Lorraine*, 18–19.
[27] McGinness, *Right Thinking*, 45, 48.
[28] O'Malley, *First Jesuits*, 16, 272, 277.

version of prostitutes.[29] In Le Picart's will, no longer extant, he left the church an annual stipend of 60li.[30]

Le Picart's sermons offer a plan of reform for both clergy and laity. He explains to his listeners the difference between the priesthood and the laity. "It is true, as you say, that we are all religious, and we are all held to follow the Christian religion and the commandments of God and our Holy Mother Church, but there are some who have chosen the stricter path . . ."[31] He asks his listeners if they want to drink from the chalice: "Are you ready to endure contempt, confusion, torment, and to give your blood and your life for me?"[32] He insists that they understand the priest's role as God's representative: "*O Mater Dei!* When the priest goes to the altar, he doesn't go there as Guillaume or Gautier, in his private personality, but in the person of Our Lord Jesus Christ, to represent Jesus Christ."[33] Unfortunately, men who carried out their duties and responsibilities as churchmen were mocked. Speaking from personal experience, he says, "the world esteems it as folly to have the means to earn goods and honors and yet to disdain them. It is said, 'He's a great fool!' It's necessary to be such a fool, to condemn the goods and the honors of the world and to carry the cross of Our Lord with faith, in order to have knowledge of God . . ."[34] It saddens him that such men are called melancholics and killjoys,[35] bigots and hypocrites.[36] Yet he fears the situation is unlikely to change, for ". . . I find another vice common today—if a young girl or boy is inspired by God and has the devotion to enter the religious life, he or she will not be received without money or property."[37] Since simple people have a greater love of God, this state of affairs is especially deplorable.[38]

---

[29] André Devèche, *L'Église Saint-Germain l'Auxerrois de Paris: Paroisse royale* (Paris: SIDES, n.d.), n.p.

[30] *Gallia christiana in provincias ecclesiasticas distributa: qua series et historia archiepiscoporum, episcoporum, et abbatum franciae vicinarumque ditionum* (Paris: Victor Palme, 1870–1874), VII:269.

[31] Le Picart, *Pasques*, fol. 61.

[32] Le Picart, *Caresme*, fol. 102.

[33] Le Picart, *Advent*, fol. 42.

[34] Le Picart, *Pasques*, fol. 213.

[35] Le Picart, *Trinité-II*, fol. 139.

[36] Le Picart, *Pasques*, fol. 213.

[37] Le Picart, *Caresme*, fol. 154.

[38] Le Picart, *Advent*, fol. 6.

One of the most prominent themes in Le Picart's sermons is the need for the clergy to become worthy of their charge and lead by example. "St. John Chrysostom tells us that the priest must be eminent above other men just as man is greater than an animal."[39] It is the responsibility of a churchman to set an example with his own life:

> As a priest, a curé, I must be the first to fast during Lent, the seasons of the church year and during the other fasts commanded by God's church. I must be the first to pray, to forgive my enemies and do good for them. I must be the first to give to the poor to set an example for the people. Because it is unworthy for a person in a public position, placed in charge of others, to look for his own profit. It is a monstrous and indecent thing when a superior, who is charged to preach, does not do so. He must be the first to put into practice what he preaches.[40]

Apathy among churchmen is lamentable, for "[w]hen we were first priests, we were marvelously devout, and now we are worse than laypeople."[41] The consequences can be seen everywhere. While "[t]he good life of a preacher will lead his listeners to do what he says and preaches,"[42] a clergyman who lives badly does so to the "great ruin and scandal of the people."[43] Le Picart insists repeatedly that ". . . if those who have the charge of souls . . . show how to live well by their example, the simple people will follow them."[44] It is a great scandal, he says, "when those who teach do not do as they say . . . Look at the example I give you. I have taught you not only with my words but also with deeds. There is an accord between my life and my words. Follow me."[45] Quoting his favorite non-scriptural source, Le Picart tells his audience that "Saint John Chrysostom, speaking of priests who have the charges of souls, says, 'I do not think among priests there are many who will be saved, but more who will perish, because it is so great a charge that I do not know who can be worthy.'"[46]

Le Picart ties the rise of heresy directly to the evil lives of monks

---

[39] Le Picart, *Pasques*, fol. 198.
[40] Le Picart, *Caresme-II*, fol. 60.
[41] Le Picart, *SL*, 118.
[42] Le Picart, *Caresme-II*, fol. 62.
[43] Le Picart, *Pasques*, fol. 28.
[44] Le Picart, *Caresme*, fol. 26.
[45] Le Picart, *Trinité-II*, fol. 191; cf. ibid, fol. 44.
[46] Le Picart, *Pasques*, fol. 28.

and priests, and does not believe Protestantism will be overcome unless something is done to remedy the problem:

> And if we want to vanquish and confound them, let us amend our bad lives: because [the heretics] are founded on nothing but the abuses that they see among us. It is necessary to amend and correct the abuses, without changing the substance. Therefore, Christians, first it is necessary to declare the holy scripture to the people, and make it speak to the morés of men—to propose scripture to them as a mirror and example.[47]

He is afraid the heretics will use this as a weapon; it could lead some to turn from religion altogether:

> The unruliness and bad lives of many in religious life, who do not observe the rules and ordinances of their order, gives occasion for the heretics to speak ill and feel wrongly about religion. But for all that we must not get rid of or abolish religion; but we must eliminate the abuses and disorders that result, and reform strictly through good works and ordinances.[48]

He goes on: "We will live so well that our life will confound them—because by arguments alone we will not be able to overcome them."[49] Le Picart's fears were well-founded. Calvin wrote:

> It is the pastors, the pastors themselves who mount their pulpits, the sacred throne of Jesus Christ, in such condition that they ought to have a purity eminent above all others, but instead they are often the patron and mirror of all ordure. And so their sermons have no more gravity or faith than a farce being played out on a platform. Such unhappy ones complain that they are held in contempt by the people, or that people give them the finger in mockery. But I am stunned by the patience of the people, that the women and small children do not throw mud and shit in their faces.[50]

Le Picart urges priests to live up to the dignity inherent in their position. Yet too often they behave worse than the laity. "Today I marvel that among us churchmen, when we are at the altar to do what Our Lord Jesus Christ did, which is so worthy and holy a mystery, we are completely irreverent. In giving holy blessings, and having Jesus Christ in our hands, it seems that we aren't even thinking

---

[47] Le Picart, *Caresme-II*, fol. 26; cf. *Caresme*, fol. 81.
[48] Le Picart, *Pasques*, fols. 245–246.
[49] Le Picart, *Caresme*, fol. 80.
[50] Calvin, *Des scandales*, 85.

about Him." He chastises churchmen who, during the elevation of
the host, "wander all around the church, just as if they were out in
the fields, which gives the heretics plenty of opportunity to say evil
things about us."[51] Other priests say mass as quickly as possible.[52]
Finally, Le Picart preaches that it is unseemly when "we gossip and
laugh with them, so that our dignity and authority is disparaged and
condemned and we do dishonor to Our Lord Jesus Christ."[53]

Avarice is at the heart of clerical abuses. Since priests do not have
wives and children to feed, they should support the poor,[54] but instead
they extort money from them. "If I give a sermon out of vainglory,
if I hear confessions for money and not out of charity, if I preach
a Lenten series to be called to the court, or to have abbeys and
similar things . . . [I am a bad priest]."[55] Priests demanding alms dishonor their estate, and render their dignity, authority and ministry
contemptible in the eyes of men.[56] Le Picart urges his colleagues to
take only what they need, following the example of Jesus, ". . . who
chose to be conceived in Nazareth, not Jerusalem, in order to show
us that we must not ask for greatness in the world, but before God."[57]
Yet the temptation proves too much for many:

> I go to the house of a great lord to be his doctor, his preacher, and
> because he is a great lord, I must be dressed in silk and velvet. And
> if someone reproaches me, I will say that it would be an affront to
> the honor of my master if I was otherwise dressed. I ask you, are you
> not a priest, a curé or the like? You are a servant and minister of
> God, you live in His house, but you do not live and dress like Him.
> Why do you dishonor Him . . .?[58]

He condemns those who seek monasteries worth two or three thousand livres a year, yet have only thirty monks to support.[59] Caring
more about revenues and cuisine, these men give little thought to
the behavior of the men in their charge.[60] The problem of individual greed is so serious that ". . . we see the beautiful religious build-

---

[51] Le Picart, *Caresme*, fol. 80.
[52] Le Picart, *Trinité-II*, fol. 156.
[53] Le Picart, *SL*, 28.
[54] Le Picart, *Trinité*, fol. 162.
[55] Le Picart, *Advent*, fol. 222.
[56] Le Picart, *SL*, 24; *Caresme*, fol. 96.
[57] Le Picart, *Advent*, 148.
[58] Le Picart, *Pasques*, fol. 34; cf. *Advent*, fol. 226.
[59] Le Picart, *Trinité-II*, fol. 188.
[60] Ibid, fol. 15.

ings that [our predecessors] constructed, and today they go to ruin."[61]

Le Picart mocks those who assume worldly honors and wealth are signs of God's love:

"I thank God, when things happen to please me. Goods come to me while I sleep, I only ask for an office, a benefice, and I already have three or four. With each one I have a great court, and I am in honor and credit of the world. I take from one, I give to another, I do whatever I please and no one can contradict me. This is why I am so happy, God shows that he loves me." Oh, poor unfeeling fool! you show well that you are blind and on the road to perdition and eternal damnation! . . . [T]his is a great and evident sign that you are unhappy, in the enmity of God . . .[62]

What is the point? He counsels churchmen to "ask only for what is necessary, not excess in food or clothing or anything else."[63] Le Picart practiced what he preached. Following the example his parents had set, he was known as the "father of the poor."[64] Nor was he interested in personal advancement. During reigns that were noteworthy for the sale of episcopal offices, Le Picart ended his days as dean of St.-Germain l'Auxerrois. As a member of one of the most important families in Paris, he could have had almost any position he desired. Moreover, when he heard that the pope intended to make him a cardinal, he sidestepped the promotion by refusing to go to Rome.[65]

If Le Picart was uninterested in promotion or honors, the same could not be said of most of his contemporaries. Although he argues that neither money nor family should induce someone to enter religion, but only vocation and devotion,[66] nepotism remained a major problem. Le Picart expresses horror that untested children are being given bishoprics and cures.[67] Simony and pluralism are rampant, worse, he says, than in the time of the Jews.[68] He exclaims, "one barters the possessions of the church as if they are commercial merchandise. What horror and damnation!"[69] He continues, "many today

---

[61] Le Picart, *Pasques*, fol. 158.
[62] Ibid, fols. 41–42.
[63] Ibid, fol. 31.
[64] Doumergue, *Calvin*, I:241.
[65] Hilarion de Coste, *Parfait ecclesiastique*, 193.
[66] Le Picart, *Pasques*, fol. 245.
[67] Le Picart, *Trinité-II*, fol. 203; *Advent*, fol. 11.
[68] Le Picart, *Advent*, fol. 173.
[69] Ibid, fol. 257.

in the church are there because of simony and patronage. We don't bother to see if these men are capable or not, but only that they come from a good house, or have the favor of some important man."[70] He complains that "you embrace and take everything, to live according to your pleasures, and do not worry about souls for Jesus Christ, or His precious blood, and however much you want to do your duty, you cannot be in two or three parishes at once to remonstrate with and teach your people . . ."[71] Personal residence is essential.[72] In a sermon consecrated to the model of the good shepherd (see Appendix B.5), Le Picart explains:

> Our good pastor Jesus Christ said: I am the good shepherd, and showed that He was a good shepherd, when He gave his soul and His life for His flock. He told us, that the condition and office of a true shepherd is to give up his life, to expose himself to perils and dangers of his life, for the good of his flock, to die for their salvation, and to make sure the wolf does not devour and choke them.[73]

The good shepherd is like "a nurse who nurses small children: I love you so much that I would give my soul, my very life, and die for you, for your salvation."[74] A priest must pray that the wrath of God does not fall on his people,[75] and be willing to bear any pain or face any danger to protect his flock.[76] This means personal involvement with one's parishioners. "The good shepherd knows his flock by name and surname."[77] To do this, he ". . . must visit his diocese, his cure, to see if everyone behaves as they should, and to condemn vices and correct them."[78] Taking responsibility is crucial: "It is up to me as a prelate or curé to look around and know what is preached in my parish and diocese, so that my parishioners are not deceived or badly taught, and so they will be in no doubt about their salvation."[79] A good clergyman must not merely condemn vices, but teach and lead people to understand what they have done wrong so that they can reform.[80] This level of involvement is not always easy:

---

[70] Le Picart, *Caresme*, fol. 34.
[71] Le Picart, *Pasques*, fol. 44.
[72] Le Picart, *Advent*, fol. 369.
[73] Le Picart, *Pasques*, fol. 25.
[74] Ibid, fol. 30.
[75] Le Picart, *Caresme-II*, fol. 58.
[76] Le Picart, *Pasques*, fol. 25.
[77] Ibid.
[78] Ibid, fol. 302.
[79] Le Picart, *Caresme-II*, fol. 12.
[80] Ibid, fol. 177.

The curé, the superior sees much poverty and abuse in his parish; if he wants to condemn them he will be slandered, ill will be said of him, and he will flee and hide through silence. . . . This is not a sign of love and the zeal of God, to keep quiet when it is necessary to speak, and principally of the honor of God, because the salvation of one's neighbor depends on this. . . . He must be a good pastor and teach good doctrine, good morés to children and servants, to take care of them, to know what condition they are in, if they serve God, if they go to Mass, to divine services, what books they read. You father, you must know this, and do your duty: because otherwise if by your fault and negligence your child or servant falters, you will be guilty.[81]

In the event that a bishop, curé or preacher could not fulfill his duties for a certain period of time, Le Picart urges him ". . . to take good men of sound reputation, who are capable of discharging these duties to aid you in serving your churches."[82] The churchman, like all Christians, should have compassion for his neighbor, and carry and sustain him when he falls.[83]

Preaching was so important to the salvation of the laity that Le Picart spends considerable time on the subject. It was the obligation of everyone from the archbishop down: "Teach the people and preach. This was the office Saint Paul held and also Saint Barnabas in Antioch. So there they were, carrying out their duties. This is good. They were not lazy. What value is there to a position if it is not exercised? What value an art that is never practiced?"[84] It is not the office that recommends a person to God, but its good exercise.[85] A preacher must be prudent and wise in his sermons, so that when he has finished none of his listeners feel any doubt.[86] What is to be preached? The basics: "[We must] preach and announce salvation to the people: to preach the Incarnation, the nativity, the Passion, the Resurrection, and the ascension of our Lord Jesus Christ, and how He will come to judge the living and the dead."[87] To be a true preacher of the word of God, a man ". . . must be willing to lose all his goods rather than alter one word of the truth."[88] His success

---

[81] Le Picart, *Pasques*, fol. 28.
[82] Le Picart, *Caresme*, fol. 161.
[83] Ibid, fol. 94.
[84] Le Picart, *Pasques*, fol. 156.
[85] Le Picart, *Trinité*, fol. 146.
[86] Le Picart, *Caresme*, fol. 72; Le Picart, *Caresme-II*, fol. 26.
[87] Le Picart, *Pasques*, fol. 14.
[88] Le Picart, *Trinité*, fol. 40.

will be his crown, for "the good life of the listeners is the glory and praise of preachers."[89] Preachers also have an obligation to spread their message far and wide, which Le Picart did by preaching in villages and small towns in northern France.[90] "It upsets me deeply that good preachers, good and knowledgeable men, do not go to preach in the villages, but leave it to young apprentices, because the former preach only good doctrine, purely and properly, and edify the people, while the apprentices sometimes preach errors that lead people astray, for there is no one to correct them . . ."[91]

Le Picart is also concerned with sexual misbehavior. The potential problems associated with acting as a spiritual director to women had been discussed by the founder of the Jesuits, who often counseled women, in his *Autobiography*:

> We must always be on our guard, and hold no conversations with women, unless they be ladies of prominence." Later in Rome, to continue on this same subject, Master Francis heard a woman's confession and once visited her to speak to her of spiritual matters. She was later found to be pregnant, but it pleased the Lord that the man who had done the wicked deed was discovered. The same happened to Jean Codure, whose spiritual daughter was caught with a man.[92]

By the time of the full implementation of the Catholic reform, the church was no longer willing to countenance the sexual misconduct of priests, monks and nuns, for church leaders believed such incontinence endangered the reforms.[93] It was often necessary to tread a fine line between publicizing clerical abuses and correcting them, but Le Picart attacks the sexual behaviors of the clergy in a general way. He maintains that no one is forced into celibacy, although it is the better choice.[94] Once chosen, however, vows of celibacy must be observed.[95] "A priest must be chaste and continent. You will say to me, I don't know how . . . It is really quite easy for those who guard themselves and avoid bad company. Look at the examples of Saints

---

[89] Ibid, fol. 90.
[90] Hilarion de Coste, *Parfait ecclesiastique*, 105. This was a concern of Le Picart's Jesuit acquaintances as well. *FN*, II:56.
[91] Le Picart, *Pasques*, fol. 50.
[92] Tylenda, *Pilgrim's Journey*, 114.
[93] Stephen Haliczer, *Sexuality in the Confessional: A Sacrament Profaned* (New York: Oxford University Press, 1996).
[94] Le Picart, *Trinité*, fol. 53.
[95] Le Picart, *Trinité-II*, fol. 133.

Catherine, Agnes, Benedict, Jerome and Joseph, all of whom kept their chastity."[96] Churchmen who seduce and then abandon a girl or woman must "demand pardon before God, and cry for the rest of your life."[97] Le Picart reprimands his erring colleagues: "Among us men of the church, I will talk with a young girl. She will be between my knees. So? What do you say? What do you do? This is to say to God, 'I'm not afraid of you.'"[98] A sinning priest does not commit simple fornication, but ". . . sacrilege, for my body is part of Our Lord Jesus Christ, and this makes a whore of His body parts."[99] He complains that when he visits ". . . a bishop, an abbot or curé, he is surrounded by a bunch of women. Horror! Abomination! . . . I go to see Monsieur, and I find him with a woman. I do not say this to provoke you against them, but so that you will pray God for them!"[100] This was yet another problem which gave ammunition to the heretics who, seeing priests and monks who could not remain chaste, allowed their priests to marry.[101]

In the wake of heresy spreading like a cancer throughout the realm,[102] Le Picart provides very specific responses to Protestantism. First and foremost it is necessary to defend the church, and Le Picart argues that a council might help: "We certainly have need of a good council, not for the faith of the Catholic Church, because it cannot err, but to reform the abuses that are in the church."[103] He describes the difference, even at the highest levels, of the church from its representatives: "The Pope, even if he is bad, is as much a pope as Saint Peter."[104] He tells his listeners that God speaks to them through the Church,[105] and that they do not need the arcane wisdom of the heretics, or scriptures in French, but only "the commandments of God, and our Holy Mother Church, and that which concerns the articles of faith."[106] As a corollary, he stresses the need for obedience, first and foremost to the Church, but also to all superiors— magistrates,

---

[96] Le Picart, *SL*, 247–248.
[97] Le Picart, *Trinité*, fol. 87.
[98] Le Picart, *Pasques*, fol. 176.
[99] Le Picart, *Advent*, fol. 228.
[100] Ibid, fol. 11.
[101] Le Picart, *Trinité*, fol. 58.
[102] Le Picart, *SL*, 56.
[103] Le Picart, *Advent*, fol. 44.
[104] Le Picart, *Caresme*, fol. 96.
[105] Le Picart, *SL*, 45.
[106] Le Picart, *Caresme*, fol. 44.

kings, or anyone in a position of authority.[107] As can be seen in his reactions to the actions taken against his Jesuit friends, Le Picart was never as strongly Gallican in his sympathies as most doctors of the Faculty of Theology. Still, he could be as critical of popes as of kings, and was no doubt aware of the political intrigues surrounding the Council of Trent. He never mentions it specifically in his sermons.

Justification by faith alone was on the lips of every heretic, so Le Picart preaches in defense of works. Although he admits that without God's grace human beings can do no good,[108] he makes clear that faith and works are interdependent: "Faith alone does not save, nor do works without faith, but both together are necessary for the justification of an adult who has the time and opportunity to do good."[109] He insists that only a living faith justifies: "I do not understand this to be a dead faith, which is vain and useless, but a living faith operating by charity. And this faith, which is a gift of God, is infused in our hearts."[110] True faith has three components: it must be firm, without doubts; it must be patient; and it must believe in heavenly rather than earthly rewards.[111] Le Picart states that

> if someone hears the word and doctrine of God and doesn't do according to what he has heard, by putting it into practice and effect, he is like those who look at themselves in a mirror and yet forget who they are. What does it profit you to look at yourself in a mirror if you don't get rid of that spot or speck that you see on your face? Thus it is that the Word of God profits nothing if you do not practice it in good works.[112]

Le Picart explains that the "tree is known by its fruit,"[113] giving numerous examples that could give hope to the worst sinner or even a heretic:

> King Saul was like a good tree before he became king. He was as simple as a one-year-old child . . . David was certainly a good tree, a good man, even though he produced bad fruit, by committing mur-

---

[107] Le Picart, *Pasques*, fol. 35.
[108] Ibid, fol. 51; Le Picart, *Caresme*, fol. 3.
[109] Le Picart, *Caresme*, fol. 145.
[110] Le Picart, *Instruction*, 12; cf. ibid, 11; *Caresme*, fol. 152; *CII*, fol. 48.
[111] Ibid, 15.
[112] Le Picart, *Pasques*, fol. 53.
[113] Le Picart, *Advent*, fol. 95; *Pasques*, fol. 54.

der and adultery, but afterwards he returned to his earlier goodness as a good tree bearing good fruit. King Manasses, was he not the worst tree in the world at the beginning? But when God afflicted him, he became better than all the other trees, fearing God and doing good works. Therefore a good tree can become bad, bearing rotten fruit, and a bad tree can be changed and produce good fruit. Wasn't St. Paul a bad tree, when he persecuted the Christians? And yet he became a tree which bore so much good fruit that it is impossible to say. And the glorious Magdalene was a rotten, barren tree, but in the end she became a tree bearing fragrant and good fruit. So however much our nature is inclined to evil more than good, if God gives us grace, we have the power and the choice with our free will to do good or ill...[114]

God gives humans the liberty to choose good or ill, life or death, and no one is constrained to do either good or evil.[115] Le Picart exhorts his listeners to cooperate with God's grace, for "just as the fall of man was voluntary, so is his justification."[116]

Le Picart's sermons fully exemplify what the cardinals at Trent would suggest in terms of exalting those doctrines and sacraments most specifically under attack from Protestants. Although he spends very little time on purgatory in his sermons, he does affirm it.[117] He explains that venial sins for which satisfaction has not been made are punished in purgatory. "God knows our fragility, and for venial sins we do not lose the grace of God. But if I die in such sin, I must be punished in purgatory."[118] It is there that the stains of the world are expunged.[119] Le Picart insists that there is a choice—one can either be punished in this world or the next, but God does not punish a human being twice. The choice is simple: "... The punishment of this world is nothing by comparison with that of the other. I would rather be punished one hundred years in this world like a woman enduring the pains of childbirth, than to be punished one hour in purgatory, because that is a more intolerable and insupportable pain."[120] But however horrific the pains of purgatory, the souls there exist in hope, knowing they will be delivered.[121] Le Picart

---

[114] Le Picart, *Trinité*, fol. 62.
[115] Le Picart, *Pasques*, fol. 57.
[116] Le Picart, *Caresme*, fol. 100.
[117] Le Picart, *Advent*, fol. 255.
[118] Le Picart, *Instruction*, 193.
[119] Le Picart, *Advent*, fol. 8.
[120] Le Picart, *Instruction*, 247.
[121] Le Picart, *Advent*, fol. 30.

justifies masses for the dead and indulgences, without mentioning them by name: "If you owe 10 *écus*, and I pay them in your name, will you not be quit of your debt? So when you do good for the dead, they will profit as well as if they had done it themselves."[122] He clarifies the differences between purgatory and Hell: "This purgation is not done in Hell, because in Hell, there is no redemption whatsoever."[123] The pains are no different; it is simply a question of duration.[124] For those who could not imagine eternity, he explains that "if a man has lived one thousand years in this world, it is still not one day compared to eternity."[125] Unlike many fourteenth- and early fifteenth-century preachers, Le Picart only rarely provides specifics about the pains of Hell. His words are surprisingly mild: "the damned endure a variety and diversity of punishments, because first they are tormented by fire, and tortured by devils. . . . What is more, they have continual memory of the faults and offenses they committed, for which they were damned."[126]

Le Picart devotes most of his attention to the sacraments, especially confession and the mass, which he was widely known to have celebrated daily.[127] He explains that the sacraments of the church were instituted for three reasons: to humble, to teach, and to excite.[128] Some sacraments, specifically baptism and the sacrament of the altar, are expressly mentioned in scripture, but others are implicit; however, all were instituted by the Lord. Baptism is the first step, without which salvation is impossible.[129] Just as water cleans away the filth and stains of the body, so holy baptism purges the soul of sin and allows it to receive the grace of God.[130] Unlike the mass and confession, baptism cannot be repeated, for it is a one-time sacrament by which humans are made children of God. "If we sin after receiving baptism, we lose that grace, which we can only recover through the sacrament of penance.[131] If baptism is the beginning, confirmation is the next step, "for it is not yet enough to be made

---

[122] Le Picart, *SL*, 168; cf. *Caresme-II*, fol. 51.
[123] Le Picart, *SL*, 167.
[124] Le Picart, *Trinité*, fol. 152; *Instruction*, 263.
[125] Le Picart, *SL*, 103.
[126] Le Picart, *Caresme*, fol. 110.
[127] *Gallia christiana*, VII:269.
[128] Le Picart, *Pasques*, fol. 314.
[129] Le Picart, *SL*, 61–62.
[130] Ibid, 91; cf. ibid, 96.
[131] Ibid, 252; *Instruction*, 198.

alive, but this must be corroborated and confirmed by the sacrament of confirmation. So the child, after he is born, is vivified and confirmed, yet he cannot live without eating and drinking . . ."[132]

This leads to Le Picart's discussion of confession and communion. He admits that confession "is a great power given to priests . . . He gave this to show us that man has power and strength on earth to remit sins."[133] Le Picart reminds confessors to bear this in mind: "In all times and all places, and at all hours, if a sinner comes to me and asks pardon with a contrite heart, I will pardon him, and think no more of his faults and sins."[134] Le Picart also insists on the education of priests, telling them they must listen attentively to their lessons so that when they are hearing confession they will have the tools to distinguish "one leper from another."[135] He urges priests to take their work as spiritual guides seriously. "When someone comes to confession, you must repeat the faults and sins to him that he has confessed, and tell him and make him understand the enormity and gravity of them so that he understands his sin. Yet when we absolve him, we are so brief that it is a marvel!"[136] A priest who recognizes that the man or woman before him has no intention of abstaining from evildoing must refuse absolution.[137] Priests must also suppress some of their natural reactions: "If I confess someone and he gets angry with me, should I in turn become angry with him? No, not at all! But I must gain him through love."[138] He demands that priests imitate God, taking into account human weakness. "To look at a woman is not a sin, because looking is natural, but to look at her with covetousness and a desire to abuse her is prohibited."[139] While blasphemy and swearing are mortal sins, ". . . a hasty word does not by itself separate oneself from the grace of God."[140] Le Picart is willing to make allowances for someone who wants to confess, but for some reason, such as the unavailability of a priest, cannot.[141] "God does not oblige you to go to confession immediately,

---

[132] Le Picart, *SL*, 62.
[133] Le Picart, *Pasques*, fol. 16.
[134] Le Picart, *Caresme-II*, fol. 3.
[135] Le Picart, *SL*, 246.
[136] Ibid, 247.
[137] Le Picart, *Advent*, fol. 116.
[138] Le Picart, fol. 73.
[139] Le Picart, *Advent*, fol. 72; cf. *Instruction*, 194.
[140] Le Picart, *Instruction*, 263.
[141] Le Picart, *SL*, 66.

but you must feel true contrition for your faults with a desire to
confess as soon as possible. For God is a good God . . ."[142] To obtain
absolution, one must purge one's soul: "Like a doctor, the surgeon
cannot cure a sickness if the sick patient doesn't reveal his symptoms and say what is wrong. So the priest cannot remit sins or cure
spiritual maladies which come from sin, if the penitent doesn't declare
those sins to him, so that the priest can give him counsel and remedy and order a satisfactory penance to atone for his guilt."[143] He
describes the three parts of confession: contrition of the heart, confession of the mouth, and satisfaction through works.[144] The first step
is to change one's will, and to be angry at oneself for having
offended.[145] "When I confess, it is necessary to say, 'I got angry and
beat up my neighbor,' and similar things, rather than saying, 'He
started it,' in order to diminish my own sin. I should not excuse but
accuse myself."[146] He urges sinners not to wait until Easter to confess.[147] They must not be overly scrupulous:

> It is necessary to believe that by the sacrament of confession your sin
> is pardoned. But if I confess ten or twenty times, I will doubt that I
> have been pardoned . . . It is impossible for your sins to be pardoned,
> if you don't have faith . . . This shows an instability of heart. . . . I must
> confide in God, and not look to push this to the last degree, for that
> arises from my pride. God sees that I travel on the right road with a
> pure heart, and do not know how to do better.[148]

The results can be quite astonishing: "After you have gone to confession, don't you feel in yourself a repose and spiritual joy in your
heart, and a discharge of your conscience?"[149]

A defense of the mass was perhaps Le Picart's most conscious
goal, as he dedicated whole collections of sermons to the subject,
and obviously felt this was the aspect of heresy that was most blas-
phemous. Although he treats it as part of his attack on heretics, Le
Picart is equally concerned with talking about the positive benefits
of the mass for a Catholic believer. Priests must be sure not to dis-

---

[142] Ibid, 68.
[143] Le Picart, *Pasques*, fol. 17.
[144] Le Picart, *SL*, 67.
[145] Le Picart, *Caresme*, fol. 64.
[146] Le Picart, *Pasques*, fol. 47.
[147] Le Picart, *Advent*, fol. 238.
[148] Le Picart, *Trinité*, fol. 187.
[149] Le Picart, *Caresme-II*, fol. 87.

courage people from frequent communion. Le Picart remarks that in the primitive church in the East, people communicated every day.[150] "If we are good Christians, we will receive every day. We must not look at whether we are poor or rich, free or slave, married or not, because these conditions do not hinder reception; only mortal sin does that."[151] He laments that "among us men of the church, we speak ill of a woman who comes to take the sacrament every Sunday, saying it is not the business of a woman to go so often."[152] Rather than murmuring against those who take the eucharist frequently, the priest should ask himself how prepared he is to receive communion.[153] On the subject of the mass, Le Picart repeats the standard doctrine that a bad priest does not affect the virtue and efficacy of the mass for the recipient,[154] but adds that "if I know a priest is living badly and does not want to change his ways, I will sooner let him die of hunger than say mass."[155] This again is bound to the problem of heresy.

> I counsel all not to hear mass from a bad priest, a thief, however much the mass itself is good—for he is an occasion of evil, and everyday the scandals grow against the holy sacrament of the altar. It is necessary to rebuild, for these malicious heretics found their errors on the irreverence of priests. So let us take this occasion to throw them into confusion by living well.[156]

Calling it the "sacrament of love,"[157] Le Picart compares its effects to food and medicine.[158] "The food of this world cannot give eternal life,"[159] but the eucharist is "the true fruit and true bread of life, by which we are made immortal and changed into God and are one with him."[160] After explaining the process of transubstantiation,[161] Le Picart develops the analogies to help make the transformation more comprehensible to the ordinary believer. A person receiving

---

[150] Le Picart, *Instruction*, 186.
[151] Ibid, 187.
[152] Le Picart, *Pasques*, fol. 296.
[153] Ibid.
[154] Le Picart, *Instruction*, 53.
[155] Le Picart, *SL*, 255.
[156] Le Picart, *Trinité*, fol. 49.
[157] Ibid, fol. 13.
[158] Le Picart, *SL*, 273; cf. *Pasques*, fol. 321.
[159] Ibid, fol. 103.
[160] Le Picart, *Epistre*, fol. 16.
[161] Le Picart, *SL*, 6, 97, 136; *Pasques*, fols. 109–110.

in a worthy state ". . . participates in divinity and is transformed into
God. Just as iron by its nature is cold, when it is put in the fire it
participates in the fire, until it is nothing but fire. So a man who
worthily receives Jesus Christ feels nothing of his terrestrial nature,
but is deified and becomes like a divine man."[162] In another example he uses the case of water placed over fire to signal the kind of
transformation provided by reception of the eucharist.[163]

The effects of worthy reception are amazing: "The Holy Sacrament
of the altar chases away the devil and chills the ardor of our passions; it purifies our heart; it appeases the wrath of God; it illumi-
nates our understanding so we can know him; it conserves man
entirely in well being; it lets him experience the memory of spiritual
sweetness; and it inflames the heart and affections toward God."[164]
But those who ignore its salutary benefits are like a sick man ". . . who
take medicine in a way other than has been prescribed, and so the
medicine does him more harm than good."[165] To receive unworthily
is a great sin: "Death comes, sickness abound, and many are so
dazed that they lose all understanding. And you often see after Easter
many illnesses, wars, plagues, and other evils reign, and many people die suddenly. This is because of the irreverence that we show
toward the Holy Sacrament."[166]

Le Picart discusses the proper reverence one should show when
approaching the host. "When I go to present a gift to the king, I
will wear my good clothes. So when you approach the most worthy sacrament, you must go properly dressed. That is, you must dec-
orate your soul with lovely virtues in all purity of conscience."[167] If
some unforeseen event occurs, proper decorum should be preserved.
"When you hear the holy mass, go down on your knees. If you
should feel sick, retire to a corner, so no one will be scandalized or
not properly edified. . . . Do not give your neighbor any occasion to
be scandalized . . ."[168] He also directs his words against "those who
during the mass babble, create a racket, and walk about, saying vile
words, violating the temple of God, or procuresses who take their

---

[162] Le Picart, *Pasques*, fol. 281; *SL*, 142.
[163] Le Picart, *Pasques*, fol. 59.
[164] Le Picart, *Épistre*, fol. 30.
[165] Le Picart, *SL*, 107; cf. *Trinité-II*, fol. 104.
[166] Le Picart, *SL*, 142.
[167] Ibid, 187.
[168] Ibid, 278.

girls up to the altar."[169] The sacrament should be refused to such transgressors.[170] But he assures men and women that the more faith and devotion they express, the more they participate in the grace of God.[171] Their eating is spiritual, based on faith, not like eating "beef, mutton, or ordinary bread."[172]

Reception is based on faith, not the misleading perceptions of the senses: ". . . To confirm my faith I do not want to see Him, because I am as sure of His presence by my faith as I would be if I saw Him. It is said that St. Louis of France was hearing mass with his chaplain, who said he visibly saw in the holy sacrament the precious body of Our Lord. The king responded that he believed enough without having to see it."[173]

Le Picart explains to the laity, who have heard Protestant attacks, that even though they do not receive in both kinds like priests, they nonetheless receive the full body and blood of the Lord. "It is not to be thought that priests, in saying mass, receive more than others who take it in only one kind, or that they have more grace than others receive . . . By which the Church makes no injury to laypeople in giving it to them in one kind."[174] In fact, the abuses of the priesthood often make them take communion to their own damnation.

Le Picart also defends other aspects of church tradition, such as the rules for Lent, the veneration of the saints, and the honor due to the Virgin Mary. He explains that if a person can fast during Lent and does not, he sins, for the practice was instituted not by man but by God.[175] As always, churchmen must set the standard. In his funeral sermon for Pierre Descornes (see Appendix B.3), Le Picart recalls that the Franciscan ". . . could have eaten meat in view of his sickness and his stomach problems, but he abstained in order to provide an example for others . . ."[176] However, a person must not fast in order to be praised for piety, which will only anger God.[177] "One should not fast or abstain indiscreetly, for this causes a loss of mental powers. Rather one should use foods in order to

---

[169] Le Picart, *Trinité*, fol. 158.
[170] Le Picart, *SL*, 229.
[171] Ibid, 42.
[172] Ibid, 176.
[173] Ibid, 89.
[174] Le Picart, *Epistre*, fols. 18–19; *Pasques*, fol. 259.
[175] Le Picart, *Instruction*, 160.
[176] Le Picart, *Pasques*, fol. 208.
[177] Le Picart, *Caresme*, fol. 3.

sustain the body without excess or delicacies ... It is necessary to give repose to the spirit, taking care of all such fantasies."[178] He advises his listeners to abstain from consensual relations during this period and refrain from celebrating a marriage, even though many do otherwise.[179]

Le Picart clarifies the proper role of the saints in the life of a Christian. He rejects the claim of idolatry made by the heretics. "One does not consider the statue or the work, but that which is represented by it—the significance and representation for which the image stands."[180] The veneration a person exhibits toward an image does not remain there, but goes to that which is signified by it, the saint.[181] Books of Hours and images aid human memory, which is feeble.[182] Addressing oneself to a saint does not dishonor God or show a lack of faith in his compassion; quite the contrary—it is a recognition of the enormity of one's faults.[183] He calls the saints God's good friends and mediators:[184] if the living aid one another, can't the saints in paradise, who have perfect love, help us even more? "They pray God for us, because they know our need. Along with us, they are of one body, of which the Lord is the head."[185] Their assistance derives from the work of Jesus Christ.[186] He tells his listeners that showing reverence by kissing the relics of the saints, through whom God has done miracles, is praiseworthy.[187] "The relics and ashes of the saints had virtue given to them by God, for they have been infused with the Holy Spirit, and so can perform miracles."[188] This also provides the opportunity for a person to reflect on how well he practices brotherly love: "Tomorrow we will carry my lady, Saint Geneviève, to Notre-Dame, and before the procession we must reconcile ourselves to our brother so that there is nothing that will prevent her from coming to our aid."[189]

---

[178] Le Picart, *Instruction*, 25.
[179] Le Picart, *SL*, 246; *Instruction*, 161.
[180] Le Picart, *Trinité*, fol. 57.
[181] Le Picart, *Advent*, fol. 347; *Trinité*, fol. 11.
[182] Le Picart, *Trinité*, fol. 238.
[183] Le Picart, *Caresme*, fol. 59; *Trinité-II*, fol. 129.
[184] Le Picart, *Pasques*, fol. 67; ibid, fol. 111.
[185] Le Picart, *SL*, 163.
[186] Le Picart, *Advent*, fol. 4.
[187] Le Picart, *Trinité*, fol. 240; *Trinité-II*, fol. 48.
[188] Le Picart, *SL*, 193.
[189] Le Picart, *Trinité*, fol. 49.

Although Désiré states in his memorial that Le Picart had loved, honored and taken as his special saint in word and deed the Virgin Mary,[190] Le Picart, quite possibly following the early Jesuit tradition, devotes less space in his sermons to the mother of God than one would expect. Nevertheless, his approach is entirely traditional. "When I am in church, I go down on my knees, and with my hands clasped before the statue of the Virgin Mary or some other saint, I feel as if I am before the crucifix or the precious body of Our Lord."[191] Her role is special, however, as she is our "mother of compassion."[192] Although Jesus Christ is the source, Mary serves as an intermediary to make God's children participants in her son's sacrifice. Through her actions, a person who is desolate can once again find joy.[193] As proof of the veneration due Mary, Le Picart points out that "Mohammed, who is an infidel, testified to the sanctity of Mary, Mother of God. How much more should we who are Christians honor and pray to her?"[194] If heretics dishonored Mary by their refusal to accept her unique role, painters in Le Picart's time did her another kind of disservice: "The painters paint the glorious Virgin Mary in her bed, as if she were in pain and travail, and as if she were in need of a midwife. What an abuse! For without any pain she gave birth to Our Lord Jesus Christ, and she alone did this. The integrity of her body was never breached. . . . This is as much an error as if one said it aloud, and should be punished."[195]

But of the saints, it is Mary Magdalene on whom Le Picart lavishes the most attention, for in Christ's most loving follower could be found all the characteristics of the female sex. Le Picart states clearly that "there are degrees of love. Our Lord shows this, because he especially loved St. John the Evangelist, Lazarus, Martha and Magdalene, and preferred to speak with them rather than others."[196] Magdalene had been a notorious sinner, a public woman given to all manner of lubricity, "but she threw herself at the feet of Jesus Christ. He made her just and returned her to a state of innocence." Le Picart describes her conversion in affective terms:

---

[190] Désiré, *Regretz*, fol. Di.
[191] Le Picart, *Caresme-II*, fol. 55; cf. *Caresme*, fol. 69.
[192] Le Picart, *Advent*, fol. 49.
[193] Ibid.
[194] Le Picart, *Caresme*, fol. 165.
[195] Le Picart, *Advent*, fol. 150.
[196] Le Picart, *Trinité*, fol. 213.

... as soon as she felt the virtue of Jesus, she was changed, and never
had her sins made her cry as she now cried to Him. A heart moved
by virtue and love of our Lord cannot be put off. . . . As soon as she
felt and recognized the force and efficacy of the name of Jesus in her
heart, without procrastination she threw herself at the feet of Our Lord
Jesus Christ at the banquet with a great effusion of tears, and bathed
His feet.[197]

Like other preachers and artists of the Catholic Reformation, Le
Picart emphasizes her tears: "She loved Our Lord Jesus Christ singularly, as the one at whose feet she found her salvation and her
life, with all consolation and joy, by her tears and the remission of
her sins."[198] Le Picart tells his listeners that this does not mean Mary
Magdalene experienced no temptations, but that she chastised her
flesh through prayer and abstinence.[199] By overcoming her lust and
putting her faith in the Lord, Mary Magdalene was made part of
the order of virgins.[200] This provided a salutary example for the fallen
women in his audience, to whom Le Picart directed many of his
sermons.[201] He explains that

> the Evangelist does not name the sin of Magdalene; he only says: *She
> was a sinner in the city.* Because when we speak of a poor girl, and call
> her a sinner, we understand the sin of the flesh. Therefore she was a
> sinner in the city and her sin was notorious, common, and manifest
> to all. Nevertheless, she converted to Jesus Christ, and not only con-
> verted, but she did not merit less than if she had always guarded her
> virginity, thanks to her great penitence, and so she was received by
> God as if she had never sinned, and she lodged and was the hostess
> for Jesus Christ.[202]

Unlike earlier preachers, Le Picart does not specifically refer to the
legendary life of Magdalene, but uses some of the story made famous
by *The Golden Legend*:

> The cause that today leads many poor girls to perdition is liberty,
> wealth and beauty, if she does not conduct herself through the fear
> of God. The Magdalene was rich, beautiful, and without fear, and she
> lived in freedom, because she had control of all her goods. Do not

---

[197] Le Picart, *Advent*, fol. 217.
[198] Le Picart, *Caresme-II*, fols. 167–168.
[199] Le Picart, *Trinité*, fol. 66.
[200] Le Picart, *Pasques*, fol. 163.
[201] Hilarion de Coste, *Parfait ecclesiastique*, 205; Désiré, *Regretz*, fol. Bi.
[202] Le Picart, *Caresme-II*, fol. 82.

give freedom to your girls. The best and most sure condition of girls is to be by their mothers' sides. But you mothers and fathers, you let them go everywhere![203]

But unlike many who increasingly called for prostitutes to be enclosed in repentant convents, Le Picart says this is counterproductive:

Nevertheless if it happens that someone falls into sin (which God does not want), do not counsel them to despair or to distrust the bounty and compassion of God if he or she is truly contrite and penitent. There are some who are so fickle and uncharitable that if they come upon a poor girl who has been ill advised, who has committed some common fault, they cry out this fault, and won't leave off their words or threats, insisting that she enter religion. If she is incapable of entering religion, why will you make her? You ought to have compassion and consider how you have gravely offended God just as much as she has offended before you and others.[204]

Le Picart places special emphasis on the role of Mary Magdalene at the cross and her part in the Resurrection. This allows him to speculate on the nature of woman. "The female is the weaker sex, and yet nevertheless Our Lord after His Resurrection manifested himself to women. Note that our Lord habitually chose the weak and fragile to manifest the truth of His majesty and to testify for Him."[205] When "Our Lord wanted to do great things, He always chose simple people and poor sinners. And in like manner He wanted first to show His Resurrection to women, who are of the fragile sex and of little virtue."[206] Le Picart praises the constancy of the women, who felt no fear, even though "woman is silly and weak, and regularly of little enterprise."[207] He contrasts these women with "some of Paris who when they get up to prepare for church, take three or four hours before they are ready ... But these women are praiseworthy for their great diligence and love."[208] Yet he compares the great faith of Magdalene and the other women favorably to the small faith of Peter:[209] "The blessed apostles and disciples of Our Lord

---

[203] Ibid, fol. 83.
[204] Le Picart, *Caresme*, fol. 10.
[205] Le Picart, *Caresme-II*, fol. 155.
[206] Ibid, fol. 59.
[207] Le Picart, *Caresme-II*, fols. 157, 186.
[208] Ibid, fol. 160.
[209] Le Picart, *Caresme*, fol. 62.

returned to their houses. But Magdalene, very upset, remained at
the monument sad and crying. . . . She remained there all by herself."[210] Ironically, the sins of her flesh had engendered her great
love. "I believe that once she had begun to obliterate the memory
of her flesh by continual exercise, she kept her body from becoming a problem . . . You will find her in contemplation at the base of
the cross of Our Lord Jesus Christ, stemming the flow of his blood.
And she was at the monument. It was love that made her do this,
and love is not idle."[211] He describes how she remained at the monument, with great anxiety and perplexity in her spirit, feeling great
sorrow that she had lost her master, and crying as she never stopped
seeking Christ.[212]

Like preachers throughout the Middle Ages, Le Picart paints an
almost mystical portrait of Mary Magdalene searching for her lord
in the garden. "She thought that Our Lord was lost to her; she felt
she had lost everything."[213] Even the presence of angels could not
console her:

> The angels had consoled the other women and had said to them,
> "Have no fear, since you are searching for Jesus Christ crucified, and
> He is resurrected and is no longer here. But nevertheless they did not
> console the blessed Magdalene who remained alone at the monument.
> Isn't the role of the angels to console the hearts of the broken-hearted
> who search for God? Certainly! But note that it is not appropriate for
> the servant to speak before his master. . . . So the angels didn't speak,
> because seeing Our Lord present (however invisible He was to the
> glorious Magdalene), they did not go forward at all to console her,
> to demonstrate the fear and reverence that the blessed angels have
> toward God.

But then Magdalene saw someone in the garden.

> So the blessed Magdalene insofar as she only saw Our Lord in the
> form of a gardener . . . and did not recognize Him, was not firm in
> her faith. But in truth Our Lord is a good gardener in the garden of
> our souls. The good thoughts and goodwill that you have, are these
> not the good seeds that the gardener Our Lord Jesus Christ plants
> and makes grow in our hearts, and in the garden of our souls, to pro-
> duce good fruit in abundance?[214]

---

[210] Le Picart, *Caresme-II*, fol. 167.
[211] Le Picart, *Trinité*, fol. 66.
[212] Le Picart, *Caresme-II*, fol. 168.
[213] Ibid, fol. 167.
[214] Ibid, fols. 169–170.

Pre-Reformation preachers, relying on *The Golden Legend,* referred often to Mary Magdalene's preaching in Aix and Marseilles.[215] But increasing concern with order in the sixteenth century and the spectre of women preaching made Catholic preachers more circumspect in describing the role of the Magdalene, and at times this verged on disparagement:

> This woman here is ignorant and foolish, and nevertheless in erring she spoke wisely through the bounty of God. . . . She erred because she did not believe at all . . . When the Magdalene recognized Our Savior after His Resurrection, she wanted to embrace him, but he said, *Do not touch me.* She wanted to hold and embrace him, so that she would not lose him all over again. She did this out of foolishness.[216]

Many preachers were uncomfortable with the absence of the Virgin Mary at the Resurrection and, following a longstanding minority viewpoint, placed her there in spite of the testimony of the gospels. Le Picart explains: "I have not spoken of the glorious Virgin Mary . . . but I believe that He manifested Himself to her before all others, however much holy scripture makes no mention of it."[217]

But it was to Mary Magdalene that Christ gave the mandate to announce his Resurrection to the apostles. "We spoke yesterday of the manner in which Our Lord Jesus Christ manifested Himself to the blessed Magdalene, and how He charged her to announce to the apostles what she had seen."[218] In the process Mary Magdalene earned the title Apostle to the Apostles, which according to Le Picart she shared with St. Catherine of Alexandria, known for her learned disputations: "This girl was of the weaker sex, and yet she had apostolic authority."[219]

If Mary Magdalene and the Virgin Mary play featured roles in Le Picart's sermons, the same cannot be said of ordinary women. Le Picart's general discussion of women shows the important changes that had taken place in the sixteenth century. He begins his discussion of the nature of woman with the scene in the Garden of Eden:

---

[215] Taylor, *Soldiers of Christ,* 176–177.
[216] Le Picart, *Caresme-II,* fols. 170–171.
[217] Ibid, fol. 171.
[218] Ibid.
[219] Le Picart, *Trinité-II,* fol. 217.

> When the snake that is, the Devil, sees that man was created by God
> and destined for blessed eternity, to be put in the place from which
> he had been chased, he got himself into the guise of the serpent and
> went to the woman, for they are known to be more easily deceived
> than man, and asked her the question, saying: "Why does God forbid
> you to eat such a fruit?" And the woman responded to him . . . "No,
> no, you will not die," said the serpent, "but will be like gods after you
> have eaten, and your eyes will be opened and you will know all." And
> this food that the Devil offered to Eve was the food of deception.[220]

Like most churchmen, Le Picart repeats the commonplace that the
beginning of man's ruin was accomplished by a woman, but his
restoration came from the Virgin Mary.[221] But his underlying doubt
remains:

> God has made marvels with women. When the city of Bethulia was
> afflicted, the good Judith cut the head off Holofernes. We also have
> the case of the king Ahasuerus who had given orders and commands
> to the good Esther, and by her counsel, the sentence was revoked. . . .
> But when a woman does evil, the Devil is not worse than she is. . . .
> The iniquity of a man is better than a woman who does good. This
> is called hyperbole. And by this is demonstrated how great is the in-
> iquity of woman when she sets herself to evil. . . . [I]t is less danger-
> ous to live with a bad man than with a good woman.

He goes on: "I say that I will not at all hesitate to dine with a good
woman. But it is necessary to guard oneself . . . [T]his passage of
Solomon shows us how great is the malice of woman when she sets
herself to evil. But we see as well that women are so devout and
do so much good when they set themselves to it that it is said that
the devout woman intercedes for us."[222] Le Picart gives the examples of Monica, who prayed God to convert her wayward son
Augustine to the Christian faith,[223] and the Canaanite woman, who
showed great faith.[224] But in a dramatic reversal of pre-Reformation
practice, Le Picart does not devote significant time in his sermons
to the concerns or problems of women or, for that matter, their vanity. This may relate to changes in gender attitudes during the sixteenth century, but the more likely explanation can be found in the
changed sermon style and structure which more closely followed the

---

[220] Le Picart, *SL*, 196–197.
[221] Le Picart, *Caresme-II*, fol. 191.
[222] Le Picart, *Trinité-II*, fol. 70.
[223] Le Picart, *SL*, 162.
[224] Le Picart, *Caresme*, fol. 60.

gospels. Occasionally, however, Le Picart offers a reflection or two on the relationship between the sexes and marriage. "The body and the flesh serve the spirit, so it is not reasonable for a woman to dominate a man, because woman is our flesh, which must be subject to and obey the spirit."[225] He berates women who behave in a wanton manner, thinking their behavior is secret. "Here you have a woman who takes care not to give offense in the presence of her husband, but she waits for the time when he will no longer be at home to go off with some man. But God is present. If you behave properly in the presence of your husband, how much more should you do so in the presence of Our Lord?"[226] One of the few attacks on vanity in his sermons involves a complaint that women are dressing up as men.[227] Yet Le Picart was equally willing to take on wayward husbands. He counsels men to live honestly and peacefully with their wives, and not consort with other women.[228] Finally, he takes a strong stand against domestic abuse: "It is too indecent a thing to beat your wife. What consolation is it to children to see their father and mother fighting?"[229]

Le Picart spends most of his time instructing lay women and men how to be good Christians. He stresses the need for people to love their neighbor, saying that you can read the entire Bible and know all of the Law, and yet it comes down to two things—loving God above all else, and loving your neighbor as yourself.[230] But as he looks around him, he finds little evidence of people fulfilling their duties. "In this city there are around three thousand paupers, and yet we find in such a great and renowned city as Paris, where the Word of God is preached like nowhere else in Christendom, that we cannot feed them."[231] All around him the poor are dying of hunger, yet no one gives a *denier*.[232] "Those who have wealth and substance in this world and do not aid their Christian brother who is needy, but let him die of hunger, are as guilty as if they murdered him."[233] He advises his listeners that it is their responsibility

---

[225] Le Picart, *Advent*, fol. 290.
[226] Le Picart, *Pasques*, fol. 176.
[227] Le Picart, *Trinité-II*, fol. 4.
[228] Le Picart, *Trinité*, fols. 98, 141.
[229] Le Picart, *Advent*, fol. 262.
[230] Le Picart, *Trinité*, fol. 176.
[231] Le Picart, *Trinité-II*, fol. 198.
[232] Le Picart, *Pasques*, fol. 151.
[233] Le Picart, *Instruction*, 188.

to pick up their neighbor when he falls, and not to defame him. "If you accuse your neighbor and reveal his turpitude, you slander and injure him. This is a fault in your love of your neighbor."[234] He sees few around him who volunteer to help those in hospitals or prisons,[235] or try to prevent a girl from turning to prostitution: "You see a poor girl in necessity, and being badly advised and needing money, she prostitutes herself and sins. If you aid her in her necessity, you will keep her from prostitution and sin."[236] But seeing so many poor girls, vulnerable to pimps, one should weep aloud.[237] He severely chastises "... bad men who go to a poor young widow and say, 'If you come along with me, I will take care of you and your children.'"[238] But while people spare nothing for the poor, they lavish their money on pet dogs and birds.[239]

Riches themselves were not inherently evil, but were a gift of God.[240] "God sends goods to test us, and to see if we will be as humble in prosperity as we were in adversity."[241] The Lord gives opulence so that people can practice charity,[242] but too often they are like thorns that prick and torment the heart of man.[243] Le Picart asks, "what will it profit you to have great pomp and ceremony at your funeral and yet be damned?"[244] Too often, "honors change morés. For example, a lawyer, counselor or president, instead of being a good advocate like when he lived more simply, becomes a prideful counselor or president."[245] Riches often lead to lawsuits and vendettas,[246] giving Le Picart the opportunity to attack the legal profession that employed so many of his family members. Judges themselves swear, saying "God's Blood!" or "God's Death!"[247] But worst of all, justice is not blind. "If a rich man brings a case to court, it will be expedited. He will play with the lawyers and procurers as

---

[234] Le Picart, *SL*, 268; *Caresme*, fol. 94; *Instruction*, 49.
[235] Le Picart, *Trinité*, fol. 162.
[236] Le Picart, *Instruction*, 189.
[237] Le Picart, *Trinité*, fol. 165.
[238] Ibid, fol. 108.
[239] Le Picart, *Trinité-II*, fol. 198.
[240] Le Picart, *Trinité*, fol. 138.
[241] Le Picart, *Caresme-II*, fol. 13.
[242] Le Picart, *Trinité*, fol. 75.
[243] Le Picart, *Pasques*, fol. 4.
[244] Le Picart, *Instruction*, 245.
[245] Ibid, 290.
[246] Le Picart, *Trinité*, fol. 76; cf. ibid, fol. 63.
[247] Le Picart, *Trinité-II*, fol. 170.

he wishes. The judge will lend his ear. But the poor man will languish. He can't get an audience, and in the meantime will die. The rich man will get his property unjustly. This is how we do things today."[248] Le Picart warns that one cannot judge by appearances, for "there are men of justice who cover their misdeeds with the color of justice. One sees paintings and images which are of gold-plated copper, but they are not gold. Just so a lie is painted as truth and justice."[249]

Le Picart offers advice to parents on household management and childrearing. He urges them not to leave their children alone with servants, for there they learn bad habits and language.[250] But he cautions servants to beware of serving in great houses, where they dare not criticize their master or mistress for fear of losing their position or favor.[251] Parents should not send their children to court, where their morals will be perverted,[252] or buy offices for them. "Your son barely has a beard, yet you buy him an office so that he will find a good patron and a rich bride."[253] Mothers must pay attention to what their children are doing: "You, mothers, if you see your daughter with fancy sleeves and bracelets, ask her where she got them. You must be watchful!"[254] The ambition of parents often leads to the ruin of their children: "'I place my daughter in a house in which they play games of dice and cards all night so that she can make a good match.' It would be better to marry her to a poor man, a porter, so that she could find salvation."[255] Parents must set an example: "You, father, mother or guardian, you play, you swear, you frolic about, you say villainous words in the presence of your children and servants, and scandalize them and give them a bad example."[256] Even worse are the actual deeds of the parents: "Fathers damn their children. As a father or mother, I go around the city wearing a mask, in disguise, which gives a bad example. I have to

---

[248] Le Picart, *Caresme*, fol. 39; cf. *Trinité*, fol. 190.

[249] Le Picart, *Trinité*, fol. 128. Curiously, Le Picart displays real invective in numerous places toward painters, complaining that they portray the Virgin and the Magdalene otherwise than they were. He complains "that the city of Paris is full of villainous and evil painters." *Pasques*, fol. 130.

[250] Le Picart, *Caresme*, fol. 123.

[251] Ibid, fol. 135.

[252] Le Picart, *Advent*, fol. 239.

[253] Le Picart, *Trinité-II*, fol. 83; cf. *Advent*, fol. 106.

[254] Le Picart, *Advent*, fol. 102.

[255] Le Picart, *Trinité-II*, fol. 83.

[256] Le Picart, *Pasques*, fol. 33.

have minstrels in my house, and teach my daughter to play [musical instruments]."[257] People are weak and indolent. "If I am sick, I must have violins and other musical instruments to help me recover. I have vexations in my spirit, but need to take all manner of human consolations to chase away my boredom."[258] Mothers and fathers are too indulgent. "Where do you find children today? At the tavern, the gambling den, the tennis court, and not at church!"[259] Boys studying far away, ". . . at Toulouse, Orléans, Poitiers or some other place, have the opportunity to learn and serve the public and their own salvation, but what do they do? Give themselves over to all manner of debauchery!"[260]

Lay religious behavior is also reprehensible. "We do worse than the Lutherans by violating the sabbath. We occupy ourselves with vanities, concluding contracts, going to the markets, getting involved in lawsuits, having banquets, trading, and committing all sorts of follies on Sundays."[261] He admonishes people who think only of their earthly goods to forget about their merchandise and negotiations and pray, hear mass, and go to sermons.[262] But instead of attending sermons, people wander about the streets[263] and play in the fields.[264] He asks such people: "Consider if you lost an *écu*, left on the windowsill, rather than the Word of God. If you were on the road to go to a sermon, and you remembered having forgotten the *écu* on the windowsill or some other place, you know you are in danger of losing it if you don't turn around to retrieve it. But on the other hand, if you return, you will lose the sermon."[265] He urges parents to teach their children well: "Take your children to confession. Instruct them well, and ask them what they learned at the sermon . . ."[266] People must express their piety sincerely:

> If you make a pilgrimage in faith and devotion, for the love you have for God and the saints, and for the grace and virtue God gave them for their merits and the suffering they endured for His honor, the pil-

[257] Le Picart, *Trinité-II*, fol. 83.
[258] Le Picart, *Trinité*, fol. 223.
[259] Le Picart, *Advent*, fol. 249.
[260] Le Picart, *Caresme*, fol. 121.
[261] Le'Picart, *Trinité*, fol. 169.
[262] Ibid, fol. 141.
[263] Ibid, fol. 159.
[264] Le Picart, *Pasques*, fol. 71.
[265] Le Picart, *Trinité*, fol. 138.
[266] Le Picart, *Advent*, fol. 248.

grimage and work is good and is helpful in your search for eternal
life. But something that is good in itself can be abused, and if it is
abused it irritates God rather than appeases Him. For example, we
see the irreverence that many have during pilgrimages. . . . "Let us take
a day and visit Saint Fiacre. It's so pleasant, such good weather to
play in the fields."[267]

Le Picart allots substantial space in his sermons to the need for
prayer in the life of a Christian. Jesus set the example: "When Our
Lord Jesus Christ raised His heart on high in praying to God His
Father, should we not do the same? He bent His knees to the earth
and His face as well, and when He prayed long on the Mount of
Olives He gave an example for us to follow."[268] Le Picart describes
prayer as an elevation of the heart and mind to God.[269] Of the many
things necessary for prayer, faith comes first.[270] Inward intentions are
paramount, with sincerity and love being essential.[271] He explains
that "at the hour of prayer, the soul is transported away from the
body."[272] God ardently desires human beings to come to him: "If I
consider my unworthiness and the great majesty of God, I will tremble, and not dare go to Him. But God doesn't want that! He gives
us the privilege that a father gives to his son to come to Him. He
tells us to call Him our Father, which is a name of love and assurance."[273] Perseverance is important—one should keep knocking at
the door until God opens it.[274] Prayers should be repeated, to further
inflame one's heart and soul.[275] Responding to his audience, he asks,
"How long? Two or three hours? As much as you want to! For
God's part He will never interrupt us when we speak with Him."[276]

In his sermons, Le Picart proposed a program of reform that he
felt had to begin with the church. He was mistaken in his belief that
if only abuses in the church could be corrected, the heretics would
be vanquished and the problems besetting the kingdom of France
would cease. Yet many of his goals—including a better-educated

[267] Le Picart, *Caresme-II*, fol. 172.
[268] Le Picart, *Instruction*, 57.
[269] Ibid, 32; *Trinité*, fol. 236.
[270] Le Picart, *Instruction*, 10–11.
[271] Ibid, 29, 46, 58.
[272] Le Picart, *Trinité*, fol. 66.
[273] Le Picart, *SL*, 111.
[274] Le Picart, *Trinité*, fol. 89.
[275] Ibid, 53.
[276] Ibid, 34.

parish clergy who were recruited from those with a vocation, bishops who lived in and visited their dioceses, and leading by example, were ideals that would be implemented by the Council of Trent. The changes he made in his preaching, especially in the structure and content of sermons, heralded this new type of clergy with its simplicity of teaching. But most of all, he led by example—by preaching, through charity, and by refusing honors and promotions.

Le Picart also spoke directly to the laymen and women in his audience, asking them to reflect upon the lives they were leading and how closely they were following the golden rule. He stressed that riches in themselves were not evil, and that the rich and the poor were interdependent in God's scheme for humanity, but he saw too many people who lived lives of luxury and sloth, ignoring the desperately poor who had become more so during his lifetime as a result of the depredations of soldiers and exactions for expensive campaigns in Italy. He urged parents to pay particular attention to raising their children well—keeping them at home where their behavior could be supervised, and teaching them about God through attendance at sermons and discussions of their meanings. He set Mary Magdalene as a model for all, both men and women, in order to show them that through love and faith even the worst sinner could become the first in God's kingdom.

CHAPTER SEVEN

AVANT LE DÉLUGE:
THE PROPHET OF PARIS?

Madame, if today we see so many debates, dissension and controversies within our Christian religion, it must not trouble or worry us, since all of
this was predicted to happen by Jesus Christ our
Redeemer and His apostles. Be careful (He said)
that you are not seduced. Because many will come
in my name saying, "I am the Christ" and they
will seduce many. At that time you will have wars
and rumors of war (as we see at present) but take
care that you are not troubled. Because it is necessary for all this to happen. But still this will not
be the end, for nation will rise against nation, kingdom against kingdom, and there will be plagues
and famines, and earthquakes in some places. All
of these things will mark the beginning of sorrows.
Then they will deliver you to afflictions and will
kill you. And you will be hated by all peoples because of my name. Others will be scandalized, and
each one will betray the other and be hated by
the other. Several false prophets will be raised up
and will seduce many. And as iniquities multiply
so the charity of many will become cold. But who-
ever perseveres to the end will be saved. St. Paul,
having learned in this same school, and enlightened
by the spirit of prophecy, said, "It is necessary for
there to be heresies in order that the good people
and the elect of God can be recognized among
you" [I Corinthians 11, II Peter 2]. And St. Peter,
in his second canon: "Just as there were false
prophets among the Israelite people, so there will
be among you false doctors who covertly introduce sects of perdition and they will deny the Lord
who redeemed them, bringing sudden perdition
onto themselves. And several will follow their in-
solent ways, by whom the way of truth will be
condemned . . ."

> These are the predictions of the end of time,
> that is, of those times in which we live . . .
>
> Paris, 17 April 1562.[1]

> Alas! How happy were our ancestors, who do not
> today live to see the sentence of Our Lord: You
> will know them by their fruits. If it is necessary for
> such cruelties, indignities, sacrileges, brigandage,
> pillaging and insolences (which are the fruits and
> practical results of such doctrine) to continue much
> longer in our France, I will be able to say along
> with Ronsard: "If religion and the Christian faith
> brings such fruits, I would rather leave it. And ban-
> ished, go live in the Indies or the Antarctic pole
> where the savages live and follow happily the law
> of nature." . . . Isaiah spoke of it in these terms:
> "We await your good sayings and good words, like
> a good vine, good reasons, and here we have wild
> grapes . . . We await some semblance of equity, and
> find troubles and oppression. We expect justice, and
> we find weeping, murders, massacres, sacrileges,
> pillages and other acts crying out for and demand-
> ing justice from God, the angels and men . . ."
>
> Paris, 19 June 1563.[2]

Writing six or seven years after the death of François Le Picart,
Nicolas Chesneau found himself living in different times, times he
believed were filled with signs of the end. In fact, Chesneau's prefaces demonstrate how much things had changed in a few short years.
Crouzet suggests that Chesneau would have felt no compulsion to
publish the sermons had he not found in them an eschatological
tone that matched his own.[3] This ignores a basic aspect of human
nature and reading habits: readers can find what they are looking
for in any writing. There is no need to cast the author of these sermons as a man for whom "violence was a soteriological necessity"[4]
simply because his publisher felt that way or because men he knew
later enunciated ideas that supported violence. More than any other
scholar, Barbara Diefendorf has traced the momentum of the years
that would build to the horrendous massacre of 1572. "There were

---

[1] Chesneau, "Preface," *Pasques,* fols. ii–iii.
[2] Chesneau, "Preface," *Trinité,* fol. iv.
[3] Personal communication, 3 January 1998.
[4] Crouzet, *Genèse,* 431–432.

three stages in the conflicts that preceded the St. Bartholomew's Day Massacre. The first, from 1557 to 1563, is characterized by the gradual breakdown of order in the city before and during the first religious war . . ."[5] Although a Reformed church was founded in Paris in 1555, while Le Picart still lived, it was not until 1557 that major riots broke out.[6] The year after his death saw a deadly conjuncture of religious conflict and military defeat that induced a feeling of panic among large segments of Paris's Catholic population. French forces suffered a disastrous defeat at Saint-Quentin, which was taken over by imperial forces on 27 August 1557. This ". . . awakened a chilling fear that the Habsburgs might put an end to their long wars with France by taking the French capital."[7] And then, only a week later, four hundred men and women were discovered gathered for a *prêche* in a house on the rue Saint-Jacques. Diefendorf points out that when the Calvinists were abused and humiliated as they were led to the Châtelet

> . . . [t]his was not the first time that Catholic Parisians had demonstrated their hatred for the followers of the new religion, but it does mark a new dimension to that hatred. In the past, the Catholic fervor of the Parisian populace had been shown by the enthusiasm with which they turned out to watch the execution of condemned heretics or their participation in processions to expiate sacrileges, but acts of violence against persons suspected of the new faith had been few in number and small in scale. After the affair of the rue Saint-Jacques, such acts multiplied.[8]

In the view of Diefendorf and others, 1557 marked a clear turning point, a point of no return in the almost inexorable slide into an atmosphere of violence, rumor and fear that would fuel religious killing. The sense that events were out of control heightened after the freak accident that led to Henri II's premature death and the accession of his young and sickly son, Francis II. Nancy Roelker admits "there were some sign of rising pressure in 1555, [but they] did not become acute until 1557. It reached the highest level so far attained in 1559–60 and lasted for four years . . . [T]he complex and

---

[5] Barbara Diefendorf, "Prologue to a Massacre: Popular Unrest in Paris, 1557–1572," *American Historical Review* 90(1985), 1069.
[6] Diefendorf, *Beneath the Cross*, 49.
[7] Ibid, 50.
[8] Ibid.

prolonged tension of 1557–63 came from the eruption of divisions within the court, formerly suppressed."[9]

As we have seen, Crouzet believes Le Picart was a prophet of panic, a preacher of the end of the world. Although the word prophetic often refers to aspects of warning and consolation, "'prophecy' is most commonly understood as the prediction of future things; more generally and more properly, it refers to any spiritually inspired preaching or warning."[10] The Hebrew word that is usually translated as "prophet" signifies "one who is called" or "one who is delegated as a messenger."[11] Many of the prophets of ancient Israel made their appeal directly to history. "They believed in and announced the judgment of God. There is no question that this second appeal was more central to their mission than the first. They looked for a tangible and terrible intervention from outside, a corrective catastrophe which bore the wrath and purpose of God."[12] One of the most characteristic features of the prophet's message was ". . . its actuality, its expectation of something soon to happen."[13] Not primarily preachers of repentance, but men who announced future events as divine intervention in history, the prophets were deeply involved in the political, social and religious life of their country.[14] Prophecy in its Old Testament context therefore encompassed two basic and sometimes differing ideas: the prophet as consoler in times of trouble and the man who spoke for God to announce his imminent intervention in human history. It is the last of these definitions that Crouzet embraces.

As should be clear from the first six chapters, Le Picart was *not* a prophet of doom, a herald of eschatological imminence, or a preacher of panic and violence. Even Le Picart's use of sources disproves Crouzet's contention. Only four percent of all Le Picart's ref-

---

[9] Nancy Lyman Roelker, *One King, One Faith: The Parlement of Paris and the Religious Reformations of the Sixteenth Century* (Berkeley: University of California Press, 1996), 184.

[10] Barnes, *Prophecy and Gnosis*, 3, 13.

[11] W. Lee Humphreys, *Crisis and Story: Introduction to the Old Testament* (Mountain View, CA: Mayfield Publishing Co., 1990), 116.

[12] James L. Mays, "Justice: Perspectives from the Prophetic Tradition," in David L. Petersen, ed., *Prophecy in Israel: Search for an Identity* (Philadelphia: Fortress Press, 1987), 156.

[13] Gerhard von Rad, *The Message of the Prophets* (New York: Harper San Francisco, 1995), 91.

[14] Gene M. Tucker, "The Role of the Prophets and the Role of the Church," in David L. Petersen, ed., *Prophecy in Israel: Search for an Identity* (Philadelphia: Fortress Press, 1987), 159, 168–169.

erences are taken from the Prophetic Books. Of these, he only quotes
substantially from Isaiah and Jeremiah, probably a function of the
length of those books. If certain elements in Le Picart's sermons can
be isolated as carrying a prophetic ring, they are those that deal
with the need for amendment. Jeremiah's Temple Sermon [Jeremiah
7:1–12] is primarily a call to repentance, to amend one's ways and
deeds,[15] and the key to his message is a person's reorientation from
a life of sin to a life in God.[16] Perhaps most significant for Le Picart
was Jeremiah's conflict with royalty, displayed in his showdown in
Jeremiah 36 with Jehoiakim.[17] Isaiah's message to the people of
Israel could have fit very well into Le Picart's understanding of mid-
sixteenth century France, for the first part of the book of Isaiah
describes a political and military crisis which the prophet believed
gave God's people the opportunity to demonstrate that they were
worthy of divine love. Isaiah felt Yahweh had been abandoned;[18] Le
Picart must certainly have felt the same as he watched heresy spread
unchecked in France. The prophets of ancient Israel often spoke up
for the poor and the weak,[19] and in this sense Le Picart was their
follower.

If there was a Hebrew prophet whom Le Picart resembled it was
Hosea. Although he takes few references from the very short Book
of Hosea, Le Picart may in some ways have modeled himself on the
prophet. Hosea's understanding of the meaning of a prophet was
". . . a figure who stood between God and the people and who was
to protect the people by warning them of approaching danger."[20]
For Hosea, ". . . love takes its place alongside fear, obedience, faith,
worship, and the like in language about human responses to the
divine initiative . . ."[21] The book of Hosea is unique for its "spiritual

---

[15] William L. Holladay, "The Years of Jeremiah's Preaching," in James Luther
Mays and Paul J. Achtemeier, eds., *Interpreting the Prophets* (Philadelphia: Fortress
Press, 1987), 132.

[16] Philip J. King, *Jeremiah: An Archaeological Companion* (Louisville, KY: West-
minster/John Knox Press, 1993), 12.

[17] Walter Brueggemann, "The Book of Jeremiah: Portrait of the Prophet," in
James Luther Mays and Paul Achtemeier, eds., *Interpreting the Prophets* (Philadelphia:
Fortress Press, 1987), 126.

[18] Humphreys, *Crisis and Story*, 139.

[19] Mays, "Justice," 154–1544.

[20] Robert R. Wilson, *Prophecy and Society in Ancient Israel* (Philadelphia: Fortress
Press, 1984), 229.

[21] John F.A. Sawyer, *Prophecy and the Prophets of the Old Testament* (Oxford: Oxford
University Press, 1987), 49.

and ethical idealism," its "demands for justice and love . . ."[22] Above all, in Hosea, Yahweh, the spurned lover, continues to love his people despite their rejection. "Israel's faithlessness is contrasted with God's abundant love,"[23] not unlike France in Le Picart's time. Like Hosea, Le Picart would criticize kings and priests who had violated the covenant with God,[24] yet also like him, ". . . his words are filled not only with profound sorrow and grief but also with a sense of hope and promise . . ."[25] Hosea's was far more a message of renewal and hope—*because of God's great love*—than a message of doom. If Le Picart is seen as a man trying to bring France back to the right course, then he can be considered a prophet in the Hebrew sense, but his was not a voice of eschatological imminence, as Crouzet claims.

We have seen in the foregoing chapters that Le Picart zealously promoted reform on both a societal and an individual level. He championed the poor and the helpless. Above all, he presented God in relational terms as a loving father, brother, husband and friend, emphasizing the consoling and forgiving aspects of God. None of this supports the notion that Le Picart was a *prédicateur panique*, so we must look for more specific evidence of eschatological strains within his sermons. Quoting from Le Picart's sermons, Crouzet says,

> [t]he prophetic panic rings in his words, even if the man who spoke them denied being a prophet: "Oh Christians! This will be a piteous and calamitous time. I am not a prophet nor the son of a prophet, but according to that which Our Lord predicts in Saint Paul, we can see well how the day of judgment approaches, because malice abounds more than ever, and charity is colder than it has ever been . . . It seems there is no God at all as we live. Christians, think on this, for there will not be time after death."[26]

The problem with reading a belief in the imminent consummation of the world into such a statement is that it takes no account of the occasion on which the sermon was preached, or the context of what preachers in earlier times had said. The sermon from which Crouzet quotes was delivered for Advent, when the most terrifying descriptions of the Judgment were frequently delivered by preachers to warn

---

[22] Ibid, 107.
[23] James D. Newsome, Jr., *The Hebrew Prophets* (Atlanta: John Knox Press, 1973), 43.
[24] Ibid, 37, 39.
[25] Humphreys, *Crisis and Story*, 125.
[26] Crouzet, *Guerriers de Dieu*, I:207–208; he quotes from Le Picart, *Advent*, fol. 54.

people of the signs of the Second Coming. A typical sermon of the late fifteenth century given by Jean Tisserand (d. ca. 1497) during Advent describes the Judgment in terrifying terms:

> But it is sufficient for now to take the signs that are mentioned in our theme. Whence it is said that the nations of the earth will be in anguish; distress will be such that people will hide in the caves of the earth. And this because of the confusion that arises with the roaring of the seas and rivers. The seas will rise wondrously over all of the hills, and then they will subside. So with the rivers, and they will make a thunderous noise . . . The rivers will bring forth great waves, and the voices of all the waters will lift themselves on high to our Lord. And then the rivers will strike against the lands, according to the gospel so that men will die of fright in the face of them.[27]

He goes on:

> O, wretched sinners, who take your gain in this or that: the fire will consume you along with your wealth . . . It will cleanse the elect who are biding their time in purgatory . . . for after the Judgment there will be no more purgatory. And after the Judgment the fire will descend with the damned into hell, for the earth will open up, and the greatest of horrors will rush to greet the damned. The damned and the fire will descend at the same moment into this pit of filth and sulfur. Immediately after the descent of the damned, the purifying fire will return to renew the earth. After the Judgment, the fire will return to its pristine state.[28]

Guillaume Pepin (ca. 1465–1533), a Dominican whose sermons usually evince little interest in signs of the Last Things, remarks in his sermons, ". . . at the end of the world a huge boulder will plunge down the mountainside, that is, Christ will come down from the heavens, and bit by bit He will tear apart the arms and torsos of sinners, and throw them into hell because of their treatment of the poor. . . . Once outside, if they look back, they will see the whole world ablaze in the fire of the great conflagration."[29]

---

[27] Jean Tisserand, *Sermones de adventu* (Paris, 1517), fol. 17.

[28] Ibid, fols. 19–20.

[29] Guillaume Pepin, *Concionum dominicalium ex epistolis et evangeliis totius anni, pars aestivalis* (Antwerp: Guillelmus Lesteenius and Engelbertus Gymnicus, 1656), 89; Guillaume Pepin, *Concionum dominicalium ex epistolis et evangeliis totius anni, pars hiemalis* (Antwerp: Guillelmus Lesteenius and Engelbertus Gymnicus, 1656), 313. Pepin's sermons went through numerous editions well into the seventeenth century, but were originally printed during his lifetime (ca. 1465–1533).

Before we turn to this theme in Le Picart's works, it is worthwhile to see how a contemporary Catholic preacher in Italy has been portrayed in French historiography. Cornelio Musso (1511–1574), a Catholic and a humanist who was also a proponent of reform from within, has also been accused of propagating a message of fear. In response to Jean Delumeau's description of Musso's *Prediche* 1.3 as terrifying and macabre, Corrie Norman asserts that

> Delumeau's brief citation of this passage did not do it justice. It is one of the most horrifying examples of *ecphrasis* in Musso's sermons. . . . But this passage does not tell the whole story. Had Delumeau looked further he would have found a balance between fearful and hopeful messages in this sermon. . . . [Musso's preaching was] "in the middle" where truth resided and [the audience] might be most receptive to moral persuasion. The kind of exaggeration and extreme that Delumeau described was exactly what Musso and these preachers were fighting against.[30]

This shows precisely how important it is to read an entire corpus rather than individual sermons, or parts of sermons. To begin with, an examination of statements in Le Picart's sermons that can be taken as signifying the approach of the end shows that they come overwhelmingly from Advent sermons, and they can only be termed mild in comparison with those of earlier preachers. Even less than Musso does Le Picart evoke terror and foreboding. Hervé Martin has shown that in times of great crisis in the fourteenth century preachers filled their sermons with a litany of horrors affecting society.[31] From a religious standpoint, the events of the mid-sixteenth century should have evoked similar dire predictions from preachers. Yet Le Picart's approach is tame compared with that of Tisserand or the even more frightening fifteenth-century preacher Vincent Ferrier. Almost all preachers spoke of the Judgment during Advent— it was part of how they were trained, and Le Picart was no exception. But let us now consider the most convincing case possible that Le Picart believed the Last Judgment was at hand.

Le Picart, who rejects the title of prophet, nevertheless defines a prophet's role as "to announce the coming and the incarnation of

---

[30] Norman, *Humanist Taste*, 100, 104.

[31] Hervé Martin, "La ministère de la parole en France septentrionale de la peste noire à la réforme," *Thèse d'état*, Université de Paris IV/Sorbonne, 1986, 653.

Our Lord."[32] The terminology is ambiguous, possibly intentionally so, as all preachers used the season of Advent when Jesus was born both to describe the blessings that were brought with the First Coming and to prefigure the Second. Le Picart spends time on the problems facing Christendom and France in his time. He frequently comments that "we are living in bad times,"[33] or "the tempest is worse today than ever . . ."[34] This, he says, is because God is no longer known.[35] It sometimes even seems that God is sleeping.[36] Le Picart explains that Saint Fiacre sought solitude so that he could come to know God better and experience no distractions, but "today the turmoil, dissension, variety of opinions, schisms and divisions hinder one from coming to know God and the truth."[37] Yet despite this being a time of grief and lamentation, "we see as many dances in these piteous and calamitous times as if it were the most tranquil and peaceful time that ever was."[38]

Heresy was a major cause of these problems, yet there was cause for hope since it was out in the open: "The times today are bad and full of scandals. It is more to be feared, however, when the infirmity is secret, for [like a sickness] it is more dangerous than when it is open and manifest. The doctor would not know anything. The heretics are like serpents—they strike with their tails!"[39] He asks his listeners to pray that these ". . . infidelities and errors, like heresies, enchantments and magical arts, will cease."[40] His optimism is palpable: "These contemptible heretics will not last but will soon be wiped out and their heresies abolished."[41] Even given an appropriate example with which to make an eschatological statement, Le Picart avoids doing so. "Saint Cyprian says that all those who were outside Noah's Ark at the time of the flood were endangered. So those who are outside the church of God are on the road to damnation."[42]

---

[32] Le Picart, *Advent*, fol. 132.
[33] Ibid, fol. 78.
[34] Le Picart, *Trinité*, fol. 50.
[35] Le Picart, *Trinité-II*, fol. 142; *Caresme-II*, fol. 121.
[36] Le Picart, *Advent*, fols. 284, 285.
[37] Le Picart, *Trinité-II*, fol. 84; cf. *Trinité*, fol. 106.
[38] Le Picart, *Trinité*, fol. 29.
[39] Le Picart, *Pasques*, fol. 123.
[40] Le Picart, *Instruction*, 91.
[41] Le Picart, *Pasques*, fol. 204.
[42] Le Picart, *SL*, 22.

Still the problems were serious enough to instill anxiety. The preacher warns:

> In past times we have so often been reprimanded, then God has deferred his anger, and it seems that He has forgotten it. We see the signs, the cities burning, people losing all their goods in this way, all is put to fire and blood, all to the sword. Are these not signs and presages which signify that in the hour when we no longer think of it, we will be struck down by God? The Jews did not see the signs, like us. It is therefore a sign that we are worse than they were. They demanded signs, and we have them.[43]

The remedy begins with prayer. "Yesterday you came together to pray to the saints, and especially Saint Geneviève. There is great occasion and need for prayer, because we are in danger of experiencing famine, plague and war. After God, the saints are your place of refuge."[44] He is philosophical about these evil times—just as the Lord sends good times, so he also sends bad.[45]

Le Picart attributes many of France's woes to war. For most of the reign of Henri II, France was involved in war with the Emperor and during part of that time with England as well. "Do we not have great cause and reason to return to God, seeing that all parts of the earth are engaged in war and that misery and poverty are everywhere? Is this not a great advertisement to convert to God and to ask His pardon and grace for our sins?"[46] Speaking of the events of 1544, he asks, "Have you not seen that for thirteen or fourteen years we fled with fear from our enemy? And those who were supposed to protect the city left the first. In despair of having peace, peace was made. Who made it? God. God permitted things to get to the point of despair, in human terms, in order that He could intervene and it would be said: 'God did that, this is not a work of men.'"[47] Referring to Henry VIII's capture of Boulogne in 1544, he asks if the capture of this city, one of the keys to France, was not a signal to recognize the sins of society.[48] The moral is that these wars will continue until the people of France correct their ways; afterwards it

---

[43] Le Picart, *Trinité*, fol. 210.
[44] Ibid, fol. 49.
[45] Ibid, fol. 100.
[46] Le Picart, *Pasques*, fol. 10.
[47] Ibid, fol. 164; cf. *Trinité-II*, fol. 120.
[48] Le Picart, *Advent*, fol. 77.

will not be necessary to fear the Emperor, the English, or any other adversary.[49] The wars, Le Picart warns, are symbolic of the war between God and humankind;[50] God hints at the possibility of future ills so that we will amend our lives.[51] Yet even when speaking of these problems, Le Picart is consolatory: "If we think that the present evil will endure forever, we must remind ourselves that the affliction is only temporal, and the good that we hope for is eternal."[52]

When assessing the eschatological content of Le Picart's sermons, several factors must be considered. On almost every occasion on which Le Picart seems to suggest the end is near, he is delivering an Advent sermon, a fact of the utmost importance. Moreover, his meaning is often ambiguous. First, there is the likelihood that he is actually referring to the First Coming, even when using the present tense. For example, he says, "[t]he time is coming, it is near, when our Redeemer and Liberator must come. There is not more than three days. And so in today's epistle, St. Paul exhorts us to rejoice . . . And why should we rejoice? Because the Lord is near. . . . When the king nears a town to make his entry, the prisoners rejoice, because they hope to be delivered."[53] Here the reference to three days and to Saint Paul show that Le Picart is alluding to the First Coming.

Second, there is a figurative connection between the First and Second Comings, just as there is a figurative relationship between the Old and New Testaments. Le Picart tells his audience that "[o]ur salvation is closer than it was in past times, because they only had the figure of it, as St. John said . . . And we have the truth! We see the thing revealed to us better than with a mirror; in times past, they only saw it as if reflected in a mirror."[54] Here the mere passage of time makes the Judgment technically nearer.

Finally, Le Picart quotes sources from the distant past which by their very nature distance the Judgment. Citing ancient sources such as the Church Fathers reduces the immediacy of the threat/promise. "Saint John Chrysostom says: 'The resurrection is near, and the terrible Day of Judgment and the Day of the Lord.' That is, the Judgment

---

[49] Le Picart, *Trinité*, fol. 24; cf. *Advent*, fol. 77.
[50] Le Picart, *Pasques*, fol. 9.
[51] Le Picart, *Trinité*, fol. 128.
[52] Le Picart, *Advent*, fol. 34.
[53] Ibid, fol. 123.
[54] Ibid, fol. 9.

of God is getting close, and so it is not the time to cause offense in these times since we are closer to the Judgment than ever."[55]

Elsewhere, Le Picart tells men and women to hasten, because their time is brief.[56] During Advent, he also speaks on rare occasions of the Antichrist, but usually in restrained language. In one sermon, he exclaims, "we grieve for the Holy Spirit in us; it only remains for the angels to depart with us, and for the Antichrist to come. You have no fear, you show no honor to the unity of the faith or baptism, you break everything, and you say that you only recognize a bad God, a bad baptism, a bad faith."[57] The other major exception is the passage quoted by Crouzet in which Le Picart rejects the title of prophet. It continues:

> ... because today, he who is Catholic vacillates and doubts, saying that when a heretic speaks he is at least partially right. Christians, if we are taken in a state of grace, it will be good, otherwise not. The damned, to their confusion, will watch the blessed mount to paradise, and they will be cast down into Hell. Oh Christians! Should we not repudiate our greediness? ... We are similar to the stupid rich man who amassed so many goods, who rejoiced that his cellar and granaries were full ... Think about the Judgment of God![58]

References to what will follow the Judgment are negligible, especially when compared with pre-Reformation sermons. In the Advent sermons, Le Picart explains that "since the coming of Our Lord, it is easier to be saved than in times past."[59] He tells those who will be saved that "after the general resurrection, my body will have the condition of spirit, and the spirit will be like that of the angels."[60] But for the damned, who wonder how long they will suffer, he responds, "Eternally, forever ... For a brief moment of delectation would you want to suffer even one moment of burning in the fire?"[61] He adds that "the bodies of the unhappy damned will also be resuscitated. But they will be more infected than with all the fetor of the world."[62] He also warns the great that they should exercise particular care over their salvation:

---

[55] Ibid, fol. 8.
[56] Ibid, fol. 33.
[57] Le Picart, *Trinité*, fol. 165.
[58] Le Picart, *Advent*, fol. 54.
[59] Ibid, fol. 10.
[60] Le Picart, *SL*, 174.
[61] Le Picart, *Trinité*, fol. 63.
[62] Le Picart, *Advent*, fol. 55.

My friends, the time will come that God will subvert all the great houses, buildings, kings and princes . . . And why will God do this? To find the lost jewel. He also makes brooms to sweep for them. The brooms are composed of several branches, by which are signified the kings and princes who gather unto them rotten soldiers who pillage the property of good people.[63]

Le Picart admits to fear that the evil will increase with time.[64]

Yet if Le Picart occasionally broaches the subject of the Judgment, he as often backs away from its implications. He uses the idea almost solely to promote moral reformation, telling his auditors, "for the first time and even the second, He doesn't get angry. But when He sees that I persist in my evil and that it is not due to weakness or ignorance, but rather because I contemplate all the means by which I can do wrong, at that point, God finally will say, 'Enough! Don't speak to me anymore.'"[65] He admits there are many signs at present that God is angry with his people.[66] But it is never too late for a change of heart:

He sent to Ezechias, that he should ready himself to die tomorrow. . . . And nevertheless, when he repented, when he did penance, God sent to tell him that he would not die after all. Similarly, he sends Jonas to tell those of Nineveh that in forty days the town will be destroyed. . . . And the king, hearing this, donned a hairshirt, and covered his head in ashes, and commanded fasts and abstinence to both men and beasts. When God saw their conversion and penitence, he did not subvert them in this time, but held his sentence.[67]

Le Picart feels the people of his day ". . . are worse than those of Nineveh. We are hardened to the very core, because no matter what war or other persecution God sends us, we only get worse."[68] He warns that "you must amend yourselves, if you do not want these menaces to come to pass. The Ninevites would not have done penance otherwise."[69] He also provides examples when God did not defer His Judgment, or not for long: "Forty years [after the Crucifixion], the Romans came to destroy the city of Jerusalem, in such a way

---

[63] Ibid, fol. 23.
[64] Le Picart, *Trinité-II*, fol. 143.
[65] Le Picart, *Advent*, fol. 75.
[66] Le Picart, *Trinité*, fol. 211.
[67] Le Picart, *Pasques*, fols. 47–48; cf. *Trinité-II*, fol. 187.
[68] Le Picart, *Pasques*, fol. 11.
[69] Le Picart, *Trinité*, fol. 165.

that it was demolished stone by stone, and 11,000 people in the city
perished. . . . And all this happened to them, to punish them for
putting Our Lord to death. By which you should understand that
the Word of Our Lord is accomplished."[70] The lesson was simple:
"When you see these evils having come in past times for which God
punished them, is there not occasion to fear? Certainly, but be penitent and you will be assured."[71] Otherwise, "God seeing that we do
not want to amend ourselves through his gentleness and friendship,
will send us calamities, just like the war afflicts us so much that our
purses are empty. We say that we have nothing, yet our tables are
filled with more kinds of meats and delicacies than ever before . . ."[72]
Le Picart tells the people of Paris that when the Day of Judgment
comes he will know he has done his duty by preaching to them—
they are his witnesses even if they choose not to listen.[73] Yet he
warns other preachers of the dangers of proceeding too far in this
direction: "The preacher must also console the people, after having
spoken of the judgments of God. He must tell them it is necessary
to have hope in God and be of good courage. Our Lord is just, but
we must have faith in His compassion. It is necessary to give good
hope and console."[74] Elsewhere he says, "we cannot know the things
that are to come—that is secret . . ."[75]

   If isolated phrases can be used to suggest conviction that the end
is near, there are at least as many that prove Le Picart did not
believe the Judgment was imminent. At one point he explains, "A
sign that the Judgment of God is not yet near, is that everyone does
not obey Him, because St. Paul says that when the Judgment of
God approaches, each one will obey God."[76] He continues in the
voice of Jesus: "Because God my Father did not send me into the
world to judge it, but He sent me to save it, to redeem the whole
world and attract each person to salvation through true penitence,
so I will defer my Judgment to another time."[77] In other places Le
Picart uses the new covenant of Jesus to comfort his hearers: "Some-

---

[70] Le Picart, *Pasques*, fol. 40.
[71] Le Picart, *Trinité*, fol. 128.
[72] Le Picart, *Trinité-II*, fol. 142.
[73] Le Picart, *Advent*, fol. 275.
[74] Le Picart, *Trinité*, fol. 39.
[75] Le Picart, *Advent*, fol. 171.
[76] Le Picart, *Instruction*, 108.
[77] Le Picart, *Caresme*, fol. 92.

times Our Lord speaks to us in terror and menace. He seems terrible, and His voice promises only menace, vengeance and death. And this voice is to make us fear. The other voice is the voice of charity, of mercy, of clemency, and *it is this voice with which he speaks to us today*"[78] [emphasis added]. It is appropriate for Christians to ponder the Judgment so that they can overcome the temptations that surround them, and learn to live in the presence of God.[79] To this end, a certain amount of fear is a good thing: "When you see the evils that have happened in past times for which God has punished the world is there not occasion to fear? Certainly, but repent and you will be assured, because the occasion of terror and surprise proceeds from our iniquities."[80] The good is always greater than the bad, because that is God's nature. "The good that God promises mitigates the fear that we are able to conceive about the Judgment of God. If we only consider the menaces of God, we will not be able to live without despair, because the terror is so horrible that who could possibly bear it?"[81]

A very large part of Crouzet's evidence in *Les Guerriers de Dieu* comes from what he characterizes as the proliferation of astrological predictions and almanacs. While this was certainly true for the Empire in the late fifteenth and early sixteenth century, and a case can be made for it in France after 1559, the proof is much less compelling for earlier in the century. Even Jean Delumeau, who acknowledges the importance of astrology in Renaissance culture, argues that "[h]istory needs to be the domain of nuances and not of systematization.... [I]t would be wrong to conclude that the entire era wallowed in pessimism; that would be an absurd generalization."[82] Most of the treatises and pamphlets cited by Crouzet are not French but German or Flemish.[83] Crouzet admits that "... [f]or the period of 1518–47 only seventeen almanacs have been inventoried ... Paris and Dijon respectively published only two."[84] He continues, asking "can we not advance the hypothesis that in France

---

[78] Le Picart, *Caresme-II*, fol. 128.
[79] Le Picart, *Advent*, fol. 55.
[80] Le Picart, *Trinité*, fol. 128.
[81] Le Picart, *Advent*, fol. 50.
[82] Jean Delumeau, *Sin and Fear, The Emergence of a Western Guilt Culture 13th–18th Centuries* (New York: St. Martin's Press, 1990), 167.
[83] Crouzet, *Guerriers de Dieu*, I:106–110.
[84] Ibid, I:106.

around 1520, almost surreptitiously, faced with the disintegration of
religious unity that was happening across the Rhine, an eschatological conscience penetrated little by little into Catholic thought?"[85]
Before at least 1559, Crouzet's viewpoint must be considered a far-
from-proven theory. As even Crouzet admits, the editor of Nostradamus' *Lettres* claims that "France remained, in effect, a land inhospitable
to astrology,"[86] a situation Jean Dupèbe contrasts with that of Germany.
The German Lutheran fascination with using astrology as a predic-
tive tool for finding the date of the Judgment[87] is not only lacking
in Catholic France in the early sixteenth century, but was rejected
by many Catholic preachers on theological grounds.

Crouzet insists that "... astrology was, from the beginning, intimately connected with the sacred Word, that of the Old Testament ..."[88] He goes on to ask if the "... ancient religion did not
find the strength to survive in France through the encounter between
astrology and eschatology?"[89] Such contentions can be examined in
Le Picart's sermons. In all of the more than 3,000 pages of sermons
by Le Picart, I have found almost no references to astrology. One
of the exceptions proves the rule: "If we have God for us, it is not
necessary to fear any creature ... Do not fear portents and the stars
in the sky ..."[90] Similarly, he almost completely ignores magic of
any sort, offering only a simple condemnation: "... the Christian
who practices magical arts pollutes the name of God ... They tac-
itly invoke the aid of devils ..."[91] The lack of a more vigorous diatribe against astrology seems a compelling argument against its
pervasiveness in early sixteenth-century French culture. Le Picart's
disinterest in astrology is based on his firm and unwavering belief
in free will. Unlike the Lutherans of Germany whose theological
beliefs eliminated the field of human action as a basis for justification,
orthodox Catholics believed that human beings infused with the Spirit
could actively cooperate with God, choosing good or evil. The deter-
ministic fatalism of the stars could have no part in such a theology.
In contrast with Lutherans who searched the stars intensely for clues

---

[85] Ibid, I:112.
[86] Jean Dupèbe, *Nostradamus: Lettres Inédites* (Geneva: Droz, 1983), 13.
[87] Barnes, *Prophecy and Gnosis*, ch. 4.
[88] Crouzet, *Guerriers de Dieu*, I:111.
[89] Ibid, I:112.
[90] Le Picart, *Instruction*, 73.
[91] Ibid, 87.

to the end, the "... French clergy ... repeatedly sought to limit or control astrological prediction."[92] In view of Catholic theology, they could hardly have done otherwise.

If there is little to suggest an obsession with astrology in early sixteenth-century France, the actions of people in high places were beginning to change that by the mid-1550s. The queen, Catherine de Medici, had been the subject of celestial scrutiny from the moment of her birth in April 1519. The elder Ruggieri, father of two men who would serve on what has been called Catherine's "astrological council," cast her birth chart. The forecast announced "the disasters of the siege of Florence which would affect her early life, her marriage to a prince of France and his unexpected accession to the throne; that three of her sons would reign in succession; that her two daughters would become queen; and that all would die childless."[93] As a result of Catherine's important but still disputed role in the St. Bartholomew's Day Massacre of 1572, her horoscope was interpreted in a much more disparaging manner after that event. In the *Discours merveilleux de la vie, actions & deportements de Catherine de Medicis*, it was said that the stars clearly menaced the place she would make her home and the house into which she would marry.[94]

During the early years of her marriage when she had trouble conceiving, Catherine had begun to consult astrologers and alchemists for a cure. It had been at her instigation that the papal astrologer, Luca Gauricus, sent his first horoscope interpretation to Henri II in 1551. Although Gauricus's initial forecast had been promising, he noted something in Henri's chart in February 1556 that alarmed him. He immediately sent a message to the king "... to avoid single combat in an enclosed place, especially near the 41st year, for in that period of his life he was menaced by a wound in his head which would quickly result in blindness and death."[95] The royal secretary l'Aubespine, present when the message was delivered, recorded Henri's response, which showed even then a rather nonchalant attitude to astrological prediction:

---

[92] Barnes, *Prophecy and Gnosis*, 141.

[93] Roelker, *One King*, 184.

[94] Nicole Cazauran, ed., *Discours merveilleux de la vie, actions & deportements de Catherine de Medicis, Royne-mère* (Geneva: Droz, 1995), 140.

[95] Claude de l'Aubespine, "Histoire particulière de la cour de Henri II," *Archives curieuses de la France*, sér. 1, 3 (1835), 295–296.

"You see, my friend, what manner of death is predicted for me?"

"Oh, sire," responded the constable, "are you going to believe in these charlatans, who are nothing but liars and gossips? Throw it into the fire!"

"My friend," replied the king, "why? Sometimes they speak the truth. I am just as willing to die one sort of death as another. I would just as soon die at the hands of whomever, as long as he is brave and valiant and my glory remains intact."[96]

Catherine was not so blasé. Having heard of the prophecies of Nostradamus, she had summoned him to her castle at Saint-Germain-en-Laye in August of 1556. After her husband's freak death in a jousting accident in 1559, Catherine gave free rein to her astrological interests. She invited Nostradamus to Blois and Chaumont to predict the fate of the royal children. Later, in 1564, when Catherine took her recently crowned son Charles IX on a royal progress, they stopped at Salon, "where Nostradamus walked alongside the king, holding his hat in his hand, leaning on a cane because of his gout."[97] Besides Nostradamus, Catherine regularly consulted Cosmo and Lorenzo Ruggieri, and the Frenchman Auger Ferrier.

In spite—or perhaps because of—support in high places, astrology still came under attack in the 1560s and 1570s, sometimes for blasphemy and sometimes for its Italian connections. In 1560, the Protestant Anthoine Couillard published his *Attack Against the False and Abusive Prophecies of Nostradamus and Other Astrologers.*[98] Couillard chastises Nostradamus and his ilk for making idolators of poor ignorant creatures. He ends his diatribe: "Oh, insatiable human curiosity! Oh, people who are far too bold and impudent! Oh, diviners full of every fallacy, children of the devil and enemies of the state! Oh, people, I say, who are notoriously suspect in this world. Cease, cease, oh unworthy of the company of Christians, your audacious presumptions!"[99] In a work published posthumously in 1566, Nostradamus says in a preface dedicated to Francis, duc d'Alençon, that ". . . I am astonished that today astrology is so vilified that those who profess it serve more as laughingstocks to men than anything else.

---

[96] Ibid.

[97] Pierre Champion, *Catherine de Médicis présenté à Charles IX son royaume (1564–1566)* (Paris, n.d.), 159.

[98] Anthoine Couillard, *Les contredicts du Seigneur du Pavillon, les Lorriz, en Gastinois, aux faulses & abbusifves propheties de Nostradamus, & autres astrologues* (Paris: Charles L'Angelier, 1560).

[99] Ibid, n.p.

I believe firmly that it is the malice of the times, since of old astrologers were in such high esteem that before all others they were chosen to advise on temporal matters."[100]

Le Picart was not a *prédicateur panique,* a prophet of doom, or a man interested in astrological prediction. But was he a preacher of the violence of God, as Crouzet also claims?[101] Again, the sermons do not support such a contention. Although Le Picart supported the burning of unrepentant heretics, there is not a single reference in any of the sermons that could broadly be construed as inciting men and women to spontaneous violence. If the man referred to as *"l'ami du feu Picard"* in 1559 called in his sermons for blood and murder, he was not basing his preaching on anything found in Le Picart's sermons. Le Picart warns his listeners not to sit by and watch the host being trampled underfoot or defamed, but *never* suggests that Catholics should commit violent acts. Mack Holt, one of Crouzet's reviewers, suggests that Crouzet writes in the tradition of the "doom and gloom" mentality of Jean Delumeau,[102] yet even Delumeau stresses the comfort and consolation that can be found in all of Le Picart's sermons. Although recognizing that he composed vigorous polemics against heretics, Delumeau goes on:

> As has been done for Hell, one could easily reconstruct the stereo-typical components of this early modern discourse on Purgatory: a predominantly tragic discourse that rarely stressed God's kindness. François Le Picart, however, a theologian who preached at Paris at the beginning of the Wars of Religion, both wrote and spoke in more positive terms. Although he does inevitably mention the all-too-notorious words of Saint Augustine, which he translates as "the pain of all the martyrs together is not so great as that of Purgatory," it is mainly to affirm that solid faith and prayers for the dead can spare us even from Purgatory . . . Throughout the liturgical year, Le Picart stressed the "mercy of God . . . greater than our infirmity and sins."[103]

Delumeau correctly stresses the "highly comforting" nature of Le Picart's sermons.[104]

---

[100] Michel de Nostradamus, *Prognostication, et amples predictions, pour l'an de Iesus Christ, mil cinq cens soixante-sept. An Embolismal* (Paris: Guillaume de Nyverd, 1566), fol. Aiiii.

[101] Crouzet, *Guerriers de Dieu,* I:208.

[102] Holt, "Putting Religion Back," 535.

[103] Delumeau, *Sin and Fear,* 388.

[104] Ibid, 369.

That Le Picart does not fit Crouzet's characterizations does not, however, prove that France was not pervaded by a climate of existential *Angst* before 1557. While it is not possible to examine every Catholic source for this period, a sample should be sufficient to test the idea, for eschatological anguish should be easy to discern. I have selected two works to try to examine Crouzet's hypothesis for the pre-1557 years.

The first work is a chronicle, Guillaume Paradin's *Continuation de l'histoire de nostre temps depuis l'an mil cinq cens cinquante iusques à l'an mil cinq cens cinquante six*. The preface indicates that the book was written on 12 December 1555, ten months before Le Picart's death. On first glance, Paradin's chronicle appears to substantiate more fully Crouzet's view of mid-sixteenth-century France, for he begins with astrological imagery. Thanking God for giving France Henri II, Paradin says ". . . it seems that the conjunction of the stars, the virtues of the stars, the disposition of the planets, the intelligences of the heavens had all worked a thousand years with nature to produce a king who would be the liberator of the Germans."[105] Much of the chronicle describes Henri II's military adventures in the 1550s, but Paradin also shows himself to be an acute observer of European affairs. He spends considerable time discussing the happy events of 1553, when God restored a Catholic to the throne of England:

> When Queen Mary was crowned the first of October in 1553, she rid the country of the foreigners who professed Lutheran doctrine, and put the English who followed the sect into prison, restoring in all things the ancient manner of living regarding religion with the recognition of the superiority of the Holy Apostolic See . . . Also certain decrees and propositions earlier established and decreed by King Edward concerning the mass of Our Lord Jesus Christ, the ceremonies of the church, the administration of the sacraments, the marriage of priests, the election of bishops and ministers of the church and the form of prayer were abrogated, declared abusive and heretical, and were condemned.[106]

Far from signalling evil days ahead, the return of England to the Catholic fold was enough to warm the cockles of a good Catholic heart. When Mary followed up these first steps with solemn pro-

---

[105] Guillaume Paradin, *Continuation de l'histoire de nostre temps depuis l'an mil cinq cens cinquante iusques à l'an mil cinq cens cinquante six* (Paris: Guillaume de la Nouë, 1575), iiii.
[106] Ibid, 130–131.

cessions and the ceremonies of the Catholic church, it was cause for rejoicing.[107]

Paradin also quotes [or purports to quote] extensively from the Duke of Guise:

> There has never been a people whose arms were more terrible than ours, and we strike our enemies, the greatest part of whom are heretical and schismatic, keeping in mind that France's prosperity depends on the defense and maintenance of the Catholic religion. Doing our duty for God, the king and the world, we will have ample reward: the eternal felicity of God, the great goods and honors of the king. The world of praise and congratulations for victories will be sculpted and engraved on the temple of honor and renown and written down in chronicles for all posterity.[108]

Referring to the demise of Duke Maurice and his funeral oration, Paradin once again mentions signs: ". . . there were some prodigies and marvelous signs which happened before his death as if they were presages, with unimaginable terror. Among others drops of blood appeared on grass, on the leaves of trees and the roofs of houses at the beginning of the month of June [1553]."[109] Interestingly, in a long digression, Paradin launches into an attack on German bishops who were involved in the war against France, saying "that burning villages and spilling human blood is a far cry from exercising the *métier* of a shepherd," and attributes many of the troubles of the church to this kind of worldliness.[110] In the context of these unworthy churchmen, Paradin expresses a longing for the great patriarchs or prophets of the Old Testament:

> . . . [T]oday . . . there are none like [Job, Noah or Daniel]. There is no Phineas, who put to death the whoremongers; there is no Moses who killed the sacrilegious, no Samuel who cried out against the disobedient ones; no Job who made sacrifice for the sins of his children; no Aaron who pronounced warnings and edicts of God to kings; and even less Noah, who in his boat made ready provision for the ark of salvation. . . . So those who formerly in the primitive church commanded emperors and kings are today nothing more than slaves of their vices and given over to the glories and vanity of the world . . .[111]

---

[107] Ibid, 133.
[108] Ibid, 162.
[109] Ibid, 186.
[110] Ibid, 187.
[111] Ibid, 187–188.

Paradin's comments show an incisive social criticism, overlaid with a spirit that wavers between optimism and pessimism, depending on how France's military ventures proceeded. While his words express alarm and fear when the Emperor wins a battle, this quickly changes to optimism when France gains the upper hand. Once again quoting the Duke of Guise, Paradin exclaims: "What we have seen and see presently by so many victories one following the other indicates that the reign of our king will be nothing but a succession of happy events."[112]

Paradin's chronicle shows a growing awareness among sixteenth-century Frenchmen of the significance of signs, prodigies and marvels, increasingly remembered as having foretold important events. Yet the chronicle is hardly different from those found in the fifteenth century—it bespeaks a military ardor and a belief that France's king would deliver the oppressed and restore freedom to subjugated peoples.[113] Except for the harangue against worldly bishops (all of them German), there is little that is new and different. If anything, the restoration of Catholicism in England was cause for joy among good Catholics.

The second source is one of the earliest sermons by René Benoist, the *Homélie de la Nativité de Iesus Crist, en laquelle est clairement monstré l'office du vray Chrestien*, the preface of which was written in January, 1557, only four months after Le Picart's death. Given during Advent, this sermon should evoke any eschatological themes current at the time. But Benoist's theme is from Luke 2: "I bring you tidings of great joy."[114] Although Benoist's sermon style differs somewhat from that of Le Picart, his themes are virtually identical. He begins

> ... Our God is very liberal to his elect and faithful in all goods, spiritual as well as temporal ... In which he resembles a good father looking after his children with love and care, not thinking to have given them enough by existence and life ... And the good father asks his children for obedience and humility, friendship, love and filial reverence in their honesty of life and good conversation.[115]

---

[112] Ibid, 248.

[113] Ibid.

[114] René Benoist, *Homélie de la Nativité de Iesus Crist, en laquelle est clairement monstré l'office du vray Chrestien, par maistre René Benoist Angevin, bacchelier en théologie à Paris* (Paris: Claude Fremy, 1558), Aiii.

[115] Ibid.

Throughout the sermon, Benoist reiterates the theme of divine good-ness, mercy and charity.[116] Like Le Picart, he explains the difference between the Law and the Gospel:

> We have not received the spirit of servitude so that we would fear, but the spirit of adoption of children by God. With great confidence we are reclaimed by God our Father as testimony that we are His children. We must therefore not fear, since the occasion of such great joy is announced and proposed to all nations, estates, sexes and con-ditions . . . It is therefore an occasion of great joy throughout the whole world . . . O what consolation, Christians, when by living faith we understand the compassion and grace of our God in the mission of Jesus Christ![117]

Also following Le Picart's example, Benoist explains the concept of the good shepherd, the pastor who cares for his sheep and does not act out of greed or desire for honors.[118] Only at the very end of the sermon does Benoist mention the Judgment:

> In conclusion, Christians, we have joy and consolation, since accord-ing to the truth of the prophets and the angels the Savior who is God is Himself born in our nature, in order to save us and pay our ran-som, which is why such an occasion of joy was given to the angels. . . . Not leaving our assembly like some customarily do, but in each one admonishing the other, and even more so as we see the day approach. Because if we sin voluntarily after having received the knowledge of the truth, there can be no more sacrifice for our sins, but a terrible wait for the Judgment, and a fury of fire which devours the inobedi-ent and adversaries of Jesus Christ.[119]

As we have seen, this one phrase at the end is nothing unusual in Advent sermons. What *is* unusual in this sermon and the sermons of Le Picart is how little the preacher elaborates upon the subject. There is absolutely nothing which suggests a present consciousness of imminence.

In his later writings and sermons, Benoist defended ". . . many aspects of Catholic doctrine and ritual, and he also wrote sweeping attacks on the 'blasphemies' of the heretics and their 'corruption' of the faith, but his favorite subjects, the ones to which he returned time and again, were the sacrifice of the Mass and the real presence

---

[116] Ibid, Aiiii.
[117] Ibid, Avii–Aviii.
[118] Ibid, Avi.
[119] Ibid, Bv–Bvi.

in the Eucharist."[120] In the 1560s and 1570s, Benoist sometimes spoke in apocalyptic terms, as when he warned in 1571 that the removal of the cross of Gastines would result in divine vengeance and damnation.[121] But unlike the sermon of 1557 examined above, Benoist's preaching after the beginning of the Religious Wars resonate[s] with calls to violence.[122] However, by the time of the League, Benoist was perceived as ". . . tolerant, but at the same weak . . ."[123] He was felt by many to be ". . . too timid and reserved in his sermons."[124] His antagonism to the League and his support of Henri IV cost him dearly. Although he was called by the memoirist Pierre de l'Estoile ". . . a good and learned man, feared and loved by his parishioners, a great theologian and preacher, who preached all things very purely, he was held back by his timidity alone."[125] Although he was appointed Bishop of Troyes by Henri IV, the pope would not allow his confirmation. He died in 1608.[126]

What general conclusions can we draw from a study of Le Picart's sermons and these other works of the same time period? Is Crouzet's contention that France was imbued with eschatological anguish unworkable? When applied to the period after 1557, and especially after 1561, Crouzet's characterization of a nightmarish religious climate in France seems closer to the mark, a view that Benoist's change in attitude seems to support. Certainly, astrology flourished with the regency of Catherine de Medici, although critics remained numerous. After 1557, forces were unleashed that increasingly and inex-

---

[120] Diefendorf, *Beneath the Cross*, 149.

[121] Ibid, 151.

[122] Diefendorf summarizes material found in his sermons and treatises from the years after 1560: "If Benoist employs ambiguous language in the cross of Gastines pamphlet, it is because he had learned from previous reprimands just how far he dared to go in stirring up popular emotions. He could get away with much more direct incitements to violence when France was at war with the Huguenots—and when his attack on the heretics did not imply a criticism of the crown. In a treatise written in August 1562 and republished at the time of the third religious war, Benoist invokes a series of Old Testament scenes in which God 'animated the people to kill the false prophets without sparing a single one, thereby teaching us how grievously and without mercy the obstinate heretics should be punished and exterminated.' He cites Moses's instructions to the Levites to buckle on their swords and go from door to door, and 'each one of you kill his brother, his friend, and his kin.'" Ibid.

[123] Labitte, *Démocratie*, 115.

[124] Ibid, 116.

[125] Quoted in ibid, 264.

[126] Labitte, *Démocratie*, 264.

orably led to violent conflict. But it is not to take away from this monumental and important work to suggest that Crouzet is reading too much into the period before the outbreak of religious war. In one review, Frederic Baumgartner questions the importance Crouzet assigns to eschatological anxiety in certain Leaguer works.[127] This seems even more true of earlier works. As Mark Greengrass points out, "... when citing from such a vast mass of published materials over such a long chronology, it is easy to construct a plausible argument on the basis of small extracts from the text rather than to reflect the flavour of a text as a whole—or to rest too much by way of explanation upon one small point of reference."[128] Philip Benedict's assessment is the most discerning:

> Crouzet has not solved adequately the problem of how to convince his audience that his depiction of the contents of the pamphlets and writings of the era is true to the actual distribution of different themes within them.... Furthermore, in insisting as strongly as he does that certain themes within the literature of the era offer *the* keys to understanding its forms of collective action—often in direct controversy with other historians who have written about the subject and who have highlighted other concerns—he underestimates the multiplicity of linguistic and conceptual traditions which may exist within any given era's universe of discourse and the variety of motives which can motivate even single actors within a given crowd.[129]

In his review of *La genèse de la Réforme française*, James Farge states that he

> ... had particular difficulty with Crouzet's handling of eschatology, in which pre-Reformation Christianity is reduced to its most negative or pejorative elements.... This thesis does not ring true. One can only conclude that the author knows more about the reformed religion than about the traditional one, and much of what he knows about the latter he learned from its bitter enemies like Beza, who is quoted throughout.... Could the great majority of French people have adhered to the traditional religion (and many thousands of Calvinists have returned to it) if it offered nothing more than a spiritual reign of terror?... The scrupulous anxiety of Martin Luther about his salvation was far from typical of Christians of his time... No, this currently popular thesis

---

[127] Frederic J. Baumgartner, "Review of Denis Crouzet, *Guerriers de Dieu*," in *Catholic Historical Review* 78(1992), 115.

[128] Greengrass, "Psychology," 473.

[129] Philip Benedict, Review of Crouzet, *Guerriers de Dieu*, in *Social History* 17(1992), 119.

that Catholic Christianity was essentially a religion of anguish and fear must eventually go the way of that other thesis that held that Calvin and Calvinists were all imbued with the spirit of Calvinism.[130]

Yet Crouzet may himself offer one answer. After lengthy passages insisting that Le Picart was a preacher of violence and Judgment, Crouzet ends with the statement that "Le Picart was without doubt a precursor."[131] That falls far closer to the mark. Le Picart was acutely aware of the troubled times in which he was living, and of the challenge to God posed by the heretics. Yet events such as military disaster, a burgeoning Calvinist church in Paris, the death of the king and the growth of factionalism were all in a future he would never know. It is impossible to say whether Le Picart's sermons would have changed dramatically had he lived into the 1560s. Perhaps he would have followed the example of Benoist; but this we cannot know. The psychology and temperament of the man (as exemplified by the sermons already presented and the eulogies in the next chapter) seem to suggest he would not have, but ultimately that cannot be known. We must try to understand him as he and his contemporaries were during his lifetime, and not project to an uncertain future. His sermons are not characterized by anguish or eschatological imminence; to the contrary, they are filled with reassurances of God's love and a call for amendment that was very closely tied to continuing earthly existence. If he sometimes felt his was a voice crying in the wilderness, this was the normal frustration of a preacher who watched his flock continuing to indulge in worldly vanities and sin. The voice of the prophet can be found instead in Le Picart's publisher, Nicolas Chesneau, who far more than his subject evinced a belief that worldly time might be coming to an end. It was Chesneau and Le Picart's eulogists, living after his death, who began to see in the events of their times a spirit of prophecy in Le Picart.

---

[130] James K. Farge, Review of Crouzet, *Genèse*, in *Sixteenth Century Journal* 28(1997), 1014–1015.
[131] Crouzet, *Guerriers de Dieu*, I:209.

CHAPTER EIGHT

ENDINGS AND BEGINNINGS

The registers of the collège de Navarre, based on contemporary writings by Aubusson de la Maisonneuve, Dupuiherbault, Désiré and others, record in great detail the funeral obsequies for the man beloved by Parisian Catholics:

On Thursday the 17th day of September, 1556, the noble and learned person Master François Le Picart, lord of d'Attily in Brie, doctor in theology and dean of Saint Germain l'Auxerrois, died in his very simple lodgings in the deanery at four o'clock in the morning. The good people of Paris felt they had had the man who died for a hundred years, because the deceased had spent his entire life making daily lessons and holy preaching, teaching the evangelical truth and pure Catholic doctrine, as much in this city of Paris where he was born as elsewhere, in the space of more than thirty years, during which he sustained and suffered many tribulations, even a long imprisonment at Saint Magloire. He was held in such reverence by the people, that he was esteemed one of the most wonderful mirrors, an exemplar of life and doctrine in this realm, and true pillar of the faith, the enemy of heresies and false doctrines which have done great damage to the Christian Republic. So at his death, a cortège and obsequies were carried out most honorably. He was conveyed from the church of Saint-Germain de l'Auxerrois to the convent of the Blancs-Manteaux, where he was buried with his father.

But first, three or four hours after his death, his body was opened and his heart taken from his body, and his body was put in the center of the lodging, surrounded by a lovely drape, his face uncovered and his hands joined, and from all parts of the city and suburbs of Paris people came to see him. Those who had known him and heard his preaching cried pitifully, and made great lamentations of having lost him in this world; and the poor and simple people who considered the sanctity of life and doctrine touched their books and paternosters to his hands.

Around five o'clock in the evening, when all the orders had passed by, his body was carried into the church, and the canons took his heart, and while singing hymns and piteous funeral chants, they interred the heart in the choir of the church of Saint Germain.

Then, clothed in grief, they marched before the criers of the body in a great number, each one having escutcheons, one in front and one behind, on which were painted [Le Picart's] arms of azure on a lion rampant d'or, and they sounded their bells or clocks in the accustomed manner.

After them marched the Children of the Trinity in great number, all barefoot, each one holding a candle or burning wax in his hand.

After marched the Cordeliers in the number of around three hundred.

Then came the Dominicans and the Augustinians. Then followed the Carmelites, and each one of the mendicants had two emblazoned torches, as above, to accompany their cross.

Following them marched twenty-four poor people, each carrying a burning torch decorated with escutcheons of the arms of the deceased.

After marched the religious of Blancs-Manteaux.

Then on one side of the road came a great number of doctors of theology, both religious and secular, and the dean of the Faculty, accompanied by their beadles and officers, the seculars carrying their furred capes. And on the other side the canons of Saint-Germain de l'Auxerrois sang and prayed God for the deceased.

Afterwards marched several doctors and bachelors who carried the exposed body.

Then followed Messieurs the presidents and counselors of the court of *parlement* wearing their black robes.

Then came Messieurs the *prévot des marchands* and the magistrates of the city clothed as above, accompanied by archers to keep the crowd in order.

In their wake marched the brothers of the deceased man, wearing long funerary robes, carrying swords above in sign of their nobility.

Then followed a great number of notable bourgeois of all estates of the city. And so they all processed to the church of the Blancs-Manteaux, where the body was buried in the nave before the crucifix of the church.

There was such a great number of people in the roads where the body passed, that although I wanted to see him for the last time, it was very hard for me to get close.

And the next day the service was held in the church of the Blancs-Manteaux, with the funeral sermon praising him . . .[1]

Hilarion de Coste adds that the crowds passing through Saint-Germain l'Auxerrois were so great that the doors to the church were broken.[2] Funeral sermons were delivered by Le Picart's friend and colleague Nicolas Maillard (d. ca. 1564–1565),[3] and Robert Ceneau, Bishop of Avranches (ca. 1483–1560).[4] In the eulogy, Ceneau refers to Sirach 31:8–11:

---

[1] Launoy, *Regii Navarii*, 430–431.
[2] Hilarion de Coste, *Parfait ecclesiastique*, 225–226.
[3] Quoted in Hilarion de Coste, *Parfait ecclesiastique*, 225–230.
[4] This is part of his *Opus quadripartitum super compescenda haereticorum petulantia* . . . (Paris: Jacques Kerver, 1556).

Blessed is the rich person who is
found blameless
and who does not go after gold.
Who is he, that we may praise
him?
For he has done wonders among
his people.
Who has been tested by it
and been found perfect?
Let it be for him a ground for
boasting.
Who has had the power to
transgress and did not
transgress,
and to do evil and did not do it?
His prosperity will be
established,
and the assembly will proclaim
his acts of charity.

Ceneau explains, "[Le Picart] is the one, this I say, who most closely matches Sirach 31. He must be called blessed by merit, who was known to be no less blessed while he lived . . ."[5] He goes on: "the entire holy church will speak of his alms. Alms, I say, not so much what he granted from his private property, but rather what he procured with pious and honest men. He poured forth and disseminated the divine Word through all of France."[6] After comparing Le Picart to a bird whose voice rang forth with a sweet and eloquent song, Ceneau adds that he was a man who ". . . hurt no one, who helped all collectively; he was created from the soul of all collectively. Among the humble and his adversaries he expressed joy. With no one was he anything but cheerful. He was ever in readiness and good natured."[7] Thinking of the followers of Calvin and Beza—men he labels *Picardomastiges*, Ceneau castigates those who had mocked Le Picart while he was still alive, using his trademark phrase, *O Mater Dei!*[8] Ceneau expresses astonishment at the good cheer of a man who was "agitated by so many annoyances, by stabs and cuts, in close combat and far away, attacked from front and back, sometimes

---

[5] Quoted in Hilarion de Coste, *Parfait ecclesiastique*, 281.
[6] Ibid, 282.
[7] Quoted in Launoy, *Regii Navarii*, 432.
[8] Quoted in Hilarion de Coste, *Parfait ecclesiastique*, 280.

exiled, ridiculed publicly... ... [Y]et he was not forgetful of the advice of Our Lord Christ." Ceneau concludes, "indeed he is dead, but it is as if he is not dead" thanks to the legacy he left the people of France.[9]

Other works appeared in the days after Le Picart's death praising the preacher for his personal qualities as well as his tireless efforts to rid the realm of heresy. Le Picart's friend Gabriel Dupuiherbault appended a tribute to Le Picart to his work on penitence, composed five days after Le Picart's death. In the form of a letter to Le Picart's cousin, Jerome, Dupuiherbault acknowledges

> I owed and will always owe so many things to my lord François Le Picart, and I wish I could have owed much more if fate had not envied me this very long friendship with one so dear and so pious. As much as I was able I rejoiced in his company. When I first came to Paris, I went to the house of your cousin. There, if I had some problem or found some difficulty in holy scripture that required explication, we would study it together amicably.[10]

Dupuiherbault had accompanied another Le Picart cousin, Louise, to the burial. He remarks in a memorial poem, how they were "... pressed closely together by the people, from all over Paris, ... who hastened to him, weeping far and wide to inundate his bier."[11] Calling him the love, the beloved object, of the people of Paris, their sanctuary and their salvation, Dupuiherbault compares his dead friend to Hercules, and ends with words he attributes to Le Picart:

> I hated the world;
> There is no care of the flesh for me,
> But care of heaven, in the favor of the Lord.
> I live in love ...
> That which I didn't love, I have left.
> That which I love I have passed to.[12]

Also appearing in the months after Le Picart's death was Barbier Aubusson de la Maisonneuve's *Deploration*, in which the author claims that Le Picart is now experiencing what he had promised in his sermons full of hope:

---

[9] Ibid, 282.
[10] Dupuiherbault, *De penitence*, n.p. (end of volume).
[11] Ibid.
[12] Ibid.

He fears no more frightful death,
He sees without end, and from his high knowledge
Which he announced in truthful sermons,
He goes to heaven to receive his reward
Now he can see Him in the face
Who governs land and sky divinely.
He does not want a mortal life,
For God has given him a divine crown.[13]

For the man who was "...more sweet than a dove,"[14] Aubusson demands of his followers that they

...each be an announcer
Of his renown perpetuated in glory.
Death has claimed the body of such a Preacher,
Of his goodness the memory will not die.[15]

René Benoist offered what he knew would be the greatest tribute to the man: "Let us follow those who have died happily, believing simply, firmly and universally with love and peace that we will find eternal life."[16] Writing in Provins, Claude Haton made a small notation in his *Mémoires*: "Death of Monsieur Picard, doctor of Paris, a celebrated preacher."[17]

All of the eulogies, verses and celebratory epistles written in the days and months after Le Picart's death took as their theme his goodness, charity and the example he had set for the people of Paris. While all mentioned Le Picart's prominent role in the fight against heresy, these references form but a small proportion of the acclamation and adulation which appeared after his death.

A year after Le Picart's death, however, the situation had changed dramatically. France was endangered from within and without, and in this atmosphere a man who had already started to make his name as a Catholic polemicist picked up his pen to praise the memory of François Le Picart. He was Artus Désiré, a priest who "...distinguished himself less for his intellectual qualities than for the violence and intransigence of his attitude."[18] Désiré probably knew Le Picart, who was his clerical ideal. But Désiré in 1557 was not yet the

---

[13] Aubusson de la Maisonneuve, *Deploration*, fol. Aiii.
[14] Ibid, fol. Av.
[15] Ibid, fol. Aiii.
[16] Benoist, "Preface," *Caresme*, fol. vii.
[17] Bourquelot, ed., *Mémoires de Claude Haton*, I:85.
[18] Giese, *Artus Désiré*, 35.

sardonic and coarse writer of the 1560s and 1570s who would praise
the St. Bartholomew's Day Massacre and pursue with "... single-
minded fanaticism ... his life-long goal: total extirpation of the protestant heresy from France."[19] Désiré apparently conceived the project
after reading Aubusson de la Maisonneuve's *Deploration*. Frank Giese
writes that in the *Regretz* Désiré "... adopted an elevated style quite
unlike anything he attempted before or since," which he attributes
to Désiré's admiration for the late preacher.[20] In this remarkable
dialogue between Passepartout and Bruictquicourt, Désiré amplifies
and reinforces the views expressed by Le Picart's earlier encomiasts.
He tells his readers that twenty thousand people, crying and wail-
ing with their grief, followed the funeral cortège in the procession
from Saint-Germain l'Auxerrois to Notre-Dame-des-Blancs-Manteaux.[21]
Even if this is one of Désiré's more restrained works, the difference
in tone and content from earlier tributes is palpable. Désiré juxta-
poses the death of the blessed Le Picart with that of Luther and his
followers. A lengthy excerpt demonstrates the differences not only
between Désiré and the earlier eulogists, but between the polemicist
and his hero:

> *Bruictquicourt*: Never in my life have I seen a doctor who in his preach-
> ing had greater devotion for the Virgin Mary, who all his life praised,
> loved and dignified her, and with all his heart honored her devoutly
> in word and deed.
> *Passepartout*: So God allowed that he ended with her in his sermons.
> Before climbing the mount mentioned by David, with a fervent affection
> he exerted himself to show the graces we can find in the kindly Virgin,
> and against that malignant sect of Martin Luther, full of error, he made
> two sermons in honor of the glorious Virgin exalting her as the most
> happy and the greatest after Jesus who sits on the throne on high.
>   And by this God wanted the deceased to have the honor and the
> merit to finish his life and his holy preaching and sweet exhortations
> in praise and glory of the name of the Holy Mother, for whom he
> made his last sermon in great joy and solemnity in celebration of her
> holy nativity as end and consummation...
> *Bruictquicourt*: Alas! The henchman of the Antichrist, the sacramentar-
> ian Martin Luther went to his death in the opposite way. Because in
> his last sermon, he was in such great choler against the holy Virgin
> that without reverence or fear, the wicked and filthy lecher exerted all

---

[19] Ibid, 32–33.
[20] Ibid, 133.
[21] Désiré, *Regretz*, fols. Aii–Aiii.

of the power of his soul to rid her of her titles of honor. He expressed
such strong feelings against her that the detestable sermon was so vile
and abominable, so full of blasphemy and error that everyone was
horrified and was so tempted to say and preach in its place that he
did not believe there was any God at all. After this miserable wretch
finished this damnable sermon full of every heresy, his feeble body full
of filth, feeling the pains approach, went to lay on his bed, on which
(note this well!) the Devil from Hell choked him. So he ended his miserable life without grace or compassion in torment. And by contrast,
the one about whom I spoke before lives eternally in joy and consolation, and the other in desolation, sorrow and grinding of teeth, captive and interned in the pit of a shadowy hell . . . One is in Heaven
and the other in Hell, captive in the lakes of Lucifer, making horrible and strange cries. One is accompanied by angels, the other tormented by devils. So look, poor people, at the great difference there
is between these two men![22]

There can be no doubt that Désiré felt a deep admiration for Le
Picart. Like Le Picart, Désiré defended all the traditions and beliefs
of the church challenged by Protestants, and traced the growth of
heresy and the ills of his time to abuses among Catholic clergymen.[23]
But the selection above shows how different was Désiré's purpose
and content from the men who eulogized Le Picart during the last
days and months of 1556. The events of September, 1557 lent themselves to a new style of rhetoric and polemic intended to rouse
Catholics to violence. Giese sums up Désiré's contribution:

> Incapable of any subtlety in evaluating the causes of division in the
> nature, and unable by his eloquence to persuade stray souls to return
> to the fold of the Catholic Church, he nevertheless had a humble part
> to play. By ceaseless repetition of his dogmatic truths in the enormous
> mass of his published works, he may have dissuaded some from aban-
> doning the religion of their fathers; and by his constant appeals for
> violence in coping with the new religion, he undoubtedly helped cre-
> ate the atmosphere in which a violent solution to the problem was
> finally attempted.[24]

In the years that would follow, there would be added to Désiré's
voice others that signalled and fomented the worsening conditions
in France. Shortly after the death of Henri II in 1559, the fiery
Dominican Pierre d'Ivollé ranted about the disorders that would

---

[22] Ibid, fols. Di–Diii.
[23] Giese, *Artus Désiré*, 186–187.
[24] Ibid, 188.

follow if the Huguenots gained the upper hand. He preached that
they would "exterminate the king and his estate," ending his sermon with the warning, "Cursed is the land that has a child for
king!"[25] Under the year 1561, Haton also mentions another preacher,
Simon Vigor, the most famous preacher in Paris in the 1560s, a
man who called for the extermination of the Huguenots.[26] As religious war followed religious war and the conciliatory policies of
Catherine de Medici toward the Calvinists increasingly frightened
Catholics, Vigor's message grew ever more violent. He insisted that
it was impossible for Catholics and Protestants to live together in
peace, for the latter would not be content until they had destroyed
the entire kingdom.[27] Diefendorf explains the joy with which Vigor
greeted the onset of the third war as due to his conviction that the
wars would have to continue until one side won or lost.[28] But even
Vigor knew limits. He admonished Parisians, "I am not saying this
to sound the tocsin against them, nor to animate you to take up
arms;" instead he asked them to pray God to exterminate them "by
a bitter death."[29] Diefendorf summarizes the situation that would
lead irremediably to the violence and hatreds of the 1560s and 1570s:

> The French Civil Wars were wars of deeds, not wars of words. And
> yet it required words to mobilize the masses to those crucial inter-
> ventions that on more than one occasion altered the larger course of
> events. In 1562 and 1567, the violent unrest of the Parisian populace
> made conciliation impossible and so encouraged the first and second
> religious wars to take place. In 1571, the affair of the cross of Gastines
> placed a serious strain on the peace of Saint Germain, and in 1572,
> the violence of Saint Bartholomew's Day was a direct cause of war.
> All of these events stand out in clearer relief if we understand that the
> Parisians were receiving from their parish pulpits the message of Simon
> Vigor and his brethren. They were being taught not only to hate pas-
> sionately the heretics that disturbed the peace of the kingdom, but also
> to question the social hierarchy, the magistracy, and even the monar-
> chy that allowed heresy to persist. Radical preachers like Simon Vigor
> placed their duty to God's truth above their duty of obedience to the
> king. Their defiant spirit as well as their words urged their listeners
> to action.[30]

---

[25] Bourquelot, *Mémoires de Claude Haton*, I:138.
[26] Ibid, I:214.
[27] Diefendorf, "Simon Vigor," 406.
[28] Ibid, 407.
[29] Quoted in ibid, 407.
[30] Diefendorf, "Simon Vigor," 410.

By 1561, inflammatory and even seditious preaching was the norm rather than the exception, with pulpits in the parishes of Saint-Benoît, Saint-Séverin, Saint-Germain l'Auxerrois, Saint-Eustache, Saint-Merry and Saint-Jacques-de-la-Boucherie resounding with calls to violence and disobedience.[31] The situation would only deteriorate as "[t]he preachers put into words the conscious and unconscious depths of distress and rage of the Catholic faithful."[32]

The years after Le Picart's death in 1556 witnessed an escalation of rumor, intrigue, and confessional violence that made any real hope of reconciliation illusory and even dangerous. In these years, Crouzet's claim of eschatological anguish is more plausible. But the differences in expression between the sermons of Pierre d'Ivollé, Simon Vigor, and the later preachers of the League on the one hand and François Le Picart on the other, cannot be overstated. Le Picart felt and expressed the distress of his co-religionists at the increasing divisions that wracked France and threatened Catholicism. He hated heresy, yet prayed for the conversion of heretics. But his message was overwhelmingly one of hope and optimism—faith that God would not let the kingdom fall into ruin or the Catholic faith be trampled upon. He urged the Catholic clergy to take the lead, reforming their lives and removing the causes (as he saw it) of Protestant criticisms and reproach. His support and assistance to the early Jesuits, even in the last days of his life, showed that he still believed it was not too late.

At the end of this study of François Le Picart, it is important to try to assess his significance. Had he truly been a prophet of doom or a preacher of panic, more glamor would attach to this study. But we must let the sources speak for themselves if we are to get a true sense of the religious climate in Paris and France in the decades between beginning of the Reformation and the Religious Wars. However tempting it is to trace an inexorable progress into violence and chaos, such an interpretation is little more than a retrospective view of history that takes little account of actual circumstances. Just as for centuries historians saw the late Middle Ages through the lens of the Reformation, so the portrayal of the early sixteenth century in France as imbued with *Angst* ignores the evidence of these years. As the man who represented Catholicism in the capital from the

---

[31] Diefendorf, *Beneath the Cross*, 61.
[32] Garrisson, *Sixteenth-Century France*, 306.

mid-1530s to mid-1550s, Le Picart speaks to us of troubled yet exciting times. If the godless heretics threatened so much that he believed
in, Le Picart nonetheless believed this was a useful wakeup call. The
Protestant onslaught offered all good Catholics—and especially those
in power in the church hierarchy—an opportunity once and for all
to address the problems that disfigured the church. God always acted
for the best, even if this was not obvious to the human beings who
tried to grasp his will.

In his sermons and by the model of his life, Le Picart exemplified
the ideal of a reformed Catholic church. Paris during his lifetime
was undergoing enormous and often threatening changes. But it was
not—yet—a place where women and men, clergy and laity, king
and *parlementaire* lived in an atmosphere of impending doom. The
darkness and fear that so characterizes Crouzet's picture of life in
sixteenth-century France may have been felt by some before 1557,
but was certainly not pervasive. The events of the years that followed Le Picart's death—international war that threatened the capital
itself, the implantation of a Calvinist church, the arrival of ministers
trained in Geneva, a peace treaty that offered both the German
emperor and the French king the first real opportunity in years to
deal with heresy effectively, the death of the king and accession of
a minor, and the embrace of astrology by the queen mother—all
led to a much-changed climate in Paris. While it is highly doubtful
that the great majority of French society was ever completely engulfed
in eschatological anguish, there can be no doubt that the atmosphere of fear, intrigue and rumor that accompanied these events
facilitated the downward spiral into violence.

As far as Le Picart's legacy, it is hard to find better words than
those of Calvin's nineteenth-century biographer Doumergue:

> His role at the beginning of the Reformation was decisive. We know
> that what stopped the Reformation [in France] was Paris and that, in
> Paris, the Catholic victory was due to the people. Le Picart was the
> soul of the people.[33]

---

[33] Doumergue, *Calvin*, I:240–241.

APPENDICES

Appendix A contains the full text of François Le Picart's *Épistre* (BN D.21840), a treatise on the sacrament of the alter which, according to publisher Nicolas Chesneau, was composed in 1533, when Le Picart was exiled to Reims by Francis I. According to the text, it was done at the behest of "Sister Jeanne" of Paris, but may have been given in the form of a sermon.

Appendix B is a selection of five complete sermons, three of which can be definitely dated. The first, a sermon for the Nativity of the Virgin Mary, was the next to last sermon given by Le Picart, in September of 1556. It can be found in the *Trinité* sermons, Part II, fols. 90–95 (BN D.41448). The second, a sermon against despair, was delivered in 1555 on the feast of the Holy Cross. It is found in folios 225–235 of the same volume. From the *Pasques* collection, folios 201–208 (BN D.41446), comes the funeral sermon for the Franciscan Pierre Descornes, who died on 21 May 1549. The final two sermons, undated, are taken from folios 19–30 of the same volume, and are both for the second Sunday after Easter.

The text has been reproduced in the exact form it can be found in the books. Spelling and use of accent marks has not been standardized, but when obvious typographical errors have been made, *sic* has been added in brackets. Quotations and citations are in the same places they can be found in the original texts, so that the reader can in most cases tell whether these were part of the original delivered sermon, or added by the printer for the use of readers. The only alteration was to change typographical abbreviations into full words.

APPENDIX A: ÉPISTRE

A TRES-ILLVSTRE
Princesse, & Reverendissime Ab-
besse de S. Pierre de Rheims,
Madame Renée de Lor-
raine, Salut.

MADAME, *nous some enseignez chasque iour par*
l'experience, que ceux qui veulent empescher le cours
d'une eau vive, outre ce qu'ilz se travaillent pour
neant, ilz se mettent en danger d'un deluge &
debordement non accoustumé. Ainsi est-il à l'endroit
de la parole de Dieu: le cours de laquelle tous ceux qui
l'ont voulu empescher, ont esté occasion de l'accroistre
& amplifier. Cela est cogneu es Apostres & autres qui
ont veu l'enfance de l'Eglise. Sainct Paul n'a iamais
plus haultement & divinement escrit, que quand il
estoit prisonnier: auβi, ce venerable Docteur, Monsieur
nostre Maistre François le Picart (lequel nous esperons
& desirons estre avec les bien-heureux) n'a iamais
mieux, & avec plus grande hardiesse & abondance,
proposé la parole de Dieu, qu'alors que (lon sçayt assez
quand, & pourquoy) la predication a esté defendue en
Paris. Qui le voudra cognoistre à l'effect lise ce petit
traicté, (composé & escript de sa propre main en ce
temps là, de la chose la plus excellente) c'est à sçavoir
de la communion du corps & sang de Iesus Christ (qui
soit es misteres de la chrestienté). Lequel, MADAME,
ayant recouvré entre autres plusieurs escritz dudit
Seigneur Picart, ay bien voulu en faire
communication à tous bons Chrestiens, sachant qu'ilz
y prendront grand proffit & contentement. Vous
suppliant, MADAME, *le recevoir soubs vostre*
protection & sauvegarde, comme avez ia receu ses
autres oeuvres ou Sermons, en aussi bonne partie,

comme de bon coeur vous l'offre, vostre plus
affectionné & obeissant serviteur,

NICOLAS CHESNEAV.

De Paris ce 28. Ianvier, 1563.

ÉPISTRE, CONTE-
nant un traicté auquel est monstré
combien est grande la charité de
Iesus Christ en l'Institution de la
saincte Communion de son pretieux
corps & sang, au Sainct Sacrement
de l'Autel.

MES TRES cheres Soeurs en Iesus Christ, vous m'avez
souvent prié, & de ma part ne l'ay pas moins desiré, de
vous faire quelque Sermon du Sainct Sacrement de
l'Autel. De quoy faire, n'ay pas eu l'opportunité,
comme sçavez par noz occupations & autres affaires.
Ce que considerant par deça, ensemble la requeste de
nostre bonne cousine & singulière amye, Soeur
Iehanne de Paris, par lettres lesquelles m'a envoyées:
me voyant du tout inutile, par l'interdiction de
prescher qui m'est faicte, dont suis fort marry: ie me
suis deliberé vous escrire ces presentes, par lesquelles
vous veux seulement reduire en memoire (estimant
qu'estes assez apprinses & trop plus de moy) la
singularité du tres-digne Sacrement: consideré que
sommes aux octaves: & la tres-singuliere charité qu'il a
pleu à nostre Seigneur Iesus Christ nous monstrer par
icelluy: afin que cognoissiez de plus en plus le coeur
fidele que i'ay en vous, & auray tant que ie vivray.
  MES tres-cheres Soeurs, nostre Seigneur Dieu le
Createur a voulu communiqué sa bonté aux creatures
en plusieurs manieres: & pour ce, au commencement
il a crée le monde, & tout ce qui est en iceluy. Et par
icelle communication, la creature a cogneu la bonté de
Dieu. D'autant qu'un bien est communicatif de soy-
mesme. & plus y a de communication, plus y a de
bonté: en quoy est facile à cognoistre la bonté infinnie
de nostre Dieu, qui se communique à ses creatures sans
diminution quelconque. Aux unes elle se

Manieres comme
Dieu a communiqué
sa bonté aux creatures.

communique par essence, en leur donnant vie,
comme aux plantes & arbres, & autres choses
semblables.

NOUS trouvons une autre communication de
la bonté de Dieu, faicte aux creatures, lesquelles outre
la vie vegetative, ont la vie sensitive, comme sont les
bestes brutes. Et dernierement à l'homme qui a esté
creé le dernier & le plus parfait, Dieu a donné vie
intellective, qui consiste en l'entendement & en la
volonté: Dont l'entendement luy a esté donné pour
parfaictement cognoistre Dieu, sa bonté, & sa
puissance. L'autre pour parfaictement aymer Dieu,
d'une pure & sincere charité, pour sa sapience, &
craindre sa puissance: qui n'est autre chose sinon, que
l'homme a esté creé le dernier, comme la fin de toutes
creatures: afin qu'il eust plus grand argument de
cognoistre & aymer Dieu: c'est à dire, la benoiste
Trinité, le Pere, le Filz, & le benoist sainct Esprit: qui
n'est qu'une bonté, une sapience, une puissance. La
bonté a esté cogneuë, & se cognoist tous les iours par
communication. La sapience, par l'ordre &
gouvernement de ses creatures, & sa puissance, par la
creation d'icelles. La bonté est attribuée au benoist
sainct Esprit, duquel procedent toutes les graces, &
auquel sont attribuez tous les dons qui sont au coeur &
en la volonté: comme est charité, amour, paix, ioye
spirituelle. La sapience est attribuée au Filz, qui est la
vraye sapience de Dieu, comme il est dit: *Ego ex ore
altissimi prodii: primogenitus ante omnem creaturam*:
& à luy sont donnez les dons, qui donnent perfection à
l'entendement: comme verité, foy, cognoissance,
puissance. La puissance est attribuée au Pere, à
l'occasion de quoy, nous appelons le peché qui est
contre le sainct Esprit, l'offence qui procede de certaine
malice. Le peché contre le Filz, l'offence faicte par
ignorance. Et le peché qui vient par infirmité ou
quelque tentation, on l'appelle, contre le Pere: combien
que les trois soyent une bonté, une sapience, & une
puissance. Et qui offence l'un, il offence l'autre, pour
la grande unité naturelle qu'est entre les trois
personnes. Tout ainsi qu'il n'est possible de pouvoir
prier le Pere, le Filz, & le S. Esprit, que lon ne prie la
saincte Trinité, qui est Dieu eternel: comme il est dict:
Qui videt me, videt & patrem meum. Et: *Ego & pater*

*En quoy a esté
cogneue la bonté,
la sapience, & la
puissance de Dieu.*

Ecclesiastes 24

*Pechez, contre le
filz, & contre le S.
Esprit.*

unum sumus. Et pource que ce n'est qu'une nature,
non seulement la bonté se communique: mais aussi la
sapience & la puissance. Et pour ce, nous sommes
appelez bons, sages, & puissans: combien que ce soit
autrement que Iesus Christ, lequel est bon par nature:
& duquel la proprieté naturelle, c'est d'estre bon. A
l'occasion de quoy, il est dict: *Nemo bonus, nisi solus*   *Luc. 13.*
Deus. Mais la creature est appelée bonne, par une
bonté empruntée. Et pour ce, il est dict: *Vidit Deus*   *Gene. 1.*
cuncta quae fecerat, & erant valde bona. Comme aussi   *I. Tim. 4.*
dict sainct Paul: *Omnis creatura Dei bona est.* Il est dict
pareillement, sage par nature: & nous avons emprunté
& mandié de luy nostre sapience. A l'occasion de
quoy, dict sainct Paul: *Christus factus est nobis*   *1. Cor. 1.*
sapientia & iustitia. Et ainsi fault-il dire, de la
puissance. Car, comme dict aussi Monsieur S. Paul:
Habemus thesaurum hunc in vasis fictilibus: ut
sublimitas sit virtutis Dei, & non ex nobis. Et en un
autre lieu: *Non sumus sufficientes ex nobis quasi ex*   *2. Cor. 4*
nobis, cogitare aliquid: sed sufficientia nostra ex Deo
est. En quoy ne veult autre chose dire Monsieur S.   *2. Cor. 3*
Paul, sinon que de nous-mesmesmes [*sic*] ne sçavons &
ne pouvons aucune chose: mais au contraire nous
sommes nays ignorans, remplis d'infirmitez, de
malice, & de peché. Et pour ce, dict S. Paul. *Nos*   *Ephe. 2.*
natura filii irae nascimur. Et puis que nous sommes
nays enfans d'ire, & conceuz en peché, desquelz la vie
est tres-dangereuse: nous devons demander sans cesse
& de grand coeur, la sapience de Dieu, pour cognoistre
les dangiers de ce monde: sa puissance, pour resister
aux adversaires que nous avons en ce monde: sa bonté,
pour estre imitateurs de Dieu, & se communiquer à
autruy, comme il se communique à nous.

APRES avoir crée le monde, nostre Seigneur
Dieu y a mis l'homme, qu'il a crée à son image &
similitude. Et ne voulant qu'il fust oisif en Paradis
terrestre, il luy a donné puissance sur toutes creatures
inferieures & de tous les fruictz qui y estoyent plantez:
excepté du fruict de science de bien & de mal. Et ce a
faict, pour tousiours le tenir en subiection &
obeissance. Aussi, afin qu'il ne mescongneut son
impuissance mais qu'il congneust sa puissance
proceder de Dieu. Lequel se voyant constitué en si
grande dignité, il a esté ingrat d'un si grande benefice,

il a oublié le commandement de Dieu son createur: &
pour obeir à sa femme, il a transgressé le
commandement de son Seigneur. Comme bien
souvent advient, que pour obtemperer à nostre chair &
à nostre sens, nous laissons Dieu: à l'occasion de quoy,
nous demeurons nudz, & destituez de tous biens: car
sans nostre Seigneur, nous sommes vuides, & avec
luy, nous sommes remplis de tous biens, & ne
pouvons avoir mal.

AVSSI, l'homme est demeuré seul apres avoir
perdu la similitude de son Dieu, qui consiste en trois
choses: c'est à sçavoir, la memoire, l'intelligence, & la
volonté: en sorte qu'il est demeuré à demy mort: & est
celuy duquel il est escrit: *Homo quidam cecidit in*
latrones, qui eum semivivo relicto spoliaverunt. Car
de deux choses que Dieu luy avoit données en sa
creation, il ne luy est demeuré que l'image, qui ne se
perdre. C'estoit indice de grande bonté, d'avoir crée
l'homme: luy avoir donnée vie & entendement:
l'avoir crée en grace & iustice originelle. Encore
d'abondant, comme l'ouvrier qui ne peult oublier son
oeuvre, luy-mesme a cerché l'homme qui estoit perdu,
en disant: *Adam ubi es.* Qui vault autant à dire,
comme, Homme, ou es-tu? quel es-tu devenu? Tu as
laissé ta place & ton lieu. Et de fait, il est ainsi que
quand l'homme est en peché mortel, il a perdu sa
place, qui est Dieu, auquel il repose: & y est logé quand
il a sa grace & son amour: comme il est escrit: *Manete*
in me, & ego in vobis. Neantmoins, l'homme
mecognoissant au lieu de prevenir la face de Dieu, en
confessant la debte, comme dict David:
Praeoccupemus faciem eius in confessione: il a voulu
reietter sa faulte sur nostre Seigneur, en disant: *Mulier,*
quam dedisti mihi, dedit mihi, & comedi: qu'est une
malice diabolique. Comme, plusieurs ne cognoissant
comme la providence divine se peult compatir avec la
liberté de l'homme, il blasphement Dieu, disant qu'il
est cause de leur mal, & de leurs faultes: d'autant qu'il
prevoit toutes choses advenir: & que rien ne peult
advenir sans sa volonté, comme dict sainct Paul:
Voluntati eius quis resistit?

MES Soeurs, il nous fault autrement croire: car nous
faillons de nous-mesmes: mais le bien & la perfection

En quoy consiste
la similitude de
Dieu, qu'a perdu
l'homme.

Luc. 10.

Gen. 9.

Ioan. 15.

Psal. 94
Gen. 3.

Rom. 9.

vient de Dieu. S. Paul dict: *Deus est qui operatur in*   *Phil. 2.*
nobis velle & perficere, pro sua voluntate. Parquoy,
comme souvent avez ouy dire, s'il est question du
bien, il se fault resouldre à la sentence de S. Paul, qui
dict: *Non est volentis neque currentis, sed Dei*   *Rom. 9.*
miserentis. Nonobstant si grande ingratitude &
extresme, nostre Seigneur a eu pitié & compassion de
l'homme: & l'a revestu, *tunica pellicea,* qu'est un   *Gen. 3*
argument d'estresme bonté, à sçavoir, faire du bien à
son ennemy. Et pour plus amplement le manifester, il
a deliberé de mourir pour l'homme, pour le revestir
de ses bons vestemens qu'il avoit perduz: laquelle
chose ne se pouvoit faire bonnement, s'il ne se
descouvroit pour couvrir l'homme qui estoit tout nud.
Ce que sainct Paul nous inculque quand il dict: *Scitis*
gratiam Domini nostri Iesu Christi: qui cùm dives
esset, propter nos egenus factus est: ut eius inopia,
divites essemus. Et en un autre lieu: *Hoc sentire in*   *2. Cor. 8.*
vobis, quod & in Christo Iesu: qui cùm in forma Dei
esset, non rapinam arbitratus est esse se aequalem Deo:
sed semetipsum exinanivit, formam servi accipiens, &
habitu inventus ut homo. Et est à noter, comme dict
S. Bernard, que Dieu avoit doué l'homme de quatre   *S. Bernard.*
pierres precieuses: à sçavoir, verité, misericorde,
iustice, & paix. Misericorde le gradoit, verité
l'enseignoit: iustice le veilloit & gouvernoit, & de ces
trois, une paix & tranquillité procedoit si grande, qu'il
n'y avoit guerre ny dedans ny dehors. Mais apres qu'il
a eu perdu iustice, en plus-tost obeissant à sa femme
que non pas à Dieu: & en accusant sa femme, &
laissant l'obligation de peché, à sçavoir peine &
calamité à ses successeurs, il a perdu pain, & senty
incontinent ce que dict Monsieur S. Paul: *Foris pugnae,*   *II. Cor. 7.*
intus timores. Mes Soeurs, ne perdons point verité qui
s'offre à nous: aymons Dieu & nostre prochain en
verité: ne soyons semblables à ceux qui referent
seulement le personnage d'autruy: ne contrefaisons
point les Chrestiens: *Habentes speciem pietatis,*   *2. Tim. 3.*
virtutem autem eius abnegantes. Gardons-nous
d'estre de ceux dont il est dit: *Non omnis qui dicit*
mihi, Domine Domine, intrabit in regnum coelorum.   *Mat. 7.*
Aymons la misericorde de Dieu: craignons sa iustice
qu'est si severe, que c'est une chose horrible que de
tomber entre ses mains. Et ainsi nous aurons une paix

si grande, & inestimable tranquillité en nous & en noz
consciences. Sentons en nous, ce que sentoit nostre
Seigneur. Cheminons en humilité, & delaissons
nostre propre volonté, laquelle est directement contre
nostre Seigneur, lequel s'est rendu commun à tout le
monde, aux pecheurs, aux publicains, aux bons & aux
mauvais. Et ne doibt estre grief à la creature d'estre
serviteur & de se communiquer & humilier, quand
elle voit son maistre soy humilier iusques à se faire
serviteur & demeurer iusques à exinanition. Lequel
voyant la perdition de l'homme estre advenuë, il a
dict: *Poenitet me fecisse hominem.* Certes s'il fault icy   *Gen. 6.*
contempler, croyez mes tres-cheres soeurs en Iesus
Christ, que c'est un des bons motz que pourrions ouyr   *L'homme doibt*
pour nostre consolation. Tout ce que nous avons est   *tout ce qu'il a.*
obligé à autruy, nous devons tout: corps, ames, &
biens, nostre vie, nostre sens, la volonté &
l'entendement, & n'avons dequoy rendre: ce qui nous
pourroit engendrer crainte & desespoir, n'estoit la
parole de Dieu qui nous console quand il dict: *Poenitet*   *Gen. 6.*
me fecisse hominem. Comme dict S. Bernard: *Poena*
me tenet facti hominis. Il fault que ie porte la peine
pour l'homme que i'ay faict & crée. Considerez
l'extresme & profonde humilité, & la charité
supereminente à toutes sciences, si ce n'est un coeur
plus dure que marbre, & obstiné en toute malice, il
n'est pas possible qu'en ce considerant, *Non*   *Gen. 41.*
commoveantur viscera eius. Mes Soeurs, si l'homme   *III. Kings 3.*
cognoissoit la multitude de ses crediteurs, il ne
s'estimeroit rien, & encore moins reputeroit ce qu'il
fait, en comparaison de ses debtes. Premierement, ie
doibs toute ma vie à nostre Seigneur Iesus Christ, car il
a mis la sienne pour la mienne: & a soustenu des
douleurs ameres, à fin que ie ne fusse damné. Quelle
chose donc me pourroit estre dure, quand, i'auray
memoire & recordation de nostre Seigneur Iesus
Christ, qui est l'image de Dieu invisible? La Splendeur
de la gloire de Dieu, & la figure de la substance, lequel
est venu en propre personne icy bas, & a voulu
prendre nostre limon? Quelle chose ne me sera douce
& delectable, si ie veux rememorer toutes les douleurs
de mon Seigneur, & ses amertumes: les necessitez de
son enfance, les labeurs qu'il a porté en preschant, les
fatigations sur les chemins, les tentations en ieusnant,

les veilles en priant, les larmes & continuelles
irrisions, exprobations, iniures & blasphemes? Certes,
si toutes les vies des hommes estoyent assemblées en
nous, pareillement tous les iours du monde, tous les
labeurs des hommes qui onte esté, qui sont & seront, ce
me seroit rien en contemplation de son pretieux corps
qui a esté livré entre les mains des loups pour nous,
auquel inhabite le S. Esprit, & auquel est coniointe la
divinité. Sa vie differe de la nostre, comme le ciel de la
terre, & neantmoins, il l'a mise pour la nostre.
Parquoy, quand ie luy auray donné tout ce que ie suis,
& tout ce que ie puis, ce ne fera qu'une estoille aupres
du Soleil, une goutte d'eau aupres de la mer. Et veu
que ie n'ay que deux deniers, encore ie n'en ay qu'un,
c'est ma volonté, ne le donneray-ie pas à mon Dieu
mon Seigneur? Si ie ne le fais, ie suis le plus ingrat de
tout le monde. Nous avons un autre crediteur, c'est
que noz pechez passez requierent toute nostre vie
passée, pour faire penitence condigne, & recogiter le
temps passé en amertume de nostre conscience: qu'est
une chose bien forte à faire, & quasi est impossible.
Mes pechez sont multipliez comme le sable de la mer.
Et comme dict David: *Multiplicatae sunt iniquitates*   *Psal. 39.*
meae super capillos capitis mei. Ie ne suis pas digne de
regarder la haulteur du ciel pour la multitude de mes
pechez: car *circundederunt me mala quorum non est*
numerus. Comme se pourra-il faire que ie compte le   *Psal. 39.*
nombre de mes maux & pechez qui sont infinis:
Comme se pourra faire la satisfaction quand ie feray
contraint rendre la debte iusques au dernier quadrant?
consideré le dict de Monsieur S. Ambroise qui dict:
Facilius inveniri eos qui innocentiam servaverunt,
quàm qui congruam egerint poenitentiam. Avons-
nous cause auiourd'huy de nous enorgueillir? Si nous
cognoissions bien nostre necessité, nous estimerions
paradventure nostre condition plus miserable que celle
des bestes brutes.

 Nous avons pour le troisiesme crediteur la
gloire de Paradis, à laquelle nous tendons tous les
iours, & n'avons dequoy la comparer. Et quant i'auray
fait & enduré toutes les castigations, labeurs, prisons,
relegations, la mort: encore *non sunt condignae*
passiones huius seculi ad futuram gloriam, quae   *Rom. 8.*

revelabitur in nobis. Outre-plus, Dieu me demande
autant que les susditz crediteurs, comme est-il possible
de rendre? Ie doibz à nostre Seigneur Iesus Christ, qui
a mis sa vie pour moy, tout ce que ie suis: à la
recordation de mes pechez. Ie doibz pareillement toute
ma vie à la gloire de Paradis, pour laquelle avoir ie suis
creé: & neantmoins ie doibs tout à Dieu, & n'y a nul
des quatre qui ne me puisse dire: *Redde quod debes.* Ie
ne voy autre moyen pour le present, sinon d'avoir
recours à la bonté de Dieu, & luy dire, Sire, de vostre
plain gré & bonté infinie, & charité inestimable, vous
avez dict: *Poenitet me fecisse hominem.* En quoy vous   *Gen. 6.*
vous estes constitué debteur pour moy, *vim patior.* A
cause de quoy *responde pro me. In manus tuas*   *Luc. 23.*
commendo spiritum meum, id est, voluntatem
meam. Tu persolve omnibus, tu ab omnibus libera,
quia tu es Deus & non homo. Et quod hominibus
impoßibile est, poßibile est tibi. Quod habui, hoc feci:
habe me excusatum Domine, quia imperfectum meum
viderunt oculi tui. Certes, nous n'avons pas plustost
prié d'un coeur contrit & humilié, que nous ne soyons
exaussez: à l'occasion de quoy pouvez vous voir la
grande & infinie bonté qui se manifeste depuis la
creation du monde iusques à l'incarnation de Iesus
Christ, que sainct Paul appelle *Sacramentum pietatis.*
Le Baptesme, les predications, les miracles d'iceluy, &
conversations avec les pecheurs inclusivement. Ce
neantmoins avant que de mourir il a voulu
demonstrer en instituant le tresprecieux & tressainct
Sacrement de l'Autel, duquel sont auiourd'huy les
octaves, en soupant avec ses Apostres la nuict qu'il fut
prins. Ce qu'il a faict afin que nous eussions tousiours
memoire de sa douloureuse & amere passion qu'il a
enduré par sa bonté pour nous. Mes Soeurs en Iesus
Christ, cognoissant l'homme par nature estre mortel,
& avoir perdu la liberté de manger du fruict de vie,
qu'estoit en Paradis terrestre, par le moyen duquel il
estoit en sa puissance de perpetuer sa vie, n'a pas
voulu laisser l'homme en telle langueur perpetuelle,
& necessité de mort. A l'occasion de quoy, le iour
devant qu'il endurast, il institua ce pretieux
Sacrement, qu'est le vray fruict & le vray pain de vie,
par lequel nous sommes faictz immortelz &

transmuez en Dieu, & sommes un avec luy. Donc, si
nous voulons cognoistre l'excellence d'iceluy
Sacrement, considerons que nostre Seigneur Iesus
Christ luy-mesme en est l'instituteur, comme dict S.
Paul: *Ego enim accepi à Domino quod & tradidi vobis.*   *1. Cor. 11.*
Et si ainsi est que nous prenions en gré le don qui
vient d'un Roy, ou de quelque autre grand personnage:
de quel coeur & quelle ioye devons nous accepter &
recevoir un si pretieux don, qui procede de la main de
Dieu, qu'est le Roy des Roys? Il est Duc, *In foemore*
eius scriptum est, Rex regum, & Dominus
dominantium. Ne devons-nous point à bonne cause
dire à Dieu, en recognoissant nostre indignité:
Domine, quid est homo quod memor es eius: Aut
filius hominis quia reputas eum?

S. Pierre considerant la multitude des poissons
qu'il avoit prins par la vert de la parole de Dieu, a dict:
Exi à me Domine, quia homo peccator sum. Et
pareillement, quand il luy voulut laver les piedz, il luy
dict: *Tu mihi lavas pedes?* Comme voulant dire, Sire,   *Ioan. 3.*
que voulez-vous faire? Ie suis vostre creature, & vous
estes mon createur, vous estes le maistre, & ie suis le
serviteur, vous estes Dieu, & ie suis homme, ie suis
mortel, & vous estes immortel, & ce-pendant vous me
voulez lavez les piedz!

SAINCTE Elizabeth, cognoissant la dignité de la
glorieuse vierge Marie, dict: *Unde hoc mihi, ut veniat*
mater Domini mei ad me? Sainct Iean Baptiste
cognoissant ce qu'il pouvoit de soy, il a dict: *Ego debeo*
a te baptizari & tu venis ad me? Sainct Paul, voyant   *Matth. 3.*
toutes graces proceder en soy, de son humilité, il a dict:
Non ego, sed gratia Dei mecum. Ego enim sum   *2. Cor. 15.*
minimus Apostolorum, qui non sum dignus vocari   *2. Cor. 15.*
Apostolus. S'il s'est appelé abortif, ne fault-il pas en
consideration de ce Sainct Sacrement auquel est
continué la divinité precieuse: le precieux corps, &
l'humanité de Iesus Christ, & son ame, chanter des
cantiques & Hymnes, & magnifier la bonté de Dieu, &
se deprimer & humilier soymesme? Certes, si un
grand seigneur auquel neantmoins i'aurois faict
beaucoup de maux, venoit à moy, qui serois destitué de
toute ayde, prest de mener au supplice de la mort: & ce
neantmoins s'offrir à moy luy ses biens & son corps &

sa vie: ie ferois bien honteux en moy-mesmes:
consideré que tousiours ie le persecute. Et nonobstant
il se vient humilier devant moy: Combien qu'à bon
droit il en pourroit prendre vengeance. Et pourtant,
consideré que nostre Seigneur Iesus Christ nous a
donné son corps tres-sacré pour nostre viande, son
sang pour nostre breuvage, ne devons-nous pas estre
confuz en nous mesmes, & sans cesse chante: *Benedic*   *Psal. 102.*
anima mea Domino, & noli oblivisci omnes
retributiones eius? C'est donc un si grand Sacrement,
pour la vertu & noblesse de celuy qui l'a institué, &
n'est pas moins excellent à l'occasion du contenu en
iceluy: Car il contient realement & personnellement
nostre Seigneur Iesus Christ. Et pour ce, il excede tous
les autres Sacremens, ausquels est seulement la vertu
& grace de Dieu. Mais à ce sainct Sacrement, Iesus
Christ y est contenu realement, apres avoir proferé les
paroles sacramentelles, à sçavoir, *Hoc est corpus*   *Matt. 26.*
meum. Et, *Hic calix novi Testamenti, &c.* Et combien   *Matth. 14.*
que pour la vertu & efficace des paroles, il n'y ayt soubz   *Luc. 22.*
l'espece de pain que le precieux corps, & soubs les
especes de vin, que le sang, combien que le corps n'est
point separé de l'ame, ny dy sang, ny de la Divinité: car
par une consequence concomitative, realement soubz
chacune espece est contenu Iesus Christ entierement.
Et ne fault pas estimer que les Prestres en disant Messe
en recoyvent plus que les autres recevant seulement
soubz une espece, ny pareillement qu'ilz ayent plus de
graces que les autres recevans soubz une espece en
vertu du Sacrement. Si ce n'estoit qu'ilz eussent plus
grande devotion. Parquoy, l'Eglise ne faict iniure aux
lays de ne leur donner que soubz une espece
seulement, comme veulent dire aucuns heretiques,
pour ce qu'il est dict: *Nisi manducaveritis carnem filii*
hominis, & biberitis eius sanguinem, non habebitis   *Ioan. 6.*
vitam in vobis. Comme dict S. Paul: *Non intelligunt,*
neque quae locuuntur, neque de quibus affirmant. Car   *I. Tim. 1.*
il est certain, que quiconque reçoit nostre Seigneur
soubz une espece, il reçoit le corps & le sang qu'il a
commandé de recevoir par le passage prealléguè, &
aussi en disant à ses Apostres: *Accipite & manducate:*
combien qu'entant que concerne le Commandement
de Dieu expres en l'escriture, l'homme ne soit tenu

plusieurs fois en sa vie recevoir le pretieux corps de
nostre Seigneur, la saincte Eucharistie: toutesfois, par
la determination de nostre mere Saincte Eglise, il est
tenu & obligé le recevoir une fois l'an, c'est à sçavoir à
Pasque: iaçoit ce que à la primitive Eglise on le recevoit
tous les iours, qu'est un signe de grande charité &
amour, laquelle est auiourd'huy tant refroidie, qu'à
grand peine on y va une fois l'an. Ie voudrois qu'il
pleust à Dieu envoyer le feu du sainct Esprit pour
embrasser noz coeurs en son amour, & que nous
puissions dire: *Nonne cor nostrum ardens erat in*   *Luc. 24.*
nobis, dum loqueretur in via? Et comme dict David:
Concaluit cor meum intra me, & in meditatione mea   *Psal. 38.*
exardescit ignis: car autrement nous ne pourrions
dignement recevoir ce tresdigne Sacrament, lequel est,
comme dict Monsieur sainct Augustin: *Sacramentum*   *S. Aug.*
unitatis & pacis, pource qu'il nous unit avec Dieu, &
avec nostre prochain. Et pour ce, dict nostre Seigneur:
Cùm offeris munus tuum ad altare, & recordatus fueris
quod frater tuus habet aliquid adversum te, relinque
ibi munus tuum super altare, & vade prius reconciliari
fratri tuo. Par ce don qui est excellent, à cause quà   *Matth. 5.*
Dieu appartient d'estre souverainement bon, on
cognoist la libertalité de luy, qui eslargit tous biens à
l'homme. Il se donne en ce tres-sainct Sacrament
comme nostre viande quotidiane. Il a donné à
l'homme le ciel, la terre, & toutes les autres creatures
irraisonnables, pour le servir, comme il est dict en
Ecclesiaste: *Deus creavit de terra hominem, & dedit ei*
potestatem eorum quae sunt super terram. Et   *Eccle. 17.*
pareillement, au Deuteronome, il est escrit: *Solem &*   *Deut. 4.*
lunam creavit Deus, & omnia astra coeli, in
ministerium cunctis gentibus. Et aux Actes des
Apostres: *Deus non sine testimonio reliquit*
semetipsum, benefaciens de caelo: dans pluvias &
tempora fructifera, implens cibo & laetitia corda nostra.   *Act. 14.*
Qui n'est autre chose à dire, sinon que nostre Seigneur
par les biens & benefices qu'il nous a faict, ne nous a
point laissé sans tesmoignage de sa bonté. Il a
d'avantage donné à l'homme les creatures
raisonnables & celestes, qui sont les sainctz Anges de
Paradis, pour luy ministrer & servir, comme dict sainct
Paul: *Omnes sunt administratorij spiritus in*   *Heb. 1.*

*ministerium mißi, propter eos qui haereditatem
capiunt salutis.* Apres, il s'est donné luy-mesme en
plusieurs manieres. Premierement, comme
compagnon en peregrination, il s'est associé avec nous,
afin que n'eussions aucune defaillance de coeur sur le
chemin, comme il est dict: *Si dimisero eos ieiunos,*   Marc. 8.
deficient in via. Et comme dict Sainct Luc: *Iter faciebat
Iesus per castella & civitates, praedicans, &
Evangelizans regnum Dei, & duodecim cum illo.* A   Luc. 8.
l'occasion de quoy, ceux qui veulent avoir la compagne
de nostre Seigneur Iesus Christ, & son association en ce
monde, le chemin ne leur semble point grief en ce
monde: mais doux & facile, & n'estoit ce, iamais nous
ne pourrions venir à fin. Et pourtant, dict David:
*Propter labia verborum tuorum, ego custodivi vias
duras.*   Psal. 16.

MES Soeurs, nous avons grand & long chemin
à faire: donc associons-nous avec nostre Seigneur, & rien
ne nous sera impossible à faire. Les ronces, les espines,
les buissons, les montagnes, & autres empeschemens
de chemin, ne nous pourront nuire. Et apres avoir
cogneu ce dangereux passage, que passerons avec l'ayde
de nostre Seigneur, association & compagnie: nous   Psal. 123.
dirons, attribuant le tout à nostre Seigneur: *Nisi quia
Dominus erat in nobis, &c. Cùm exurgerent homines
in nos, fortè vivos deglutissent nos. Torrentem
pertransivit anima nostra, forsitan pertransisset anima
nostra aquam intollerabilem.* C'est à dire, apres avoir
passé les dangereux passages, & estre eschappez
d'iceux, nous cognoistrons qu'il estoit, & est
impossible les evader, sans avoir pour compagnon
Iesus Christ, qui est fidele & loyal. Il n'a pas esté
content d'estre compagnon, si encore il ne se donnoit à
nous, comme serviteur de nostre necessité. C'est une
charité indicible, de ne vouloir seulement estre nostre
compagnon sur le chemin: mais aussi nous servir en
nostre necessité. C'est ce que dict S. Paul: *Formam*   Phil. 7.
servi accepit. Ce que pareillement il a monstré en
lavant les pieds à ses Apostres. Et comme sçavez,
Filius hominis non venit ministrari, sed ministrare.
Et en un autre lieu: *Ego sum in medio vestrûm, sicut*   Luc. 22.
qui ministrat. N'est-ce pas une grande presomption à
l'homme, qui n'est que cendre & poudre: n'est-ce pas

une grande hebetation de sens, de demander gloire &
honneur & domination, & mettre tout son estude en
ambition, veu que son Seigneur, son maistre, son
Dieu, a voulu estre si pauvre, si abiect, & de si petite
reputation en ce monde? Nous sommes auiourd'huy
si loing d'aller apres luy! Nostre conversation est si
differente de la sienne, que nous monstrons plustost
estre Mahometistes, Sarazins prophanes, & serviteurs du
diable & ses enfans, que Chrestiens. Et peu s'en
fault que nous n'ayons perdu ceste appellation de
Chrestien, si excellente: laquelle a esté premierement
aux disciples de Iesus Christ en Antioche, & devons à
meilleure raison estre nommez Antechristes, que
Chrestiens: car nous faisons pour la plus part, les
oeuvres de l'Antechrist. Et pource, dict sainct Iean,
quod Antichristus iam venit: & quod multi sunt
Antichristi. Prions Dieu qu'il y vueille remedier, &   *I. Iean. 2.*
prenons peine de nous sauver en la crainte & tremeur
de Dieu.

   D'avantage, il s'est donné pour le pris de nostre
redemption: comme dict S. Paul: *Christus dilexit nos:*
& tradidit semetipsum pro nobis, hostiam &
oblationem Deo, in odorem suavitatis. Et encore: *Eph. 5.*
Filius hominis venit dare animam suam in
redemptionem pro multis. Et d'avantage, il a donné   *Matth. 20.*
son precieux corps à l'homme pour sa viande, comme
il est dict en S. Iean: *Panis quem ego dabo, caro mea est*
pro mundi vita. Et en cela, il est demonstré sa grande   *Iean. 6.*
largesse & liberalité. Car combien que ce soit grande
chose, que de nous accompagner en nostre
peregrination, de se constituer serviteur de nostre
necessité, de payer pour nous, de prendre la debte pour
soy: neantmoins, en cela il y a encore separation entre
Dieu & l'homme: mais quand il s'est donné pour la
viande de l'homme, ç'a esté pour soy unir totalement
à l'homme. Comme la viande, & celuy qui la prend
sont un corporellement, comme il dict en S. Iean: *Qui*
manducat meam carnem, & bibit meum sanguinem,   *Iean. 6.*
in me manet, & ego in eo. Iaçoit que la viande
corporelle se convertisse par l'operation de nature, en
celuy qui la prend: si est-ce que au contraire, nostre
Seigneur en la recevant dignement, nous transmue en
soy, il nous convertist en luy & transforme, tellement

que nous sommes deiformez & deifiez.

CESTE liberalité est si extresme que non
seulement il se donne à ses serviteurs: mais aussi il ne
se sustrait point aux mauvais, comme il dict:
Appropiant super me nocentes, ut edant carnes meas,   *Psal. 26.*
Car, comme il s'est permis crucifier à gens iniques, &
par les mains des pecheurs, aussi il permet contraicter
son pretieux corps par gens remplis d'iniquité. En
signe de quoy, comme disent plusieurs, il donna son
corps à Iudas, duquel il cognoissoit le peché. Laquelle
chose nous enseigne que lon ne doibt point refuser le
precieux corps de nostre Seigneur à un pecheur
occulte, duquel le peché est incogneu à un chacun,
sinon à celuy qui le ministre, & ce quand il le demande
en public, combien qu'il ne luy faille donner quand il
le demanderoit à part: mais à un pecheur public &
manifeste, iamais ne luy fault donner, ny administrer
ensuyvant la sentence de Dieu qui dict: *Nolite*   *Matt. 7.*
sanctum dare canibus. Pource que nostre Seigneur
Iesus Christ ne se substrait non plus aux mauvais
qu'aux bons: car combien que le fruict soit bon, on
cognoist amplement sa bonté. C'est un franc coeur de
donner grand don à ses prochains & amys, c'est plus de
donner à ses serviteurs, & tres-grand de donner à gens
incogneuz & pelerins mais c'est une chose trop
excessive de se donner & livrer soy-mesme à ses
ennemys. De ceste viande, Sainct Paul a dict: *Omnes*   *I. Cor. 10.*
eandem escam spiritualem manducaverunt, & omnes
eundem potum spiritualem biberunt. Ceste viande a
esté figuré par la Manne qu'avoyent les enfans d'Israël,
& par les pains de propositions qu'estoyent pour les
prestres. Aussi par le sacrifice de pain & de vin,
qu'offroit le grand prestre Melchisedech à Dieu, pour la
victoire qu'avoit eu Abraham des cinq Roys: dont est
ensuyvie l'appellation des prestres, & de la Loy
Evangelique, lesquelz sont appelez: *Sacerdotes*
secundum ordinem Melchisedech: car ilz offrent à
Dieu tous les iours en leurs sacrifices, le pain & le vin,
c'est à dire, le tres-precieux corps de nostre Seigneur
soubz les especes de pain & de vin. Laquelle oblation
durera en l'Eglise iusques au iugement universel.
Comme dict St. Paul: *Quotienscunque manducabitis*
panem hunc & calicem bibetis, mortem Domini

*Il ne se fault
estonner si nostre
Seigneur souffre
son corps estre
touché & pris par
gens pecheurs.*

annunciabitis donec veniat, ad iudicium, supple.   *I. Cor. 11.*

CE tres-sainct Sacrement, combien que pour le
contenu en iceluy il precede en dignité & excellence
tous les autres Sacremens, encore il les excede, pource
que les autres Sacrements ne profitent sinon à ceux qui
les reçoivent: mais le Sacrement de l'Autel, en
consideration que c'est un sacrifice et oblation faicte à
Dieu, profite non seulement à ceux pour lesquelz ceste
oblation & sacrifice est faict. Et ne se fault ingerer de le
recevoir sinon avec grand foy, esperance & charité,
qu'est: la robe nuptiale. A l'occasion de quoy, dict S.
Paul: *Probet autem seipsum homo, & sic de pane illo
edat, & de calice bibat.* Car ce seroit grande   *I. Cor. 11.*
presomption de recevoir tel don, sans precedente
probation, attendu ce que dict Sainct Paul: *Qui
manducat & bibit indignè, iudicium sibi manducat &
bibit.* Et pour ce, il est facile à cognoistre & iuger, qu'il   *I. Cor. 11.*
est requis d'avoir autre discretion à se confesser, &

*Il fault autre
discretion à se
confesser, qu'a
se communier.*

autre à se communier. Car toute discretion
indifferemment suffit à se confesser dignement. Mais
il est requis, & de necessité, d'avoir digne discretion
devote, & reverence pour acceder à ce tres-digne
sacrement de l'Autel. Et par ce, les enfans qui ont
discretion suffisante pour eux confesser, ilz n'ont pas
encore ceste devotion & reverence, & ne doivent estre
participans de la communion sacramentale. Et est
besoing à celuy qui veult dignement participer ledict
Sacrement, qu'il ayt devotion actuelle audict
Sacrement, non seulement en consideration de la
volonté qu'il a de communier: mais aussi par
meditation du tres-sainct Sacrement, en desirant &
voulant repaistre son ame de ceste viande, de nostre
Seigneur Iesus Christ: de sa vie, de l'imitation d'iceluy,
de son humilité, de sa sapience, constance & charité. Et
si l'homme n'a ce desir, & ne le procure avoir, il ne
faict suffisamment ce qu'est en soy pour le recevoir
dignement.

MES Soeurs, pour plus encore cognoistre
l'excellence de ce sainct Sacrement, est à considerer,
qu'en la consecration se sont trois choses de grande
admiration. La premiere c'est, que le vray corps de
Iesus Christ qu'il a prins au ventre virginal, & qui a
esté mis en croix, & au tombeau, est soubz les especes

*Trois choses se
font en la
consecration.*

de pain, comme dict Sainct Augustin: *Accedit verbum ad elementum, & fit sacramentum.* C'est à dire, la parole instituée de nostre Seigneur Iesus Christ est prononcée sur le pain, & incontinent est faict un secret, c'est à sçavoir, le precieux corps de nostre Seigneur soubz l'espece du pain. Et dict S. Augustin, que le sainct Sacrement de l'Autel consiste de deux choses: c'est à sçavoir, de l'espece visible, & de la chair, & sang de Iesus Christ invisibles. Parquoy, nous voyons une chose, & en entendons une autre. Nous voyons l'espece du pain & du vin, soubz quoy nous croyons fervesment estre le precieux corps de nostre Seigneur & son sang. Et soubz icelles especes de pain & de vin, qui sont visibles, nous adorons la chair & le sang de nostre Seigneur.

LA seconde chose digne d'admiration, c'est que la substance du pain, est muée, au corps de Iesus Christ. Ce qui est faict en vertu de la parole de Dieu. Et combien qu'il ne faille doubter de ce, neantmoins il se peult persuader & prouver: car nostre Seigneur peult muer une substance en une autre, comme aux nopces il mua l'eau en vin. Et s'il est ainsi, qu'une substance puisse estre muée en une autre, comme un voirrier mue de la cendre à un voirre, par plus forte raison, la parole de Dieu & sa vertu infinie, pourra muer le pain & le vin, au corps & sang de Nostre Seigneur Iesus Christ. Et comme il est dict, au premier chapitre de l'Ecclesiastique: *Sermo Dei, potestate plenus est: ec quisquam potest contradicere &c. Quare ita facis?* A ce propos dict Eusebe: *Invisibilis sacerdos, visibiles creaturas in substantiam corporis & sanguinis sui, verbo suo secreta potestate sua facit & commutat.* Si pareillement par l'operation de nature, une substance est transmuée en une aultre: comme lon voit en la vigne, ou l'eau se mue en vin: & le pain quotidian que nous mangeons se convertit en nostre chair: beaucoup plus la vertu de Dieu pourra muer le pain & vin en la substance du corps & sang de Iesus Christ. Et oultre, par la grace que Dieu donne à l'homme, aucunefois il transmue une substance en l'aultre: comme Moyse par grace especiale, mua sa verge en un serpent: & de l'eau en sang. C'est chose admirable que l'homme, ny par plusieurs paroles, ny

Seconde chose, qui se fait en la consecration.

Eccles. 1.
Eusebius.

par benefices, ny par menasses, ny par comminations
ne se veult convertir de mal en bien, qui est signe &
argument evident de grande obstination.

LA troisieme chose est, que combien que toute la
substance du pain est transmuée *in corpus Domini
nostri Iesu Christi,* non obstant, les accidens du pain,
comme la couleur, la sauveur, & aultres, demeurent
sans estre corrumpez. Et c'est ce que nous voyons au
Sacrement. Et ceste transmutation, est appellée
conversion & transsubstantiation. Et est à noter,
comme dessus est dit, qu'en ceste viande sacrementale,
il y a deux choses: le Sacrement, & la vertu d'iceluy. Le
Sacrament contient l'espece visible du pain & du vin,
& la chair de Iesus Christ & son sang invisible. La
vertu du Sacrement, c'est la santé spirituelle, &
delivrance de la mort eternelle. De laquelle vertu ont
creu & gousté spirituellement tous ceux qui doivent
estre sauvez des la constitution du monde: &
continuellement le goustent tous les bons Chrestiens
qui reçoivent tous les iours nostre Seigneur
spirituellement par une foy & ardante charité: comme
dit S. Augustin: *Crede, & manducasti.* En vertu de
ceste tres-digne reception, nous avons remission de
noz pechez. Comme dit aussi monsieur S. Augustin,
etiam mortuos vivificat. Nous sommes delivrez de la
mort eternelle, & sommes fais vrais membres du corps
mistique de Iesus Christ, qui est l'Eglise. A l'occasion
de quoy, il nous fault aorner & vestir de ce tres-digne
Sacrement, pour continuellement resister à noz
adversaires, qui ne nous laissent à repos iours ne nuict.
Et pour ce, *Induimini Dominum nostrum Iesum
Christum. Induite & vos sorores chariẞimae in
Christo Iesu, armaturam Dei, ut possitis resistere
adversus insidias diaboli in die malo.* C'est à dire, au
iour de la mort. Et n'y a chose qui à ce nous ayde tant
que le sainct Sacrement de l'Autel: car il chasse le
diable, & refrigere l'ardeur de noz concupiscences: il
modifie nostre coeur: il appaise l'ire de Dieu: il
illumine nostre entendement pour se cognoistre: &
conserve l'homme entierement en bien: il delecte la
memoire d'une douceur spirituelle: & enflambe le
coeur & l'affection en l'amour de Dieu. Et combien
que quelqu'un pourra dire, qu'il fait tout son pouvoir

*Troisiesme chose
qui se faict en la
consecration.*

S. Aug.

& toute sa disposition pour dignement recevoir nostre
Seigneur: & consequemment les fruicts dessusdits: &
neantmoins il ne sent rien de devotion, ny de douceur
spirituelle, ny aucune consolation interieure. Il fault
noter, que la viande sacramentalle, est comme une
medecine. Et tout ainsi qu'un bon medecin donne à
leur goust: aux aultres une medecine amere à leur
goust: combien que selon raison elle soit doulce en
consideration de la santé corporelle: tout ainsi nostre
Seigneur donne à ses serviteurs son precieux corps, &
quant & quant sa doulceur: mais differemment ainsi
qu'il cognoist estre expedient à un chacun. A
l'occasion de quoy, aucuns sentent une consolation &
douceur spirituelle, par affection & fervente dilection
en leurs volontez. Les autres, le sentent par foy en leur
entendement, & rapportent suffisant utilité de la
reception d'iceluy, en ce qu'ilz croyent & entendent par
ceste viande obtenir la vraye vie, qu'est la vision de
Dieu: laquelle vous donne nous Seigneur Iesus Christ.
Gratia Domini nostri Iesu Christi, & communicatio
Sancti Spiritus, & charitas Dei, sit semper cum
omnibus vobis. Amen.

APPENDIX B

1. *Autre sermon pour le iour de la Nativité nostre Dame*

CE PRESENT SERMON, EST le *penultiesme que feist feu Monsieur Picard, se sentant ia fort preßé de la maladie de laquelle il mourut bien tost apres le dixseptiesme de September l'an 1556.*

Iacob genuit Ioseph utrum Mariae. Matth. I. Ignorance est cause de tout mal. Il n'y a peché qui ne procede d'ignorance, encores qu'un homme peche par malice, & contre sa propre conscience. Nul peché sans ignorance, nul peché sans erreur. On dit aussi communement, *Omnis malis est ignorans.* Il est escrit, *Errant qui operantur malum.* Il n'y a donc peché & malice sans erreur. C'est donc à dire ce que i'ay dit au commencement, Tout peché vient d'ignorance, *etc.* En l'escriture nostre Seigneur distingue trois sortes de peché, aucunesfois l'homme offense contre le Pere, aucunesfois contre le Fils, & regulierement ces deux fautes se pardonnent, aucunesfois l'homme offense contre se [*sic*] S. Esprit. Peché contre le Pere s'appelle peché d'infirmité, contre le Fils peché d'ignorance: contre le S. Esprit peché de malice. Dieu nous donne ceste distinction en l'Evangile, & dit que celuy qui peche contre le Pere & contre le Fils, aura remission, mais qui peche contre le S. Esprit, iamais ne l'aura. Or ceste distinction n'est pas contraire à ce que nous avons dit, que nul peché est sans ignorance & erreur. Est-ce pas grande ignorance de Dieu, que l'offenser par malice? Celuy qui n'obeyt point aux commandemens de Dieu, ignore Dieu. Et ainsi tout peché & mal, n'est point sans erreur & ignorance. Pour ce dient les docteurs, que ignorance est grand peché: c'est à dire bien perilleux. Proprement malice, c'est un aveuglement, cecité & ignorance. Vous me pourriez

*Tout peché est commis par ignorance.
Prover. 14.
Matth. 12.*

L'homme desobeissant aux commandemens de Dieu, il ignore dieu.

dire: ce n'est pas à propos du iourd'huy que nous
faisons la feste de la Nativité de la glorieuse vierge
Marie: ce n'est pas hors de propos. Nous voyons
auiourd'huy que nostre Seigneur Iesus Christ n'est
point aymé, craint, obey, reveré ainsi qu'il appartient,
& en est digne. Nous voyons auiourd'huy que la
glorieuse vierge Marie n'est point honorée selon sa
dignité. D'où vient cela? d'ignorance. Ie ignore Iesus
Christ & la vierge Marie. Aucunesfois ie parleray à
une personne & ne cognoissant pas sa qualité,
condition, & dignité, cela est cause que ie ne luy fais
pas tel honneur qu'il luy appartient. Ie rencontreray le
Roy, ne le cognoissant point, ne luy feray plus
d'honneur qu'à un autre cela vient que ie ignore sa
qualité. Ainsi auiourd'huy ignorance nous est cause
de grand malheur. Nous ne donnons point l'honneur
qui appartient à nostre Seigneur. Pourquoy? nous
ignorons pour la plus part Iesus Christ. Et aussi nous
ne cognoissons pas pour la plus part la condition de la
vierge Marie, pourtant ne le reverons ny aymons
comme elle est digne. Voyla dequoy ignorance est
cause. Et si est encores cause d'un grand mal. Ie donne
auiourd'huy à l'homme plus qu'il ne luy appartient, &
le crains plus qu'il ne faut, car i'ay plus grand peur de
l'offenser que Dieu. Ie laisseray Dieu pour servir à
l'homme, ie luy fais plus d'honneur qu'il ne luy
appartient. Cela vient d'ignorance. Ie ignore la
condition de l'homme. C'est bien ignorer sa qualité,
quand on luy attribue ce qui appartient au createur.
Aymez la createur comme createur, dessous Dieu, &
craignez Dieu plus que la createur. Mais nous faisons
tout au contraire. Si auiourd'huy on me propose
chose qui soit pour mon salut, ie respondray, Si ie fay
cela que dira on? mais que dira Dieu? Auiourd'huy
nous conduisons noz affaires & noz choses comme
nous pensons que plairons ou desplairons aux
hommes. Et en cela Dieu n'est point appelé.
Aucunesfois nous dirons, I'ay gaigné un tel, Dieu n'y
est point appelé. D'où vient cela? d'ignorance, nous
donnons trop à l'homme & auiourd'huy nous
recommençons nostre idolatrie. Auiourd'huy
l'homme veut prendre pour sa reigle & voye, sa
volonté. Il me plaist de faire ainsi. Est-ce à vous à me

*La vierge Marie
n'est reverée
comme il
appartient à
cause que lon
ne cognoist sa
qualité & dignité.*

reprendre? Tu ne parles point comme l'homme, tout
homme est suiect à reprehension: ce n'est parler en
homme que cela c'est parler en Dieu. Tu dis, il me
plaist de faire ainsi, cela vient d'ignorance. Ie suis
homme, la verité de l'homme est defectible. Or il faut
qu'une reigle soit droicte. Puis donc que la volonté de
l'homme est oblicque & defectible, l'homme ne peut
prendre icelle pour reigle. Donc quiconque soit, soit
grand ou petit, il ne peut dire, il me plaist ainsi.
L'homme ne veut point parler en homme, il veut
parler comme s'il estoit Dieu, se attribuant ce qui
appartient à Dieu. Nous avons bien dit au
commencement, par ignorance tous maux viennent, &
ne sçauroit-on faire un mal sans ignorance & erreur:
en tout peché y a ignorance & erreur. Le monde
auiourd'huy est en grande ignorance & erreur.
Autrefois nous vous avons dit ce qui est escrit aux
Actes, quand S. Paul vint en Athenes entre autres   *Act. 17.*
choses superstitieuses qu'il trouva y avoit un autel,
auquel estoit escrit, *Ignoto Deo*, au Dieu incogneu. Et
auiourd'huy ie croy que le Dieu des Chrestiens, qui est
le vray Dieu, est incogneu, c'est à dire, le Dieu pour
lequel on ne fait rien, duquel on ne fait grand compte.
C'est le Dieu, mis avec les pechez oubliez: Il n'est point
obey. Que Dieu & l'homme parlent, on laissera Dieu,
& prendre-on l'homme. Il n'y a homme tant soit-il
passioné, qui ostast dire en despit du Roy, ie le despite
(aussi ne le faut-il pas dire) neantmoins pour un satras,
nous dirons en despit de Dieu, Ie renonce dieu, &c.
Estce pas grande ignorance? certes si est, & nous en
sommes auiourd'huy à cela. Or il faut cognoistre la
qualité de Dieu. Faute de cognoistre la qualité de   *Hiere. 17.*
l'homme, ie luy attribue ce qui ne luy appartient pas. Il   *Psal. 46.*
ne luy appartient pas que ie m'appuye sur luy: mais
sur Dieu. Et auiourd'huy ie tiens plus stable ce que
l'homme dit, que le commandement de Dieu, cela est
tout evident. Que dit Dieu? Fay mes commandemens,
& tu auras vie eternelle. *Hoc fac & vives. Si vis ad*   *Luc. 10.*
vitam ingredi serva mandata. Il a fait ce marché avec   *Matt. 19.*
moy qu'en gardant ses commandemens, me donnera
vie eternelle. Comment? *Convenit mecum ex*   *Matt. 20.*
denario diurno. Il me menace de damnation eternelle,   *Iacob. 2.*
si ie transgresse un seul commandement. Que dit

l'homme, venez à moy, que me donnerez vous? Il me
promet seulement du temporel. Ie le suy & laisse
Dieu. Voyci deux hommes qui m'appellent, & tous
deux me font promesses & menaces, en suyvant l'un
plustost que l'autre, ie monstre bien que ie tiens sa
promesse la plus stable. Auiourd'huy Dieu m'appelle.

Matt. 11.

Vien apres moy. *Tollite iugum meum super vos, et
invenietis requie animibus vestris.* Suyvez moy. Le
monde d'autre costé dit, Suyvez moy. Vous voyez qui

*Le monde a plus
de suite que
Dieu.*

a plus de suyte, c'est le monde. Et cela est un
tesmoignage que nous tenons sa parole plus stable &
ferme que celle de Dieu. Et encores tant plus est grande
nostre ignorance & erreur, que voyant mon
compagnon qui a esté trompé, ou qui est demeuré les
mains vuides, ie me voys mettre à sa place. Voyci
cestuy qui s'est mis à suyvre le monde, il meurt
pauvre comme Iob, & a destruict soy & ses amys,
neantmoins ie me voys mettre à sa place pour estre
mangé des pour comme luy, est-ce pas grand erreur?
Neantmoins cela est à nostre iugement &
condemnation, que nous tenons plus de compte, &
plus ferme la parolle de l'homme que de Dieu. Et de là

Hierem. 17.
Hiere. 2.
I. Cor. 8.

vient que nous sommes maudits par le prophete,
Maledictus qui confidit in homine. Faisons nous pas
cela tous les iours? Voyci que dit Dieu par Hieremie.
Transitè ad insulas Cethim, &c. Auiourd'huy le
monde est comme l'idole qui n'est que par apparence,
ce n'est rien. C'est grande pitié qu'ignorance. Nous
ignorons Dieu, & si ignorons nous-mesmes. Et par

*Qui se iuge ne
cognoit pauvreté.*
Luc. 7.
*Qui se cognoist il
se humilie.*
Matt. 18.
Matt. 8.
Luc. 7.
Psal. 72.
*Humilité n'a
indignation
contre autruy.*
Matt. 1.

cela nous pensons & sentons de nous plus qu'il ne
faut, & nous complaisons. C'est faute d'entendre. Si
i'entendois bien, ne verrois en moy, que pauvreté,
indigence, *etc.* En voyant cela, iamais ne serois fier &
orgueilleux, i'aurois pitié de mon prochain. Mais
nous sommes ainsi que ce Pharisee qui desdaignoit
Magdaleine, il se ignoroit, il pensoit estre iuste, & ne
valloit rien, comme ce Pharisee qui desdaignoit le
publican, disant: *Non sum sicut caeteri hominum,
etiam velut hic publicanus, &c.* Nous sommes tant
faciles à une elation de cueur. D'où vient cela?
d'orgueil & ignorance. Ie ignore ma condition &
qualité. Centurion entendoit bien sa qualité quand il
disoit: *Nam homo sum sub potestate constitutus.* Et

David disoit bien, *tanquam nihilum sum ante te. Ut iumentum factus sum.* En une vraye humilité iamais n'y aura indignation contre son prochain, trop bien contre vice. Et si en humilité se trouve indignation, c'est contre soymesme. Or passons outre, il faut cognoistre la qualité de Iesus Christ. L'evangile du iourd'huy nous la declare *Iacob genuit Ioseph virum Mariae.* Pour entendre cecy il faut noter que sainct Matthieu au commencement de son Evangile, nous declare la qualité de Iesus Christ quand il dit, *Liber generationis Iesu Christi.* Aucunesfois le nom qu'on impose à une personne declare la nature & condition d'icelle. Dieu a imposé nom à Abraham, qui au commencement avoit nom Abram. Ce nom Abraham declare sa condition. En ce nom Dieu vouloit demonstrer qu'Abraham devoit estre pere des Gentils par foy, *In spem contra spem credidit, ut fieret pater multarum gentium per fidem, &c.* Iacob faut autant à dire que *supplantator:* car il a prevenu la benediction de son frere Esau. Sainct Iean Baptiste, ce nom Iean declare sa qualité, c'estoit à dire qu'il devoit estre rempli de la grace de Dieu, *Ioannes, id est, in quo est gratia.* Aussi nostre Seigneur a imposé nom à Sainct Pierre, *Imposuit nomen Simoni Petro.* Ce nom Pierre declare sa qualité. Dieu l'a mis sous luy pour fondement de son Eglise. *Rogavi pro te ut non deficiat fides tua.* Ainsi la firmité de l'Eglise Romaine est monstrée par ce nom Pierre. *Hieronymus ait, à firmitate dicitur Petrus.* Or regardons quel est le nom de nostre Seigneur. Son nom c'est Iesus. *Vocabis Iesum:* car il delivrera le peuple de ses pechez. Son nom donc declare sa qualité, delivrer de peché c'est le propre de Dieu. Son nom donc monstre vrayement qu'il est Dieu. Si vous dites que le prestre absoult, il est vray: mais c'est en autre degré que Iesus Christ, lequel en son nom remet le peché, mais le prestre le remet au nom de Iesus. Ainsi Iesus Christ comme maistre remet le peché, le prestre soubs Dieu, de sorte que la puissance de Iesus Christ est d'authorité, & le prestre est comme ministre, qui le remet en son nom. C'est donc à dire que ce nom Iesus declare apertement sa qualité, car il est Dieu. Les Iuifs combien qu'ils fussent en grandes erreurs, si avoient ils ceste foy, qu'il n'ya

Matt. 1.
Le nom est declaritif du naturel de la personne.
Gene. 17.
Rom. 4.
Marc. 3.
Ioan. 1.

Luc. 22.

Matt. 1.
Iesus Christ en autre degré absoult le pecheur, qui ne fait le prestre.

avoit que Dieu qui remet les pechez. Ils ignoroient la
qualité de Iesus Christ, pensans qu'il ne feust homme
& Dieu, *Hic blasphemat.* Ils ignoroient, mais par leur
malice: Pource sont tombez en ce blaspheme. Il leur
dit: *Quid cogitatis inter vos, &c.* Venez-ça, lequel de
deux est le plus facile à dire, *Dimittuntur tibi peccata,*
an surge, tolle grabatum tuum & ambula? ut autem
sciatis, etc. Et ses euvres donnoient tesmoignages de
sa qualité. Et il dit luy mesmes: *Si opera on fecissem*
quae nemo alius fecit, excusationem haberent. Rupert
dit sur ce passage. *Cum audisset Ioannes in vinculis*
opera christi, etc., id est, que nul autre peut faire, & ses
euvres monstrent bien qu'il est Dieu. Iesus Christ
disoit de Nathanael: *Ecce verè Israelita, in quo dolus*
non est? Il luy demande. *Inde me nosti?* Il respond:
Priusquam Philippus te vocaret cum esses sub ficu,
vidite. Ce que il luy reveloit, ne se pouvoit sçavoir par
une voye humaine, incontinant va dire: *Tu es filius*
Dei rex Israel. Par cela entendit sa qualité qu'il estoit
fils de Dieu. Et S. Pierre disoit: *Tu es Christus filius*
Dei vivi. Ainsi par ses euvres & sa doctrine, on
cognoist sa qualité, car les escritures n'on autre but, que
nos monstrer que Iesus Christ est fils de Dieu eternel:
Haec scripta sunt ut credatis, quia Iesus est filius Dei.
Et S. Philipe [sic] disoit, *Quem scripsit in lege Moyses,*
invenimus Meßiam. Celuy duquel les prophetes
portent tesmoignage, nous l'avons trouvé. Qui est-il?
Iesus. Quand S. Iean Baptist l'eust monstré au doigt, S.
André le suyvit, Il luy demande: Que cherchez vous:
& il luy demande, Où demourez vous? *Veni & vide,*
&c. Et en si peu de temps qu'a esté avec luy, a entendu
sa qualité: c'est a sçavoir qu'il estoit le Messias, fils de
Dieu. Voila sa qualité. Il est le sauveur du monde, &
n'en y a point d'autre en ce degré. Il nous a sauvez &
rachetez. Pour autant que les Iuifs n'entendoient ceste
qualité, il les renvoyoit aux escritures. Il est impossible
estre sauvé, qui ne luy exhibe l'honneur & reverence
qui luy appartient, & qui ne le cognoist, ne luy peut
exhiber. Les Iuifs qui ne cognoissoient pas sa qualité,
l'appellent demoniacle, parquoy afin qu'ils
cogneussent sa qualité, les renvoyoit aux escritures.
Scrutamini scripturas, ipsae enim testimonium
perhibent de me. Le mauvais riche prioit Abraham

Matt. 9.
Marc. 2.

Matt. 9.

Ioan. 15.
Matt. 11.

Ioan. 1.
Nathanael confesse
Iesus Christ estre
fils de Dieu.
Ioan. 1.
Matt. 16.
Ioan. 21.

Ioan. 1.

Ioan. 1.

Les escritures
tesmoignent que
Iesus Christ est le
sauveur du monde.
Ioan. 5.
Ioan. 7.
Luc. 16.

envoyer le Lazare à ses cinq freres, Il repond, *Habent
Moysem & prophetas, audiant illos.* Comme s'il eust
dit: Ils ne sçauroient estre mieux advertis de la qualité
de Iesuschrist, que par Moyse & les prophetes. *Finis*   *Rom. 10.*
legis Christus: La fin où nousmesme la loy, c'est
cognoistre la qualité de nostre Seigneur, afin que nous
soyons sauvez. Et auiourd'huy nostre Evangile donne
à entendre cela. Aucunesfois l'homme peut pretendre
cause d'ignorance, il dira, Ie ne sçay rien. On demande
à un homme de village: Es tu Chrestien? il dira: Ie ne
suis pas clerc. Or afin que nul pretend excuse de son
ignorance, car *vult Deus omnes homines salvos fieri.*   *I. Tim. 2.*
Toute la loy nous monstre sa qualité pour la
cognoistre. Il ne faut seulement que regarder son nom.
Or ie ne cognois pas son nom: Il ne tient qu'à toy, car il
a esté annoncé par tout le monde, & a esté verifiée la
prophetie de David avant la destruction de Ierusalem,
c'est à sçavoir: *In omnem terram exivit sonus eorum,*   *Psal. 18.*
& in fines orbis terrae verba eorum. S. Paul dit:
Praedicamus Christum crucifixum, Iudaeis   *I. Cor. 1.*
scandalum, gentibus autem stultitiam. Et S. Pierre
dit: *Non enim aliud nomen est sub caelo datum
hominibus, in quo oporteat nos salvos fieri.* Pourtant   *Act. 4.*
nous ne pouvons ignorer son nom, qui vault autant à
dire que sauveur. Cognoissons donc un peu sa qualité.
Toute la perfection d'un Chrestien gist en l'amour de
Dieu, quelque vertu que i'aye, ie ne suis en l'estat de
perfection Chrestienne, si ie n'ay amour de Dieu. Qui   *Enquoy gist la*
m'induit à aymer aucun? Les bien-faits. Vien-ça,   *perfection du*
peux-tu avoir plus grands bien-faits qu'estre delivré de   *Chrestien.*
peché & d'enfer, & avoir salut? Qui te fait ce bien?
C'est Iesus: pourtant pense, offenseray-ie celuy duquel
i'ay tant receu de bien? sans luy ie fusse damné. Donc
ce nom Iesus m'attire à aymer, & me retire de mal.
Nous n'ignorons point son nom. Pourtant dient les
Docteurs, Nul auiourd'huy ne se peut excuser par
l'ignorance de son salut, fay ton devoir, & ce qui est en
toy, le S. Esprit t'enseignera interieurement ou
exterieurement. Et si tu demeures en ignorance du
nom de Iesus, c'est ta faute. Voila donc son nom,
Iesus, id est, salvator, Iesus, c'est tout l'appuy & attente   *Le nom de*
de l'homme, me peux-ie bien appuyer sur luy? ouy, le   *Iesus, c'est*
nom de Iesus me montre qu'il est tout puissant: s'il   *l'appuy de l'homme.*
                                              Luc. 1.

l'est, *Non erit impoßible apud eum omne verbum.* Ie
peux bien donc me fier en luy. Aucunesfois
continuation en mon peché me fait desesperer de mon
salut. I'ay tant fait de mal. Regarde le nom de Iesus.
Est-il pas Dieu? Il n'y a donc peché qui ne soit sous
luy. Et pource qu'il est tout puissant, il n'y a peché,
qu'il ne puisse remette: son nom monstre qu'il me
peut sauver. O mais il a le pouvoir, mais ie ne sçay s'il
le veult: Son nom te declare qu'il le veult, son nom est
Iesus, id est, salvator, Il est venu pour ceste fin. Et pout
monstrer qu'il te veut sauver, il a prins ce nom. Son
nom declare autant sa bonté que sa puissance. Et ainsi
que sa puissance est infinie, aussi est sa bonté. Bonté se
veult communiquer, & tant plus grande est la
communication, tant plus grande est la bonté, pourtant
il me peut sauver. Apres il le peult & veult, mais ce
n'est pas tout. Voicy un homme qui me peult & veut
ayder, mais il peult changer, ou il ne durera pas
tousiours. Ah Iesus dure tousiours. *Christus heri &*
hodie ipse & in secula, In principio erat verbum. Or ie
ne sçay s'il changera point: Ce nom de Iesus me
monstre qu'il est immuable. *Ego Deus & non mutor.*
Apud quem non est transmutatio nec vicißitudinis
obumbratio. Comme ce nom Iesus me monstre qu'il
est puissant & veritable, aussi il me monstre son
immutabilité. Et ainsi ie m'appuye sur luy. Donc tout
cela me manifeste sa qualité & condition. Que luy
dois-ie rendre maintenant? entant que ie le cognois
tout puissant, ie le craindray par dessus tout, en tant
qu'il est bon par dessus tout, & que bonté luy convient
par essence, ie l'aymeray par dessus tout. D'autant
qu'il est veritable, ie m'asseure de luy, & qu'il dure
tousiours, & ne peut changer. Voila donc que ie luy
vueil exhiber toute reverence & crainte, tout amour &
fiance. Voila qu'il nous faut entendre de la qualité de
nostre Seigneur. A-il point d'autre qualité que ceste
là? S'y a, il est homme. *Est filius Dei, & hominis, &*
conveniunt in persona. Comme sçavez vous cela? En
deux passages l'escriture nous monstre sa qualité
d'homme. *Liber generationis Iesu Christi filii David,*
filii Abraham. Le fils est de mesme nature que le pere.
Apres vous avez en la sentence qui est prinse pour le
thesme, *De qua natus est Iesus.* Pour estre sauvé ne

Dieu a vouloir
de sauver un
chacun. Bonté
se veut tousiours
communiquer à
autruy.

Heb. 13.
Ioan. 1.

Iac. 1.

Ce que nous
devons rendre
à Iesus Christ.

Ioan. 1.

Matt. 1.

suffit sçavoir sa qualité, entant qu'il est Dieu: mais
aussi entant qu'il est homme, *Deus est ex substantia*
patris ante secula genitus, homo ex substantia matris
in seculo natus. Or-ça que luy convient il en ceste
qualité d'homme? Estre passible, mortel, subiect à
toute passion excepté peché, *Debuit per omnia fratribus*   *Hebr. 2.*
aßimilari, ut pontifex fieret Hebraeorum. Pourtant
dit sainct Iean: Aucuns qui ont ignoré sa qualité, ont
dit qu'il n'estoit homme: les autres qu'il n'estoit Dieu.
Mais nous qui sommes son peuple & ses hommes,
devons confesser tous les deux, qu'il est vray Dieu &
vray homme. *Verbum caro factum est.* Et ceux qui   *Ioan. 1.*
nyent cela, sont Antechrists. *Qui negat christum in*
carne venisse, est Antichristus. O mater Dei! Voila   *I. Ioan. 2.*
                                               Psal. 32.
une grande qualité, mais la qualité de Dieu est bien
plus grande. *Verbo Domini caeli firmati sunt.* En
qualité d'homme il a respandu son sang. Est-ce pas
grand chose de nostre Dieu? Il est Dieu & homme, &
en qualité d'homme il a faict plus grandes choses
qu'en qualité de Dieu. Comme Dieu, il a creé le
monde, comme homme il a racheté, & si a monstré
ceste qualité de Dieu par la qualité d'homme,
tellement qu'il a convaincu tous de dire, Il est fils de
Dieu, il est plein d'infirmité, comme homme,
neantmoins en souffrant comme homme, a contraint
de dire qu'il estoit fils de Dieu. Et si comme homme a
chassé le diable de sa principauté. Or il est Dieu &   *Ioan. 21.*
homme, mais il n'est moins fort estant homme que
Dieu, & toute la force de Dieu a esté monstrée estant
homme, ainsi il est Dieu & homme. En quelle qualité
sommes nous plus tenus à luy, en qualité de Dieu, ou
en qualité d'homme? Il a demonstré son infirmité
comme homme, enquoy sommes nous plus obligez à
luy comme Dieu, ou comme homme? Monsieur
Sainct Augustin dit, *plus debemus infirmitati eius*
quàm virtuti: car son infirmitee m'a sauvé, iustifié: de   *St. August.*
son infirmitee i'ay tiré paradis, remission de mes pechez,
reconciliation avec Dieu. Et cela est un plus
grand benefice, que cela que i'ay de sa vertu, qui est
creation. Estre sauvé, est-il pas meilleur, qu'estre &
estre damné? Mais vivre en esperance de vie
eternelle, ie tire cela de son infirmité qui est sa passion.
Crucifixus ex infirmitate, Apres il est Roy & prestre.   *I. Cor. 13.*

Rupertus in Matthaeum. Dit que ses armoiries est
Dieu & homme, Roy & prestre. Il a succedé à son pere
David, qui estoit Roy, à son pere Abraham qui estoit
prestre, *quia olim primogeniti erant sacerdotes.* A-il
pas escrit en sa cuisse. *Rex regum & Dominus
dominantium. Ego autem constitutus sum rex ab eo
super Syon montem sanctum eius. Deus iudicium
tuum regi da.* Or-ça il est le Roy d'Israel, Pourtant
Pylate (ne sçachant toutesfois qu'il faisoit, il estoit
beste, mais le sainct Esprit parle aucunesfois par les
bestes) a mieux dit que il n'entendoit, escrivant *Iesus
Nazarenus Rex Iudaeorum.* Il est aussi prestre selon
l'ordre de Melchisedech. S'est il pas offert à Dieu son
pere pour le salut du monde? y a-il en sacrifice auquel
Dieu se soit pleu pour la remission des pechez que de
luy? *Impoßibile est sanguine tantorum & hyrcorum
aufferri peccata, &c. Sed semetipsum obtulit Deo, & c.
Holocausta & pro peccato non postulasti, tunc dixi ecce
venio. In qua volunte omnes sanctificantur.* Il a offert
une fois son corps en sacrifice en l'arbre de la croix,
pour le salut des hommes, & a esté tant aggreable à
Dieu, qu'il a mis fin à tous les sacrifices de la loy
ancienne. Voila les tiltres de nostre Seigneur, *Deus &
homo quia de virgine natus, rex & sacerdox unxit eum
prae participibus suis oleo laetitiae.* Voila ses qualitez,
Roy pour nous deffendre, Sauveur pour nous delivrer,
& mort grand prestre pour offrir à Dieu son pere. Il
s'est offert une fois visiblement, mais tous les iours
s'offre soubs les especes de pain & de vin
invisiblement au sainct sacrement de l'Autel.

Exod. 22.
Apoc. 19.
Psal. 2.
Psal. 71.

Luc. 23.
Hebr. 5.

Hebr. 10.

Matth. 1.
Hebr. 1.

2. *Sermon auquel est amplement traicté des remedes contre la tentation de Desespoir: fait par feu monsieur Picard, le iour de l'exaltation saincte croix, 1555.*

Mihi absit gloriari nisi in cruce, Gal. 6. Quand un homme a quelque affaire, ce luy est un grand bien estre bien appuyé. Voila un homme qui est en quelque necessité s'il est bien appuyé, luy sera facile de sortir son besoing & venir à bout de son affaire. Un homme qui est bien apparenté, qui a grande faveur & bon port, peut entreprendre & venir à bout de beaucoup de choses: mais un homme mal appuyé, ne sçauroit pas faire grande chose. Aucunesfois en ce monde nous prendrons alliance en une maison pour avoir appuy. Le colloqueray ma fille un tel lieu pour avoir port & faveur. C'est donc à dire que ce n'est pas peu, estre bien appuyé. Un homme qui a port & faveur du Roy, fait beaucoup de choses. Puis qu'il aura l'oreille du Prince, la faveur & le credit, il fera tout ce qu'il voudra. En ce monde, un homme qui est porté d'un grand seigneur, d'un Cardinal, fait beaucoup de choses à cause du support & appuy. I'ay une lettre de monsieur tel, ie la presente à un president, la voyant il est stimulé d'accomplir ma requeste. Ainsi c'est grand chose d'avoir port & appuy. Or ie vous diray, ie suis d'opinion que nous cherchions à bien nous appuyer. Il nous fault chercher port, faveur & credit: mais il faut bien garder qu'en se cuidant bien appuyer, on ne tombe. Bien souvent ie prendray un homme pour mon appuy, & à la fin ie me trouve trompé, quand ie pense estre bien appuyé, c'est quand ie me laisse tomber au milieu de l'eau & de la boüe. Ainsi c'est bien fait de chercher port & appuy pour estre sousteneu. Ie suis de cest advis: mais aussi il faut bien garder qu'en cherchant appuy, nous ne soyons trompez: & qu'en pensant estre bien appuyé, nous ne tombions à terre. C'est chose toute asseurée, que qui prend

Il est mal appuyé qui se confie en l'homme.

l'homme pour son appuy, se trouve trompé &
tousiours à terre: il est mal soustenu qui est porté de
l'homme: c'est à dire il est mal appuyé, qui se confie en
l'homme, c'est Ieremie qui le dit, *Maledictus qui
confidit in homine & ponit carnem brachium suum.* Ierem. 17.
Celuy est maudit que se confie en l'homme, & qui faict
son fort de la chair. Vous sçavez bien que le chair n'est
pas forte, il n'est rien si fresle & si imbecille. Combien
en voyez vous en ce monde qui pensent estre bien
appuyez & avoir grand port, car incontinant qu'on leur
fait quelque chose, ils disent, Ie suis à un tel: tellement
que bien souvent pour mieux venir à bout d'une
tyrannie & oppression qu'ils font à un pauvre homme,
disent, ie suis à un tel: toutesfois se trouvent à la fin
trompez. Maudit est qui prend l'homme pour son
appuy: on pense par ce moyen estre bien fort, intimider
& donner terreur à autruy, mais on n'en vient pas à
bout. Or ie vous diray pour estre bien soustenu &
porté, il faut prendre la croix pour nostre appuy, &
suyvre S. Paul en la sentence prinse pour le thesme,
Mihi absit gloriari nisi in cruce: toute ma gloire, tout
mon fort, tout mon appuy, & toute mon attente n'est
autre chose que la croix de Iesus Christ: voila mon fort
& ma defense. Vous voyez que nostre ennemy faict
des boulevers, des forteresses pour se garentir &
defendre contre nous, & de nostre costé nous nous
sont que les toupes & nids de pie: mais nous avons
bien un ennemy plus à craindre & plus dangereux,
contre lequel il nous faut armer & fortifier. Vous
sçavez bien que le monde est l'un de ceux qui nous
molestent, la chair est l'autre, mais la principale guerre *Nostre principale
vient de satan: nostre principale guerre vient du* *tentation vient de
maling esprit. Ce qu'a tresbien descrit sainct Paul,* *Satan.*
disant en l'epistre aux Ephesiens. Pour vous guetter &
garder d'estre surprins de vostre ennemy le diable
d'enfer: Armez vous des armures de nostre
redempteur: *quoniam non est nobis colluctatio* Ephe. 6.
adversus carnem, car nous n'avons pas seulement à
nous guetter à resister contre les passions qui
procedent de charnalité, comme gourmandise, ou
paillardise, *& sanguinem,* ny contre les passions qui
viennent du sang, c'est à dire, contre ire & courroux
qui procedent d'une esmotion de sang, quand on vous

dit iniure, ou qu'on vous fait tort. Non sans point de
faute, mais outre cela vous avez affaire, *Adversus
principes & potestates, adversu mundi rectores
tenebrarum harum, contra spirituales nequitias in
caelestibus.* Sçavez vous bien contre qui vous avez à
batailler? Sont les Princes, les Potentats, &
gouverneurs de ce monde & de ces tenebres, c'est à
dire, vous avez affaire contre le diable, qui domine sur
gens mondains obtenebrez de peché. Et en ce monde
qu'il domine, car apres la consommation du monde, il
n'aura plus de puissance. D'avantage vous avez
affaire contre la malice & iniquité spirituelle, c'est a
dire, contre le maling esprit, qui est bien plus sçavant
& plus subtil que l'homme, qui s'applique à toute
meschanceté. Voila pourquoy il est dit meschanceté
spirituelle, par ce qu'est bien plus dangereuse que la
malice de l'homme. Est si sçavez vous bien pourquoy
il s'addresse contre vous? ce n'est pas pour un
royaume temporel: non, mais *est in caelestibus*, c'est
pour vous priver de paradis, pour lequel nous
defendre de nostre ennemy si cauteleux & dangereux
que serons nous? Il nous faut armer & faire un fort.
Quel fort prendrons nous? Demandez à sainct Paul
qui dit. *Mihi absit gloriari nisi in cruce domini nostri
Iesu Christi.* Tout mon appuy, toute ma defense, c'est
la croix, la mort & passion que nostre Seigneur Iesus
Christ a endurée pour nous. Voila qui est bon. Or
comme i'ay dit souvent, l'homme est tenté & assailly
par satan, de desespoir, de lascheté, & de pusillanimité,
de descouragement: aucunesfois l'homme se trouve
tant descouragé qu'il luy est advis que iamais ne sera
sauvé. A l'encontre de ces tentations que faut-il faire?
de quelles armes se doit on armer? Prenez pour vostre
fort & lieu d'asseurance la croix de nostre Seigneur
Iesus Christ, ce qu'il a enduré pour nous tous. Et
comment se pourra descourager l'homme, quand il
pensera que Iesus Christ a esté mis en croix pour son
salut? Qui me fait perdre l'espoir que i'ay en
l'homme? C'est de deux choses l'une, ou que
l'homme en qui i'ay mis mon esperance, n'a pas la
puissance de me secourir en mon besoing, ou bien
aucunesfois il a bien puissance de m'ayder, mais ie voy
que la volonté qu'il avoit est changée: & ceste

mutation de sa volonté est argument de me degouster
que ie puisse parvenir à ce que ie pretendois par son
moyen & fiance en luy. Outre cela il peut advenir qu'il
aura le pouvoir & le vouloir de m'ayder, mais ie crains
qu'il me faille & meure quand i'aurois à faire de luy: &
ceste apprehension que i'ay qu'il ne me faille, me fait
diminuer mon esperance que i'avoye en luy & suis
descouragé. Or voila les causes pourquoy il ne faut
mettre son appuy en l'homme. Mais sçavez vous bien
que nous prendrons pour nostre appuy, afin que ne
soyons frustrez de nostre esperance? C'est la croix de
Iesus Christ, en laquelle est monstrée la puissance de
Dieu, combien Dieu est puissant de m'ayder. Car en
icelle ie voy le triomphe & la victoire que Iesus Christ
a eu du diable: car ie voy que satan qui est tant puissant
que merveilles, & duquel dit Iob, *Non est potestas*
super terram quae comparetur ei, qui factus est ut
nullum timeret. Sa puissance est si grande qu'elle
passe toutes les forces de ce monde & est si fort qu'il ne
craint homme, & pource s'est fait appeler Prince de ce
monde. Mais par la croix il a esté chassé de la
principauté. Et c'est ce que dit nostre Seigneur, *Nunc*
princeps huius mundi eiicitur foras. Le prince de ce
monde Satan, qui avant la venue de Iesus Christ par sa
tyrannie avoit usurpé domination & seigneurie par
tout le monde, & avoit tant eniambé sur Dieu, que
quasi tous le recognoissoient pour le grand maistre,
Seigneur & monarque du monde, mais Iesus Christ,
qui est le fort armé, venant en ce monde pour le
combattre, luy a bien abbaissé ses cornes. Par quel
moyen? Par la croix. Ie cognoy donc que peché & satan
sont vaincus spoliez & chassez de ce monde par la
croix, & le monde est converti à Dieu. La croix de Iesus
Christ me demonstre cela. Donc quand ie suis tenté de
desespoir & ie regarde à la croix de Iesus Christ,
laquelle est pour moy, i'ay matiere de tenir bon. Outre
cela i'ay la volonté de nostre Seigneur qui ne change
point, laquelle m'est donnée à entendre par la croix: la
croix me dit, Dieu se veut sauver & pardonner tes
pechez: car par la croix il a destruit peché & satan. Or
dira quelqu'un, Ie sçay bien que Dieu me peut sauver,
mais ie ne sçay s'il le veut. Tu ne sçais? regarde la
croix, & tu cognoistras assez la grande affection &

Nous devons
prendre nostre
appuy en la croix.

Iob. 14.

Ioan. 12.

bonne amour qu'il te porte. Premierement il veut que
tous soient sauvez. *Vult omnes homines salvos fieri,* *I. Tim. 2.*
Rom. 5.
& ad agnitionem veritatis venire, dit S. Paul.
D'avantage il dit en un autre passage. *Commendat*
autem charitatem suam Deus in nobis quoniam adhuc
peccatores essemus, secundum tempus Christus pro
nobis mortuus est. Nostre Seigneur nous rend en
grande recommandation sa bonne volonté qu'il a
envers nous, car nous qui ne vallions rien sommes
iustifiez par la mort de son fils Iesus Christ qui est
mort pour nous. Peut on monstrer plus grande charité
& dilection à un homme que mourir pour luy? C'est
bien donc à dire qu'il nous veut sauver, puis qu'il est
mort pour nous encores, *quum inimici essemus,* lors
que nous estions ses ennemis, & a espandu, pour ce
faire, son sang en croix pour nous. Donc il me peut
sauver, quant & quant il me veut sauver: & ceste
puissance & volonté est demonstrée par la croix.
Notez un bon petit mot que dit S. Iean Chrys. *Copia* *Chrysost.*
peccatorum non trahit hominem in desperationem
sed animus impius: etiam si omnem malitiam
exercueris noli desperare. L'abondance & multitude
des pechez ne fait point tomber la personne en
desespoir: mais la meschante volonté. Mon amy,
pense un petit. Dieu desire mon salut & ne veut point
ma mort: car dit-il par son Prophete Ezechiel, *Quare*
moriemini domus Israel? Nolo mortem peccatoris, sed *Ezech. 18.*
magis ut convertatur & vivat. Et quoties ingemuerit
peccator omnium iniquitatem suarum non recordabor.
Pensez à cela & vous trouverez consolez. O ie ne sçay
si Dieu a ce desir de me sauver: Dy tu? Et tu vois qu'il
est mort pour toy & a porté sa croix pour toy. *Esa. 9.*
Principatum super humerum eius, dit Esaye: ne doute
plus de cela. La croix me monstre clerement la vertu &
puissance de Dieu & de son fils Iesus Christ, car par la
croix peché est destruit, le diable vaincu, paradis
ouvert, & l'homme a remission de son peché: c'est à
dire que celuy qui a pendu en croix est omnipotent,
outre plus qu'il est omnipotent, il monstre bien qu'il
nous veut sauver: car il n'a eu autre motif d'estre
pendu en croix, que le salut de l'homme, c'est que dit
S. Iean, *Sic Deus dilexit mundum, ut filium suum* *Ioan. 3.*
unigenitum dares. Dieu a tant aymé l'homme qu'il a

donné son fils pour sa redemption. Est-ce pas donc à
dire, que la croix monstre evidemment que Dieu veut
sauver l'homme? Tu as donc deux choses où tu te
peux bien appuyer & en faire ton fort. La puissance de
Dieu & sa volonté: ainsi le declare S. Paul, *Vult omnes
homines salvos fieri.* Ouy: mais peut estre que c'est *I. Tim. 2.*
pour un astre que la volonté de Dieu est determinée:
Non, elle est determinée pour tous & comme dit S. *Act. 10.*
Pierre. *Non est acceptio personarum apud Deum: sed* *En Dieu n'y a*
in omni gente qui timet eum & operature iustitiam, *point acceptation*
acceptus est illi. En Dieu n'y a point acception de *de personnes.*
personnes. Mais toute personne de quelque estat ou
condition qu'elle soit, craignant Dieu, & gardant ses
commandemens, elle est aggreable à Dieu. Crains Dieu
& mets peine de garder ses commandemens, asseure
toy que tu seras sauvé par sa croix: il est mort pour tous
indifferemment. Et si quelqu'un ne se sent du fruit de
ceste passion, il ne tient qu'à luy, c'est pour autant
qu'il ne se rend capale [*sic*]. C'est ainsi de Dieu envers
nous, comme si quelqu'un me disoit: va labourer en
ma vigne, & ie te donneray escu. Si ie n'y vay ie
n'auray pas l'escu, qui excede beaucoup la peine ou
travail que ie prendois en labourant, mais celuy qui ira
aura un escu, puis qu'on luy a promis. Aussi si
l'homme n'a part & portion à la mort de Iesus Christ,
il ne tient qu'à luy, c'est pour autant qu'il ne fait pas ce
que Iesus Christ luy a dit, & ne luy obeit pas, qui est
moins que rien au regard du loyer qu'il promet, qui est
infini, & celuy qui fait son commandement gaigne
cela, non l'autre, qui est lasche & pusillanime & qui ne
veut travailler. Et c'est ce que dit S. Paul, *Factus est* *Hebr. 5.*
omnibus obtemperantibus sibi causa salutis aeternae.
Iesus Christ est cause de salut, à qui? à tous ceux qui
luy obeïssent. Et font son commandement. Aussi
nous voyons la force & puissance de nostre Seigneur
Iesus Christ, qui nous peult ayder, d'avantage l'autre
argument que i'ay de me confier en luy, est qu'il me
veult ayder. Faisons donc là nostre fort & nous
appuyons sur luy contre tous tentation de desespoir.
Ouy, mais me durera-il tousiours? aucunesfois un pere
fault trop tost à ses enfans, un oncle à ses nepveux, &
un qui aura bonne volonté de m'ayder, sera prevenu
de mort aucunesfois, & ainsi voila mon fort qui est

tombé. Mais voicy le point, où il se fault arrester.
Iesus Christ ne nous peult iamais faillir, il n'est pas
mortel comme un homme, il dure tousiours. *Semper*   *Hebr. 7.*
vivens ad interpellandum pro nobis. Et en un autre
passage dit sainct Paul, *Christus heri & hodie ipse & in*
secula. C'est à dire Iesus Christ est eternel. Il ne
sçauroit donc me faillir au besoing. Voila trois grands
moyens d'avoir ayde & secours contre mes ennemis,
qui me doivent inciter à prendre Iesus Christ pour
mon appuy & protecteur en toutes mes affaires. Il
advient que ie suis tenté souvent de desespoir, &
comme dit David, *Domine quid multiplicati sunt qui*   *Psal. 30.*
tribulant me? Multi dicunt animae meae, non est salus
ipsi in Deo eius. Et, sire, que ceux qui me tourmentent
& affligent sont en grand nombre. Il en y a tant qui
s'eslevent à l'encontre de moy & me cuident
persuader, que vous ne me sauverez-point, mon Dieu,
mais, sire, ie ne perdray pas courage pour tout cela. Ie
me confie en vous. *Tu es susceptor meus.* C'est vous
qui me deffendez contre tous mes ennemis, & en vous
non pas en moy ie me glorifieray. Aussi, ie suis tenté
aucunesfois de desespoir. Ie voy la grandeur de mes
pechez, & ma continuation en mal: ie considere que
i'ay passé la pluspart de ma vie en toute ordure &
iniquité. Ie ne fis donc bien, plusieurs-fois i'ay receu
mon sauveur en mauvais estat. Que feray-ie là? Ce
sont moyens que prend Satan aucunesfois pour nous
descourager de nostre salut. Il nous souffle aux
aureilles. Comment est il possible que tu faces
penitence, veu que tu as si longuement continué en
ton peché, & encores de pro-pos deliberé. Or contre
telles tentations ie me veux armer des armeures que
nous presente sainct Paul, pour me garder des dards
envenimez de mon ennemy. Sainct Paul apres avoir
declaré la force, astuce & cautelle de nostre ennemy,
vient à armer le chevalier Chrestien de toutes pieces, &
luy baille deux armeures comme les principales, &
ausquelles se doit fier, disant: *In omnibus sumentes*   *Ephe. 60.*
scutum fidei, in quo poßitis omnia tela nequissimi
ignea extinguere: & gladium spiritus, quod est verbum
Dei. Contre toutes tentations prenez l'escussion de foy,
par lequel vous puissiez esteindre tous les dards
enflambez du maling esprit: & le glaive de l'esprit, qui

est la parole de Dieu. Or de tous les dards de satan, le   *Desespoir.*
plus dangereux c'est desespoir. Et n'y en a point qui
appellées *ignea*. Presomption ne vault rien, & sçay   *Presomption.*
bien que Satan tente plusieurs de ce vice, & faict
tresbucher en peché: mais ce n'est rien au regard de
desespoir. Parce que plus facile est de descendre au
milieu, qu'il n'est de monter au milieu. Pource sainct   *S. Bernard.*
Bernard appelle desespoir la consommation de tout
mal. Orgueil, presomption, est le commencement de
tout mal: mais desespoir est le comble &
consommation: & depuis que Satan tient une
personne en desespoir, c'est avec grande difficulté s'il
en eschappe. Or contre telle tentation, il fault prendre
l'armeure de Iesus Christ. Comment a vaincu IESVS
CHRIST le diable? Par la croix: pren donc la croix & la
presente comme un bouclier à l'encontre des durs
assaults & frequentes impugnations que te donne
Satan pour te mener à desespoir, afin que le dard de
desespoir ne te face aucun mal, mets au devant ce
bouclier de la croix. Car en icelle tu cognoistras la
puissance qu'a ton Dieu de t'ayder & son bon vouloir.
Rien ne luy est impossible: autant luy est facile de
pardonner une infinité de pechez, qu'un peché tout
seul. Mets cela au devant de la tentation, pensez, Dieu
me peult pardonner mes pechez, ores qu'ils
excedassent l'arene de la mer, ouy mais incontinant
Satan me mettra devant les yeux, O penses-tu que Dieu
se soucie de toy, & qu'il te vueille ayder, veu que tu
l'as offensé si griefvement, & que tant de fois es
recidive en adioustant peché sur peché & qui pis est, tu
l'as fait de certaine malice & propre industrie?
D'avantage il est si maling & cauteleux, que bien
souvent pour mieux nous accabler, s'ayde de la saincte
escriture en nous suggerant. Viens-ça ton peché n'a
point esté commis par ignorance, mais de certaine
malice & cognoissance, qui est un peché directement
contre le sainct Esprit. Or sçay tu pas bien, que ce peché
là ne se remet point, *neque in hoc seculo neque in*   *Matth. 23.*
futuro? Tu sçays bien que dit l'escriture: Qui peche
contre le pere, ou contre le fils, c'est à dire par fragilité,
ou par ignorance, son peché se remet: mais toy, tu as
peché de certaine malice & volonté deliberée, tu ne le
sçaurois nier: tu as prins plaisir à mal faire, tu as

prevenu la tentation: & si tu n'eusses pensé porter
nuisance à ton prochain, tu ne l'eusses pas fait: & Dieu
sur lequel tu t'appuyes, est il pas veritable? Or il dist
d'un tel peché, que ie tien, *quòd non remittetur, neque
in hoc seculo, neque in futuro*: Ie confesse cela. Outre
plus il exaggerera, disant: Sçays tu pas bien qu'il a dit
par sainct Iean. *Est peccatum ad mortem: non pro illo
dico ut roget quis.* Or ton peché est tel, car de propos
deliberé tu as contamné ton salut. Que veux tu dire?
O Mater Dei! M'allegues-tu l'escriture? Ie feray ainsi
que m'a enseigné Iesus Christ, lequel tenté de
l'ennemy au desert, & qui luy avoit allegué l'escriture,
luy repliqua par l'escriture. Aussi à son exemple,
Clavum clavo retundam. Quand Satan vint au desert
tenter nostre Seigneur, il luy presenta des pierres,
disant: *Dic ut lapides isti panes fiant.* Nostre Seigneur
luy respond, ce qui est escrit en Deuteronome. *Non in
solo pane vivit homo.* On vit bien sans pain materiel.
Apres il mena nostre Seigneur sur le pinnacle du
temple, & puis luy dit: Iecte toy du hault en bas, car il
est escrit, *Angelus suis mandavit de te,* & en ce lieu il
alleguoit l'escriture faulsement, car elle ne s'entend
que de l'homme iuste, non pas de Iesus Christ. Pource
luy respond nostre sauveur, *Non tentabis Dominum
Deum tuum.* Pour le tiers assault apres l'avoit mené
sur une haulte montagne, il luy monstra tous les
royaumes du monde, & luy dit: Ie suis un grand
Prince, tel que tu me veois, tout ce que ie te monstre
m'appartient, & le donne à qui il me plaist: & pource
que te cognois grand personnage, si tu me veux adorer,
ie te donneray tout. Nostre Seigneur luy respond.
Retire toy arriere Satan. Il est escrit. *Dominum Deum
tuum adorabis, ut illi soli servies.* Tu adoreras un seul
Dieu vivant de l'adoration souveraine, c'est à dire: Tu
recognoistras un seul Dieu comme souverain. Voila
comme Iesus Christ pour nostre exemple a vaincu les
tentations de Satan par l'escriture, laquelle il luy avoit
allegué fausement. Faisons ainsi que luy. Quand donc
Satan me dira & alleguera, Sçays tu pas bien, que tant
long temps tu as continué en tes maux & pechez de
propos & volonté deliberée? Ne sçays tu pas bien que le
peché contre le sainct Esprit ne se remet point? Ouy ie
le sçay bien. Mais il s'entend de celuy qui ne se veult

I. Ioan. 8.

Matth. 4.

Deut. 8.

Psal. 90.

Deut. 6.

pas repentir. Et faire penitence. Car puis que tu
m'allegues l'escriture, i'ay l'escriture qui faict pour
moy. Il a dit & n'est point menteur. *Non est Deus*   *Num. 23.*
quasi homo ut mentiatur, nec ut filius hominis, ut
mutetur. Or il a dit, & n'est point muable &
inconstant, comme l'homme. Ie ne vueil point la
mort du pecheur, mais toutesfois & quantes qu'il
gemira son peché, & fera penitence, ie mettray en
oubly toutes ses iniquitez. Et quand il dit: *Peccator,* il *Ezech. 18.*
n'entend parler d'un tel ou tel peché en particulier,
mais de tous en general. O mais ton peché est contre le
sainct Esprit, qui ne se remet point, tu seras donc
damné? O ie m'en garderay bien si Dieu plaist:
sanctum, aussi a il dit: *Quoties ingemuerit peccator,*
omnium iniquitatum illius non recordabor.
I'entendray donc par l'escriture, que celuy qui peche
contre le sainct Esprit, sera damné: ouy bien s'il ne se
repent & fait penitence. Mais aussi, ie suis asseuré par
l'escriture, si le pecheur se repent, il sera sauvé, & aura *Matth. 5.*
pardon en faisant penitence. Outre plus les faicts de *Rom. 6.*
Dieu sont une bonne & vraye interpretation de   *2. Cor. 1.*
l'escriture. En un passage nous trouverons escrit: Ne *Iere. 4.*
iure nullement. *Dico vobis. Non iurate omnino.* Et
nous trouvons en un autre passage, que sainct Paul a
iuré, & que nostre Seigneur mesme a dit par son
prophete. *Et iurabis, vivit dominus, in veritate et in*
iudicio, et in iustitia; c'est donc à dire que quelquefois *2. Par. 33.*
il est licite de iurer. Or voyons qu'a fait nostre
Seigneur. Il a pardonné à un Manasses, Roy de Iuda:
qui avoit mené une vie la plus meschante du monde,
& si son peché estoit par malice: Il avoit remply la ville
de Ierusalem du sang des Prophetes, à la fin il fut mené
en captivité où il recogneust son peché, & en grande
contrition de cueur fit penitence, demandant pardon à
Dieu: & il luy pardonna: c'est donc à dire que quand on
se repend en demandant à Dieu pardon, il faict grace &
remet tous les pechez. Parquoy i'opposeray cela contre
les dards de Satan, qui sans cesse me flagorne aux
aureilles, *Non est tibi salus in Deo tuo.* Tu t'abuses *Psal. 3.*
bien d'esperer & attendre salut & confort de ton Dieu,
il t'a delaissé pour la multitude de tes pechez, &
continuation en malice. Penses-tu qu'il a y pitié de
toy? Ouy ie le pense & mets du tout ma fiance en luy:

parce qu'il est puissant pour me pardonner, &
d'avantage, il veult me pardonner. Ie suis asseuré
qu'en faisant penitence, il me fera grace par sa grande
bonté & misericorde. Voila mon fort & mon appuy. O
mais tu te fies en toy. Non faicts, mais en la bonté &
clemence de mon Dieu, & suis asseuré qu'en faisant ce
qu'il m'a dit, c'est à dire penitence, il me pardonnera.
C'est ainsi que qui auroit promis dix escus à un
homme, qui feroit quelque petite chose legere, & qui
ne seroit respondante à ladite somme, en faisant la
chose commandée on est tenu luy tenir promesse, &
baillir les dix escus, ausquels volontairement on s'est
obligé: aussi ie sçay bien que ce que ie fay n'est suffisant
pour avoir paradis ny condigne de la vie eternelle que
i'attens. *Non enim sunt condignae passiones huius*
temporis ad futuram gloriam quae revelabitur in
nobis. Mais Dieu qui est liberal, accepte si peu que ie   *Rom. 8.*
fay, & a pour aggreable ma penitence en m'appuyant à
sa promesse. Et là où ie me fieray qu'il me donnera
pardon & ne feray sa volonté, c'est presomption &
temerité, ie m'abuse. Et pensez vous que ce ne fut pas
grande folie estimer, le Roy m'aidera & m'accordera ce
que ie luy demande & ie luy fay le pire que ie peux? Et
un Lutherien dit qu'il sera sauvé sans rien faire en
croyant seulement, & au rest vivra à son plaisir disant
que les euvres ne sont que superstitions. Or ce n'est
pas assez de croire: mais outre cela il fault faire service
à Dieu, en obeissant à son commandement. Voyla
mon appuy & mon fort. Ainsi donc ie me vueil
appuier en ceste croix de Iesus Christ: *Mihi absit*
gloriari nisi in cruce Domini nostri Iesu Christi.
Contre tous les dars & sagettes de l'ennemy, dont la
pire est desespoir, ie vueil mettre comme un bouclier
la croix de Iesus Christ. Vous voyez Chrestiens que
tout le commencement du christianisme, & la fin c'est
la croix. Le premier sacrement de l'Eglise c'est le
Baptesme, auquel on commence par la croix: & la
dernier c'est le sacrement d'extreme onction, lequel se
baille avec le signe de la croix: & tous les autres
sacremens ont efficace par la croix. S. Iean
Chrysostome dit, Il semble que la croix n'a point de
vertu: mais si nous regardons de pres, nous
trouverons que tout le bien de l'homme vient de la

croix de Iesus Christ. Un Lutherien dira, si par la croix
nous avons salut, les euvres n'y font rien: voila bien
argué, si font. Or escoutez que dit S. Paul. *Speramus*   *I. Tim. 4.*
in Deum vivum qui est salvator omnium maxime
fidelium. Nous esperons en Dieu vivant, qui est
salvateur de tous, mais principalement des fideles. Et
par ces parolles de S. Paul, nous confermons une
distinction de theologie, a sçavoir: La mort & croix de
Iesus Christ est suffisante pour sauver tous, mais elle
n'est pas efficace pour tous: c'est à dire combien que la
croix & passion de Iesus Christ soit suffisante pour
sauver tout le monde s'il se vouloit disposer, si est-ce
que tous n'ont pas le fruict de ceste croix. Et pourquoy,
ie vous prie, mettroit S. Paul ceste distinction. *Maxime*
fidelium, c'est à dire, & ceux qui croyent en luy: s'il
estoit ainsi comme dit le Lutherien, que par la seule
foy, & par la croix tous estoient sauvez. Si tous sont
sauvez par la seule mort de Iesus Christ, S. Paul
n'avoit que faire d'adiouster ceste distinction,
Specialement des fideles. Et ce que S. Paul a dit
Maxime, les theologiens disent *Efficaeciter.* Dieu baille
à tous un moyen d'estre sauvé, c'est la croix de Iesus
Christ. D'où vient que tous ne sont sauvez? Par ce
que tous ceux qui croyent en Iesuschrist ne font ce que
Dieu a commandé faire poure estre sauvé. Mais pour
monstrer ceste efficace de la croix & passion de Iesus
Christ, & qui sont ceux qui la reçoivent, S. Paul dit: *Et*
consummatus, factus est omnibus obtemperantibus
sibi, causa salutis aeternae. Nostre Seigneur Iesus
Christ, par ce qu'il a esté offert en croix à Dieu son pere,
il est cause de salut à ceux qui luy obtemperent. Donc
pour estre sauvé il ne suffit pas croire, il fault obeir, &   *Heb. 10.*
qui obeit fait ce qu'on luy commande. Il fault donc que
ie obeisse à nostre Seigneur, & face ses
commandemens & en obeissant ie seray sauvé par sa
croix. Ainsi ie vay à confesse, puis qu'il me le
commande, & me recognoissant pecheur, i'ay pardon.
Qui me pardonne? Iesus Christ qui est l'autheur de
remission des pechez, Ie sçay bien que c'est Dieu qui
remet le pechez comme souverain. *Ego sum, ego sum*
ipse, qui deleo iniquitates tuas propter me, &
peccatorum tuorum non recordabor: Mais le prestre
les commend comme ministre institué de Iesus Christ:

& en me confessant au prestre, & proposant de
n'offenser Dieu iamais, moyennant sa grace, & sentant
cela en mon cueur, Dieu me pardonnera mon peché.
Pourtant prenons la croix comme un bouclier contre
toutes tentations. Nous voyons auiourd'huy si
quelcun est offensé, & soit appuyé d'un grand
Seigneur, il dira incontinant: ha un tel sera adverty de
ce que vous me faictes: ie vous en feray remercier par
un tel: pour monstrer que i'ay du credit, ie dy ces
propos, & pour empescher qu'on ne me moleste
d'avantage. Ainsi pour vostre appuy contre les
fascheries que vous fait sathan, par ses suggestions,
renommez vous de Iesus Christ crucifié. Et c'est ce que
dit S. Paul, & l'avons prins au commencement du
sermon. *Mihi absit gloriari nisi in cruce Domini nostri
Iesu Christi.* Ha ie ne me vante nullement sinon de la
croix de mon redempteur Iesus Christ. Ie n'ay d'autre
appuy ny esperance qu'en la croix. Voila un bon appuy
& n'en sçaurions avoir de meilleur, ny plus fort
bouclier, pour mettre au devant des dards & sagettes de
satan. Donc, puis que Iesus Christ a esté fiché en croix
pour toy, ne te descourage point: fie toy en la croix de
Iesuschrist. Escoutez fault faire comme S. Paul qui dit.
*Nos autem, non spiritum huius mundi accepimus, sed
spiritum qui ex Deo est: ut sciamus quae à Deo donata
sunt nobis in doctrina spiritus, spiritualibus spiritualia
comparantes.* Nous appelons choses spirituelles, qui
ne sont sinon par la vertu de Dieu & du Sainct Esprit.
Comme est que la vierge Marie a conceu demeurant
vierge: que Iesus Christ est au sainct sacrement de
l'autel, car par la seule vertu de Dieu, le pain est
converty au vray corps de Iesus christ, & le vin en son
vray sang: que la mer rouge a esté ouverte pour faire
passage aux enfans d'Israël, & ça esté faict par la vertu
de Dieu, & est chose spirituelle: *quia sola virtute
spiritus hoc factum est.* Aussi est chose spirituelle que
la remission des pechez: car l'homme par sa vertu
propre, n'y peut rien: cela vient de la vertu de Dieu.
Pourtant en figure de cecy, Nostre Seigneur disoit au
Paralytique. *Confide fils, remittuntur tibi peccata tua.*
C'est donc une chose spirituelle, que la remission des
pechez. Ainsi quand ie suis tenté de desespoir, & que
satan me souffle aux aureilles: comment est il possible

Esa. 47.

*Choses spirituelles
qui se font par la
vertu de dieu et du
sainct Esprit.*

Matth. 9.

que tu ayes remission de tes pechez? Or il fault
conferer une chose spirituelle à une autre. Est-ce pas
une chose spirituelle que par la croix satan ait esté
vaincu & spolié? que peché ait esté destruict, & le
monde converty à Dieu? Apres que Iesus christ fut
expiré en croix, le cueur de Centurion fut tellement
gaigné, qu'il commença à dire, vrayement cestuy estoit
fils de Dieu. Et un larron pendu en croix avec Iesus
christ à l'heure que le moins on pensoit que il se deust
convertir, c'est quand il a faict penitence, & a obtenu
pardon. Il a esté asseuré par nostre Seigneur. *Hodie
mecum eris in paradiso.* Tout cela est spirituel car il se
fait par la vertu de la croix de Iesus Christ. Donc, satan
quand tu me demandes si ie m'attends d'avoir pardon.
Ie te responds qu'ouy & n'en fay doubte: car Iesus
christ a il pas acquis tout le monde & attiré à luy par la
croix? *Si exaltatus fuero à terra omnia traham ad
meipsum.* Et n'est-ce pas luy qui se compare au grain   *Ioan. 12.*
de fourment, lequel apres avoir esté mortifié en croix,
a apporté beaucoup de fruict? Donc en faisant
penitence, & ce que Dieu m'a commandé, ie ne fais
difficultee que ie n'aye remission de mes pechez. Et
voyla comparer choses spirituelles à choses
spirituelles. Comme auiourd'huy un heretique qui
fait difficulté croire que quand le prestre a proferé les
parolles sacramentales *Hoc est corpus meum*, Le vray
corps de Iesus Christ soit soubs l'espece du pain. Vien ça
tu fais difficulté de croyre cela, ie te demande, le
premier homme a il pas esté formé de terre & la
premiere femme a elle pas esté formée de sa coste?
d'avantage, *Quod ex invisibilibus visibilia facta sunt*,
Comme dit S. Paul. *Fide illud intelligimus.* Et tu crois   *He. 11.*
bien tout cela, que de rien toutes choses ont estés faites,
par la vertu de dieu, & ce sont choses spirituelles que
tu crois estre faictes par l'omnipotence de Dieu, ainsi   *Luc. 1.*
est il du S. sacrement de l'autel auquel est le corps de
Iesus par la vertu divine. *Et mater Dei!* fais tu
difficulté de croire cela? il fault en ceste maniere
comparer, *Spiritualia spiritualibus.* L'ange m'a
apprins ceste leçon, quand il annonça à la vierge Marie
qu'elle concevroit le fils de Dieu, & la vierge a bien
creu cela: mais luy a demandé seulement la maniere
du fait, & pour luy faire entendre, l'Ange luy va dire &

mettre une chose spirituelle devant les yeux, voila ta
cousine Elizabeth, qui est hors d'aage de porter enfans
& qui est sterile, toutesfois elle a conceu un fils sur ses
vieux iours. Il fault donc bien dire que c'est par la
vertu de Dieu. Ainsi contre les ennemis de la virginité
de la glorieuse mere de Dieu, i'allegueray. *Partus
mulierum sterilium in lege veteri.* Semblablement s'il
est question auiourd'huy pour vaincre les tentations
de desespoir: qui est la chose qui plus trouble la
personne, & quand le diable tient là une personne liée,
c'est grand coup d'aventure s'il en reschappe iamais
mais pour resister il fault mettre bouclier au devant, &
quand il me viendra souffler aux oreilles, tu as fait tant
de maux. Ie respondray: Encores plus que tu ne penses.
Tu es donc damné, non, Dieu aidant, ie m'en garderay
bien: car ie sçay bien qu'en faisant penitence, il me
pardonnera. Comment le sçais tu? & il a pardonnée à
un Manasses le plus meschant homme qui fut sur
terre. Et qui avoit remply la ville de Ierusalem du sang
des prophetes. D'avantage il a fait misericorde à un
David, lequel a cuidé couvrir sa faute, en adioustant
peché sur peché. Et puis ie te responds ce que nostre
Seigneur dit à S. Pierre, Sire, combien de fois
pardonneray-ie à mon frere, qui m'aura offensé, sera ce
iusques à sept fois? Ce n'est pas ce que ie te dy, respond
Nostre Seigneur, mais ie veux que tu luy pardonnes
iusques à septante fois sept fois: non qu'il determine
combien de fois on doit pardonner à son frere, mais
c'est autant que s'il disoit, toutesfois & quantes que ton
frere chrestien te demandera pardon, tu luy dois
pardonner de bon cueur. Aussi, c'est autant que s'il
disoit à toute heure que le pecheur se repentira, il aura
pardon de moy. Iesus Christ que tu es bon. Disons
donc avec S. Paul *Mihi absit gloriari nisi in cruce
Domini nostri Iesu Christi.* Ie ne me veux vanter, &
renommer sinon de Iesus Christ. Qu'as tu fait pour
estre sauvé? Rien. Et seras tu sauvé sans rien faire?
Non, mais ie feray penitence, & garderay les
commandements de mon Dieu, au moins mal que ie
pourray. Ie me mettray avec la pauvre vefve, *aera duo
minuta in gazophilacium Domini:* c'est mon
entendement & ma volonté, que i'appliqueray au
service de mon dieu. O mais tu n'as plus qu'une

*Desespoir est chose
qui trouble plus la
personne.*

Matth. 18.

heure de temps: Dieu ne mesure point la penitence à la
longueur du temps. En moins d'une heure ie peux   *Presumption.*
recouvrer tout le bien que i'ay perdu en cinquante ans.
Regardez le bon larron, lequel en moins de demie
heure a eu salut & remission de ses fautes. Or ie ne dy
pas cecy pour vous induire à presumption & vous
enhardir à mal faire: car ie sçay bien qu'il en y a que
sous umbre de ceste grande misericorde de Dieu,
l'offensent continuellement: mais ils sont bien
trompez, car souvent il advient qu'au besoing & à
l'article de la mort, ils meurent sans cognoissance de
Dieu & de soy mesme, il ne se fault pas tant fier au gros
de l'arbre, qu'on ne se tienne aux branches tousiours.
Mais ie parle tant de la grande misericorde de Dieu,
pour donner courage aux pusillanimes & descouragez.
Il ne se fault pas tant deiecter. Mon amy ne te deffie
point, quand viendra l'heure de la mort: mais appuye
toy du tout sur la mort & croix de Iesus Christ. O, ie
n'ay plus que demie heure de temps pour me repentir!
Et i'ay tant faict de mal que ne sçaurois dire la quantité.
Mon amy, en si peu de temps que tu as, ne perds
courage, mais ayme Dieu de tout ton cueur, & de tout
ton pouvoir, & de toute ta pensée, apres confesse toy à
Dieu. Ouy, mais i'oublieray la moytiée de mes pechez
à confesser. Fay devoir de t'accuser au moins mal que
tu pourras, & ainsi s'il advient que tu en ayes oubliez
aucuns, Dieu ne laissera à te pardonner tout. Or
prenons la croix pour nostre appuy. Iesus Christ est
mort pour nous, qui me donne courage de luy alleguer
sa bonté, sa passion, & ce qu'il a faict pour moy, non
pas ce que i'ay fait: car en regardant ma vie, qui est si
meschante, ie diray: Mon Dieu, ie suis indigne de
grace: mais ie luy allegueray sa croix & ce qu'il a
souffert pour moy: & comme dit sainct Bernard,
Quand tout bien me deffault i'ay encores quelque
chose pour presenter à nostre seigneur. Et quoy?
Calicem salutaris accipiam, c'est le calice duquel il
disoit à Dieu son Pere au iardin d'Olivet, *Pater si fieri*
potest, transfer à me calicem istum. Il entendoit sa
passion qu'il devoit souffrir: c'est comme si ie disois,
Mon Dieu ie n'ay rien de mon costé que ie vous puisse
presenter: mais ie vous presente la croix, la passion de
vostre fils Iesus Christ, & en vertu d'icelle ie vous prie,

Sire, avoir pitié de moy. Avez vous pas dit que
quiconque vous invoquera au nom de vostre fils, que
vous l'exaucerez? Et luy il a dit en sainct Iean, *Si quid* *Ioan. 15.*
petieritis patrem in nomine meo, dabit vobis. Prenons
là nostre appuy. *Mihi absit gloriari nisi in cruce.* C'est
grande chose que de ceste croix, apprenons quelque
chose en icelle. Que verrez vous en la croix? Ie voy *Iustice &*
misericorde en la
croix.
beaucoup de choses. Quoy? Iustice & misericorde.
Qu'est-ce que vous dites? sont choses contraires que
iustice & misericorde, si est-ce que la croix nous
apprend tous les deux. En une maniere ie voy
misericorde en la croix, ie voy que mes pechez sont
pardonnez, que la redemption de nature humaine est
faicte, que a paix est payée, & Dieu nous est reconcilié,
n'est-ce pas grande misericorde & bien pour nous? Et
d'autre costé voy-ie pas la iustice, laquelle est faicte de
mon peché, non en la personne de moy, qui ay failly,
mais en un autre qui est innocent, c'est Iesus Christ
mort pour moy en croix. Et iamais Dieu le Pere n'a
voulu reprendre l'homme en grace, que
premierement Iesus Christ Dieu & homme n'ayt
souffert mort honteuse & ignominieuse en la croix.
Ha dit Dieu. Iustice sera faicte du peché de l'homme
avant que ie luy pardonne. Pource a tresbien dit
David, *Universae viae domini misericordia & veritas.* *Psal. 24.*
En la croix vous voirrez d'un costé sa iustice, & de
l'autre sa misericorde infinie. Mourir pour le pecheur
& qui est son ennemy, ce n'est pas peu de chose: car à
grand peine en trouverez vous un qui vueille mourir
pour son amy, encores qu'il soit homme de bien &
pour une iuste querelle, c'est ce que dit S. Paul, *Vix*
enim pro iusto quis moritur: nam pro bono forsitan
quis audeat mori. Et Iesus Christ l'a fait, il est mort *Rom. 5.*
pour nous, *Quum adhuc inimici et peccatores*
essemus. Et en cecy voyez vous pas la iustice de Dieu?
Il fault que iustice soit faicte de celuy qui a failly, c'est
bien raison, mais en faisant iustice, misericorde est
faicte: punition & iustice est faicte en la personne de
celuy qui n'a iamais failly. *Qui peccatum non fecit,* *I. Petr. 2.*
nec inventus est dolus in ore eius, car comme dit
sainct Paul, *Talis decebat ut nobis esset pontifex*
impollutus et innocens. Et qui peccatum non fecit, pro *Hebr. 7.*
nobis peccatum fecit. Iesus Christ qui iamais ne fit

mal. *Pro nobis peccatum fecit. i. hostia fuit pro peccato nostro.* C'est autant que qui diroit, Le peché a esté puny, & bien rigoureusement: mais en la personne de l'innocent: & à cause de cela, Dieu a espandu largement sa misericorde sur le pecheur. Parquoy le pecheur est iuste par la punition & iustice faicte sur le iuste, *Ut iustitia Dei in illo efficeremur,* dit sainct Paul, afin que nous fussions iustes devant Dieu, c'est à dire que nous eussions misericorde & pardon de noz pechez. Apres, en ceste croix nous voyons iugement & misericorde. Un iuge quand il tient son iugement, il est assis en son throsne. Chrestiens le throsne de Iesus Christ, c'est sa croix, en laquelle il faict iugement & misericorde l'un quand & l'autre. Sçavez vous pas bien qu'à la consommation du monde, quand Iesus Christ viendra tenir son dernier iugement & universel, il mettra d'un costé les boues, c'est à dire les meschans, & d'autre costé sont les brebis, par lesquelles nous entendons les gens de bien, ausquels il dira, *Venite benedicti patris, poßidere regnum*: mais aux meschans qui seront en la senestre, il dira: *Ite maledicti in ignem aeternum.* Or en la croix nous trouvons la figure de ce iugement general. Iesus Christ fait grace au bon larron & luy dit. Au iourd'huy tu seras avec moy en paradis. Le mauvais larron qui demeure obstiné & ne se repent point de son peché, est la figure des malheureux damnez, ausquels il dira, *Ite maledicti in ignem aeternum.* Pensez vous que c'est de la croix de Iesus Christ? Encores fault-il dire un mot. En l'escriture nous trouvons deux manieres de iugemens de Dieu. Un de rigueur, duquel dit S. Iacques, *Iudicium sine misericordia fiet illi qui non fecerit misericordiam.* Iugement sans misericorde sera fait à celuy qui ne fera misericorde à son prochain. Et c'est ce iugement de condamnation, duquel parle nostre Seigneur en sainct Iean, *Qui non credit, iam iudicatus est.* D'avantage en la croix nous trouvons un autre iugement qui est de misericorde & benevolence, duquel dit David, *Secundum iudicium vivificas me,* & en un autre passage, *Exaudi me secundum iustitiam tuam.* Comme David, demandez vous la iustice de Dieu, & vous dites en un autre passage, *Si iniquitates observaveris Domine, Domine quis sustinebit?* Si

I. Cor. 5.

2. Cor. 5.

Matth. 25.
La croix figure
du iugement
general.

Iaco. 2.

Ioan. 5.

Psal. 118.

Iesus Christ use de sa iustice, toy & moy serons
damnez (ce qui n'adviendra pas si Dieu plaist.) Or il
fault entendre qu'il y a difference des iugemens de
Dieu, l'un de rigueur, duquel avons parlé, l'autre de
grace. Et de cestuy de grace entend parler David, lequel
iugement a esté faict en la croix, & d'iceluy s'entend ce
qui est escrit en S. Iean, *Nunc iudicium est mundi:*
nunc princeps huius mundi eiicietur foras. N'est-ce

Ioan. 12.

pas grace que Dieu a faict à l'homme, il estoit possedé
du diable, & l'a iecté hors par sa mort & passion: &
n'est-ce pas faire grace à l'homme? Et c'est selon ce
iugement que nous demandons à Dieu qu'il nous
vivifie. Apres, selon sa iustice. Qu'appellez vous
iustice? Aucunesfois on vient au Roy. Sire, faictes
moy iustice. Il ne s'en faut pas soucier, aussi sera-il. Et
souvent ceux qui demandent iustice, se trouvent bien
estonnez, quand pour leurs larcins & pilleries on les
envoye au gibet & tout leur bien est confisqué: où s'ils
se fussent humiliez, on leur eust faict grace. Or nous
demandons à Dieu qu'il nous face selon sa iustice, non
pas selon la nostre, qui n'est demander autre chose,
sinon qu'il nous face selon que Iesus Christ a merité
pour nous: non pas que i'aye merité, comme de moy,
la iustice de Dieu, de laquelle dit S. Paul, *Iustitia Dei*

Rom. 1.
Qu'est-ce que la
iustice de Dieu.

revelatur in evangelio. Qu'appellez vous la iustice de
Dieu? Nous n'entendons pas la iustice de laquelle il est
iuste, mais le moyen par lequel l'homme est iuste
devant Dieu, qui est la croix de Iesus Christ. Parquoy
quand nous demandons à Dieu qu'il nous face iustice,
c'est à dire qu'il nous face ainsi que Iesus Christ a
merité pour nous. Et qu'est-ce autre chose, que
demander grace & misericorde? Et à propos dit S. Paul,
Factus est nobis iustitia, &c.: Donc demander ainsi à

I. Cor. 1.

Dieu iustice, c'est luy demander grace, misericorde &
reconciliation avec luy. Apres, que trouvez vous en
ceste croix? S. Paul dit, *Flecto genua ad patrem domini*

Ephe. 3.

nostri Iesu Christi, & c. ut det vobis Christum habitare
per fidem in cordibus vestris, in charitate radicata et
fundata, ut poßitis comprehendere cum omnibus
sanctis quae sit longitudo & latitudo, sublimitas &
profundum. Ie prie Dieu à genoux que vous puissiez
entendre qui est la latitude, la longitude, la hautesse, &
la profonditee, de qui? De Iesus Christ crucifié. O
Chrestiens! qu'appellez vous la latitude? c'est la

Qu'est-ce que
latitude.

charité que est monstrée en ceste croix. Sçavez vous
pas bien que le commandement de charité est de
grande estendue? il s'estend iusques à aymer son
ennemy. *Latum mandatum tuum nimis* dit David.
Pourtant en la croix nostre Seigneur a prié pour ses
ennemis, & pour ceux qui le crucifioient, disant, *Pater
ignosce illis quia nesciunt quid faciunt,* & nous a
commandé prier pour les nostres. *Diligite inimicos
vestros, orate pro persequentibus.* Apres la largeur il y   *Matth. 5.*
a longueur, qui est perseverance. Il ne suffit pas avoir
bien commencé, il faut perseverer, *Qui perseveraverit
usque in finem hic salvus erit.* Soit en bien soit en   *Perseverance.*
mal, il n'y a que la perseverance qui le gaigne.
Pourtant perseverons en cest amour, & nous serons
sauvez. Outre-cela il y a la hauteur comme vous diriez
le tiltre de la croix qui est esperance. Où est ton
esperance? Elle est en haut. Qu'esperes tu? Paradis.
Esperes tu point les honneurs de ce monde, les plaisirs
& delices? Non, ie regarde en hault non en terre, mon
esperance est avoir vie eternelle. Et qui est la
profondeur de la croix, que nous ne voyons point?
C'est la foy, laquelle est des choses qui transcendent
tout entendement humain. Prenez donc pour bouclier
ceste croix, contre les tentations & alarmes que vous
livre sathan.

3. Sermon Funebre
Faict aux Obseques de Feu
nostre Maistre de Cornibus.

*Omnia in sapientia fecisti Domine. Repleta est terra
creatura tua.* Il est dit en l'Apocalypse, que sainct Iean
a veu une femme paillarde, estant acoustrée de
pourpre, dorée d'or, & de pierres precieuses: laquelle
avoit une coupe d'or en sa main, pleine
d'abomination & immondicité de sa fornication.
Sainct Iean dit: *Et miratus sum eùm viderem illam.
Et angelus: Quare miraris?* Pourquoy t'esmerveilles
tu? Dequoy t'estonnes tu? *Ego dicam tibi
sacramentum mulieris in mysterium.* S. Iean qui
s'esmerveille, nous represente les infirmes & vacillans
en la foy, qui s'emerveillent de voir les mauvais
prosperer, & les gens de bien endurer. Dieu ostera
aucunefois les bons de ce monde qui bien
entretiennent la paix, & prouffitent beaucoup à la
chrestienté, & laissera vivre les mauvais. L'homme à
ceste heure qui n'a point de foy, ou bien peu, s'estonne
& est scandalisé de veoir ainsi prosperer les meschans,
& les bons endurer, & estre persecutez: & luy est advis
que Dieu ne soit pas iuste. Il ne faut point estre
scandalizé pour cela. *Et beatus, ait Christus, qui non
fuerit scandalizatus in me.* Nostre Sauveur fait tout en
sapience, & ne fait aucune chose, sans bonne cause &
raison. Et c'est ce que i'ay prins pour le theme: *Omnia
in sapientia fecisti Domine.* En general, nous sçavons
bien que nostre sauveur fait tout par sa sapience, & par
raison: mais nous sommes infirmes & imbeciles, &
nous esmerveillons des choses qui adviennent, disans:
Pourquoy Dieu prend-il par devers luy les gens de bien
qui prouffitent beaucoup en ce monde, & qui sement
sa saincte parole: & les meschans & iniques,
impugnans nostre foy, il les laisse vivre iusques à
soixante ou quatre vingt ans? Si l'homme n'est ferme
en la foy, & s'il ne sçait que Dieu fait toutes choses en
sapience, & tout par raison, il ne fera que tituber &
vaciller, & l'esperance & asseurance que Dieu donne à

*Psal. 130.
Apoc. 17.*

*Matth. 11.
Nostre Sauveur
fait tout en
sapience.*

l'homme pour estre ferme en cela, c'est d'entendre que
Dieu fait tout pour cause & raison, par sa sapience.
Omnia in sapientia fecisti domine. L'escriture dit: *In
operibus Dei, noli esse multum curiosus.* De se
vouloir enquerir pourquoy Dieu fait cecy, ou cela, c'est
trop curieusement demander: car il faut sçavoir &
entendre, que Dieu ne fait aucune chose sans bonne
cause & raison: s'il fait tout en sapience. Il ne faut
donc s'esmerveiller des choses qui adviennent contre
la capacité & intelligence humaine, comme dit l'ange à
sainct Iean: *Quare miraris?* Si un homme de bien
endure, & qu'il meure plustost que non pas un
meschant, pourquoy t'en esmerveilles tu? Un homme
de bien meurt *quidem* de corps, mais il vit
eternellement devant Dieu. *In memoria aeternae erit*   Psal. 111.
iustus. Iusti in perpetuum vivent. Et si les gens de
bien nous ont aydé & prié pour nous, ce pendant qu'ils
estoient en ce monde, combien d'avantage prieront ils
pour nous eux estans en paradis? La charité qu'ils ont
euë envers nous, ne sera point diminuée, pour leur
absence corporelle, mais sera plus augmentée, à raison
de leur perfection, & auront memoire de la stabilité &
perseverance de nostre foy, & de nostre mere l'Eglise.
S. Paul dit: *Charitas nunquam excidit. Omnia in*   I. Cor. 13.
sapientia fecisti, Domine, idem: Quàm magnificata   Psal. 91.
sunt opera tua, Domine: nimis profundae factae sunt
cogitationes tuae. Augustinus ibi dicit. *Revera fratres*
mei, nullum mare tam profundum est, quàm ista
cogitatio Dei, ut mala floreant, & boni laborent. Si iam
Christianus es, & bene eruditus, dicis: Deus in iudicio
suo reservat omnia, boni laborant, quia flagellabuntur
ut filii: mali exultant, quia damnabuntur ut alieni.
Duos filios habet homo, alterum castigat, alterum
dimittit: facit unus malè, & non corripitur à patre: alter
mox ut se moverit, corripitur, & colaphis caeditur &
flagellatur. Unde ille dimittitur, et ille caeditur, nisi
quia huic caeso haereditas reservatur: ille autem
dimissus, exhaeredatus est, etc. Vous voyez ce bon
personnage icy, qui est allé de ce monde en l'autre, il
ne le vous faut point prescher, vous le sçavez bien: il a
vescu tousiours tant religieusement, & a esté si bon
pour defendre la foy contre les meschans & heretiques:
& sincerement en toute pauvreté il a presché & declaré

l'evangile, & la foy de nostre sauveur & redempteur
Iesuschrist, & iamais ne devoya en un seul point, de la
tradition de nostre mere l'Eglise: & neantmoins, au
plus fort de noz affaires, & que nous en avions tant
affaire, il nous defaut. Il y a huict ans qu'il y avoit tant
d'heretiques, contre lesquels il a si bien resisté: mais
auiourd'huy, & pour le present, il a en a plus grande
abondance qu'il n'y avoit. La Cité du diable a esté
edifiée plus haute que non pas la Cité de Dieu: c'est à
dire par apparence faulse & detestable. Nous ne
trouvons pas en la saincte escriture, qu'il y ait eu qui
ait edifié que Caïn: Abel son frere, ne les autres n'ont
point voulu edifier. Nostre Seigneur dit à ses disciples.
Nolite timere, pusillus grex. Il les appelle petit
troupeau, à la comparaison des meschans & mauvais
qui sont en si grand nombre, que nous ne pourrions
aller en lieu & place, par maniere de dire, qu'on n'en
trouve. Nous voyons l'Eglise de Dieu diminuer &
endurer des tribulations & adversitez innumerables,
par les assaux du diable, & des heretiques. Et à ceste
heure que nous avions bien affaire de ce bon
personnage, pour les debouter & repousser, comme il
avoit acoustumé, nous estans au plus fort de la bataille
& de la besongne, Dieu le prend, & le nous a osté.
Pourquoy Dieu l'a il prins, que plustost il ne prenoit
les meschans, & ne nous laissoit ce bon personnage,
qui en valoit bien dix mille comme dit le peuple à
David, qui vouloit aller en la guerre, quand il leur dist:
Egrediar vobiscum. Respondit populus: Non exibis
hodie. Sire, vous n'y entrerez-ia. *Sive enim*
fugerimus non magnopere ad eos de obis pertinebit:
sive media pars è nobis caeciderit, non satis curabunt:
quia tu unus solus per decem milibus computaris.
Melius est igitur ut sis nobis in urbe praesidio. Aussi
de cest homme icy qui en valoit bien dix mille,
pourquoy Dieu le nous a il osté? Qui estes vous qui
demandez cela à Dieu? Voulez vous resister à sa
volonté comme dit S. Paul: *O homo, tu quis es, qui*
respondeas Deo? Voluntati enim eius quis resistit? Et
chrestiens! ne vous esmerveillez pas, mais dites avec
David: *Omnia in sapientia fecisti.* Nous ne pourrions
sçavoir les effects & iugemens de Dieu, ne perscruter &
excogiter pourquoy il fait cecy ou cela, sinon qu'il luy

Les tiltres d'un
homme Catholique.

Luc. 12.

L'esglise de Dieu
endure des
adversitez par
les heretiques.

2. Reg. 17.

Il ne faut
resister à la
volonté de Dieu.
Rom. 9.

pleust le nous reveler. Et comme dit sainct Iean
Chrysostome: *Plurimum mirari debemus in his quae*
ingenium nostrum transcendunt, & quod rationes
operum Dei non intelligamus. Nous devons
grandement louer Dieu aux choses qu'il fait, qui
passent nostre entendement & intelligence. Et quand
nous n'entendons pas les raisons des effects de Dieu,
sçavoir la maniere comme un enfant au ventre de sa
mere est fait, & semblables choses: cela passe nostre
intelligence *quia nunc arte nunc natura efficitur.*
Nous pourrions tituber en la foy, si nous n'entendions
bien, que toutes les euvres de Dieu se font par raison &
par sapience. *Omnia in sapientia fecisti, Domine:*   *Psal. 91.*
nimis profundae factae sunt cogitationes tuae. Quand
nostre Seigneur Iesus Christ demande de l'eau à la
Samaritaine pour boire, elle luy dit *Domine, neque in*
quo haurias habes, et puteus altus est.i.profundus.   *Ioan. 4.*
Aussi le puits de la sapience de Dieu, est si profond
qu'il n'y a entendement qui fut capable & suffisant de
sçavoir entendre, & scruter les raisons des effects &   *Combien est profond*
operations de Dieu. Doncques gardons nous de faillir   *le puits de la*
& succomber, en voulant trop enquerir des secrets &   *sapience de Dieu.*
iugemens de Dieu, & pourquoy c'est qu'il prend les
bons, & qu'il laisse vivre les mauvais: car *omnia in*
sapientia facit. Sainct Paul considerant la profondité &
altitude des secrets & operations de Dieu dit: *O altitudo*   *Rom. 11.*
divitiarum sapientiae et scientiae Dei quàm
incomprehensibilia sunt iudicia eius, & investigabiles
viae eius! Quis enim cognovit sensum Domini?&c.
Ne nous estimons donc és choses qui passent nostre
entendement, mais en louons Dieu, & le magnifions
grandement, *qui est excelsior caelo, longior terra,*
profundior mari: qui fecit caelum & terram, mare, &
omnia quae in eis sunt. Augustinus, *Si omnia quae in*   *Psal. 145.*
eis sunt, ergo & te. Le prophete Ieremie plorant sur la
cité de Ierusalem, laquelle nous represente l'Eglise, dit:
Quis enim miserebitur tui Ierusalem? aut quis   *Ierem. 15.*
contristabitur pro te? aut quis ibit ad rogandum pro
pace tua? Nous en pouvons ainsi dire auiourd'huy
sur l'Eglise de Dieu, laquelle a esté privée d'un si
vaillant personnage, lequel batailloit si vaillamment
pour la foy. En compassion d'iceluy, nous pouvons
dire à l'eglise: *Quis miserebitur tui Hierusalem?* Hierusalem,

qui aura pitié de vous, qui avez esté
destituée d'un si noble personnage, vous deffendant si
bien de voz ennemis & adversaires? Lequel n'a point
devoyé des traditions de l'Eglise, car il a esté bien
nourry & alaicté du laict de la saincte Theologie.
Chrestiens, ne beuvons point d'autre laict que cestuy-
là, n'allons point chercher ailleurs d'autre doctrine.
Nostre Seigneur parlant par la prophete Esaye, se
complaint de ceux qui n'ont point gardé ses
commandemens, & sa doctrine, disant: *Dereliquerunt*   *Iere. 7.*
me Deum, fontem aquae vivae foderunt sibi cisternas
veteres, non valentes continere aquas. Nous cuidons
aucunesfois que la meschante doctrine soit du bon
laict, combien que ce n'est que venin. Mais ce bon
personnage a tousiours purement & sincerement
presché, & donné le laict, & la vraye doctrine de nostre
mere saincte Eglise. Il n'a point devoyé de la rectitude,
ne adulteré la parole de Dieu, comme font d'aucuns,
qui soubs umbre de sincerement prescher l'Evangile, ils
l'adulterent. Sainct Paul dit: *Non enim sumus*   *2. Cor. 4.*
adulterantes verbum Dei, sicut plurimi: sed ex
sinceritate sicut ex Deo, coram Deo in Christo
loquimur. Ie le dis afin que prenne exemple sur ce
personnage là. Vous direz: C'est trop loué les
hommes. Non est: Nous ne faisons point d'iniure à   *On ne faict point*
Dieu, en preschant la vertu d'un homme, *Non quòd*   *d'iniure à Dieu en*
sufficientes simus cogitare aliquid ex nobis, quasi ex   *louant un homme.*
nobis, sed sufficientia nostra ex Deo est. Item: Quid   *I. Cor. 3.*
autem habes quòd non accepisti? Et pource nous   *2. Cor. 4.*
    I. Cor. 3.
    Rom. 2.
louons & preschons Dieu, en preschans les vertus d'un
homme de bien, lequel a cooperé avec Dieu, comme
dit saint Paul: *Dei enim coadiutores sumus.* Et par
ainsi l'homme est digne d'estre presché. Sainct Paul
ne dit il pas: *Gloria autem, honor & pax omni*
operanti bonum. Iudaeo primum & Graeco? Et ce bon
personnage en a tant fait: pourquoy ne le preschera on
pour ses bonnes vertus, qu'il a euës? Soyons ses
imitateurs. Il a esté nourry du laict de sa mere la
saincte theologie, & iamais n'a devoyé de la tradition   *Quel est le vray*
de l'Eglise, mais purement & sincerement a presché la   *laict que nous*
verité de l'Evangile non point selon son propre sens &   *devons prendre.*
entendement: mais suyvant tousiours l'interpretations
des saincts Docteurs, approuvez de nostre mere S.

Eglise: & tel est le vray laict que nous devons prendre.
Mais auiourd'huy nous an abusons & soubs couleur
du laict, nous prenons du venin, cherchans autre
interpretation que de l'Eglise. Il n'y a que ceux là qui
soient deceuz & trompez, car ce sont enfans qui
contemnent leur pere & leur mere, & qui vont hors de
la maison de l'Eglise, pensans mieux trouver, combien
qu'ils ne pourroient. Voila Dina fille de Lya: regardez-
ce qui luy est advenu pour estre sortie hors de la
maison de ses parens, & a regardé les passans: *Princeps
adamavit eam & rapuit, & dormivit cum ea.* Elle a
estee violée & corrompue. Aussi ceux qui veulent
prendre autre doctrine que de l'Eglise, sont suspects &
facilement corrompus. Et pource ce bon personnage a
esté nourry & alaicté de la mammelle de sa mere la
saincte theologie, & n'a point fourvoyé de la verité
evangelique. *Defunctus est in signo fidei:* il est mort
bon Chrestien avec le signe de la foy: & l'Eglise ne prie
que pour ceux qui meurent en cest estat là, comme il
est fait mention au Canon de la messe. *Decedere cum
signo fidei,* c'est mourir bon catholique, ou mourir
apres avoir receu les saincts sacremens de l'Eglise: &
pour ceux qui meurent ainsi, l'Eglise prie. Ce n'est pas
chose nouvelle, ne doctrine inventée de nouveau,
comme dit sainct Iean Chrysostome, qui fut introduit
dès la primitive Eglise, qu'en la messe on feroit
memoire des trepassez, defuncts avec le signe de la foy.
Cest homme icy a esté un vray homme de bien, nourry
du laict evangelique, & entretenu en iceluy, de sorte
qu'il a si bien communiqué sa doctrine, qu'il n'y a rue
ne cornet en la ville de Paris, qui ne s'en sente. Vous
sçavez les labeurs, veilles, abstinences & travaux qu'il a
prins pour manifester l'honneur de Dieu il n'a cessé
tousiours de lire, ou de prescher. Mais par adventure
vous direz, que tant de labeurs luy ont advancé ses
iours, & que s'il n'en eust tant prins, qu'il fust encore
en vie, & bonne santé. Ouy, par adventure: mais ie
vous responds avec sainct Iean Chrysostome: *Et hoc
nomine gloriosus.* O qu'il est glorieux d'estre mort au
service de Dieu. Il est escrit que Dieu disoit à Iosué:
Moyses servus meus mortuus est. Voila Moyse mon
serviteur qui est mort en mon service. Quel honneur
pourroit avoir l'homme plus grand que de mourir au

Dina fille de Lya.

Genes. 34.

*Un homme est
glorieux de mourir
au service de Dieu.
Iosué. 1.*

service de Dieu? Auiourd'huy l'Eglise est privée de
ceste homme, qui l'a tousiours si bien defendue de ses
ennemis. Mais entendez qu'elle n'est privée sinon de
sa presence corporelle: car puis qu'il l'a bien defendue,
luy estant en ce monde icy, il la defendra encores
mieux, presentement qu'il est en paradis: car qu'il
n'avoit ce pendant qu'il estoit encore en ceste vie
mortelle & passible. *Charitas nunquam excidit*, dit S.   *I. Cor. 13.*
Paul: *sed perfectior erit in patria, quam in via.* Or
voila: *Moyses mortuus est*, au service de Dieu. Aussi
quand nous disons que cest homme icy est mort au
service de Dieu, c'est à dire qu'il est mort en labourant
& travaillant pour Dieu: il ne s'est point estimé de
luymesme il n'a fait compte de soy, *seipsum negavit*, il
s'est denié suivant ce qui est dit en l'Evangile: *Si quis*   *Matth. 16.*
vult post me venire, abneget semetipsum, & tollat
crucem suam & sequatur me. Dieu sçait quel homme
c'estoit: ie le sçay aussi bien qu'un autre: ie m'en
rapporte aussi à ceux qui le sçavent bien, & qui ont
conversé avec luy, de ce que ie dis, s'il n'est pas vray.
Et pource, nous pouvons bien dire à l'Eglise: *Quis*   *Iere. 1.*
miserebitur tui Ierusalem, aut quis contristabitur pro
te? à cause de cest homme de bien qui est separé d'elle,
il est dit qu'il y avoit des gens de bien qui eurent le
soing d'ensevelir S. Estienne, & qui en firent grand
dueil. *Curaverunt Stephanum viri timorati, &*
fecerunt planctum magnum super eum. Aussi nous
pouvons bien faire le dueil, & lamentation sur ce bon
personnage icy. Ie sçay bien qu'il est mieux d'estre
avec nostre Seigneur & veoir Dieu, qu'il ne seroit en ce
monde: car nous ne voyons que toute pauvreté &
meschanceté, regner. Et comme dit l'escriture:
Laudavi magis mortuus, quàm viventes. I'ay plus   *Eccle. 4.*
loué les morts que les vivans pour la misere &
calamité qu'on a en ce monde. Et S. Paul qui se
complaint disant: *Infoelix ego homo, quis me liberabit*
de corpore mortis huius? Gratia Dei per Iesum   *Rom. 7.*
Christum. Il est donc bien heureux d'estre mis hors
des miseres de ce monde, comme il est escrit: *Iustus de*   *Prov. 11.*
angustia liberatus est. L'homme iuste par la mort est
delivré de toutes peines, angusties & tribulations. Il est
dit iuste, car il est mort avec les signes de la foy, & d'un
homme iuste. Le iuste vit par foy operante par charité,

non pas d'une foy morte, inutile, & ocieuse, comme
dit sainct Iaques: *Vis scire, ô homo inanis, quoniam*
fides sine operibus mortua est. Et S. Iean: *Beati mortui*
qui in domino moriuntur: à modo enim iam dicit
spiritus, ut requiescant à laboribus suis, opera enim
illorum sequuntur illos. Secundum opera quae in hac
vita exercuerunt, recipiunt mercedem, & praemium.
Puis doncques qu'il a pleu à Dieu de le prendre, disons
sans demander pourquoy: *Omnia in sapientia fecisti,*
Domine. Comme Elie a esté translaté en un chariot de
feu, aussi ce iuste icy, *de angustia liberatus est.* Ne
nous esmerveillons point. Tout ainsi que Dieu fut
avec Moyse, il promit à Elie qu'il seroit avec luy disant:
Nullus poterit tibi resistere cunctis diebus vitae tuae:
sicut fui cum Moyse, ita ero tecum: non te dimittam
neque derelinquam. Nous ne serons point delaissez,
car Dieu oit les prieres des defuncts comme des vivans.
Si ce personnage a prié pour nous, ce pendant qu'il
estoit en ce monde encore priera il d'avantage en
paradis. Et bien, Dieu laisse vivre les mauvais, s'ils
s'amenderont, ou pour exercer les bons, & que les bons
en endurans patiemment des mauvais, pour
l'honneur de Dieu, en ayent plus grand merite &
gloire en paradis. Et les meschans pour avoir persecuté
les bons & enfans de Dieu, en seront plus griefvement
damnez & punis. *Non miremur igitur, sed cum*
David dicamus, Omnia in sapientia fecisti, Domine.
Voire mais, nous en avions encore bien affaire
pourquoy le nous a il osté? *Non Dei possumus*
resistere voluntati? Item: Scrutator maiestatis
opprimetur à gloria. Ce que nous estimons aucunesfois
estre mal, c'est tout bien & sapience, & cuidons que soit
folie, quand c'est vraye sapience. Iamais nous
n'eussions pensé que la croix de nostre Seigneur eust
esté vraye sapience de Dieu, sa vertu & puissance, par
laquelle il a surmonté les cueurs des hommes, &
l'ennemy d'enfer, comme bien le prouve monsieur
Sainct Paul, disant: *Verbum enim crucis pereuntibus*
quidem stultitia est, his autem qui salvi facti sunt à
nobis, Dei virtus est. Nonne fecit Deus stultitiam
sapientiam huius mundi? Nam, quia in Dei sapientia
non cognovit mundus per sapientiam Deum placuit
Deo per stultitiam praedicationis salvos facere

Iac. 2.
Apoc. 14.

Psal. 103.

Prov. 25.

credentes. Nos praedicamus Iesum crucifixum.
Iudaeis quidem scandalum, Gentibus autem stultitiam:
quia quod stultum est Dei, sapientius est hominibus: &
quod infirmum est Dei, fortius est hominibus. Et
pource ne nous esmerveillons doncques point si Dieu
a prins cest homme icy au plus fort de noz affaires, qui
estoit comme une tour, un propugnacle, & une
forteresse contre noz ennemis de la foy, ne cherchans
sinon à destruire l'Eglise: mais ils n'en feront rien, si
Dieu plaist, comme on dit communement. Nous
n'avions que cestuy-là qui nous donnast support &
soulagement en noz affaires, aussi estoit cestuy là. O
que noz ennemis sont doncques bien aises, & se
resiouissent de sa mort. Ils feront ce qu'ils voudront,
on ne leur sçauroit plus que faire. Dictes vous? Si ne
sont ils pas ou ils pensent. Dieu permet qu'ainsi se
face, & laisse aucunesfois regner les choses, iusques au
bout: en telle sorte, que selon le cours naturel &
iugement des hommes, il n'y a point d'espoir d'en avoir
bonne issue. N'avons nous pas de la bonne Susanne,
que Dieu permit estre si au bas par le tesmoignage des
faux viellards, qu'elle estoit toute preste, & condamnée
pour estre lapidée? mais à ceste heure là, Dieu suscita
l'esprit de Daniel, qui dit *Revertimini ad iudicium:*
quia falsum testimonium loquuti sunt adversus eam.
Il convainquit les deux viellards, qui furent lapidez, &
saincte Susanne fut ainsi delivrée. Aussi Dieu nous
permet bien endurer des meschans, lesquels il
confondra, & nous delivrera finalement s'il luy plaist.
Mais apres que nous aurons esté ainsi delivrez, ne
nous attribuons point la victoire, comme dit David:
Non nobis Domine, non nobis, sed nomini tuo da
gloriam. Ils se reiouissent dequoy leur adversaire est
mort, & qu'on ne leur pourra plus que faire. Dictes
vous? Iesus Christ les a confondus par luy qui est mort,
& les confondra encores par d'autres s'il luy plaist. Ils
ressemblent aux Egyptiens & à Pharao, avec son
exercice qui persecutoient les enfans d'Israël, Ils
disoient: *Evaginabimus gladium super eos,*
dimidiabimus panem. Nous titerons nostre cousteau,
nous leur monterons sur la gorge: nous leurs
taillerons leurs morceaux, & trancherons du gros, & du
menu, ainsi que bon nous semblera. Vous le dictes.

Dieu laisse aucunesfois regner les choses iusques au bout Susanne.

Dan. 13.

Quand on a eu victoire, il en faut attribuer la louange à Dieu. Psal. 113.

Vous comptez sans vostre hoste: car Dieu ne fit sinon
souffler, comme on souffleroit: une plume: &
incontinant ils ont esté submergez en la mer, & tous
leurs chariots & harnois ont esté mis au dessus
dessous: *Et ecce respiciens Dominus super castra*
Aegyptiorum per columnam ignis & nubis, interfecit
exercitum eorum. Aussi ces malheureux icy, qui
veulent faire des lourdaux, Dieu en un instant les fera
descendre en enfer, aussi facilement que de souffler
une plume, s'ils ne se hastent d'eux amender. Quand
l'antechrist sera venu, il fera merveilles: *& tunc*
revelabitur ille iniquus, quem Dominus Iesus
interficiet spiritu oris sui. Nostre sauveur ne fera que
souffler, & incontinant il sera destruict, Chrestiens,
iamais l'Eglise n'eust autant à faire, comme elle a pour
le present: mais si ne sera elle pas pourtant surmontée,
car elle a bon fondement: elle est fondée sur une forte
pierre, & sur un bon rocher: *fundata enim erat supra*
firmam petram. Petra autem, inquit Paulus erat
Christus. Et pourtant chrestiens, ne vous decouragez
point, car nostre sauveur ne fera que souffler, &
comme on souffleroit une plume, & incontinant il les
annichilera & mettra au neant. Et en le remerciant en
toutes graces & honneurs, nous chanterons comme fit
Moyse avec les enfans d'Israël: *Cantemus Domino,*
gloriosè enim magnificatus est: equum & ascensorem
eius, proiecit in mare. Per currus sont entendus les
faveurs & supports qu'ont les adversaires, mais ils ne
durent point: comme quand vous voyez venir tout à
sac en un flot, une pluye vehemente, c'est signe qu'elle
ne durera gueres, mais sera bien tost passée. Aussi ces
meschans heretiques ne dureront gueres mais bien tost
seront annichilez & abolis. Mais nostre vie est si
mauvaise, nous ne vivons point en chrestiens, c'esst
une pitié, amendons nous, & bien tost les meschans
seront confondus: car la stabilité de l'Eglise n'est point
fondée en la parole de l'homme, mais en la parole de
Dieu: *Ego mitto vos, &c.* Sainct Iean Chrysostome dit
que *errores non praevalerent, nisi hominum peccata*
praecederent. Peché engendre erreur, & erreur est la
peine de peché. Quand nous aurons osté peché, & que
nous nous serons amendez, Dieu sera appaisé. Mais
quelle sapience de Dieu c'est d'avoir prins ce

Exod. 13.

I. Thessa. 2.

L'Eglise est fondée
sur une forte
pierre.
Matth. 7.
I. Cor. 10.

Exod. 15.

Matth. 10.

personnage en nostre necessité, & au plus fort de noz
affaires? Il est dit que quand David eust entendu
qu'Absalon son fils estoit mort, & qu'il estoit demeuré
pendu par les cheveux à un chesne, combien qu'il fust
mauvais, il en fut grandement faché, & le pleura
amerement: *Et sic loquebatur vadens: fili mi Absalon,
Absalon fili mi. Quis mihi tribuat, ut ego moriar pro
te?* Combien doncque devroit-on pleurer ce bon
personnage icy, qui est mort fidele & catholique? Si
David pleuroit son fils Absalon, qui estoit si mauvais,
& qui le persecutoit, & qui disoit: *Quis dabit mihi, ut
ego moriar pro te?* comme Prisca & Aquila, *qui pro
anima Pauli suas cervices supposuerunt*: c'est à dire,
qu'ils vouloient mourir pour garder la vie à sainct
Paul, lequel se recommande à eux, disant: *Salutate
Priscam & Aquilam adiutores meos in Christo Iesu,
&c.* Et vouloient mourir pour luy, pource qu'ils le
voyoient plus prouffitable & utile à l'eglise, qu'ils
n'estoient. Ainsi qui est celuy là qui dira à cest homme
de bien trespassé: *Quia mihi dabit, ut ego moriar pro
te?* Lequel a esté tousiours pour l'eglise & iamais ne
luy fut contraire. C'est un signe merveilleux quand
Dieu oste ainsi les bons de ce monde icy, c'est une
punition que Dieu nous fait. Ie crains bien que nous
ne soyons au temps de ceux qui furent tant persecutez,
dont sainct Paul dit: *Sancti per fidem vicerunt regna,
etc. Alii verò ludibria & verbera experti, insuper &
vincula & carceres: lapidati sunt, fecti sunt, tentati
sunt, in occisione gladii mortui sunt.* Puis apres il dit:
Quibus dignus non erat mundus. Aussi ce bon
personage a beaucoup enduré de calomnies,
d'opprobres & de detractions pour soustenir la foy: & le
monde par adventure n'estoit pas digne de l'avoir, car
les meschans ne sont pas dignes des gens de bien. Dieu
nous envoye la lumiere & la bonne doctrine, mais
nous aymons mieux les tenebres que la lumiere: *Hoc
est autem iudicium, quia lux venit in mundum: &
dilexerunt homines magis tenebras quàm lucem: erant
enim mala eorum opera.* Chrestiens, qui dira avec
David: *Quis mihi tribuat, ut moriar pro te?* N'y a il
point de Prisca & d'Aquila, qui eussent bien voulu
exposer leur vie pour luy? Ie le dis pour vous inciter à
l'imitation de luy: comme dit S. Paul, qu'on ait à

*I. Reg. 17.
David pleure la
mort de son fils
Absalon.
Rom. 6.*

Hebr. 11.

Ioan. 3.

l'ensuivre, disant: *Rogo ergo vos, imitatores mei
estote, sicut & ego Christi.* Nostre maniere de vivre
n'est qu'un contemnement de Dieu. Nous chercheons
les cours des princes, & grandes maisons des seigneurs,
& autres, pour avoir des benefices, abbayes, & eveschez,
ils s'ingerent de demander. Attendez qu'on vous
appelle. Vous devez bien refuser, comme a fait
Ieremie qui dit *Domine Deus, ecce nescio loqui, quia
puer ego sum.* Et Moyse disoit qu'il ne pouvoit parler,
car il estoit begue, disant: *Domine non sum eloquens
ab heri, & nudiustertius.* Mesme Iesus Christ? s'il est
ingeré pour estre Evesque? Nenny non, comme dit
sainct Paul: *Nec quisquam sumit sibi honorem, sed
qui vocatur à Deo tanquam Aaron. Sic & Christus non
semetipsum clarificavit ut pontifex fieret, sed qui
loquutus est ad eum: filius meus es tu, ego hodie genui
te.* Il n'en fault qu'un pour faire devoyer tous les
autres, en leur donnant mauvaise exemple, de s'aller
ainsi ingerer à demander les benefices. Et puis on dit:
Voyez comme il court apres pour en avoir. Ie ne dis
pas qu'il soit faict en ceste maniere: mais ie vous en
adverty, afin qu'il ne soit fait. Nostre ambition &
cupidité d'avoir honneurs & benefices, c'est une
machine, & bombarde ruée contre l'eglise, pour le
scandale que nous faisons. Prenez ce bon personnage
icy pour exemple, & regardez s'il en a eu. Il n'a tenu
qu'à luy qu'il n'en ait bien eu: car il avoit le moyen
assez pour parvenir, & avoit entrée aux grandes
maisons, aussi bien qu'un autre: mais il a mieux aymé
n'en avoir point, pour faire son salut. Nous ne
sommes pas moins qu'heretiques, de faire ce que nous
faisons. Nous renonçons pas Dieu de bouche, mais par
noz faicts & maniere de vivre, nous le renonçons,
comme dit monsieur sainct Paul: *Confitentur se nosce
Deum, factis autem negant, cùm sint abominati, &
incredibiles, et ad omne bonum reprobi.* Nous valons
pis qu'heretiques: *quia error cui non resistitur,
approbatur, & veritas cùm minime defenditur,
opprimitur. Negligere quippè, cum poßis perturbare
perversos, nihil aliud est quàm fovere, nec caret
scrupulo societatis occultae, qui manifesto facinori
definit obviare.* Il fault estre pour Dieu, ou contre luy,
comme dit nostre sauveur: *Qui non est mecum, contra*

I. Cor. 4.
Il ne se fault
point ingerer des
Evesques.
Exod. 4.

Hebr. 5.

*Ambition
d'honneur et
benefices.*

Tit. 1.

me est: & qui non congregat mecum, spargit. *Matth. 12.*
Chrestiens, prenez exemple sur ceste homme de bien,
& vous ne serez pas tant cupides d'en avoir. Il y a tant
d'ennemis domestiques, que ie ne sçay que s'en sera:
mais à la fin Dieu fera qu'ils seront cogneus: *Nam* *I. Cor. 11.*
oportet haereses esse, ut & qui probati sunt, manifesti
fiant in vobis. Tenons nous en Dieu, & en la tradition
de l'eglise, & nous n'errerons point. Qu'est-ce que la
tradition de l'eglise? S. Augustin dit: *Traditio Ecclesiae*
est bombarda & invincibilis machina contra omnes
haereticos: est profeßio concors, & unanimis omnium
doctorum sacrorum, qui unanimiter testimonium
dederunt scripturae sacrae, & doctrinae Iesu Christi. Il
se fault arrester à l'eglise, car c'est elle qui donne le *Il ne se fault arrester*
à l'eglise.
vray nourrissement, & une parole & doctrine
irreprehensible: il n'en fault point chercher ailleurs,
pour en trouver de meilleur. Et pource qu'on ne peult
tout prouver par la saincte escriture, on a recours à la
tradition de l'eglise, qui est un tesmoignage invincible
contre tous les heretiques, qu'ils ne sçauroient nier, &
si nient bien les escritures sainctes: car ils disent
qu'elles ne se doivent pas entendre selon le sens &
interpretation de l'eglise, mais eux-mesmes la veulent
interpreter à leur plaisir, & à leur sens particulier.
Quand S. Paul veult montrer que les femmes doivent
prier en l'eglise le chef couvert, il n'ameine point la
saincte escriture, mais seulement la coustume &
tradition de l'eglise, disant: *Vos ipsi iudicate: decet* *I. Cor. 11.*
mulierem non velatam orare Deum? Si quis autem
videtur contentiosus, nos talem consuetudinem non
habemus, neque ecclesia Dei. Suivons doncques
l'eglise, & ses traditions, si nous voulons estre sauvez:
quia extra Ecclesiam non est salus. Pour la
commendation & louenge de ce bon personnage, nous
le comparerons à Timothée disciple de sainct Paul,
lequel exhortoit de labourer pour l'Evangile,
singulierement de veiller, reprendre, & increper en
toute patience & doctrine: *Noli itaque erubescere* *2. Tim. 1.*
testimonium Domini nostri, neque me vinctum eius:
sed collabora Evangelio Dei, secundum virtutem Dei.
Item: Praedica verbum, iusta opportunè, argue,
obsecra, increpa, in omni patientia & doctrina. Tu
verò vigila, in omnibus labora, opus fac Evangelistae,

ministerium tuum imple, sobrius est. Item: Attende
lectioni, & exhortationi doctrinae. Aussi cest homme
icy avoit toutes les conditions que nous avons recitées.
Il ne cessoit de lire, ou de prescher, & soustenir
l'Evangile, & la foy de Iesus Christ, iusques à endurer
calomnies, opprobres & iniures des adversaires. En
apres sainct Paul dit à Timothée: *Noli adhuc aquam*   I. Tim. 5.
bibere, sed modico vini utere propter stomachum
tuum, & frequentes tuas infirmitates. Ie sçay du
personnage comme il estoit angustié & travaillé de
l'estomach, lequel toutesfois ne vouloit avoir rien
d'avantage que les autres religieux. Il pouvoit manger
de la chair à cause de sa maladie, & de son estomach:
mais il s'en abstenoit pour donner exemple aux autres,
comme fit un homme de bien nommé Eleazarus, aagé
de nonante ans, lequel ayma mieux mourir que de
transgresser la loy, & manger de la chair de pourceau,   *Eleazarus ayma*
ou seulement faire semblant d'en manger: *Sed cum*   *mieux mourir que*
plagis perimeretur, ingemuit & dixit: Domine qui   *de transgresser la loy*
habes sanctam scientiam, manifestè tu scis, quia cum à   *de Dieu.*
morte possem liberari, duros corporis sustineo dolores: 2. Mach. 6.
secundum animam verò propter timorem tuum,
libenter haec patior. Et iste hoc modo vita disceßit:
non solùm iuvenibus, sed & universae genti
memoriam mortis suae, ad exemplum virtutis &
fortitudinis derelinquens. Aussi ce bon personnage a
mieux aymé endurer mort, que de prendre de la chair,
combien qu'il luy fust licite d'en manger, pour donner
exemple aux autres: car il estoit de la lumiere, &
comme la chandelle qui est au chandelier, mise sur la
table pour illuminer & faire veoir ceux qui sont en la
maison. Et comme une cité construite sur une
montagne ne peult estre cachée: aussi estoit il eminent
par dessus les autres. Et de peur de donner scandale, il
aymoit mieux ne point manger de la chair, suivant la
doctrine de S. Paul, disant: *Bonum est manducare*   Rom. 14.
carnem, & non bibere vinum, neque in quo frater tuus
offenditur, aut scandalizatur, aut infirmatur. Item: Si
esca fratrem meum scandalizat, non manducabo
carnes in aeternum, ne fratrem meum scandalizem. Il   I. Cor. 8.
ne fault pas que les subiects, & inferieurs donnent
scandale, ou occasion de scandale: mais encore moins
les prelats & superieurs, & s'en doivent garder: car ils

sont comme un signe, & le blanc auquel chacun tire.
Licet autem hoc sit observandum in subditis,
diligentiùs tamen est observandum in praelatis, qui
quasi signum sunt positi.i.ad sagittam. D'avantage, S.
Paul dit à Timothée: *Sollicitè cura teipsum probabilem*
exhibere Deo, operarium inconfusibilem, rectè
tractantem verbum veritatis. Alia litera habet: rectè
secantem, dividentem verbum veritatis. Aussi ce
personnage icy n'a il pas eu le soing de bien
sincerement traiter la parole de Dieu, & la diviser &
distribuer à un chacun & tant en ses leçons, comme en
ses sermons? Ouy en verité. Il n'y a ne grand ne petit,
qui ne s'en sente. O que la perte en est grande!
Chrestiens, resiouïssons nous que ce bon personnage
iuste, est mort au service de Dieu. Mais nous avons
bien grande matiere de pleurer, car auiourd'huy il est
cheut un bon & vaillant gendarme à l'Eglise de Dieu.
Il fut fait grand dueil & lamentation de Moyse, quand
il fut mort. *Fleuerunt eum filii Israel in campestribus*
Moab, triginta diebus. La femme veufve pleuroit à la
porte de la cité de faim, de son fils qu'on portoit en
terre: mais nostre Seigneur l'a consolée, disant: Ma-
mie ne pleure plus. Et commande à l'adolescent qu'il
eust à se lever: & l'adolescent qui estoit mort se leve:
& nostre Seigneur le rend à sa mere. Rachel a pleuré
ses enfans, mais elle n'a point esté consolée: *Rachel*
plorans filios sos, noluit consolari, quia non sunt.
Rachel c'est l'eglise qui pleure pour l'absence de son
espoux Iesus Christ, lequel est avec elle tousiours par
grace: & realement est au S. Sacrement de l'autel: mais
elle est veufve de sa presence visible. Et pource l'eglise
pleure. Consolons la, Chrestiens, & gardons sa
doctrine. L'escriture dit: *Non desit plorantibus in*
consolationem, et cum lugentibus ambula. Faisons le
dueil de ce bon personnage qui nous estoit bien
necessaire, & nous est failly au besoing: mais comme a
dit l'Ange à S. Iean, qu'il n'eust à s'esmerveiller: aussi
ne nous esmerveillons point, car Dieu faict tout en
sapience, & par raison, comme dit David: *Omnia in*
sapientia fecisti domine. Et S. Augustin: *Noli turbari,*
tranquillus esto, ut scias quoniam rectus dominus, &
non est iniquitas in eo.

2. Tim. 2.

Moyse fut beaucoup
pleuré quand il
fut mort.
Matth. 2.

Eccle. 7.

S. Augustin.

4. *Pour le Second Dimenche d'apres Pasques.*

CHristus passus est pro nobis, nobis relinquens exemplum &c. L'homme par sa grande ignorance, & imbecilité qui est en luy, a besoing d'estre instruit & enseigné: car de luy il ne peut venir à la cognoissance de salut & de verité: il faut venir à l'escole de nostre Seigneur, pour apprendre Dieu & nostre salut, & non pas à l'escole du monde. Ceux qui ont cogneu Dieu, s'ils suivent l'escole du monde, ils oublieront tout ce qu'ils avoient apprins, ils seront faicts bestes, & semblables aux iumens. Adam, cependant qu'il a esté à l'escole de Dieu, il s'est rendu obeissant selon la forme que Dieu luy avoit donnée, il estoit sçavant: mais il s'est dereiglé, & a voulu suivre le train, & prendre la voye du monde, qui est le chemin de perdition: & en un moment, il a oublié la cognoissance de Dieu & l'a perdue. Il a oublié ce qu'il sçavoit, & a esté faict beste par faute d'entendre le bien que Dieu luy avoit faict. Aussi nous semblablement, si nous voulons tenir, & ensuivre l'instruction de nostre Seigneur, infalliblement nous trouverons nostre salut: & quelque part que pouvions estre, nous serons bien-heureux, pourveu que ne sortions point de l'escole de Dieu, & que nous soyons enseignez de luy. Le Psalmiste dict: *Beatus quem tu erudieris domine. & de lege tua docueris eum.* Il est bienheureux qui est enseigné de Dieu, & en la loy de nostre Seigneur: car en l'escole de Dieu: il n'y a que bon exemple, bon propos, bonnes paroles: mais en l'escole du monde on n'y oit que mauvais exemple, on y desaprend Dieu, & vient on à estre endurci & obstiné en mal, comme si on n'eust faict autre mestier, que de suivre le monde. Si celuy est bien heureux qui estudie à l'escole de Dieu, au contraire celuy est malheureux qui estudie à l'escole du monde: car on y oit tout mal, & n'y peut on apprendre autre chose: & si on a quelque bien, & quelque vertu, il est corrompu, comme dit S. Paul: *Corrumpunt bonos mores colloquia prava.* Il faut apprendre Dieu, & non pas le monde: & pour

A l'escole du monde on oublie Dieu.

Psal. 93.
En l'escole de Dieu est bonne exemple.

I. Cor. 15.

l'apprendre il faut venir à l'escole de Dieu, afin que
vous voyez & entendiez ce que Dieu vous commande
& enseigne. Et pour ce, S. Pierre dit: *Christus passus
est pro nobis, &c.* En l'escole de Dieu on y apprend
premierement que nostre Seigneur Iesuschrist vray
Dieu & vray homme, est mort pour nous, pour nostre
redemption. La premiere doctrine de ceste escole, c'est
d'entendre que Dieu nous ayme, comme ses enfans
tresaymez: *Sicut filii chariſſimi.* C'est grand chose que
quand le disciple cognoist que son maistre l'ayme, il en
apprend de meilleur courage: & au contraire, il ne peut
apprendre s'il n'a bon vouloir envers son maistre, &
son maistre envers luy. En l'escole de Dieu, Iesus
Christ est nostre maistre, nous le devons ouir: car Dieu
le pere dist en son baptesme, & en sa transfiguration:
*Hic est filius meus dilectus, in quo mihi bene
complacui: ipsum audite.* Faictes ce qu'il vous dict &   *Matth. 7.*
commande: c'est vostre maistre. Iesus Christ nostre
maistre nous porte si bon vouloir, & si bonne
affection, qu'il a pour nous enduré mort & passion.
Nous estions tous brigans, larrons, & deputez à
damnation eternelle, & escoliers du diable. Mais Jesus
Christ par sa bonté & misericorde, a eu pitié de nous, &
nous a ostez de ce malheur & misere extreme, en nous
prenant pour ses escoliers, quand il nous a reconciliez,
& faicts amys de Dieu. Il ne luy a pas suffi de nous
aymer en son cueur, mais aussi exterieurement, & en
payant, & satisfaisant pour nous par sa mort & passion.
Nous n'estions pas puissans pour satisfaire, & appaiser
l'ire & inimitié de Dieu, & pour payer la debte que
nous debvions pour nostre peché: & pourrant Iesus
Christ en a eu pitié, & s'est offert liberalement en
l'arbre de la croix, pour payer nostre debte & rançon.
Redemit nos. Et pource, dit S. Pierre: *Christus passus*   *I. Petr. 2.*
est pro nobis, vobis relinquens exemplum, ut
sequamini vestigia eius. Et pource si nous voulons
prouffiter en son escole, il faut que nous exhibions tels
envers luy, & envers nostre prochain, qu'il s'est exhibé
envers nous. Si quelqu'un m'enseigne, & ie cognois
qu'il ne me porte pas bonne affection, ie ne puis
prouffiter soubs luy: mais nous avons grande occasion
d'ouir Iesus Christ, de faire ce qu'il nous dict, & de
prouffiter soubs luy, consideré l'amour & charité qu'il

nous porte. Et pour ce, nous devons estre diligens
d'apprendre à son escole l'amour qu'il nous porte, & le
besoing qu'il nous veult, & peult faire: à ceste cause dit
S. Paul: Ie prie Dieu que vous puissiez entendre la   *Ephes. 3.*
haulteur, & la latitude, la largeur, & la profondité de la
charité de nostre Seigneur envers vous, & de sçavoir la
supereminente science de sa charité. Elle est si grande
que l'entendement humain ne la peult comprendre:
c'est qu'il a voulu mourir pour les pecheurs, &
satisfaire pour eux, combien qu'ils fussent indignes de
vie, de grace, & de pardon. Voila la charité
supereminente de nostre Seigneur, c'est un exces
d'amour qu'il monstre envers nous. Et pourtant il
fault apprendre cela à son escole, & en faire son
prouffit. Il nous a bien aimez, il est nostre
reconciliation, nostre souverain Seigneur. Nous
sommes fais le peuple de Dieu, par l'acquisition du
precieux sang de Iesus Christ son fils. Il est aussi nostre
docteur, & nostre maistre. Il nous enseigne ce que   *Nous sommes le*
nous devons faire: *Christus passus est pro nobis, etc.*   *peuple de Dieu par*
Ne pensez pas qu'il suffise à vostre salut, de croire que   *le sang de nostre*
Iesus Christ est mort pour vous: mais aussi avec ce, il   *Seigneur.*
fault que vous entendiez qu'il veult que vous
l'ensuiviez: *Vobis relinquens exemplum, ut*
sequamini vestigia eius. C'est à dire, qu'ainsi que il a   *I. Petr. 2.*
enduré, il veult aussi que vous enduriez avec luy, en
appuyant toutes voz euvres sur luy, & sur le merite de
sa mort & passion: autrement elle ne vous prouffitera
de rien, mais plustost vous fera à plus grand comble de
mal. Notez que nostre Seigneur Iesus Christ nous est   *La passion de nostre*
opposé en deux manieres. Premierement comme un   *Seigneur est don de*
don & grace de Dieu. Si le Roy me fait quelque don, il   *grace.*
me donne une ville, ou un chasteau, ie ne l'ay pas
merité, mais il est ainsi liberal, & luy plaist que ie l'aye:
& le me donne soubs condition que ie face quelque
chose. Dieu nous a fait un grand don: il nous a donné
son fils, avec lequel il nous a tout donné, comme dit S.
Paul: *Quomodo non etiam cum illo omnia nobis*   *Rom. 8.*
donavit? Et Esaie dit: *Puer natus est nobis, etc.* Dieu
dit: Ie vous donne mon fils, & en le vous donnant, ie
vous donne tout ce qu'il a fait, c'est à dire, de sa mort
& passion, tout ce que il a enduré, & toute sa
peregrination, & veult que vous en ayez le prouffit &

l'emolument: comme quand le Roy donne quelque terre, il donne quant & quant tous les droits & appartenances d'icelle. Malediction à celuy qui repudie ce don, & ceste offre de nostre Seigneur: mais en faisant ce don, il y a opposé une condition, qu'il fault faire, qui veult avoit le don, & le prouffit d'iceluy: c'est ce qu'il dit: *Ut sequamini vestigia eius.* Il vous fault faire à l'exemple de nostre Seigneur: ainsi qu'il a contemné le monde, il fault que vous le contemniez. Il ne s'est point vengé de ses ennemis, ne de ceux qui l'ont accusé fausement: il a prié pour ses ennemis: Aussi ne demandez pas vengeance contre voz ennemis, mais priez pour eux, & soyez imitateurs de Iesus Christ crucifié. Il fault crucifier nostre chair à vice & à peché, comme dit S. Paul: *Qui christi sunt, carnem suam crucifixerunt cum vitiis et concupiscentiis.* Il se fault crucifier & mortifier, non pas reallement d'un cousteau mais il fault mortifier ses passions & les surmonter. Iesus Christ a ieusné, il a peregriné, il a enduré beaucoup de maux, prié pour ses ennemis, il a faict de bonnes euvres, & iamais ne feit mal ne peché: car il estoit impecable par nature. Faites ainsi, & vous iouïrez du don que Dieu vous fait de son fils, & de tout le merite d'iceluy: mais si vous n'estes imitateurs de nostre Seigneur, autant qu'il vous sera possible, & selon vostre fragilité, soyez certains que iamais sa mort & passion ne vous prouffitera. Et pourtant, combien que Dieu me vueille pardonner mes fautes & pechez, il veult neantmoins que ie face penitence, laquelle a trois parties. Premierement il fault que i'aye contrition de mon peché: apres que ie m'en confesse distinctement au prestre. Et tiercement que i'en face satisfaction. Ouy mais Iesus Christ n'a il pas satisfait pour moy? Ouy, mais avec ce qu'il a satisfait pour toy, il veult aussi que tu satisfaces de ton costé, ce que tu pourras, en faisant de bonnes euvres, tant par ieusnes & abstinences, par aumosnes & autres bonnes euvres: combien que tes euvres, d'elles ne vallent rien, & ne sont pas satisfactoires, ne meritoires, si elles ne sont fondées & appuyées au merite de la mort & passion de nostre Seigneur Iesus Christ. Et si ainsi vous le faites, elles seront acceptées de Dieu, comme le propre euvre de Iesus Christ. Et pourtant ne

La passion de nostre Seigneur ne prouffite de rien à ceux qui ne l'ensuivent.

Penitence a trois parties.

vous abusez point, car il fault que nous soyons
imitateurs de Iesus Christ & que nous facions à son
exemple, que nous ensuyvions ses vestiges: *Ut
sequamini vestigia eius.* Pour bien faire noz euvres, il
nous fault touriours regarder Iesus Christ, nous y
fonder, & reigler totalement par luy ou autrement
nous gasterions tout, & ne ferions chose qui vaille:
comme vous voyez que si un enfant ne regarde à son
exemple en escrivant, il va tortu, & n'escrit pas bien.
Nostre Seigneur a surmonté le diable, qui l'a tenté de
gloutonnie. Il luy a dit: *Non in solo pane vivit homo.*
Aussi n'acquiessons point à la tentation: mais nous
recommandons à nostre seigneur, & il nous la fera
surmonter, Mais nous nous oublions, & gastons tout:
car nous ne regardons point à nostre exemple Iesus
Christ, & à sa parole. Faisons comme David qui avoit
tousiours la parole de Dieu en son cueur, afin qu'il ne
l'oubliast, & qu'il n'offensast point: *In corde meo
abscondi eloquia tua, ut non peccem tibi.* Et en
l'Ecclesiastique il est dit: *Eqa quae praecepit tibi Deus,
cogita semper.* Et Tobie à son fils. *Omnibus diebus
vitae tuae habe Deum in corde tuo.* Pense que Dieu te
veoit & penetre ta pensée. *Cave ne malo consentias.*
Le maistre, la maistresse ne voudroient pas mal faire
devant leurs enfans, devant leurs serviteurs, mais les
envoyent dehors, car ils les craignent. Combien donc
d'avantage devez vous craindre Dieu, qui est tesmoing
des cogitations & intentions? Et pource, tous les iours
de vostre vie, ne vueillez consentir à mal, estre
provoquer à mal. Ce n'est pas peché, si vous pourray
bien provoquer à mal: mais vous n'offensez pas
pourtant, si vous n'y consentez. Retenez donc que
vous devez tousiours avoir nostre Seigneur devant
voz yeux, pour exemple, & pour lumiere. Tenez vous
à son escole, & soyez de ses escoliers: & si vous n'y
estes, entrez y tout à ceste heure: car il reçoit facilement
& volontairement, & n'est difficile d'y avoir accez,
comme envers les hommes. Nostre Seigneur nous
porte bon vouloir, & aussi nous luy devons porter bon
vouloir, en mettant sa doctrine, & ses commandemens
à execution: car la science de Dieu, que Iesus Christ
nous enseigne, gist en l'euvre, & autrement ne
prouffite pas. Un boulenger, combien que il sçache

*Pour bien faire, il
faut regarded Iesus
Christ.*

Matth. 4.

*Psal. 118.
Eccl. 3.
Tob. 4.*

*La science de nostre
Seigneur gist en
l'euvre.*

bien faire du pain, il mourroit de faim, s'il n'en faisoit:
car c'est un acte, & mestier qui gist en pratique: aussi la
theologie. Ce n'est pas assez de sçavoir la loy de Dieu,
mais aussi la fault mettre en euvre & execution, qui y
veult prouffiter. La parole de nostre Seigneur, c'est vie
eternelle, comme disoit S. Pierre à nostre Seigneur:
Verba vitae aeternae habes. Apprenez donc la science   *Ioan. 6.*
de Dieu, en laquelle gist la vie eternelle: mais si vous
ne la mettez en execution, vous perdrez temps, comme
dit saint Iean. Celuy qui dit qu'il sçait Dieu, & ne garde
ses commandemens, il est menteur. *Ut sequamini*   *I. Petr. 2.*
vestigia eius. Mais comment pourray ie ensuivre
nostre Seigneur, & faire comme il a fait, consideré que
ie ne sçaurois faire miracles, comme luy, cheminer sur
l'eau, resusciter les morts, & semblables? Aussi il ne
nous commande pas de l'ensuivre en ses euvres là:
mais vous sont proposées pour les avoir en
admiration: mais il vous commande sur peine d'estre
damné, de l'ensuivre aux choses qu'il a mises en
vostre capacité & puissance: comme est de l'aimer sur
toutes choses, comme il vous a aimez, & de faire les
autres bonnes euvres à son exemple. Il s'ensuit: *Qui*   *I. Petr. 2.*
peccatum non fecit, nec inventus est dolus in ore eius.
Iesus Christ est innocent, iamais ne pechea, & dol &
fraude n'a point esté trouvé en sa bouche, c'estoit un
aigneau sans macule. Si vous dites: Ie ne sçaurois me
garder de pecher, vous faites iniure à Dieu de dire cela,
car peché est volontaire, & ne pecheriez pas si vous ne
vouliez: car s'il eust esté impossible à l'homme de s'en
garder, Dieu ne l'eust pas defendu. Dieu ne
commande pas à l'homme, de faire ce qu'il ne peult,
comme de toucher le ciel au doigt, & semblable. Sainct
Hierome dit que c'est blaspheme & anatheme, de dire
que Dieu commande chose impossible, ou trop difficile
à faire. O que cela est aliené & estrange de raison: Il
m'est commandé de m'abstenir de peché, c'est donc
signe que cela est en ma puissance, & liberal arbitre de
m'en abstenir moyennant l'aide de Dieu, & sa grace.
Donc vous devez ensuivre nostre Seigneur, en fuyant
tous vices & pechez: considerez combien Dieu est bon,
& quelle est sa nature. David dit: *Quoniam non Deus*
volens iniquitatem tu es. Odio est peccatum Deo, &
iniquitas. Dieu a en horreur tout peché quel qu'il soit.

Doncques puis que vous cognoissez la nature de Dieu,
& de peché, vous devez aimer Dieu: & luy servir, &
haïr peché, & le fuïr & eviter, puis qu'il est desplaisant
à Dieu. Un bon enfant fait ce qu'il cognoist qui plaist à
son pere, & fuit & evite ce qu'il sçait luy desplaire: il
s'adapte & accommode au vouloir de son pere. Aussi
entendez la nature de nostre Dieu, qu'il hait tous vices
& pechez, & aime vertu. Doncques estant à son escole,
exercez vous à vertu, & faictes tout au plaisir de Dieu,
estimans que Dieu se complaist en vostre bon euvre.
Et quand vous pensez, & entendez que Dieu se
complaist en vostre bon euvre, vous vous y
resiouïssez, & estes plus diligens & fervens à luy
servir. Voila la condition d'un bon escolier, & bon
Chrestien, qui a bien estudié à l'escole de nostre
Seigneur. Il sçait son texte par cueur, & ne fait point
crier apres luy. Ouy mais cela est tant difficile à faire:
ouy bien à celuy qui est pusillanime, & lasche de
courage: mais à un bon cueur il n'est rien difficile, tout
est faile? *Amanti nihil difficile.* Et s'il est ainsi que
celuy qui aime d'un meschant amour, ne demande
sinon que de faire le vouloir de celle qu'il aime
meschamment, & pour luy complaire il ne trouve rien
difficile: que doit d'avantage faire le bon Chrestien
pour son Dieu? Sainct Ambroise recite de saincte
Agnes, à laquelle on presentoit tant de dons & de
presens, afin que elle se voulust consentir d'estre
mariée au fils du prevost, qui estoit enflambé, & ravy
de meschant amour lubrique, & elle n'en voulut
point, mais refusa tout cela pour le grand amour
qu'elle avoit en nostre Seigneur. Ceux qui font
enragez de meschant amour, combien de peine
prennent ils pour en iouïr? Et neantmoins, cela ne
leur semble pas estre peine, tant sont transferez de ce
meschant amour damnable. Ils n'en dorment iour ne
nuit, & qui plus est, s'ils ne peuvent iouïr de celle
qu'ils aiment ainsi meschamment, ils feront
despeindre son image, pour la porter sur eux en leur
sein, cela est plus penible que chose qui soit en ce
monde. C'est le meschant amour qui les a ainsi
transferez. Et vous dites qu'il y a difficulté à bien faire.
Et s'il y a tant de peine à faire mal (ce neantmoins
encore le fait on, & ne semble pas estre peine) combien

doncques d'avantage de bon cueur ferez vous le bien,
si vous le voulez faire? Si vous avez bon amour en
Dieu, vous n'y trouverez pas de peine, mais vous
semblera plus doux que miel, c'est merveille que le
diable peut tant faire. Si un meschant prend en gré le
mal & la peine qu'il a pour faire mal, & commettre
peché (on le battra, on luy dira iniure: & neantmoins il
est tant enragé de mechant amour, qu'il ne pense point
au mal qu'on luy sçache faire, il ne s'en soucie:) &
vertu, l'amour de Iesus Christ, n'aura il pas plus
d'efficace à bien, que le meschant à mal? Doncques il
faut fuir tous pechez, à l'exemple de nostre Seigneur,
& non seulement peché mortel, pour lequel on est
obligé à peine eternelle: mais aussi peche veniel, qui
n'oste pas la grace de Dieu, mais il diminue & refroidit
la charité, & on en est retardé de la vision de Dieu,
pour quelque temps. N'est ce pas une grosse peine que
cela? Si un homme meurt en peché veniel, il va en
purgatoire, & y est detenu pour quelque temps: &
iusques à ce qu'il ait satisfaict pour iceluy peché veniel,
il est retardé de la vision de Dieu. Si une femme,
aymant bien son mary, sçavoir qu'il fust venu de
quelque lieu bien loing, ne luy feroit il pas bien mal, si
elle iouït pas du bien qu'il desire, quelle peine
doncques est ce à une ame, qui est en purgatoire,
combien qu'elle ne soit pas separée de la grace de Dieu,
si elle est retardée de sa vision? Doncques il faut fuir &
eviter tous pechez & mortel & veniel. Il est facile de se
garder de peché mortel, car il fault grande deliberation
avant que pecher mortellement, & Dieu n'est pas facile
à irriter. On dit que celuy est homme de bien, qui n'est
pas facile à irriter, & à courroux, & s'il est irrité, il
s'appaise aisement: & d'avantage il ne fait pas
seulement bien, à ceux là qui l'ont merité, mais à ceux
qui ne l'ont pas merité: cela est ensuivre la condition
de nostre Seigneur Dieu, qui n'est pas facile à irriter &
à punir: & s'il est irrité, il s'appaise, & pardonne
facilement. D'avantage il fait bien, non seullement
aux bons, & à ceux qui l'ont merité & derservy: mais
aussi aux mauvais, qui en sont indignes, comme dit
l'escriture: *Solem suum facit oriri super bonos &
malos, pluit super iustos & iniustos.* Toy qui es trop
craintif, tu cuides que tout ce que tu fais soit peché: tu

*Il faut grande
deliberation devant
que pecher
mortellement.*

Matth. 5.

es chagrin, tu te fasches, tu dis: Ie ne fais rien de bien.
Que gaignes tu de dire cela, puis que tu as bon vouloir
en Dieu, & que tu fais du mieux que tu peux selon ta
fragilité humaine? Si tu sens de Dieu en tout bien, tu *Sentir de Dieu en*
penseras comme nous venons de dire, qu'il n'est pas *toute humilité.*
facile à se courroucer, n'y à punir, & qu'il est facile &
prompt à pardonner, & faire grace & misericorde à
ceux qui luy demandent, & sont vrayement contris. Le
petit enfant se presente à son pere avec humilité, en
asseurance qu'il a en luy, & qu'il l'ayme: aussi asseurez
vous en Dieu, qui est vostre bon pere, & luy presentez
vostre infirmité, en disant avec David: *Non est sanitas* *Psal. 37.*
in carne mea. Et si vous avez ceste confience en Dieu,
qu'il vous ayme, & qu'il se complaist en vous, comme
en ses enfans, vostre conscience sera establie, & vous
vous asseurerez en luy, & vous serez stables. On peut
facillement passer, & eviter peché mortel toute sa vie,
car comme nous avons dit, il est requis un grand
consentement, avant que d'offenser mortellement. Et
Dieu n'est pas facile à irriter: mais peché veniel est *Peché veniel est*
difficile à eviter, mesme celuy qui procede d'infirmité, *difficile à eviter.*
comme est de se resiouyr subitement du mal de son
ennemy, estre esmeu en mal, quand on le voit, qu'on
en oit parler, & semblable: sans toutesfois y donner
consentement, & que si tost que on vient à penser à
foy, & iuger, on seroit marry qu'il eust mal. Il y a une
autre maniere de peché veniel, duquel on se peut
facillement garder, comme de peché mortel, par la
grace de Dieu, comme est de mentir en choses ioyeuses
& facetieuses, qui ne portent point de dommage à
autruy, rire, & folastrer, & semblable ie m'en puis bien
garder: car ie ne diray pas de mensonge ioyeuse, si ie ne
peche pas pourtant si ie n'y consens: car ce
mouvement est d'infirmité, & les premiers *Tentation à pecher*
mouvemens ne sont peché mortel ne veniel: car les *n'est pas peché.*
premiers mouvemens ne sont point en la puissance de
l'homme, il ne pourroit faire, qu'il ne les ait: la
passion previent toute deliberation & raison, mais par
grand estude & labeurs, il n'y a passion qu'on ne
puisse eviter & ranger. Monsieur Sainct Thomas
appelle ces vertus un esprit purgé, comme estoit Adam
en paradis terrestre, & l'homme qui y peult facilement
resister, *habet notam perfectionis humanae.* Et si

vous n'estes parvenus là, desirez d'y parvenir: soyez
marris que vous n'y estes parvenus, & priez Dieu qu'il
vous face de la grace d'y parvenir. Et en ce faisant,
vous meritez d'estre du nombre de ceux, desquels
nostre Seigneur dit: *Beati qui esuriunt & sitiunt*   *Matth. 5.*
iustitiam. Gaignez auiourd'huy un petit sur vous, &
tousiours de mieux en mieux, de iour en autre, &
soyez diligens à refrener & oster ces passions: & à la fin
vous en viendrez à bout par la grace de Dieu. Ie ne vay
gueres bien, mais si ie voulois entreprendre d'aller à
Rome, i'y pourrois aller petit à petit: mais aussi qui ne
met la main à l'euvre, qui ne gaigne païs, il demeure
tousiours là. Les femmes qui alloyent au monument   *Marc. 16.*
pour y oindre le corps de nostre Seigneur, estoyent en
peine & soucy, qui leur osteroit la pierre du
monument: & en y allant, elles ont veu la pierre du
monument ostée. Aussi en nous exerçans & mettans
en euvre, nous serous, tous esbahis, que nous serons à
bout, & nous nous trouverons à fin de ce que nous
desirons, combien qu'il nous semblast bien difficile d'y
parvenir. Voyla comme Dieu satisfaict au bon vouloir
& desir des siens, qui labourent, & font leur devoir.
Fuyons donc tous pechez, à l'exemple de nostre
Seigneur, *dolus non est inventus in ore eius.* Il
n'estoit point simulateur, ne menteur, comme sont
ceux qui de bouche se monstrent favorables à leur
prochain, & non pas de cueur, comme dit David: *Psal. 11.*
Corde & corde locuti sunt. Ie ne sçay où c'est qu'il y a   *Chacun cherche*
pour le iourd'huy fidelité. Chacun cherche son   *son prouffit*
prouffit particulier, & on ne se soucie de celuy   *particulier.*
d'autruy. On ment, on se pariure, pour decevoir son
prochain: ce n'est pas là le chemin de paradis, mais
plustost d'enfer. Et pensans faire ainsi vostre prouffit,
vous faictes vostre grand dommage, car vous vous   *I. Petr. 2.*
damnez. *Qui cum pateretur, non comminabatur.*   *Nostre Seigneur*
Voyla nostre maistre Iesus Christ, qui nous est proposé   *ne rendoit mal*
pour exemple, afin de l'imiter & ensuyvre. Quand il   *pour mal.*
enduroit, & qu'on le maudissoit, il ne rendoit pas mal
pour mal, ny iniure pour iniure, il n'a pas demandé
vengeance, mais *tradebat iudicanti se iniustè.* Il s'est
laissé iuger iniustement, entre les mains de Pilate, c'est
nostre exemple. Il ne rend point iniure pour iniure,
mal pour mal. Si quelcun m'a donné une buffe, ie ne

luy en doy pas rendre une autre: prohiber & empescher
qu'il ne me frappe & moleste, & me pourveoir par
iustice, sans me vanger: mais ie doy laisser la
vengeance à Dieu, qui dit: *Mihi vindicta & ego*
retribuam. Que pensent donc faire nos gentils-
hommes, qui disent: Et que sera ce de moy, si ie ne me
venge? moy & ma race serons deshonorez. Et pour
cela, vous offensez Dieu, vous en aurez louenge en la
bouche des mondains & pecheurs: mais vous en serez
en confusion devant Dieu, & devant les gens de bien,
qui le craignent & ayment. Que prouffite il à Cesar & à
plusieurs autres, d'avoir eu plusieurs victories, &
d'avoir subiugué & molesté leurs ennemis, si à present
ils sont damnez? Tu demandes la luicte & le combat,
pour monstrer ton innocence, & le monde dit, que tu
es homme de bien: mais au contraire Dieu dit, que tu
es un meschant: car tu n'es pas imitateur de nostre
Seigneur, qui pouvoit en un moment confondre &
abismer ses ennemis, neantmoins il endure qu'ils le
battent & tourmentent, qu'ils le mettent à mort: &
encores prie il Dieu son pere pour eux. *Tradebat*
autem se iudicanti iniustè, scilicet Pilato. Vel tradebat
se iudicanti iustè: c'est à dire, qu'il remettoit sa cause à
Dieu, qui iuge iustement. Il n'a point demandé
vangeance, mais a remis sa cause entre les mains de
Dieu, il luy propose son innocence: aussi vous pouvez
demander au iuge iustice, non pas vangeance. Vous
demandez que vostre prochain soit puny, & corrigé
pour l'honneur de Dieu, & pour son salut. Il ne fault
pas qu'il y ait d'affection particuliere. Si la perte & le
mal qu'on vous a fait, vous esmeut plus que l'offense
commise contre Dieu, vous n'estes pas chrestiens en
verité, & n'appartenez à Iesus Christ: *ut sequamini*
vestigia eius. Si pour l'honneur & charité de nostre
Seigneur, vous endurez iustement, ce vous est grande
grace, & merite devant nostre Seigneur, vos endurez
iustement: car vous estes imitateurs, & ensuyvez les
vestiges de nostre Seigneur: *Qui peccata nostra pertulit*
ipse in corpore suo super lignum, ut peccato mortui
iustitiae vivamus. C'est à dire que Iesus Christ nostre
redempteur a enduré la peine deüe à nos pechez.
Parquoy à son exemple, nous le devons imiter & porter
le fardeau, la peine, le labeur, & travail les uns des
autres, estre marris de la perte & du dommage

Rom. 12.
Ezech. 9.
Deut. 32.

Il ne fault demander
combat ne duel.

L'homme peut
demander au iuge
iustice, &c non pas
vengeance.

I. Petr. 2.

Nous devons
supporter les uns
les autres.

d'autruy, comme du nostre: *Alter alterius onera
portae, & sic adimplebitis legem Christi.* Il fault avoir
charité, *quae operit multitudinem peccatorum.* Il se
fault accuser, & excuser autruy, à l'exemple de nostre
Seigneur, qui a porté nos pechez, & enduré la mort
pour iceux, *ut iustitiae vivamus.* Il vous fault vivre à

Galat. 6.

iustice, c'est à dire, faire les commandemens de Dieu &
de son Eglise, ordonner toute vostre vie à l'honneur
de Dieu, & au salut de vostre prochain, alors vous
vivez à Dieu, & à iustice. Faictes ce que vous pourrez,
& que toute vostre vie soit à louer & magnifier Dieu,
que tout ce que vous dictes, pensez & faictes, soit pour
avancer Dieu, c'est à dire afin qu'il soit tousiours de
mieux en mieux cogneu, loué & honoré, & nous
faisons le contraire quand nous l'offensons. *Cuius
livore sanati estis.* Les playes de Iesus Christ, sa mort
& passion, c'est nostre santé, ce nous est une medecine
efficace pour guerir nos pechez, & nous en purger. Et
combien que vostre prochain vous ait offensé, & vous
cognoissez que si premierement vous n'allez à luy
pour vous reconcilier, qu'il ne viendra pas à vous,
vous devez aller à luy, si vous avez coniecture que son
cueur en sera amolly, & qu'il recognoistra sa faulte &
peché: car vous estes tenus d'imiter nostre Seigneur,
lequel combien que nous l'ayons irrité & offensé, il n'a
pas attendu que nous nous soyons premierement
retournez à luy, mais par sa bonté, grace & misericorde
il est venu à nous, & a payé la rançon & la debte que
nous devions pour nostre peché: en mourant pour
nous oster la mort, & nous faire vivre eternellement.
*Is qui non noverat peccatum, pro nobis peccatum fecit,
id est, hostiam pro peccato.* Vous estiez comme brebis
errantes, mais maintenant vous estes convertis au
pasteur de vos ames, c'est à Iesus Christ: c'est ce que dit
Sainct Pierre à la fin de L'Epistre: *Erratis sicut oves
errantes, sed conversi nunc estis ad pastorem &
Episcopum animarum vestrarum.* Dieu nous face la
grace d'estre tellement imitateurs & de nostre Seigneur
& bon pasteur, que nous puissions continuer à son
service, iusques à la fin. Amen.

I. Petr. 2.
*Les playes et la
mort de nostre
Seigneur, sont nostre
santé.*

I. Corint. 5.

I. Petr. 2.

5. *Pour le Second Dimenche d'apres*
Pasques.
SERMON.

Ego sum pastor bonus: bonus pastor animam suam dat
pro ovibus suis, &c. Le pasteur doit conduire ses brebis
& les paistre. Celuy qui est nostre vray pasteur, c'est
nostre Seigneur Iesus Christ, qui nous regit &
gouverne. Ainsi que le bon pasteur & bergier va
devant ses brebis, & elles vont apres: aussi nostre
Seigneur Iesus Christ va devant nous, & nous
enseigne, & monstre à faire ses commandemens.
Coepit Iesus facere, postea docere. C'est ce que dit
sainct Pierre: *Christus passus est pro nobis, &c.* Vous
estes ses brebis, oyez donc la voix de vostre bon
pasteur, & le suyvez. Nostre Seigneur qui est nostre
vray pasteur, declare les conditions du pasteur, afin
que nous les cognoissions, & que nous soyons asseurez
de ce que nous devons faire, & de ce que nous devons
laisser, eviter & fuyr. Nostre bon pasteur Iesus Christ
dit: *Ego sum pastor bonus.* & monstre qu'il est bon
pasteur, quand il met son ame, & sa vie pour ses brebis
& oüailles. Il nous dit, que la condition & office d'un
vray pasteur, c'est mettre sa vie, se mettre & exposer à
tous perils, & dangers de sa vie, pour le bien de ses
brebis, mourir pour leur salut, & pour empescher que
le loup ne les devore & estrangle. Si le bergier s'ensuyt
quand il voit le loup venir, & laisse ses brebis, il n'est
pas bon pasteur: mais le vray pasteur, qui ne crainct
point sa vie, afin qu'il mette & tienne ses brebis en
seureté, se met en danger, & n'espargne rien pour les
bien garder & faire prouffiter. Voyla la condition d'un
vray pasteur. Il fault voir si nostre Seigneur a eu ceste
condition. Il vous est plus evident que le Soleil, qu'il
s'est mis en danger. Ne voyez vous pas que les
ministres de Pilate, avec les scribes, sont venus en la
bergerie, pour prendre nostre Seigneur, au iardin
d'Olivet? Il dist: *Ego sum,* Il se presente, mais
touchant ses disciples, il dist: *Sinite eos abire.* Laissez
les aller, & ne leur faictes aucun mal. Il a mis son ame

Ioan. 10.
L'office du pasteur.

Act. 1.
I. Petr. 2.

Ioan. 18.

pour plusieurs, & est mort, pour nous oster de la
tyrannie du diable. Doncques, il monstre qu'il est bon
pasteur, car il est mort pour ses brebis: & pourtant, à
bonne cause, il dit bien: *Ego sum pastor bonus.* La
condition du vray pasteur, c'est non seulement de
chercher, mais aussi de mettre sa vie pour ses subiects,
s'exposer à tous dangers & perils de la vie corporelle:
aussi nostre Seigneur est le pasteur de noz ames,
comme dit sainct pierre en l'Epistre du iourd'huy.
*Conversi enim estis ad pastorem & Episcopum
animarum vestrarum.* En l'Evangile, il est fait
mention de trois personnages, du pasteur, du larron, &
du mercenaire. La condition du pasteur, c'est mettre sa
vie pour le bien de ses brebis, & aller devant elles, leur
monstrer bon exemple, les conduire, & les delivrer de
mal, les oster de perils & dangers & les asseurer.
Davantage le pasteur cognoist ses brebis par noms &
surnoms. Ces conditions ont esté en nostre Seigneur
Iesus Christ: il nous monstre exemple de patience, &
que nous devons veincre le mal par le bien, & non pas
rendre le mal pour le mal, mais supporter le prochain,
& commettre à Dieu la cause, ne demandant
aucunement de partie. Davantage, l'exemple du bon
pasteur, qui est nostre Seigneur Iesus Christ, est, que ne
soyez faciles à ire & courrous, les uns contre les autres,
& de vous bien tost rappaiser, & remettre d'accord, &
en vostre amitié & charité. D'avantage, il vous donne
exemple, de non seulement faire bien à ceux que vous
aymez, mais aussi à ceux qui vous luy donniez à boire,
& à manger, & semblable, & s'il en a besoing, que vous
prier Dieu pour luy. Regardez comme a fait vostre
exemple Iesus Christ, il va devant, Seigneur dit:
Omnes quotquot venerunt, fures sunt & latrones.
Ouy, mais n'y a il pas eu de bons prophetes, comme
Ieremie, Esaie, & autres qui sont venus devant nostre
Seigneur? Ouy. Et par ainsi il fault entendre, de ceux
qui sont venus, & se sont ingerez d'entrer sans avoir
esté envoyez de Dieu: que tous ceux là sont larrons. Il
n'y a seulement qu'un moyen d'entrer en la bergerie
de nostre Seigneur, en l'Eglise, c'est entrer par l'huis,
qui est I E S V S C H R I S T. On cognoist quelcun
avoir entré par l'huis, quand il est esleu & choysi de
nostre Seigneur, qui luy donne les moyens, & la grace,

*Nostre Seigneur
est mort pour
nous oster de la
tyrannie du diable.
I. Petr. 2.*

*La condition du
pasteur.*

*Il fault bien faire
à ceux qui font mal
à l'exemple de
nostre Seigneur.*

Ioan. 10.

*Les larrons sont
ceux qui se sont
ingerez d'entrer
en la bergerie.*

pour conduire ceux qui sont en sa charge. Quand
i'applique seulement à mon prouffit particulier, ie ne me
soucie des brebis, & ne les cognois point, ce m'est
assez qu'on m'apporte de l'argent, ie ne prouffite en
ma charge, c'est signe que ie ne suis pas entré par
l'huis, *sed aliundè*. Parquoy il s'ensuit, que ie suis un
larron: ie suis appellé pasteur, de nom seulement, &
non pas d'euvre. Vous ne devez pas chercher &
demander, mais vous devez attendre que Dieu vous y
appelle, comme dit monsieur sainct Paul: *Nemo*
sumit sibi honorem, nisi qui vocatur à Deo, tanquam
Aaron. Nul ne se doit ingerer à demander l'honneur
& charge: car Iesus Christ, combien qu'il fust digne
d'estre Evesque, il n'a rien demandé: mais il a attendu
qu'il ait esté appellé de Dieu son pere, qui l'a ordonné
& estably grand prestre, selon l'ordre de Melchisedech,
comme il est dit: *Tu es sacerdos in aeternum,*
secundum ordinem Melchisedech. Si Dieu vous y
appelle, vous ne devez pas refuser, car vous pourriez
bien autant ou plus offenser en le refusant par
pusillanimité, qu'en le demandant par presumption.
Si on le vous offre, recommandez vous à Dieu, le
priant vous faire digne de le bien exercer à son
honneur & gloire, & au salut de ceux qui vous sont
donnez en charge. C'est un grand bien d'estre bon
pasteur, & s'exposer pour le salut de ses subiects. Et si
vous n'avez cette condition, vous n'estes pas bon
pasteur, mais larron. *Fur,* c'est celuy qui n'a droict au
benefice. En voyla un autre qui a vray droict & tiltre
au benefice, mais toy, tu es intrus, Ie crains qu'il y ait
plusieurs larrons & larronnesses en l'Eglise de Dieu,
comme sont ceux qui y sont entrez par force, par
faveur, & par simonie, & semblables. Quand tu
difformes & dereigles la maison bien formée & reiglée,
que des religieux tu en fais des seculiers, afin de faire
ton plaisir du revenu de la religion, es tu pas larron? Il
semble advis que nostre Seigneur face difference *Inter*
fures & latrones. Les uns desrobent appertement &
sans craincte pechent, comme les ravisseurs: les autres
desrobent sous umbre de bien & iustice, comme un
larron qui desrobe secrettement, craignant qu'on le
sçache. Doncques, pour faire l'honneur de Dieu, & son
salut en la maison de Dieu, il ne fault pas estre

*Nul ne se doit
ingerer, mais
attendre qu'il
soit appellé.
Hebr. 5.*

mercenaire, ne larron: mais il fault estre bon pasteur, à l'exemple de nostre Seigneur. Regarde ton cueur, ton vouloir & affection, & tu voiras comment c'est que tu y es entré, & si tu es larron, mercenaire ou bon pasteur. Le bon pasteur met son ame pour ses brebis, il n'y espargne pas sa vie, à l'exemple de nostre Seigneur. Le mercenaire n'est pas si mauvais que le larron: mais il ne vault gueres mieux, il ne regarde sinon à l'argent, & à faire son prouffit particulier. *Omnes quae sua sunt quaerunt. Omnes sequuntur munera & retributiones. Omnes socij furum.* Lequel vault mieux, ou de fuyr, ou se taire quand il fault parler? Ie me tais, & ne resiste pas aux mauvais & meschans, de peur de perdre le fruict: ie m'en fuis, & laisse les brebis entre les loups. Nostre Seigneur I E S V S C H R I S T est bon par nature, par proprieté, & par essence: il est le bon pasteur, & ne fait pas comme le larron, & le mercenaire: car il a mis son ame pour nous, il est mort pour faire vivre ses brebis, & les oster de la gorge du loup. *Mercenarius, à mercede dicitur*: car il ayme le loyer & retribution, le gain temporel, & non pas la charge de Dieu. Puis qu'il tient le lieu de Dieu, il est tenu de faire comme Dieu, il doit mettre son ame & sa vie pour le salut des autres. Avoir un bon benefice, de grand valeur & revenue, c'est avoir de bons parroissiens, s'employer pour l'amour de nostre Seigneur à leur salut. Mes amis, nous ne serons pas tousious [*sic*] en ce monde: il fault estre eternellement sauvé, ou eternellement damné. Et quand nous penserons bien à cela, il n'y aura partie sur nous qui ne tremble. Le peché d'un prelat & superieur, ne peut estre petit: s'il vit bien, c'est à la grande edification du peuple, mais au contraire, s'il vit mal, c'est aussi à la grande ruine, & scandale du peuple. I'en cherche, & en ay ia trois ou quatre, & n'y vas n'y viens. Nous serons damnez si nous ne faisons penitence. Dieu ne se change point, sa loy demeurera tousiours. Consideré nostre ambition, & nostre maniere de vivre, ie ne sçay qui sera sauvé. Sainct Iean Chrysostome, parlant des prestres qui ont charge d'ames, dit: *Non puto inter sacerdotes multos qui salui fiant, sed plures qui pereant*: car c'est une si grande charge que ie ne sçay qui en est digne. Ils ne sont pas icy, mais il y en

Le mercenaire n'est außi mauvais que le larron.
Philip. 2.
Esa. 1.

Avoir un benefice de grande revenu, est avoir de bons parroißiens.

peut avoir, qui pourront parvenir là. Toute nostre fin,
nostre souhait, doit estre de plaire à Dieu, de chercher
le Royaume de Dieu. Si vous avez l'amour, & la
craincte de Dieu, n'avez vous pas tout? Autrement
Dieu seroit menteur, car il dit: *Timentes Dominum,*   *Psal. 33.*
non minuentur omni bono. Et pourtant, cherchez de
tout vostre cueur, d'avoir Dieu avec vous. Vous ne   *Le meilleur*
pourrez avoir de meilleur benefice, que de servir à   *benefice est de*
Dieu, & d'avoir sa grace. Ne faictes rien qui desplaise à *servir à Dieu &*
Dieu, & vous serez bien heureux. Le curé, le superieur   *d'avoir sa grace.*
voit beaucoup de pauvretez, & d'abus en sa paroisse:
s'il les veult reprendre, on le calumniera, on luy
voudra mal, il s'ensuit, il se cache par silence. *Quia*
verbum exhortationis subtrahit, ne perdat
emolumenta. Ce n'est pas un signe d'amour, & de
zele de Dieu, de se taire quand il fault parler, &
principalement quand l'honneur de Dieu, & le salut
du prochain y pend. Il ne fault pas seullement
entendre d'un curé, d'un pasteur, mais aussi d'un pere
de famille en sa maison. Il doit estre comme un bon
pasteur, & enseigner bonne doctrine, bonnes meurs à
ses enfans & serviteurs, avoir soing d'eux, sçavoir de
quelle condition ils sont, s'ils servent à Dieu, s'ils vont
à la Messe, & au sainct service divin, quels livres ils
lisent. Toy pere, tu dois sçavoir cela, & faire ton
devoir: car autrement si par ta faulte & negligence ton
enfant, ton serviteur faillent, tu en es coupable. Et
encores, consideré le temps present, qui est si mauvais
& si dangereux, pour l'enormité & multitude des   *L'enfant ne doit*
pechez du peuple qui regnent. Et si d'aventure le pere   *obeir au commande-*
commande à son fils d'aller ouyr un predicateur, &   *ment contraire au*
gens suspects, ou faire quelque autre chose contre   *commandemens de*
l'honneur de Dieu, l'enfant ne luy doit pas obeir, mais *Dieu.*
se separer de luy, suyvant la doctrine de l'Evangile, qui *Matth. 18.*
dit: *Si oculus tuus, si pes, &c. Scandalizat te, erue &*
proiice abs te. C'est à dire, que si mon pere, ma mere
qui me doivent estre comme l'oeil, le pied, pour me
conduire, enseigner, soustenir, nourrir, s'ils me
veulent faire faire quelque chose contre Dieu, ie les
dois arracher de moy, c'est à dire, ne leur point obeir.
Et si l'enfant endure du mal, pour telle & semblable
cause, il est martyr, quand il resiste, & tient tousiours
bon pour nostre Seigneur. Et si le pere, le maistre, a un

enfant, un serviteur, qu'il sçait estre meschant, & de
mauvais gouvernement, & neantmoins il ne luy dit
mot, il endure, & ne le corrige pas, pource qu'il luy
semble qu'il le sert bien, & qu'il crainct que s'il le
battoit & chastioit, qu'il le laissast, & que ses affaires &
son mesnage demourassent en arriere: cestuy-là est
mercenaire, & non pas pasteur, car il regarde à son
prouffit particulier, & pour iceluy il delaisse l'honneur
de Dieu, & le salut de ceux dont il a charge &
gouvernement. Il ne se faut point servir de meschans
gens, car ils empeschent l'aide de Dieu & l'execution
de son bon vouloir. Et pourtant, toy pere, maistre, &c.
ne soys mercenaire, mais pasteur, ayant le soing de
l'honneur de Dieu sur toutes choses, & du salut &
prouffit de voz enfans ou serviteurs: ou autrement,
iamais vous ny eux ne prouffiterez. C'est grand pitié
de les perdre, & les damner: au lieu de les bien
conduire & enseigner. Ils estoient simples & innocens
quand on te les a baillez en charge, pour les faire
prouffiter, & tu les fais estre meschans. Ils ne sont pas
si tost au college, qu'ils sont diables: pour le mauvais
exemple & mauvaise instruction qu'on leur baille. Le
pere, le maistre, le regent, iurent & yvrongnent devant
leurs enfans & serviteurs: ce n'est pas faire l'office
d'un bon pasteur qui entre par l'huys, qui ne dit rien
qu'il n'ayt ouy de Iesus Christ, & selon la doctrine de
son Eglise. Mais le larron contorque l'escriture, il ne
l'interprete pas selon le sens de Dieu mais selon son
iugement & affection privée. Il faict comme les
taverniers qui meslent l'eau parmy le vin. Aussi les
heretiques meslent leur doctrine, qui n'est qu'eau, à la
doctrine & parolle de nostre Seigneur, & de son Eglise,
qui est le bon vin. Et ainsi ils meslent de l'eau parmy
le vin, & vendent leur eau parmy le bon vin: ils
meslent leur doctrine parmy l'Evangile, afin qu'elle
semble avoir bon goust, & qu'elle soit receuë: car
autrement ils ne la pourroient faire passer. Ils ne sont
pas envoyez de Dieu, parquoy *sunt fures & latrones.*
Les vrayes brebis oyent la voix de leur pasteur, & non
past d'un estrangier. Et si vous l'oyez, c'est signe que
vous estes les brebis de Dieu. Les estrangiers, les
heretiques, ont l'Evangile, & l'escriture saincte à la
bouche: mais ils y mettent de leur eau parmy, &

*Les meschans gens
empeschent l'aide
de Dieu.*

*Le larron contorque
l'escriture, quand
il ne l'interprete
selon le sens de Dieu.*

Esa. 1.

gastent le bon vin, qui est l'escriture: c'est à dire, qu'ils
l'entendent & interpretent mal, à raison qu'ils suyvent
leur sens propre & particulier: ils parlent & inventent
d'eux mesmes. Et en ce faisant, ils sont larrons, car ils
desrobbent & perdent les ames: mais au contraire, le
bon pasteur n'excogite rien du sien, il ne dict sinon ce
qu'il a ouy, comme faict monsieur sainct Paul, qui dit:
Ego enim accepi à domino quod & tradidi vobis. Ce
que ie vous ay dit & enseigné, ie l'ay apprins de nostre
Seigneur Dieu. Sainct Paul, c'est celuy entre les autres,
qui a eu les conditions du bon pasteur, & qui a esté
plus imitateur de nostre Seigneur Iesus Christ, vray
pasteur de noz ames, il dit aux Corinthiens: *Ego autem
libentißimè impendam, & superimpendar ipse pro
animabus vestris.* La condition du bon pasteur, c'est de
mettre sa vie & ses biens pour ses brebis: il n'a à
regarder sinon au salut des ames, & non pas s'il est
aymé de cestuy cy, ou de cestuy-là. Quand nostre
Seigneur voulut instituer sainct Pierre, pasteur de son
Eglise, il luy demanda par trois fois: *Petre, diligis me
plus his? diligis me plus quàm te? plus quàm tua?
plus quàm tuos?* Le bon pasteur doit plus aymer Dieu
que soy-mesme, que ses biens, ne que ses parens &
amys. Et aussi qui n'a charité à son prochain, & qui ne
l'ayme, il ne peut aymer Dieu, comme dit S. Iean en sa
canonique: Si vous n'avez amour & charité à vostre
prochain, que vous voyez, comment l'aurez vous à
Dieu que vous ne voyez pas? Parquoy, le moyen pour
estre bon pasteur, c'est charité. Sainct Paul dit: *Nem &
ipsi scitis fratres, introitum nostrum ad vos, quia non
inanis fuit.* Sainct Paul n'a enseigné que toute
saincteté, & bonne doctrine, salutaire: & au contraire,
l'heretique enseigne erreur, immundicité, que les
prestres ne doivent point garder chasteté, qu'il ne faut
point obeir aux prelats, ne point ieusner, qu'il ne faut
point faire penitence, que les prestres seront mariez. Ie
te dis, qu'homme vivant ne sçauroit dispenser de cela:
car c'est un voeu solennel. Et encores plusieurs sont
en ceste opinion, que le simple voeu oblige: combien
doncques plus le voeu solennel? *Neque in dolo.* Il ne
faut rien prescher ne dire de bouche, qui ne soit au
cueur. La doctrine de S. Paul n'a point esté pour nous
tromper, ne en paroles d'adulation. *Neque enim*

I. Cor. 11.
S. Paul a les
conditions du
bon pasteur.

2. Cor. 12.

Ioan. 21.

I. Thessal. 2.
Comment S. Paul
enseigne toute
saincteté,
l'heretique au
contraire.

I. Thessal. 2.

aliquando fuimus in sermone adulationis. Et les
heretiques cherchent ces moyens là. *Neque in*
occasione avaritae, Deus testis est. Sainct Paul iure
qu'il n'a point presché par avarice, comme il dit aussi:
Argentum & aurum, aut vestem nullius concupivi,   *Act. 20.*
sicut ipsi scitis: quoniam ad ea quae mihi opus erant, &
his qui mecum sunt, ministraverunt manus istae.
Pour monstrer sa liberté, il n'a rien voulu prendre, il
en appelle Dieu à tesmoing, & dit, que ce pendant qu'il
vivra, qu'il ne prendra rien d'eux, afin que la parole &
Evangile de nostre Seigneur ne vienne à scandale. Et
luy a esté besoing de labourer de ses mains, pour
gaigner sa vie. *Neque quaerentes ab hominibus*   *I. Thessal. 2.*
gloriam, neque à vobis, neque ab aliis, cùm possemus
vobis oneri esse, &c. Ie ne demande point, dit-il, la
gloire des hommes, ne de vous, mais seulement
d'informer Iesus Christ en voz cueurs. Aussi a-il eu
ouverture, Dieu luy a ouvert l'huys: *Ostium enim*   *Dieu a ouver [sic]*
mihi apertum est. Dieu, voyant la grande affection de   *l'huys à sainct*
Sainct Paul, il luy a ouvert l'huys, c'est à dire, les   *Paul, voyant sa*
cueurs des auditeurs, afin d'avoir affection à la parole   *grande affection.*
de Dieu: & autrement on ne sçauroit proufiter: c'est
luy, *qui habet clavem David: claudit, & nemo aperit:*
aperit, & nemo claudit. Comme dit sainct Iean: *Et*
angelo Philadelphiae scribe Angelus. En cest endroit   *Apoc. 3.*
là, c'est à dire, *episcopus, pastor Philadelphiae, id est,*
amor fraternus. Escris à l'Evesque, au Pasteur, qu'il ait
devant ses yeux l'amour & charité de son frere, de son
prochain. L'huys, le cueur du prochain est ouvert
pour recevoir doctrine, & la parole de Dieu, quand il
voit son pasteur, & superieur parler d'amour, & de
charité fraternelle. *Non quaerentes ab hominibus*   *I. Thess. 2.*
gloriam. Nous avons presché, comme Iesus Christ
nous a faict dignes de l'Evangile, selon la probation
que Dieu a faict de nous, ne demandans point de
complaire à cestuy-cy, ny à cestuy là par flatterie: mais
Dieu qui regarde noz cueurs, que nous avons
seulement faict purement & simplement nostre charge
& office. I'ay esté entre vous comme une nourrice qui
nourrit ses petis enfans: ie vous aymois tant, que
i'estois content de donner mon ame, ma vie, & mourir
pour vous, pour vostre salut, *Ita desiderantes vos*

cupidè, volebamus tradere vobis, non solùm
evangelium Dei, sed etiam animas nostras, quoniam
chariβimi noviβimi facti estis. Vous sçavez en quelle
sincerité de cueur, nous vous avons admonestez de
vivre, comme il appartient à un bon Chrestien, pour la
reverence de nostre sauveur, & redempteur Iesus
Christ. Voyla la condition & maniere de faire du vray
pasteur. Toy pere, maistre, pedagogue, &c. tu dois ainsi
estre envers tes enfans, serviteurs & escoliers,
aucunesfois aspre & severe, mais plustost doux &
mansuet: car mansuetude gaigne, & faict plus que
rigueur, qui ne gaigne gueres ou point le cueur de
l'homme. Sainct Paul monstre bien l'amour &
affection qu'il a au prochain, quand il dit: *Quotidie*
morior propter vestram gloriam, fratres. O quel
pasteur, d'estre en ce vouloir de mourir tous les iours
pour ses brebis, pour ses subiects! Et pource, ne
defaillez point en la foy pour mes tribulations, quand
vous me voirrez endurer, & estre persecuté pour
soustenir la verité, le nom de nostre Seigneur: aussi les
subiects doivent prier pour leur pasteur & superieur,
afin qu'il plaise à Dieu, luy faire grace de bien faire son
office & sa charge, à l'honneur de Dieu, & au salut de   *Hebr. 13.*
ses subiects. Sainct Paul dit: *Obedite propositis vestris,*
& subiacete eis: Ipsi enim pervigilant quasi rationem
pro animabus vestris reddituri, ut cum gaudio hoc
faciant, & non gementes: hoc enim non expedit vobis.
C'est grand pitié, il en y a tant qui tiennent le lieu des
Apostres, & il n'en y a point, ou bien peu, qui s'en
rendent dignes. Nostre Seigneur dit qu'il cognoist ses
brebis, & elles le cognoissoient: aussi dit il qu'il a
d'autres brebis, qu'il doit amener à sa bergerie. *Habeo*
autem alias oves, quae non sunt ex hoc ovili. Le
commencement de l'Eglise a esté des Iuifs: *De Sion*
exibit lex, & verbum Domini de Ierusalem. Sont esté
les premiers congregez & assemblez, pour faire l'Eglise
de nostre Seigneur, il y avoit autres brebis, c'estoient
les Gentils: aussi nostre Seigneur n'y a pas esté
personnellement: mais il y a envoyé ses Apostres, pour
les prescher, les mener à la bergerie, à l'Eglise de
nostre Seigneur Iesus Christ. Et de ces deux bergeries
en a esté faicte une, soubs nostre Seigneur Iesus Christ,

grand pasteur, & soubs sainct Pierre son vicaire, qui est
Pape, & pareillement soubs son legitime successeur. Et
c'est ce que dit nostre Seigneur: *Fiet unum ovile, &
unus pastor.* Dieu nous doint grace d'estre tousiours
en ce tropeau, & la grace de Dieu pour parvenir au
Royaume de Paradis. Amen.

BIBLIOGRAPHY

Manuscript Sources

BN Dossiers bleus 429, "de Marle."
BN Dossiers bleus, 521, 13638.
BN Ms. fr. 4752, "Champagne."

Primary Sources

Aubespine, Claure de l'. "Histoire particulière de la cour de Henri II," *Archives curieuses de l'histoire de France*, sér. 1, 3 (1835), 295–296.
Aubusson de la Maisonneuve, Barbier. *Deploration sur le trespas de noble & vénérable personne monsieur maistre François Picard, Docteur en Théologie, Doyen de Sainct Germain de lauxerrois, qui mourut à Paris le dixseptiesme iour de Septembre, l'an mil cinq cens cinquante & six. Par un poète François*. Paris: Estienne Denise, 1556.
Benoist, René. *Homélie de la Nativité de Iesus Crist, en laquelle est clairement monstré l'office du vray Chrestien, par maistre René Benoist Angevin, bacchelier en théologie à Paris*. Paris: Claude Fremy, 1558.
Bèze, Théodore de. *Le passavant de Théodore de Bèze. Épître de Maître Benoît passavant à Messire Pierre Lizet*. Paris: Isidore Liseux, 1875.
──. *Histoire ecclésiastique des églises réformées au royaume de France. Édition nouvelle avec commentaire, notice bibliographique et tables des faits et des noms propres*, eds. G. Baum and E. Cunitz, vol. 1. Paris: Fischbacher, 1883.
Bobadilla Monumenta. Rome: MHSI, 1970.
Bourquelot, Félix, ed. *Mémoires de Claude Haton*. Paris: Imprimerie Impériale, 1857.
Bourrilly, V.-L., ed. *Le journal d'un bourgeois de Paris sous le règne de François Ier (1515–1536)*. Paris: Alphonse Picard, 1910.
Budé, Guillaume. *Epistolae Guilelmi Budaei*. Paris: Josse Bade, 1520.
──. *Epistolae Guilelmi Budaei, Secretarii Regii, Posteriores*. Paris: Josse Bade, 1522.
Calvin, John. *Des scandales qui empeschent auiourdhuy beaucoup de gens de venir à la pure doctrine de l'Évangile, & en desbauchent d'autres*. Geneva: Jean Crespin, 1550.
──. *Tracts and Treatises in Defense of the Reformed Faith*, trans. Henry Beveridge, vol. III. Grand Rapids: W.B. Eerdmans, 1958.
──. *Opera quae sunt omnia*. Braunschweig and Berlin: Schwetschke, 1890.
Campardon, Émile and Tuetey, Alexandre. *Inventaire des registres des insinuations du Châtelet de Paris: Règnes de François Ier et de Henri II*. Paris: Imprimerie Nationale, 1906.
Catalogue des actes de François I. Collection des ordonnances des rois de France. Paris: Imprimerie nationale, 1885–1908.
Cazauran, Nicole, ed. *Discours merveilleux de la vie, action & deportements de Catherine de Médicis, Royne-mère*. Geneva: Droz, 1995.
Clerval, Jules-Alexandre, ed. *Registre des procès-verbaux de la faculté de théologie: 1505–1523*. Paris: Lecoffre and Gabalda, 1917.
Concasty, Marie-Louise, ed. *Commentaires de la faculté de médécine de l'université de Paris (1516–1560). Documents inédits sur l'histoire de France*. Paris: Imprimerie nationale, 1964.

Couillard, Anthoine. *Les contredicts du Seigneur du Pavillon, les Lorriz, en Gastinois, aux faulses & abbusifves propheties de Nostradamus, & autres astrologues.* Paris: Charles L'Angelier, 1560.

Coyecque, Ernest. *Recueil d'actes notariés relatifs à l'histoire de Paris et de ses environs au XVIᵉ siècle.* Paris: Imprimerie nationale, 1905–1924.

Crespin, Jean. *Histoire des martyrs persecutez et mis à mort pour la veritee de l'evangile, depuis le temps des apostres iusques à present (1619).* Toulouse: Société des livres religieux, 1885.

De Bujanda, J.M., Higman, Francis M., and Farge, James K., eds. *Index de l'Université de Paris 1544, 1545, 1547, 1549, 1551, 1556.* Sherbrooke: Librairie Droz, 1985.

Delisle, Léopold. "Notice sur un régistre des procès-verbaux de la faculté de théologie de Paris pendant les années 1505–1533," *Notices et extraits des manuscrits de la Bibliothèque Nationale et autres bibliothèques* 36(1899), 317–407.

Désiré, Artus. *Les regretz et complainctes de Passe partout et Bruictquicourt, sur la mémoire renouwellée du trespas et bout de l'an, de feu tres noble et venerable personne Maistre Françoys Picart, docteur en théologie et grand doyen de sainct Germain de l'Aucerroys.* Paris: Pierre Gaultier, 1557.

De Thou, Jacques-Auguste. *Histoire universelle, depuis 1543 jusqu'en 1607.* London, 1734.

Dupèbe, Jean, ed. *Nostradamus: Lettres Inédites.* Geneva: Droz, 1983.

Duplessis-d'Argentré, Charles. *Collectio judiciorum de novis erroribus qui ab initio duodecimi saeculi . . . usque ad annum 1632 in ecclesia proscripti sunt et notati . . .* Paris: A. Cailleau, 1727–1736.

Dupuiherbault, Gabriel. *De penitence, et des parties d'icelle, selon la verité de l'Eglise orthodoxe & catholique, & la necessité de salut . . . auquel sont adiouxtez les Epitaphes de feu Monsieur Picart.* Paris: Jean de Roigny, 1557.

Epistolae PP. Paschasii Broëti, Claudi Jaji, Joannis Codurii et Simonis Rodericii. Madrid: Gabriel Lopez del Horno, 1903.

Farge, James K., ed. *Registre des procès-verbaux de la Faculté de Théologie de l'Université de Paris de janvier 1524 à novembre 1533.* Paris: Aux amateurs du livre, 1990.

Fontaine, Simon. *Histoire catholique de nostre temps, touchant l'estat de la religion chrestienne, par F. Simon Fontaine de l'ordre de S. François & Docteur en Theologie à Paris. Enrichie de plusieurs choses notables depuis l'an 1546 iusques à l'an 1550.* Paris: Claude Frémy, 1562.

Fontes narrativi de S. Ignatio de Loyola et de Societatis Iesu initiis. I: Narrationes scriptae ante annum 1557. Rome: MHSI, 1943.

Fontes narrativi de S. Ignatio de Loyola et de Societatis Iesu initiis. I: Narrationes scriptae 1557–1574. Rome: MHSI, 1951.

François, M., ed. *Correspondance du Cardinal François de Tournon.* Paris, 1946.

Gallia Christiana in provincias ecclesiasticas distributa: qua series et historia archiepiscoporum, episcoporum, et abbatum franciae vicinarumque ditionum. Paris: Victor Palme, 1970–1874.

Genin, F., ed. *Lettres de Marguerite d'Angoulême, soeur de François I, reine de Navarre.* Paris: J. Renouard, 1851.

Guiffrey, Georges, ed. *Chronique du Roy Françoys Premier.* Paris, 1860.

Grenier, Nicole. *Le bouclier de la foy, en forme de dialogue, extraict de la saincte escripture, et des sainctz peres, et plus anciens docteurs de l'eglise, dedié au roy tres chrestien Henry, deuxiesme de ce nom, nouwellement imprimé à Paris en 1548 nouwellement reveu et augmenté par l'autheur.* Paris: Vivant Gaulteroit, 1548.

Herminjard, A.-J. *Correspondance des réformateurs dans les pays de langue français.* Geneva and Paris, 1886–1897.

Hilarion de Coste, F. *Le parfait ecclesiastique ou l'histoire de la vie et de la mort de François Le Picart, Seigneur d'Atilly & de Villerson, Docteur en Théologie de la Faculté de Paris & Doyen de Saint Germain de l'Auxerrois.* Paris: Sebastian Cramoisy, 1658.

Ignatius of Loyola. *The Spiritual Exercises and Selected Works*, ed. George E. Ganss. New York: Paulist Press, 1991.

———. *The Spiritual Exercises of St. Ignatius: Based on Studies in the Language of the Autograph*, ed. and trans. Louis J. Puhl. Chicago: Loyola University Press, 1951.

———. *The Spiritual Exercises of Saint Ignatius of Loyola and the Directorium in Exercitia*, ed. and trans. W.H. Longridge. London: A.R. Mowbray, 1955.

Lalanne, L., ed. *Journal de Bourgeois de Paris sous le règne de François I.* Paris, 1854.

Launoy, Jean de. *Regii Navarrae Gymnasii Parisiensis Historia.* Paris, 1677.

———. *Opera omnia.* Cologne: Fabri & Barillot et Marci-Michaelis Bousquet, 1732.

Le Picart, François. *Épistre, contenant un traicté auquel est monstré combien est grande la charité de Iesus Christ en l'institution de la saincte communion de son pretieux corps & sang, au S. Sacrement de l'Autel.* Paris: Nicolas Chesneau, 1564.

———. *Instruction et forme de prier Dieu en vraye & parfaite oraison, faite en forme de sermons, sur l'Oraison Dominicale, par M. François le Picart, Docteur en Théologie.* Reims: Nicolas Bacquenois, 1557.

———. *Les grans souffrages et oraisons.* Rouen: Nicolas Vaultier, n.d.

———. *Le second livre du recueil des sermons.* Reims: Nicolas Bacquenois, 1560.

———. *Les sermons et instructions chrestiennes, pour tous les Dimenches, & toutes les festes des saincts, depuis la Trinité iusques à l'Advent,* 2 parts. Paris: Nicolas Chesneau, 1566.

———. *Les sermons et instructions chrestiennes, pour tous les iours de caresme, & Feries de Pasques,* 2 parts. Paris: Nicolas Chesneau, 1566.

———. *Les sermons et instructions chrestiennes, pour tous les iours de l'Advent, iusques à Noël: & de tous les Dimenches & Festes, depuis Noël iusques à Caresme.* Paris: Nicolas Chesneau, 1566.

———. *Les sermons et instructions chrestiennes, pour tous les Dimenches & toutes les festes des saincts, depuis Pasques iusques à la Trinité.* Paris: Nicolas Chesneau, 1566.

Lestocquoy, J., ed. *Correspondance des nonces en France: Carpi et Ferrerio 1535–1540 et légations de Carpi et de Farnèse.* Paris: E. de Boccard, 1961.

Litterae quadrimestres ex universis praeter Indiam et Brasiliam locis in quibus aliqui de Societate Jesu versabantur Romam missae. Madrid: Augustinus Avrial, 1895.

Longéon, Claude, ed. *La farce des théologastres.* Geneva: Droz, 1989.

Marchand, Charles. *Documents pour l'histoire du règne de Henri II.* Paris, 1902.

Maugis, E. *Histoire du parlement de Paris à l'avènement des rois Valois à la mort d'Henri IV.* Paris, 1913–16.

Maur, Rabanus. *In ecclesiasticum commentarii, recens in lucem editi.* Paris: Simon Colinoeum, 1544.

Nostradamus, Michel de. *Les propheties de M. Michel de Nostradamus dont il y a trois cens qui n'ont encore jamais été imprimées.* Lyon: Benoist Rigaud, 1568.

———. *Prognostication, et amples predictions, pour l'an de Iesus Christ, mil cinq cens soixante-sept. An Embolismal. A Monseigneur François Duc d'Alençon.* Paris: Guillaume de Nyverd, 1566.

Palladius. *Dialogue on the Life of St. John Chrysostom*, ed. Robert T. Meyer. New York: Newman Press, 1985.

Paradin, G. *Continuation de l'histoire de nostre temps depuis l'an mil cinq cens cinquante iusques à l'an mil cinq cens cinquante six.* Paris: Guillaume de la Nouë, 1575.

———. *Histoire de nostre temps.* Lyons, 1550.

Pasquier, Estienne. *Lettres historiques pour les années 1556–1594*, annot. D. Thickett. Geneva: Droz, 1966.

Pepin, Guillaume. *Concionum dominicalium ex epistolis et evangeliis totius anni, pars aestivalis.* Antwerp: Guillelmus Lesteenius and Engelbertus Gymnicus, 1656.

———. *Concionum dominicalium ex epistolis et evangeliis totius anni, pars hiemalis.* Antwerp: Guillelmus Lesteenius and Engelbertus Gymnicus, 1656.

Polanco, Joanne Alphonso de. *Vita Ignatii Loiolae et rerum Societatis Jesu.* Madrid: MHSI, 1894.

Possevino, Antonio. *Apparatus sacer.* Venice: Venetian Society, 1603.

Rabelais, François. *Garantua and Pantagruel*, trans. Burton Raffael. New York: W.W. Norton, 1991.

Ronsard, Pierre. *Poésies choisies*. Paris: Boradas, 1989.

Tisserand, Jean. *Sermones de adventu*. Paris, 1517.

Tuetey, Alexandre. *Inventaire des registres des insinuations du Châtelet de Paris, règnes de François Ier et de Henri II*. Paris: Imprimerie nationale, 1906.

Vacquerie, Jean de la. *Remonstrance adressée au roy, aux princes catholiques, et à tous Magistrats & Gouverneurs de Republiques, touchant l'abolition des troubles & emotions qui se sont auiourd'huy en France, causez par les heresies qui y regnent & par la Chrestienté*. Paris: Jean Poupy, 1574.

Viret, Pierre. *De la communication des fideles qui cognoissent la verité de l'Evangile, aux ceremonies des Papistes, & principalement à leurs baptesmes, mariages, messes, funerailles, & obseques pour les trespassez*. Geneva: No publisher given, 1547.

——. *Dialogue du desordre qui est à present au monde, et des causes d'iceluy, & du moyen pour y remedier: Desquelz l'ordre & le tiltre sensuit*. Geneva: No publisher given, 1545.

——. *La necromance papale, faites par dialogues en maniere de devis*. Geneva: No publisher given, 1553.

Secondary Sources

Armstrong, Megan. *The Franciscans in Paris, 1560–1600*. Unpublished Ph.D. dissertation, University of Toronto, 1998.

Aveling, J.C.H. *The Jesuits*. London: Blond & Briggs, 1981.

Babelon, Jean-Pierre. *Nouvelle histoire de Paris: Paris au XVIᵉ siècle*. Paris: Hachette, 1986.

Baker, Joanne. "Female Monasticism and Family Strategy: The Guises and St. Pierre de Reims," *Sixteenth Century Journal* 28(1997), 1091–1108.

Bakhtin, Mikhail. *Rabelais and His World*. Bloomington: Indiana University Press, 1984.

Bangert, William V. *Claude Jay and Alfonso Salmerón: Two Early Jesuits*. Chicago: Loyola University Press, 1985.

——. *To the Other Towns: A Life of Blessed Peter Favre, First Companion of St. Ignatius*. Westminster, MD: The Newman Press, 1959.

——. *A History of the Society of Jesus*. St. Louis: The Institute of Jesuit Sources, 1972.

Barnes, Robin Bruce. *Prophecy and Gnosis: Apocalypticism in the Wake of the Lutheran Reformation*. Stanford: Stanford University Press, 1988.

Baumgartner, Frederic J. *Henri II: King of France 1547–1559*, Durham: Duke University Press, 1988.

——. *Change and Continuity in the French Episcopate: The Bishops and the Wars of Religion, 1547–1610*. Durham: Duke University Press, 1986.

——. *France in the Sixteenth Century*. New York: St. Martin's, 1995.

——. *Louis XII*. New York: St. Martin's, 1994.

——. "Review of Denis Crouzet, *Guerriers de Dieu: La violence au temps des troubles de religion (vers 1525–vers 1610)*," in *Catholic Historical Review* 78(1992), 113–116.

Bellenger, Yvonne, ed. *Le mécénat et l'influence des Guises: Actes du colloque tenu à Joinville du 31 mai au 4 juin 1994*. Paris: Honoré Champion, 1997.

Benedict, Philip, "Review of Denis Crouzet, *Guerriers de Dieu*," in *Social History* 17(1992), 117–120.

Bense, Walter F. "Noël Beda and the Humanist Reformation at Paris, 1504–1534." Unpublished Ph.D. dissertation, Harvard University, 1967.

——. "Noël Beda's View of the Reformation," *American Society for Reformation Research* 1(1977), 93–107.

Bernard-Maître, Henri. "Les 'théologastres' de l'université de Paris au temps d'Érasme et de Rabelais (1496–1536)," *Bibliothèque de l'humanisme et renaissance. Travaux et documents* 27(1965), 248–264.

———. "François Le Picart, docteur de la faculté de théologie de Paris et les débuts de la Compagnie de Jésus (1534–1556)," *Bulletin de littérature ecclésiastique (1954)*, 90–117.

———. "Ignace de Loyola, étudiant de théologie à Paris?" *Revue d'histoire de l'église de France* 45(1959), 72–76.

———. "L'inquisiteur dominicain Mathieu Ory et son *Alexipharmacon* contre les hérétiques (1544)," *Revue des sciences religieuses* 30(1956), 241–260.

———. "Un théoricien de la contemplation à la Chartreuse parisienne de Vauvert: Pierre Cousturier dit Sutor (c. 1480–18 juin 1537)," *Revue d'ascétique et mystique* 32(1956), 174–196.

———. "La préréforme humaniste de l'Université de Paris aux origines de la Compagnie de Jésus (1525–1536)," in *L'homme devant Dieu: Mélanges offerts au Père Henri de Lubac*, vol. 2. (Paris: Aubier, 1964), 223–233.

———. "Calvin et Loyola," *Association Guillaume Budé, 3ème sér.* 2(1953), 74–85.

———. "Les fondateurs de la compagnie de Jésus et l'humanisme Parisien de la Renaissance (1525–1536)," *Nouvelle revue théologique* 72(1950), 811–833.

Berthoud, Gabrielle. "La 'confession' de Maître Noël Beda et le problème de son auteur," *Bibliothèque d'humanisme et renaissance* 29(1967), 373–397.

———, ed. *Aspects de la propagande religieuse*. Geneva: Droz, 1957.

Bibliothèque Nationale. *Guillaume Budé*. Paris: BN, 1968.

Boussinesq, Georges and Laurent, Gustave. *Histoire de Reims depuis les origines jusqu'à nos jours. Tome I: Reims ancien des temps préhistoriques à la mort d'Henri IV*. Reims: Matot-Braine, 1933.

Bouwsma, William J. *John Calvin: A Sixteenth-Century Portrait*. New York: Oxford University Press, 1988.

Bower, H.M. *The Fourteen of Meaux*. London: Longmans, Green and Co., 1894.

Brodrick, James. *The Origin of the Jesuits*. Westport, CT: Greenwood Press, 1971.

Brueggemann, Walter. "The Book of Jeremiah: Portrait of the Prophet," in James Luther Mays and Paul J. Achtemeier, eds., *Interpreting the Prophets*. Philadelphia: Fortress Press, 1987, pp. 113–129.

Burke, Peter, ed. *A New Kind of History from the Writings of Febvre*. New York: Harper & Row Publishers, 1973.

Busson, Henri. "Les églises contre Rabelais," *Études rabelaisiennes* 7(1967), 1–81.

Cameron, Richard M. "The Charges of Lutheranism Brought Against Jacques Lefèvre d'Étaples (1520–1529)," *Harvard Theological Review* 63(1970), 119–149.

Carrière, Victor. "La Sorbonne et l'Évangélisme au XVIᵉ siècle," in *Aspects de l'Université de Paris*. Paris: Albin Michel, 1949, pp. 159–186.

———. "Guillaume Farel: Propagandiste de la Réformation." *Revue d'histoire de l'église de France* 20(1934), 37–78.

Cesareo, Francesco C. "Penitential Sermons in Renaissance Italy: Girolamo Seripando and the Pater Noster," *Catholic Historical Review* 83(1997), 1–19.

Champion, Pierre. *Catherine de Médicis présenté à Charles IX son royaume (1564–1566)*. Paris: n.d.

Chaunu, Pierre. *Église, culture et société: Essais sur réforme et contre-réforme 1517–1620*. Paris: SEDES, 1984.

Chevalier, Bernard. "Olivier Maillard et la réforme des Cordeliers (1482–1502)," *Revue d'histoire de l'église de France* 65(1979), 25–39.

Clancy, Thomas H. *An Introduction to Jesuit Life: The Constitution and History through 435 Years*. St. Louis: The Institute of Jesuit Sources, 1976.

Conwell, Joseph F., S.J. *Impelling Spirit: Revisiting a Founding Experience: 1539 Ignatius Loyola and His Companions*. Chicago: Loyola Press, 1997.

Crimando, Thomas. "Two French Views of the Council of Trent," *Sixteenth Century Journal* 19(1988), 169–186.

Crouvezier, G. *La vie d'une cité Reims au cours des siècles*. Paris: Nouvelles Éditions Latines, 1970.

Crouzet, Denis. *Les guerriers de Dieu: La violence au temps des troubles de religion (vers 1525–vers 1610)*. Paris: Champ Vallon, 1990.

——. *La nuit de la Saint-Barthélemy*. Paris: Fayard, 1994.

——. *La genèse de la Réforme française, 1520–1562*. Paris: SEDES, 1996.

Crozet, René. "Les églises rurales de la Champagne orientale et méridionale du XIIIe au XVIe siècle," *Bulletin monumental* 89(1930), 355–397.

Dagens, Jean. *Bibliographie chronologique de la littérature de spiritualité et de ses sources (1501–1610)*. Paris, 1952.

Dahmus, John. "Preaching to the Laity in Fifteenth Century Germany: Johannes Nider's 'Harps,'" *Journal of Ecclesiastical History* 12(1982), 55–68.

Darricau, Raymond. "La réforme des reguliers en France de la fin du XVIe siècle à la fin des guerres de religion," *Revue d'histoire de l'église de France* 65 (1979), 5–12.

Delaruelle, Louis. *Guillaume Budé: Les origines, les débuts, les idées maîtresses*. Paris: Honoré Champion, 1907.

——. "L'étude du Grec à Paris de 1514 à 1530," *Études Rabelaisiennes* 9(1922), 132–149.

——. *Répertoire analytique et chronologique de la correspondance de Guillaume Budé*. Toulouse: Édouard Privat, 1907.

Delumeau, Jean. *Sin and Fear: The Emergence of a Western Guilt Culture 13th–18th Centuries*. New York: St. Martin's, 1990.

——. "Une histoire totale de la Renaissance," *Journal of Medieval and Renaissance Studies* 22(1992), 1–17.

De Nicolas, Antonio T. *Powers of Imagining: Ignatius de Loyola*. Albany: State University of New York Press, 1986.

Denifle, H. "Quel livre servait de base à l'enseignement des maîtres en théologie dans l'Université de Paris?" *Revue Thomiste* 2(1894), 149–162.

Desportes, Pierre. *Histoire de Reims*. Toulouse: Privat, 1983.

——. "La population de Reims au XVe siècle," *Moyen Age* 72(1966), 463–508.

Devèche, André. *L'église Saint-Germain l'Auxerrois de Paris: Paroisse royale*. Paris: SIDES, n.d.

Diefendorf, Barbara. *Beneath the Cross: Catholics and Huguenots in Sixteenth-Century Paris*. New York: Oxford University Press, 1992.

——. *Paris City Councillors in the Sixteenth Century: The Politics of Patrimony*. Princeton: Princeton University Press, 1983.

——. "Prologue to a Massacre: Popular Unrest in Paris, 1557–1572," *American Historical Review* 90(1985), 1067–1091.

——. "Recent Literature on the Religious Conflicts in Sixteenth-Century France," *Religious Studies Review* 10(1984), 362–367.

——. "Les divisions religieuses dans les familles parisiennes avant la Saint-Barthélemy," *Histoire, économie et société* 7(1988), 55–78.

——. "Houses Divided: Religious Schism in Sixteenth-Century Parisian Families," in Susan Zimmerman and Ronald F.E. Weissman, eds., *Urban Life in the Renaissance*. Newark: University of Delaware Press, 1989, pp. 80–99.

——. "Simon Vigor: A Radical Preacher in Sixteenth-Century Paris," *Sixteenth Century Journal* 18(1987), 399–410.

——. "Review of Denis Crouzet, *Guerriers de Dieu: La violence au temps des troubles de religion (vers 1525–vers 1610)*," in *American Historical Review* 99(1994), 241–242.

Doucet, Roger. *Les bibliothèques parisiennes au XVIe siècle*. Paris, 1956.

Doumergue, Émile. *Jean Calvin: Les hommes et les choses de son temps*, vol. I. Lausanne: Georges Bridel, 1899.

——. "Paris Protestant au XVIe siècle," *Bulletin de la société de l'histoire du protestantisme français* 45(1896), 113–132.

Evennett, H. Outram. *The Cardinal of Lorraine and the Council of Trent: A Study in the Counter-Reformation*. Cambridge: Cambridge University Press, 1930.

——. *The Spirit of the Counter-Reformation: The Birkbeck Lectures in Ecclesiastical History Given in the University of Cambridge in May 1951.* Cambridge: Cambridge University Press, 1968.

Farge, James K. *Biographical Register of Paris Doctors of Theology 1500–1536.* Toronto: Pontifical Institute of Medieval Studies, 1980.

——. *Orthodoxy and Reform in Early Reformation France: The Faculty of Theology of Paris, 1500–1543.* Leiden: E.J. Brill, 1985.

——. *Le parti conservateur au XVIᵉ siècle: Université et parlement de Paris à l'époque de la Renaissance et de la Réforme.* Paris: Documents et Inédits du Collège de France, 1992.

——. *Registre des conclusions de l'université de Paris (1533–1550), vol. II.* Paris: Klincksieck, 1994.

——. "Marguerite de Navarre, Her Circle, and the Censors of Paris," in Régine Reynolds-Cornell, ed., *International Colloquium Celebrating the 500th Anniversary of the Birth of Marguerite de Navarre* (Birmingham, AL: Summa Publications, 1995), 15–28.

——. Review of Denis Crouzet, *La genèse de la Réforme française 1520–1562,* in *Sixteenth Century Journal* 28(1997), 1013–1016.

——. "Early Censorship in Paris: A New Look at the Roles of the Parlement of Paris and of King Francis I," *Renaissance and Reformation* 13(1989), 173–183.

Favier, Jean. *Nouvelle histoire de Paris: Paris au XVᵉ siècle 1380–1500.* Paris: Hachette, 1974.

Febvre, Lucien. *The Problem of Unbelief in the Sixteenth Century: The Religion of Rabelais,* trans. Beatrice Gottlieb. Cambridge: Cambridge University Press, 1982.

——. *Au coeur religieux du XVIᵉ siècle.* Paris, 1957.

——. "Dolet propagateur de l'évangile." *Bibliothèque d'humanisme et renaissance* 67(1945), 98–170.

Febvre, Lucien and Martin, Henri-Jean. *The Coming of the Book: The Impact of Printing, 1450–1800.* NLB, 1979.

Féret, Pierre-Yves. *La faculté de théologie de Paris et ses docteurs les plus célèbres. Époque moderne,* vols. *1–2: 16th Century.* Paris: Picard, 1900–1910.

Foisil, Madeleine. "Guillaume Budé (1467–1540)," in R. Mousnier et al., *Le Conseil du Roi* (Paris, 1970), 277–292.

Fosseyeux, Marcel. "Processions et pélérinages parisiens sous l'ancien régime," *Bulletin de la Société de l'histoire de l'Ile-de-France* 71–72(1944–45), 19–43.

Galpern, A.N. *The Religions of the People in Sixteenth-Century Champagne.* Cambridge: Harvard University Press, 1976.

Ganoczy, Alexandre. *The Young Calvin.* Philadelphia: Westminster Press, 1987.

Garrisson, Janine. *A History of Sixteenth-Centurh France, 1483–1598: Renaissance, Reformation and Rebellion.* New York: St. Martin's Press, 1995.

Garside, Charles, Jr. "'La farce des théologastres': Humanism, Heresy, and the Sorbonne, 1523–1525," *Rice University Studies* 60(1974), 45–82.

Giese, Frank. *Artus Désiré: Priest and Pamphleteer of the Sixteenth Century.* Chapel Hill: North Carolina Studies in the Romance Languages and Literatures, 1973.

Gilmont, Jean-François. *Les écrits spirituels des premiers jésuites: Inventaire commenté.* Rome: Institutum Historicum S.I., 1961.

Gilmore, Myron P. "Valla, Érasme, et Bédier à propos du Nouveau Testament," in *L'humanisme français au début de la renaissance. Colloque International de Tours (XIVᵉ stage).* Paris: Vrin, 1973.

Godet, Marcel. "Consultation de Tours pour la réforme de l'église de France (12 novembre 1493)," *Revue d'histoire de l'église de France* 2(1911), 175–196, 333–348.

——. *La congrégation de Montaigu (1490–1580).* Paris: Honoré Champion, 1912.

Godineau, G. "Status synodaux inédits du diocèse de Bourges promulgués par Jean Coeur en 1451," *Revue d'histoire de l'église de France* 72(1989), 49–66.

Greengrass, Mark. *The French Reformation.* Oxford: Basil Blackwell, 1987.

Gray, Janet. "The Origin of the Word Huguenot," *Sixteenth Century Journal* 14(1983), 349–359.

———. "Review Article: The Psychology of Religious Violence." *French History* 5(1991), 467–474.

Gregory, Timothy E. *Vox Populi: Popular Opinion and Violence in the Religious Controversies of the Fifth Century A.D.* Columbus: Ohio State University Press, 1979.

Griffiths, Gordon. "Louise of Savoy and Reform of the Church," *Sixteenth Century Journal* 10(1979), 29–36.

Guibert, Joseph de. *The Jesuits: Their Spiritual Doctrine and Practice: A Historical Study.* Chicago: Loyola University Press, 1964.

Guignard, Jacques. "Imprimeurs et libraires parisiens 1525–1536," *Bulletin de l'Association Guillaume Budé, 3ème sér.* 2(1953), 43–73.

Gundersheimer, Werner L., ed. *French Humanism 1470–1600.* New York: Harper Torchbooks, 1969.

Guy, Jean-Claude, "Les 'Exercices Spirituels' de Saint Ignace," *Nouvelle revue théologique* 107(1985), 255–260.

Haliczer, Stephen. *Sexuality in the Confessional: A Sacrament Profaned.* New York: Oxford University Press, 1996.

Hauser, Henri. *Les sources de l'histoire de France au XVIe siècle.* Paris, 1909.

Heller, Henry. "Marguerite of Navarre and the Reformers of Meaux." *Bibliothèque d'humanisme et renaissance* 33(1971), 271–310.

Hempsall, David. "Measures to Suppress 'La Peste Luthérienne' in France, 1521–2," in *Bulletin of the Institute of Historical Research* 120(1976), 296–299.

Higman, F.M. "Theology in French: Religious Pamphlets from the Counter-Reformation," *Renaissance and Modern Studies* 23(1979), 128–146.

———. *Censorship and the Sorbonne: A Bibliographical Study of Books in French Censured by the Faculty of Theology of the University of Paris, 1520–1551.* Geneva, 1979.

Holladay, John S., Jr., "Assyrian Statecraft and the Prophets of Israel," in David L. Petersen, ed., *Prophecy in Israel: Search for an Identity.* Philadelphia: Fortress Press, 1987, pp. 122–143.

Holt, Mack P. *The French Wars of Religion, 1562–1629.* Cambridge: Cambridge University Press, 1995.

———. "Putting Religion Back into the Wars of Religion," *French Historical Studies* 18(1993), 524–551.

Humphreys, W. Lee. *Crisis and Story: Introduction to the Old Testament.* Mountain View, CA: Mayfield Publishing Co., 1990.

Hyrvoix, A. "Noël Bédier d'après les documents inédits, 1533–1534," *Revue des questions historiques* 72(1903), 578–591.

Imbart de la Tour, Pierre. *Les origines de la réforme.* Geneva: Slatkine Reprints, 1978.

Jadart, Henri. *Les débuts de l'imprimerie à Reims et les marques des premiers imprimeurs 1550–1650.* Reims: Imprimerie et lithographie de l'indépendant Rémois, 1893.

Jouanna, Arlette. *La France du XVIe siècle: 1483–1598.* Paris: Presses universitaires de France, 1996.

Kelley, Donald R. *The Beginning of Ideology: Consciousness and Society in the French Reformation.* Cambridge: Cambridge University Press, 1981.

King, Philip J. *Jeremiah: An Archeological Companion.* Louisville, KY: Westminster/John Knox Press, 1993.

Kingdon, Robert M. *Geneva and the Coming of the Wars of Religion in France 1555–1563.* Geneva: Droz, 1956.

Knecht, R.J. *Francis I.* Cambridge: Cambridge University Press, 1982.

———. *Renaissance Warrior and Patron: The Reign of Francis I.* Cambridge: Cambridge University Press, 1994.

Kraus, Michael J. "Patronage and Reform in the France of the Prereform: The Case of Clichtove," *Canadian Journal of History* 6(1971), 45–68.

Labitte, Charles. *De la démocratie chez les prédicateurs de la Ligue.* Paris: Joubert, 1841.
Ladurie, Emmanuel Le Roy. *The Royal French State 1460–1610.* Oxford: Blackwell, 1994.
Larmat, Jean. "Picrochole est-il Noël Beda?" *Travaux d'humanisme et renaissance* 8(1969), 12–25.
Lebeuf, l'Abbé. *Histoire de la ville et de tout le diocèse de Paris*, ed. Fernand Bournon. Paris, 1883–1891.
Leff, Gordon. *Paris and Oxford Universities in the Thirteenth and Fourteenth Centuries: An Institutional and Intellectual History.* New York: John Wiley, 1968.
Lemaître, Nicole. *Le Rouergue flamboyante: Le clergé et les fidèles du diocèse de Rodez 1417–1563.* Paris: Cerf, 1988.
Levi, A.H.T., ed. *Humanism in France At the End of the Middle Ages and in the Early Renaissance.* New York: Barnes & Noble, 1970.
Lhote, Amedée. *Histoire de l'imprimerie à Châlons-sur-Marne, 1488–1894.* Chalons, 1894.
Marcel, Raymond. "Pic de la Mirandole et la France de l'Université de Paris au Donjon de Vincennes," in *L'Opera e il pensiero di Giovanni Pico della Mirandola nella storia dell'umanesimo, Convegno Internazionale Mirandola 15–18 Settembre 1963: I: Relazioni.* Florence: Nella Sede Dell'Instituto, 1965, 205–230.
Margolin, Jean-Claude. "Humanism in France," in Anthony Goodman and Angus MacKay, eds., *The Impact of Humanism on Western Europe.* New York: Longman, 1990.
Marichal, Robert. "Rabelais et les censures de la Sorbonne," *Études Rabelaisiennes* 9(1971), 135–150.
Marlorat, Guillaume. *Histoire de la ville, cité et université de Reims: Métropolitaine de la Gaule Belgique.* Reims: L. Jacquet, 1846.
Martin, A. Lynn. *The Jesuit Mind: The Mentality of an Elite in Early Modern France.* Ithaca: Cornell University Press, 1988.
———. "The Jesuit Émond Auger and the Saint Bartholomew's Massacre at Bordeaux: The Final Word?" in Jerome Friedman, ed., *Regnum, Religio et Ratio: Essays Presented to Robert M. Kingdon.* Kirksville: Sixteenth Century Essays and Studies, 1987, 117–124.
Martin, Hervé. "La ministère de la parole en France septentrionale de la peste noire à la réforme," *thèse d'état*, Université de Paris IV, 1986.
Marvick, Elizabeth. "Pyschobiography and the Early Modern French Court: Notes on Method with Some Examples," *French Historical Studies* 19(1996), 943–965.
Mays, James L. "Justice: Perspectives from the Prophetic Tradition," in David L. Petersen, ed., *Prophecy in Israel: Search for an Identity.* Philadelphia: Fortress Press, 1987, pp. 144–158.
Mays, James Luther and Achtemeier, Paul J. *Interpreting the Prophets.* Philadelphia: Fortress Press, 1987.
McFarlane, I.D. *A Literary History of France: Renaissance France, 1470–1589.* New York: Barnes & Noble, 1974.
McGinness, Frederick J. *Right Thinking and Sacred Oratory in Counter-Reformation Rome.* Princeton: Princeton University Press, 1995.
McGrath, Alister E. *A Life of John Calvin: A Study in the Shaping of Western Culture.* Oxford: Basil Blackwell, 1990.
McNeil, David O. *Guillaume Budé and Humanism in the Reign of Francis I.* Geneva: Droz, 1975.
Meissner, W.W. *The Psychology of a Saint: Ignatius of Loyola.* New Haven: Yale University Press, 1992.
Michaud, Hélène. *La grande chancellerie et les écritures royales au seizième siècle (1515–1589).* Paris: Presses universitaires de France, 1967.
Millin, Aubin-Louis. *Antiquités nationales, ou recueil de monuments, pour servir à l'histoire générale et particulière de l'Empire François.* Paris: M. Drouhin, 1792.

Mitchell, David. *The Jesuits: A History*. London: MacDonald Futura Publishers, 1980.

Monter, William. "Review of Denis Crouzet, *Guerriers de Dieu: La violence au temps des troubles de religion (vers 1525–vers 1610)*," in *Sixteenth Century Journal* 22(1991), 557–558.

Newsome, James D., Jr. *The Hebrew Prophets*. Atlanta: John Knox Press, 1973.

Nicholls, David. "The Social History of French Reformation: Ideology, Confession and Culture," *Social History* 9(1984), 25–43.

———. "Inertia and Reform in the Pre-Tridentine French Church: The Response to Protestantism in the Diocese of Rouen, 1520–1562," *Journal of Ecclesiastical History* 32(1981), 185–197.

———. "The Theatre of Martyrdom in the French Reformation." *Past and Present* 121(1988), 49–73.

———. "The Nature of Popular Heresy in France, 1520–1542," *The Historical Journal* 26(1983), 261–275.

Norman, Corrie E. *Humanist Taste and Franciscan Values: Cornelio Musso and Catholic Preaching in Sixteenth-Century Italy*. New York: Peter Lang, 1998.

Nugent, Donald. *Ecumenism in the Age of Reformation: The Colloquy of Poissy*. Cambridge: Harvard, 1974.

O'Leary, Brian. "The Discernment of Spirits in the *Memoriale* of Blessed Peter Favre," *The Way* 35(1979), 1–140.

Olin, John C. *Catholic Reform from Cardinal Ximénes to the Council of Trent, 1495–1563*. New York: Fordham University Press, 1990.

O'Malley, John W. *The First Jesuits*. Cambridge: Harvard University Press, 1993.

Paetow, Louis John. *The Arts Course at Medieval Universities with Special Reference to Grammar and Rhetoric*. Champaign, IL: University of Illinois Press, 1910.

Pannier, Jacques. "L'abbaye de Notre-Dame et les Budés, seigneurs d'Yerres aux XVI et XVIIe siècles," *Bulletin de la société de l'histoire du protestantisme français* 48(1899), 386–388.

Pasquier, Émile. *René Benoist: Le pape des Halles (1521–1608)*. Paris: Alphonse Picard, 1913.

Peter, Rodolphe. "La réception de Luther en France au XVIe siècle," *Revue d'histoire et de philosophie religieuse* 63(1983), 67–89.

Petersen, David L., ed. *Prophecy in Israel: Search for an Identity*. Philadelphia: Fortress Press, 1987.

Piton, M. "L'idéal épiscopal selon les prédicateurs français de la fin du XVe siècle et du début du XVIe," *Revue d'histoire de l'église de France* 52(1966), 77–118, 393–423.

Popoff, Michel. *Prosopographie des gens du parlement de Paris (1266–1753)*. Paris: Références, 1996.

Potter, David. *A History of France 1460–1560: The Emergence of a Nation State*. New York: St. Martin's, 1995.

Prethes, Frederic M. *Life of John Chrysostom, Based on the Investigations of Neander, Böhringer, and Others*. Boston: John P. Jewett, 1854.

Reinburg, Virginia. "Popular Prayers in Late Medieval and Reformation France." Unpublished Ph.D. dissertation, Princeton University, 1985.

Renaudet, Augustin. "L'humanisme et l'enseignement de l'Université de Paris au temps de la Renaissance," in *Aspects de l'Université de Paris*. Paris: Albin Michel, 1949, pp. 135–155.

———. *Préréforme et humanisme à Paris pendant les premières guerres d'Italie (1494–1517)*. Paris: Argences, 1953.

Roberts, Penny. *A City in Conflict: Troyes During the French Wars of Religion*. Manchester and New York: Manchester University Press, 1996.

Rodriguez-Grahit, I., "Ignace de Loyola et le Collège Montaigu: L'influence de Standonk sur Ignace," *Bibliothèque d'humanisme et renaissance* 20(1958), 388–401.

Roelker, Nancy Lyman. *One King, One Faith: The Parlement of Paris and the Religious Reformations of the Sixteenth Century*. Berkeley: University of California Press, 1996.

Rolland, Romain. "Le dernier procès de Louis de Berquin, 1527–1529," *Mélanges de l'école française de Rome* 12(1892), 314–325.

Roussel, Bernard. "Martin Bucer et Jacques Sadolet: La concorde possible (automne 1535)?" *Bulletin de la société de l'histoire du protestantisme français* 122(1976), 525–550.

Royannez, Marcel. "L'eucharistie chez les évangeliques et les premiers réformés français (1522–1546)," *Bulletin de la société de l'histoire du protestantisme français* 125(1979), 548–576.

Salmon, J.H.M. *Society in Crisis: France in the Sixteenth Century*. London: Methuen, 1975.

——. "Review of Denis Crouzet, *Guerriers de Dieu: La violence au temps des troubles de religion (vers 1525–vers 1610)*," in *Journal of Modern History* 63(1991), 775–779.

Samouillan, Alexandre. *Olivier Maillard: Sa prédication, son temps*. Toulouse: Privat, 1891.

Saulnier, V.L. "La correspondance de Marguerite de Navarre: Complément et répertoire," *Bibliothèque d'humanisme et renaissance* 33(1971), 571–603.

Sawyer, John F.A. *Prophecy and the Prophets of the Old Testament*. Oxford: Oxford University Press, 1987.

Schmidt, Charles. *Gérard Roussel: Prédicateur de la reine Marguerite de Navarre*. Geneva: Slatkine Reprints, 1970.

Schurhammer, Georg. *Francis Xavier: His Life, His Times, Vol. I: Europe, 1506–1541*. Rome: Jesuit Historical Institute, 1973.

Stevens, Linton C. "A Re-evaluation of Hellenism in the French Renaissance," in Werner L. Gundersheimer, ed., *French Humanism 1470–1600*. New York: Harper Torchbooks, 1969, pp. 181–196.

Sutherland, Nicola. *The Huguenot Struggle for Recognition*. New Haven: Yale University Press, 1980.

Sypher, G. Wylie. "'Faisant ce qu'il leur vient à plaisir': The Image of Protestantism in French Catholic Polemic on the Eve of the Religious Wars," *Sixteenth Century Journal* 11(1980), 59–84.

Tatarenko, Yves. "Les 'Sorbonnistes' face à Genève. La perception de Calvin et de la Réforme Genevoise par les théologiens catholiques Parisiens (1536–1564), in Olivier Millet, ed., *Calvin et ses contemporains: Actes du Colloque de Paris 1995*. Geneva: Droz, 1998, 135–148.

Taylor, Larissa. *Soldiers of Christ: Preaching in Late Medieval and Reformation France*. New York: Oxford University Press, 1992.

——. "Comme un chien mort: Preaching About Kingship in France," *Proceedings of the Western Society for French History* 22(1995), 157–170.

——. "The Influence of Humanism on Post-Reformation Catholic Preachers in France," *Renaissance Quarterly* 50(1997), 115–130.

——. "The Good Shepherd: François LePicart (1504–56) and Preaching Reform from Within," *Sixteenth Century Journal* 28(1997), 793–810.

——. "Out of Print: The Decline of Catholic Printed Sermons in France, 1530–1560," in Robin B. Barnes, Robert A. Kolb, and Paula Presley, eds., *Books Have Their Own Destiny: Essays in Honor of Robert V. Schnucker*. Kirksville, MO: Sixteenth Century Essays and Studies, 1998, 105–113.

——. "Funeral Sermons and Orations as Religious Propaganda in Sixteenth-Century France," in Bruce Gordon and Peter Marshall, eds., *The Place of the Dead in Early Modern Europe*. Cambridge: Cambridge University Press, 1999.

Tucker, Gene M. "The Role of the Prophets and the Role of the Church," in David L. Petersen, ed., *Prophecy in Israel: Search for an Identity*. Philadelphia: Fortress Press, 1987, pp. 159–174.

Turner, Victor. *Dramas, Fields, and Metaphors: Symbolic Action in Human Society*. Ithaca: Cornell University Press, 1987.

Tylenda, Joseph N. *A Pilgrim's Journey: The Autobiography of Ignatius of Loyola*. Wilmington, DE: Michael Glazier, 1985.

——, ed. *Counsels for Jesuits: Selected Letters and Instructions of Saint Ignatius Loyola.* Chicago: Loyola University Press, 1985.

Veissière, Michel. "Croyances et pratique religieuse à Meaux au temps de Guillaume Briçonnet (1525)," *Revue d'histoire de l'église de France* 67(1981), 55–59.

Venard, Marc. "Une réforme Gallicane? Le project de concile national de 1551," *Revue d'histoire de l'Église de France* 67(1981), 201–225.

——. "L'église d'Avignon," *thèse d'état*, Université de Paris IV, 1977.

von Rad, Gerhard. *The Message of the Prophets.* New York: Harper San Francisco, 1995.

Weiss, Nathanaël. "La Sorbonne, le parlement de Paris et les livres hérétiques de 1542 à 1546," *Bulletin de la société de l'histoire de Protestantisme Français* 34(1885), 19–28.

——. "La réformateur Aimé Meigret." *Bulletin d'humanisme et renaissance* 39(1890), 245–269.

——. *La chambre ardente: Étude sur la liberté de conscience en France sous François Ier et Henri II (1540–1550).* Paris: Fischbacher, 1889.

Weiss, Nathanaël and Bourrilly, Victor-Louis. "Jean Du Bellay, les Protestants, et la Sorbonne (1529–1535)," *Bulletin de la société de l'histoire du Protestantisme français* 52(1903), 97–127; 53(1904), 97–143.

——. "Une victime inconnue sous Henri II (Jean Thuret, 11 décembre 1550)," *Bulletin de la société de l'histoire du protestantisme français* 35(1886), 97–111.

Wilson, Robert R. *Prophecy and Society in Ancient Israel.* Philadelphia: Fortress Press, 1984.

INDEX OF NAMES

INDEX OF PLACES

SUBJECT INDEX

STUDIES IN MEDIEVAL
AND REFORMATION THOUGHT

EDITED BY HEIKO A. OBERMAN

15. KEMPFF, D. *A Bibliography of Calviniana.* 1959-1974. 1975 *out of print*
16. WINDHORST, C. *Täuferisches Taufverständnis.* 1976
17. KITTELSON, J. M. *Wolfgang Capito.* 1975
18. DONNELLY, J. P. *Calvinism and Scholasticism in Vermigli's Doctrine of Man and Grace.* 1976
19. LAMPING, A. J. *Ulrichus Velenus (Oldřich Velenský) and his Treatise against the Papacy.* 1976
20. BAYLOR, M. G. *Action and Person.* Conscience in Late Scholasticism and the Young Luther. 1977
21. COURTENAY, W. J. *Adam Wodeham.* 1978
22. BRADY, Jr., Th. A. *Ruling Class, Regime and Reformation at Strasbourg, 1520-1555.* 1978
23. KLAASSEN, W. *Michael Gaismair.* 1978
24. BERNSTEIN, A. E. *Pierre d'Ailly and the Blanchard Affair.* 1978
25. BUCER, Martin. *Correspondance.* Tome I (Jusqu'en 1524). Publié par J. Rott. 1979
26. POSTHUMUS MEYJES, G. H. M. *Jean Gerson et l'Assemblée de Vincennes (1329).* 1978
27. VIVES, Juan Luis. *In Pseudodialecticos.* Ed. by Ch. Fantazzi. 1979
28. BORNERT, R. *La Réforme Protestante du Culte à Strasbourg au XVIe siècle (1523-1598).* 1981
29. SEBASTIAN CASTELLIO. *De Arte Dubitandi.* Ed. by E. Feist Hirsch. 1981
30. BUCER, Martin. *Opera Latina.* Vol I. Publié par C. Augustijn, P. Fraenkel, M. Lienhard. 1982
31. BÜSSER, F. *Wurzeln der Reformation in Zürich.* 1985 *out of print*
32. FARGE, J. K. *Orthodoxy and Reform in Early Reformation France.* 1985
33, 34. BUCER, Martin. *Etudes sur les relations de Bucer avec les Pays-Bas.* I. Etudes; II. Documents. Par J. V. Pollet. 1985
35. HELLER, H. *The Conquest of Poverty.* The Calvinist Revolt in Sixteenth Century France. 1986
36. MEERHOFF, K. *Rhétorique et poétique au XVIe siècle en France.* 1986
37. GERRITS, G. H. *Inter timorem et spem.* Gerard Zerbolt of Zutphen. 1986
38. ANGELO POLIZIANO. *Lamia.* Ed. by A. Wesseling. 1986
39. BRAW, C. *Bücher im Staube.* Die Theologie Johann Arndts in ihrem Verhältnis zur Mystik. 1986
40. BUCER, Martin. *Opera Latina.* Vol. II. Enarratio in Evangelion Iohannis (1528, 1530, 1536). Publié par I. Backus. 1988
41. BUCER, Martin. *Opera Latina.* Vol. III. Martin Bucer and Matthew Parker: Florilegium Patristicum. Edition critique. Publié par P. Fraenkel. 1988
42. BUCER, Martin. *Opera Latina.* Vol. IV. Consilium Theologicum Privatim Conscriptum. Publié par P. Fraenkel. 1988
43. BUCER, Martin. *Correspondance.* Tome II (1524-1526). Publié par J. Rott. 1989
44. RASMUSSEN, T. *Inimici Ecclesiae.* Das ekklesiologische Feindbild in Luthers "Dictata super Psalterium" (1513-1515) im Horizont der theologischen Tradition. 1989

45. POLLET, J. *Julius Pflug et la crise religieuse dans l'Allemagne du XVIe siècle.* Essai de synthèse biographique et théologique. 1990
46. BUBENHEIMER, U. *Thomas Müntzer.* Herkunft und Bildung. 1989
47. BAUMAN, C. *The Spiritual Legacy of Hans Denck.* Interpretation and Translation of Key Texts. 1991
48. OBERMAN, H. A. and JAMES, F. A., III (eds.). in cooperation with SAAK, E. L. *Via Augustini.* Augustine in the Later Middle Ages, Renaissance and Reformation: Essays in Honor of Damasus Trapp. 1991 *out of print*
49. SEIDEL MENCHI, S. *Erasmus als Ketzer.* Reformation und Inquisition im Italien des 16. Jahrhunderts. 1993
50. SCHILLING, H. *Religion, Political Culture, and the Emergence of Early Modern Society.* Essays in German and Dutch History. 1992
51. DYKEMA, P. A. and OBERMAN, H. A. (eds.). *Anticlericalism in Late Medieval and Early Modern Europe.* 2nd ed. 1994
52, 53. KRIEGER, Chr. and LIENHARD, M. (eds.). *Martin Bucer and Sixteenth Century Europe.* Actes du colloque de Strasbourg (28-31 août 1991). 1993
54. SCREECH, M. A. *Clément Marot: A Renaissance Poet discovers the World.* Lutheranism, Fabrism and Calvinism in the Royal Courts of France and of Navarre and in the Ducal Court of Ferrara. 1994
55. GOW, A. C. *The Red Jews: Antisemitism in an Apocalyptic Age, 1200-1600.* 1995
56. BUCER, Martin. *Correspondance.* Tome III (1527-1529). Publié par Chr. Krieger et J. Rott. 1989
57. SPIJKER, W. VAN 'T. *The Ecclesiastical Offices in the Thought of Martin Bucer.* Translated by J. Vriend (text) and L.D. Bierma (notes). 1996
58. GRAHAM, M.F. *The Uses of Reform.* 'Godly Discipline' and Popular Behavior in Scotland and Beyond, 1560-1610. 1996
59. AUGUSTIJN, C. *Erasmus. Der Humanist als Theologe und Kirchenreformer.* 1996
60. McCOOG SJ, T. M. *The Society of Jesus in Ireland, Scotland, and England 1541-1588.* 'Our Way of Proceeding?' 1996
61. FISCHER, N. und KOBELT-GROCH, M. (Hrsg.). *Außenseiter zwischen Mittelalter und Neuzeit.* Festschrift für Hans-Jürgen Goertz zum 60. Geburtstag. 1997
62. NIEDEN, M. *Organum Deitatis.* Die Christologie des Thomas de Vio Cajetan. 1997
63. BAST, R.J. *Honor Your Fathers.* Catechisms and the Emergence of a Patriarchal Ideology in Germany, 1400-1600. 1997
64. ROBBINS, K.C. *City on the Ocean Sea: La Rochelle, 1530-1650.* Urban Society, Religion, and Politics on the French Atlantic Frontier. 1997
65. BLICKLE, P. *From the Communal Reformation to the Revolution of the Common Man.* 1998
66. FELMBERG, B. A. R. *Die Ablaßtheorie Kardinal Cajetans (1469-1534).* 1998
67. CUNEO, P. F. *Art and Politics in Early Modern Germany.* Jörg Breu the Elder and the Fashioning of Political Identity, ca. 1475-1536. 1998
68. BRADY, Jr., Th. A. *Communities, Politics, and Reformation in Early Modern Europe.* 1998
69. McKEE, E. A. *The Writings of Katharina Schütz Zell.* 1. The Life and Thought of a Sixteenth-Century Reformer. 2. A Critical Edition. 1998
70. BOSTICK, C. V. *The Antichrist and the Lollards.* Apocalyticism in Late Medieval and Reformation England. 1998
71. BOYLE, M. O'ROURKE. *Senses of Touch.* Human Dignity and Deformity from Michelangelo to Calvin. 1998
72. TYLER, J.J. *Lord of the Sacred City.* The *Episcopus Exclusus* in Late Medieval and Early Modern Germany. 1999

Prospectus available on request
BRILL — P.O.B. 9000 — 2300 PA LEIDEN — THE NETHERLANDS